DICTIONARY OF FINE ARTS

DICTIONARY OF

# FINE ARTS

*Denis Thomas*

## HAMLYN

LONDON · NEW YORK · SYDNEY · TORONTO

First published in 1981 by
The Hamlyn Publishing Group Limited
London · New York · Sydney · Toronto
Astronaut House, Feltham, Middlesex, England

ISBN 0 600 32995 X

Phototypeset by Page Brothers (Norwich) Ltd in
$9\frac{1}{2}$ on $10\frac{1}{2}$pt Linotron 202 Baskerville

Printed in Great Britain by
Hazell Watson & Viney Ltd,
Aylesbury, Bucks.

# INTRODUCTION

To try and embrace the world of fine art and architecture within the compass of a single, manageable dictionary seems a formidable undertaking. Its value, however, must lie not so much in breadth of scope as in clarity of presentation. For the author's aim is to appeal to the general reader or aspiring student whose interest may be limited by lack of readily available knowledge, and who would also benefit from an element of art appreciation.

This dictionary contains clear definitions of the terms and techniques, and outlines the main schools, movements and forms of expression as they have developed in the western world from the earliest times to the present day. It also includes short biographies of painters, sculptors, architects and engravers who are regarded as having made significant contributions to the history of art. Through them may be traced the development of the fine arts from the mysterious, quasi-religious works of prehistoric times to the blossoming of intellectual and spiritual sensibility epitomized by the religious architecture of the Middle Ages; and so on through the rediscoveries of the Renaissance and the upsurge of Romanticism to the explorations of the present age, in which conventional notions of form and structure have given way to abstraction and ephemeral performance. If artists and movements of the 20th century seem especially prominent, it is because they are the more likely to occur in the general reading and day-to-day experience of students and vistors to galleries.

Inevitably, some of the technical terms and descriptions have more than one application, and recur in several entries. These could be helpful for a layman viewing buildings of architectural interest – a cathedral, for instance, where reference might be made to a rood screen or clerestory – or when confronted with a picture painted in, say, tempera or gouache.

The black-and-white reproductions have been chosen not so much for their decorative value as for their use in providing visual examples of the period, technique or style to which they refer. They complement a text which aims to present a balanced, though necessarily selective, account of the achievements and ideas that make up the artist's world.

# DICTIONARY OF FINE ARTS

**abacus** In Classical architecture, the flat block that forms the upper member of a capital, and on which the architrave rests. In the Doric capital it is a plain square slab; in the Ionic, a small thin member interposed between the volutes and the architrave. In the Corinthian it is more prominent, with slightly concave sides and moulded edges.

**Abbate, Niccolò dell'** (*c.*1509–71) Italian painter and fresco artist. He is best known for his decorations at the château of Fontainebleau. His landscape paintings are Mannerist exercises on Classical themes, such as the *Rape of Proserpine* (Louvre, Paris) and the *Orpheus and Eurydice* (National Gallery, London).

**Abbott, John White** (1763–1851) English painter of landscape, figure and classical subjects. An amateur and pupil of Francis Towne, he was a surgeon by profession in Exeter and rarely ventured outside the West Country. His manner, close to that of Towne, is essentially ink outline and clear grey wash.

**Aboriginal art** Early Australian art, as practised by the indigenous people of that continent. It takes the form of body painting, cave and rock painting, engraving on stone or wood, and decoration of domestic objects. Aborigines have a concept of their place in a cosmological 'dream time' that is the basis of much of their imagery and has produced some of their most impenetrable art. There are centres of cave painting in Arnhem Land, the Kimberleys, and Queensland. An apparently different style, of linear and geometrical design, is found in an inland area extending from the south-west into the district beyond Lake Eyre.

**abozzo** An Italian term meaning sketch. it refers to the first outline or underpainting on the canvas; or in sculpture to material which has been chiselled, carved or moulded into the rough form of the finished work.

**absorbent ground** A porous ground, made of chalk or gesso, which absorbs the liquid with which the colour is applied, leaving the surface very quick drying. Egg tempera paintings become permanent when applied to an absorbent ground.

**Abstract art** An imperfect but indispensable term for distinguishing non-objective, non-figurative art from other categories or styles. 'Abstract' has come to mean the opposite of 'concrete' in recognition of values which have nothing to do with literal truth but which have been integral to art since prehistoric times. The conventional sense of the verb 'to abstract', meaning to draw off or remove, and thus to separate elements from one form and turn them into another, is also applicable, especially to such modern masters as Paul Klee, who has written of turning forms into 'images which, in the abstract, may be called constructions, but which may be named after the associations which they have prompted, such as star, vase, plant, animal, head or man'.

The awareness that art is not necessarily born of the material world but also resides in private forms that belong to the spirit, was acknowledged by Cézanne, who said: 'One must make a vision for oneself, an optic.' Braque explained his method in similar terms: 'Without having striven for it, I do in the end change the meaning of objects and give them a pictorial significance which is adequate to their new life.' Kandinsky, one of the most influential of Abstract artists, wrote that all the forms he ever used 'came from themselves, or created themselves while I was working, often surprising me.' Abstraction is therefore as much an attitude or intellectual stance as an artistic language.

**Abstract Expressionism** The term usually applied to the flowering of American painting that began in New York towards the end of the Second World War and continued until the late 1950s. During this period the New York School largely supplanted the School of Paris as the main impulse of Western art, and Abstract Expressionism was its major innovation. The term was first applied in 1946 to describe the painting of Arshile Gorky and Jackson Pollock and was extended to cover the products of other New York artists such as De Kooning, Motherwell, Kline, Still and Rothko, whose work was often neither abstract nor expressionist. In fact the unity of the school owed more to geography than to stylistic uniformity. In 1952 the critic Harold Rosenberg coined the term Action Painting which quickly gained more general currency.

Despite its diversity, Abstract Expressionism was almost as radical a departure from precedent as Cubism had been earlier in the century. It was a vigorous revolt against traditional styles and aesthetic criteria with an emphasis on spontaneous, gestural expression. The painting was to be regarded not as a finished, formally complete object, but as an expression of the moment of its making, a record of the artist's performance. Thus, De Kooning would deliberately leave traces of changes of mind during the course of composition, and Pollock abandoned the control of painting from the wrist in favour of gestures of his whole arm and body. The finished work was to be understood as embodying the mental state of the artist as he made it.

For all their declarations, the Abstract Expressionists could not reject form and control. In fact, their formal innovations have been as influential as any other. They were responsible for the concept of 'wholistic' composition, in which each area of the canvas is considered equally important, and this 'all-over' style has had a considerable influence on later generations. See also **Action Painting**.

**Abstract Illusionism** A development of Abstract Expressionism in the 1970s which uses the Cubist concept of 'shallow space' to create free-floating forms close to the picture plane.

**Abstract Image Painting** A variant of Abstract Expressionism in which simplified forms and motifs predominate, the intention being to strip the painting of any elements that might communicate by traditional painterly means.

**Abstraction-Création** An international artists' association formed in the early 1930s in Paris to bring together Abstract painters of all persuasions, from Constructivism to Neo-Plasticism. Members included Hans Arp, Kupka, Naum Gabo, Mondrian, Van Doesburg, Lissitsky and Kandinsky. They exhibited together until 1936 and published an annual review of non-figurative art under the group's title.

**abutment** The masonry at the base of the spring of an arch. It supports the weight and the downward thrust of the arch.

**academic** A descriptive adjective meaning adherence to traditional standards, or to the usually conservative criteria of a recognized academy. It is also used in a pejorative sense, implying pedantic or unoriginal work.

**academy** Usually enjoying official or semi-official status, academies are institutions charged with the promotion of national traditions in art. They are responsible for the training of young artists, the encouragement of higher learning, technical disciplines and scholarship, for upholding standards of taste and judgement and for the enhancement of their own members' reputations.

Academies of fine arts first flourished in 16th-century Italy with the principal purpose of raising the social standing of artists. The autocratic French Academy was founded in 1648. By the end of the century it was both a state-sponsored school and a learned body, its members graded into a strict hierarchy according to the form of art they practised, and with exclusive rights to public exhibition. Under the presidency of Sir Joshua Reynolds the Royal Academy in London was founded in 1768, receiving royal patronage but no state subsidy or control. The Scottish and American Academies were both founded in 1826.

During the 19th century, most academies of art resisted innovative work and encouraged the worthy second-rate. The damage thus done to their own avowed function and growing competition from public and private galleries and museums largely accounts for the peripheral place these institutions occupy today.

**academy figure** A study of a nude figure, usually half life size, executed as an exercise.

**acanthus** A sculptured leaf which resembles the foliage of the acanthus. A design incorporating this was used by the Greeks and the Romans, and in Gothic architecture and that of the Renaissance. The acanthus leaf forms the decoration of Corinthian capitals.

**acid bath** In etching, the tray of mordant in which the plate is immersed so that the acid may bite along the etched lines. Sometimes instead of the acid bath a walling wax is used to build a containing barrier around the edges of the plate, into which the mordant is poured.

**acropolis** The citadel of an ancient Greek city.

**acroterion** A pedestal placed at the apex and the ends of a pediment, usually supporting an ornament, statue or vase.

**acrylic paint** A recently developed synthetic paint of great versatility, properly called acrylic vinyl polymer emulsion. It can be applied with water in washes with a polymer medium that acts like oil in oil painting, or as impasto, enabling it to be used with both traditional oil and watercolour techniques. It dries fast and is thought to be completely durable.

**Action Painting** One of a group of terms used to describe the dominant style of the New York School during the late 1940s and 1950s. It was first coined by the American critic Harold Rosenberg in 1952 in an attempt to find a more apposite definition of the work of the New York artists than Abstract Expressionism. The new term was appropriate because it referred directly to the crucial innovation of the group – the concept that a painting should be a record of its own creation, expressing the artist's state of mind and emotions at the time of its making.

Action Painting is literally an action performed by the painter on a canvas, with no associations beyond itself. According to Harold Rosenberg, artists who practised this style of painting began to think of the canvas 'as an arena in which to act – rather than as a space in which to reproduce, redesign, analyse, or "express" an object, actual or imagined. What was to go on the canvas was not a picture but an event.' See also **Abstract Expressionism**.

**Adam** Family of French sculptors from Lorraine, notably the brothers Lambert Sigisbert (1700–59), Nicolas Sebastien (1705–78) and François-Gaspard (1710–61). Lambert Sigisbert (known as Adam the Elder) is best known for the *Triumph of Neptune* group at Versailles, on which he collaborated with Nicolas Sebastien (known as Adam the Younger). François-Gaspard worked at the court of Frederick II at Potsdam, and decorated the gardens at Sans Souci with sculptures of mythological figures.

**Adam** Family of Scottish architects whose name denotes a decorative style combining the tenets of Classicism with 18th-century urban and domestic taste. The brothers Robert (1728–92), James (1730–94) and William (c. 1738–1822) were patronized by George III and by English families building or embellishing their ancestral homes. In addition to architecture they paid attention to interior decoration, contents and fittings, from tapestry to doorknobs, thus helping to achieve complete unity of concept in their most typical work. They are credited with some 100 separate buildings, including such masterpieces as Syon House and Osterley Park in Middlesex, and in Edinburgh the Register House and old University buildings. In London Fitzroy Square remains one of their most conspicuous exercises in graceful town planning.

**Adler, Jules** (1865–1952) French painter. He trained at the École des Beaux-Arts and made his first appearance at the Salon in 1889. Thereafter he steered a course between the new naturalism and the academism of the day. His *Young Flower Girl*, 1899 (Petit Palais, Geneva) was exhibited at the Post-Impressionist exhibition in London in 1979–80.

**adobe** Walling of clay or mud bricks which have dried hard in the sun. The term is also applied to buildings made with sun-dried materials. Adobe is used by the Indians in Latin America, and also in New Mexico.

**advancing colour** Warm colours in a painting (reds and oranges) which have the effect of seeming to be near at hand are said to advance, whereas the cool colours (blues and violets) tend to be perceived as distant or receding.

**adytum** A place that only priests may enter. It was the name given to the innermost and secret chambers of a Greek temple.

**aedicule** A small temple used to house a statue.

**Aeolic** In Classical architecture, a type of capital decorated with scrolls; an early form of Ionic.

**affiche originale** A term appearing in French catalogues applying to a poster created by a named artist, usually for a short run and sometimes signed.

**affronted** In architecture, two animals placed symmetrically on a capital facing each other.

**African art** As with other ancient peoples, Africans have no word for what the West understands as art. It is only in recent times that the term 'art' has been applied to such objects as idols, totems and head-dresses brought back from Africa; or, if it was applied, it was designated 'primitive' art. Though there are considerable variations across the continent in style, materials and purposes, the African art most easily recognizable to non-Africans is sculpture and carving. Since its discovery at the beginning of this century, it has influenced the way European artists have regarded form, from the incipient Cubism of Picasso to the abstract sculptures and constructions of the Modern Movement.

The essence of African tribal art is its innate, mysterious comprehension of form, which is neither functional nor intellectual. Technically it is often of a very high order, as in ceremonial masks, ivory carving, or the bronzes of Benin. In some ways, for example body painting, the West has unwittingly followed ancient African traditions, perhaps in response to a shared, though uncomprehended, impulse towards ritual expression.

**after** A term used to indicate that a work is influenced by, executed in the manner of, or copied from the work of another artist.

**Aglio, Agostino** (1777–1857) Watercolour painter of landscapes and Italian views. He was born in Cremona and came to England in 1803, working first as a scene painter and decorator. His coastal sketches are broad and simple, not unlike those of Constable, with whom he has been confused. His son and namesake, Agostino Jnr, became a drawing master and worked in a similar style.

**Agnus Dei** Latin for Lamb of God, referring to images of Christ as a lamb, bearing a banner.

**Agora** Marketplace and meeting place of ancient Greek cities. The most famous is in Athens.

**Agostino di Duccio** (1418–81) Italian sculptor. He was born in Florence, where the altar at Modena is taken to be his earliest surviving work. He was responsible for the tombs and relief sculptures at the Tempio Malatestiano, in Rimini, and the façade of the Oratory of S. Bernadino, Perugia, where he died. There is a Madonna and Child by him in the Victoria and Albert Museum, London.

**airbrush** A small, precision version of a spray gun. An airbrush uses compressed air to spray paint in smooth gradations of tone and colour. Although it is mainly a tool of the commercial artist, the Pop and Photo-realist movements of the 1960s have established the airbrush technique as an accepted medium.

**aisle** The lateral division of a church, parallel to the nave.

**Alberti, Leon Battista** (1404–72) Italian architect, writer, painter and poet, born in Genoa and educated in Padua and Bologna. His treatise on the arts, *Della Pittura*, includes the first description of the applications of perspective. He worked in Florence, Rimini, Rome and Mantua. His humanist beliefs and his concept of art as resting on a rational base are developed in his writings, which are among the most eloquent of early Renaissance texts.

**alette** A small extension to or wing of a building.

**Alexander, Edwin John** (1870–1926) Scottish painter of bird, flower and animal studies. An early companion of his fellow Scot, Joseph Crawhall, with whom he travelled to

North Africa, he eventually settled in Inveresk, where he established a private zoo to help his studies of birds and animals.

**Alexander, William** (1767–1816) Painter of architectural views and landscapes. A pupil of William Pars and of Julius Caesar Ibbetson, he studied at the Royal Academy Schools, and travelled to China in 1792 as official draughtsman to a diplomatic mission. His drawings of Chinese subjects remain the most important work of his career. In 1808 he was appointed Keeper of Prints and Drawings at the British Museum.

**Algardi, Alessandro** (*c.*1596–1654) Italian sculptor born in Bologna, where he was a pupil of Ludovico Carracci. He moved to Rome, and became second in renown only to Bernini, whose work he sometimes imitated. He remained closer to classical tradition than did Bernini, and was rewarded with high office under Pope Innocent X when Bernini lost favour at the Papal court. His most important works are the tomb of Pope Leo XI and the relief sculpture of Pope Leo driving Attila from Rome, both in St Peter's.

**Alken** Family of Danish artists whose work became the epitome of English sporting life. Samuel (1750–1815) painted hunting scenes. His sons, Samuel (1784–1825) and Henry (1785–1851), followed him in style and subject matter with popular success. Henry, in particular, made a name with his aquatints of English sporting subjects, especially fox hunting. The work of his son, Henry Gordon Alken (1810–92), shows the family style in its long decline.

**all-over painting** A term which first became associated with the Abstract Expressionist painters to describe the way in which artists such as Jackson Pollock, Barnett Newman and Mark Rothko used every area of the picture surface to contribute to a single image. In all-over painting the image seems to bleed off the edge of the canvas, each part having equal emphasis so that the edges of the picture are as important and as intensly realized as the centre. Pictures painted in this style have no internal structure in the conventional sense and no particular focus of interest, but give the impression that they might extend indefinitely beyond the edge of the canvas.

The Abstract Expressionists were not the first to use the technique: many of Monet's late works, particularly the waterlilies series, have a uniform distribution of pictorial interest. The Abstract Expressionists were the first to develop its possibilities, and later American artists have carried it further.

**alla prima** Italian term for a method of oil painting using only a single layer of paint with no underpainting to complete a canvas in one sitting. Once regarded as a sloppy and irregular practice, it has been common since the 19th century. The equivalent French term is *au premier coup*.

**Allingham, Helen** (1848–1926) English artist and illustrator. She studied at Birmingham and at the Royal Academy Schools and was influenced by the dainty workmanship of Birket Foster. In 1874 she married the Irish poet William Allingham and so joined the London literary set. She worked in cool, bright colours, with a touch of sentiment in her figures and subjects that is still appealing.

**Allom, Thomas** (1804–72) English topographical artist and illustrator. He spent much of his life travelling in Europe and the Near East on commissions from publishers of illustrated travel books. His drawings are in wash or watercolour, neatly drawn in the professional manner that he shared with his contemporary and fellow traveller, William Henry Bartlett.

**Allston, Washington** (1779–1843) American painter. He divided his time between Boston and London, where he was elected ARA during the Presidency of his compatriot, Benjamin West. His early work, in the grand Romantic style, is of thunderstorms, shipwrecks and similar examples of nature's wilder moods. His later work, for which he is best remembered, is less dramatic and more lyrical. He ranks as the first American landscape painter of academic stature.

**Alma-Tadema, Sir Lawrence** (1836–1912) Dutch-born painter. He spent most of his life in Britain, rising to eminence as a specialist in tableaux from ancient Greece and Rome, painted with a high degree of unconvincing realism. Elected a Royal Academician in 1879, he was knighted in 1899.

**altarpiece** The decorative structure, often portable, which is set upon, behind or above an altar. It can consist of paintings or of ornamental screens incorporating a combination of painting, carving and statuary, often divided into a number of panels. An altarpiece with two panels is called a diptych; with three a triptych, and with any more than three a polyptych, although this is strictly a generic term meaning any altarpiece with more than two panels.

Typically, a Renaissance altarpiece is a triptych with the principal subject depicted on the central panel, and related ones on either side. Below the main panels there is often a predella, a smaller strip of paintings showing scenes from the lives of the saints represented above. A large altarpiece carved of stone or wood is called a reredos or retable. If it contains a painting, the term for it is a pala; if more than one painting, though still in one panel, an ancona.

**Altdorfer, Albrecht** (*c.*1485–1538) German artist, trained in Austria, where he was influenced by Lucas Cranach. Dürer and Mantegna are other influences on his work, which includes landscapes with figures, altarpieces and battle scenes. His *Birth of Venus*, in Munich, is a successful early exercise in the handling of perspective.

**alto-rilievo** see **relief**

**Aman-Jean, Edmond** (1860–1936) French painter. He was an associate of Seurat, with whom he shared a studio. A Salon artist, he was influenced by Puvis de Chavannes and, in later years, by Pierre Bonnard. His most fruitful period was the 1890s, when his explorations of naturalism and symbolism in portraiture, somewhat in the manner of the Pre-Raphaelites, were much admired.

**Amberger, Christoph** (*c.*1505–62) German portrait painter. His paintings show Venetian influence in the attention to ornate detail and revelation of character. His portrait of the

emperor Charles V, in Berlin, appears to be the only one he signed.

**ambo** In church architecture, a stand raised on two or more steps from which the Gospels may be read.

**ambry** A store for sacred vessels.

**ambulatory** An enclosed space, either open or covered, forming an arcade or cloister. The term is applied chiefly to the aisle behind the altar in a large church and means, literally, a place for walking.

**American Scene Painting** A recurrent genre in American art, in which reaction against big-city values has found expression in realistic but undemonstrative imagery of lives and landscapes often closer to the pioneer era than to modern times. Thomas Hart Benton (b. 1889), John Steuart Curry (1897–1946), Charles Burchfield (1893–1967), Grant Wood (1892–1942) and Andrew Wyeth typify the tradition.

**amorino** An Italian term for an infant cupid, especially common in 16th-century Italian art; it may also be called a putto. Though often used purely decoratively, the amorino can have a more central significance in the subject of the work.

Small cupids and cherubs often occur as carved or painted decoration in the architecture of the Italian Renaissance.

**amphiprostyle** A temple with porticos at each end.

**amphitheatre** Oval or circular building invented by the Romans for gladiatorial tournaments and displays. The seating rose in steeply banked tiers round an open arena and held many thousands of spectators.

**amphora** Greek two-handled jar, generally used for storing wine.

**anaglyph** A piece of carving or sculpture executed in **relief**, as opposed to a **diaglyph**, which is worked in **intaglio**.

**Analytical Cubism** see **Cubism**

**anamorphosis** An image that is distorted or almost unrecognizable for what it really is unless viewed through a special lens or mirror or from a particular angle. The best-known instance is probably the elongated skull in the foreground of Holbein's *Ambassadors* in the National Gallery. See **Trompe l'oeil**, p. 184.

**Anastasis** Greek for Resurrection.

**anastatic printing** A method of relief print making in which all except the areas of the plate which are to be inked are etched away, leaving upstanding only those parts that are to be reproduced. In this it is distinct from **etching** proper, which is an intaglio process. Relief etching, as it is sometimes called, is done by first painting the design to be printed directly on to a zinc plate using an acid-resistant varnish. When the plate is immersed in an acid bath the mordant bites away the unpainted areas, leaving the plate ready for inking and printing. William Blake used this process to reproduce both text and illustrations in some of his books.

**ancona** see **altarpiece**

**ancones** Brackets on each side of a doorway to support a cornice. They are often scrolled.

**Andrea del Sarto** (1486–1531) Italian painter, a contemporary of Leonardo, Michelangelo and Raphael and himself the embodiment of Florentine classicism. His major works include the decorations to the Annunciata (1510) and to the Chiostro dello Scalzo (1511–26), both in Florence, the *Madonna of the Harpies* (1517) in the Uffizi Gallery, Florence, and the *Assumption of the Virgin* (1530) in the Pitti Palace.

**Angelico, Guido di Pietro,** called Fra Angelico (1387–1455) Italian painter, born in Tuscany. He entered the Dominican convent in Fiesole in 1407 and in 1449 became Prior. His earliest work may have been with miniatures or illumination. Altarpieces painted in the 1440s show an advanced sense of spatial composition, which also distinguishes his high altar at S. Marco, Florence and the *Coronation of the Virgin* in the Louvre. He was entrusted with the restoration of the convent of S. Marco and

with painting a chapel in the Vatican (1447).

Highly regarded in his lifetime, he owes his pre-eminence to the breadth and dignity of his approach to what were essentially didactic themes, elevated by painterly skill and untroubled faith.

**Angell, Helen Cordelia** (1847–84) English flower painter who first exhibited under her maiden name, Coleman. She was much admired by the acknowledged master of rustic still life, William Henry Hunt. She succeeded Valentine Bartholomew as Flower Painter in Ordinary to Queen Victoria.

**Anglo-Saxon** Although the period extends from the early 5th century, no datable architecture exists from before the 7th century. Surviving examples are to be found only in churches characterized by apses and triple arcades, rough stonework and pilaster strips. Anglo-Saxon towers date back to the 10th century. Churches of the 11th century are Anglo-Saxon in structure but often have Norman decoration.

**Angrand, Charles** (1854–1926) French painter. His work shows many of the characteristics of more prominent painters of his time, such as Bastien-Lepage, Seurat and Van Gogh. He ranks among the minor members of the Post-Impressionist movement. He stopped painting altogether by about 1900.

**angular capital** An Ionic capital with all four sides matching and the volutes turned outwards. This is a 16th-century style attributed to Vincenzo Scamozzi (1552–1616), a follower of Palladio.

**annulet** A band or ring decoration used around a column in architecture of the 12th and 13th centuries.

**Anquetin, Louis** (1861–1932) French painter. He joined with Emile Bernard, Toulouse-Lautrec and Van Gogh to found the Groupe du Petit Boulevard (1886–7). Subsequently he met the group of painters headed by Gauguin at Pont-Aven, and also the **Nabis**, through his friendship with Bernard.

**antefixa** Decorated blocks used to screen the edge of the tiles on a roof.

**antependium** A screen or tapestry that covers the front of an altar.

**anthemion** A honeysuckle flower and leaf decoration used in Greek and Roman architecture. The word is also used to denote fan-shaped palm-leaf decoration. See **palmette**.

**antic work** A general term used to describe work of a fantastic or grotesque character, particularly groupings of human, animal and vegetable figures.

**Antonello da Messina** (*c.*1430–79) Italian painter of the early Renaissance. In his work an Italian sense of form is combined with a Flemish attention to detail and finish, derived from Jan van Eyck. Antonello is credited with having introduced the process of oil painting from northern Europe to Italy through his connections with Netherlands painters. His own work shows an impressive mastery of the medium, used in conjunction with smoothly rounded forms.

**apex stone** The top stone in a gable construction.

**Apollinaire, Guillaume** (1880–1918) French poet, critic and literary journalist. His membership of the Paris avant-garde from the early days of Cubism, and his propaganda for such friends as Picasso, Matisse and Braque, established him as one of the formative influences of the time. He invented the term **Orphism** to describe the work of Robert Delaunay, as well as coining **Surrealism**, the successor to **Dada**, in 1917.

**Appel, Karel** (b.1921) Dutch painter. He works in Paris, is a member of **COBRA** and an Abstract Expressionist in the mould of William de Kooning. He frequently applies paint straight from the tube in such a way as to give it a separate presence from surrounding pigment applied by conventional means.

**applied arts** General term for practical, man-made objects such as ceramics, leatherwork or textiles in which artistic skill or motivation can be regarded as intrinsic to the design.

**apse** The vaulted, semicircular end of a chancel. In Classical architecture, an apse is a semicircular recess in a wall.

**Apt, Ulrich the Elder** (*c.*1465–1532) German portrait painter. He was active in Augsburg in the 1480s, working in the manner of Holbein. There is an example of his work, a portrait of a man and his wife, at Hampton Court.

**aquarelle** A French term for watercolour or wash drawings.

**aquatint** A form of etching which is not confined to the use of line only, but is capable of tonal effects in some ways similar to those of a wash drawing: the name is derived from its resemblance to drawings done with watercolour washes. The transparent tones are obtained by using a porous ground through which the acid can penetrate.

A copper or zinc plate is first dusted with a fine sprinkling of powdered resin, usually by means of a dust box to ensure an even covering. This is then carefully fused to the metal by heating so that the mordant in the acid bath will bite around each grain, causing the plate to be pitted all over with little dots. These, when inked, result in a uniform, grainy-toned print. The amount of resin powder used, its coarseness, and the length of time the plate is immersed in the bath all regulate the depth and texture of the tone. The artist can achieve a variety of tones on the same plate by **stopping out** some areas – protecting them from further attack from the acid – while biting others more deeply. This process can be repeated until a large number of different tones have been obtained. Areas that are to print completely white have to be stopped out before the first immersion in the acid bath.

A variation on this technique is the sugar aquatint, which dates from the 18th century. This enables the artist to draw directly on to the plate, instead of having to rely on stopping out. A mixture of watercolour and sugar is used to make the drawing, and the plate is then varnished and immersed in water. The water causes the sugar to swell and burst the crust of the varnish, exposing the bare metal where the drawing was made. By next dusting the plate with resin and allowing acid to bite in the normal way, the artist can make a print

**Arabesque** Design with a griffin from a 14th-century niello attributed to Peregrino (Edmund de Rothschild Collection, Louvre, Paris).

in which the background, protected by the varnish, remains white, while the design stands out in an aquatint texture.

Aquatint technique is seldom used alone. Usually a plate so treated is then incised by **line engraving** or **drypoint**. Paul Sandby was the first to demonstrate its potential. Until modern times it had not been widely used by artists, though during the 19th century it was a popular method of colour printing with different plates being used for each colour.

**aqueduct** An artificial masonry channel invented by the Romans to convey water.

**arabesque** A flowing, curvilinear decoration, sometimes incorporating floral motifs, in common use since Graeco-Roman times and probably originating in the earlier Arabic and Moorish cultures. It is sometimes applied more loosely to a rhythmic line inside a pictorial composition.

In architecture, the term refers to a carved or painted panel showing geometrical, human, animal and grotesque symbols interwoven with flowers and foliage. In Greek, Roman and Renaissance architecture the arabesques are intertwining plants and animals. Muslim arabesques have foliage intertwined with geometric patterns.

**arcade** In modern architecture, a covered pathway between shops. More generally, an arcade consists of a series of arches supporting a roof.

**arch** A curve-shaped structure made with wedge-shaped blocks of stone or brick.

A drop arch is pointed, and its span is greater than its radius.

A four-centred Tudor arch has two outer arcs and two lower arcs rising from the centres on the springing line. The two inner and upper arcs rise from centres below the springing line.

A horseshoe arch can be either pointed or round.

A lancet arch is a narrow pointed arch with radii much larger than the span.

An ogee arch is constructed with two convex arcs above and two lower concave arcs.

A pointed arch or equilateral arch has two curves, each with a radius equal to the span and meeting in a point at the top.

A relieving arch or discharging arch is placed in a wall above an arch or opening to relieve it of a great deal of the weight.

A segmental arch is a section of a circle drawn from a centre below the springing line.

A shouldered arch has projecting lintels resting on the horizontal course.

A trefoil arch is a rounded or pointed arch rising from the apex of two separate rounded arches.

**Archaic** The period of Greek art between about 700 and 480 BC.

**Archer, Thomas** (1668–1743) English architect whose travels acquainted him with the continental Baroque, on which his subsequent style was founded. His works include the Cascade House at Chatsworth and St John's, Smith Square, Westminster, his most handsome surviving church.

**Archipenko, Alexander** (1887–1964) Russian sculptor, born in Kiev. He worked in Paris during the early years of the Cubist movement, of which he was an active member, and eventually settled in the United States. His early work is valued for his attempts at Cubist structure by means of concave forms, and for his use of materials such as wood, metal and glass. His later Plexiglass sculptures of the 1940s, illuminated from within, were further explorations of ways to liberate sculpture from naturalistic forms.

**architrave** In Roman and Greek architecture, the lowest of the three main parts of the entablature which stretches from column to column. The word also refers to the masonry frame or moulding round a doorway or a window.

**architrave-cornice** An entablature, used by Inigo Jones, from which the frieze has been elided.

**archivolt** A moulding around an arch. The word is also used of the under-curve of an arch.

**Arcimboldi, Giuseppe** (1537–93) Italian painter, noted for his grotesque heads and figures composed of fruit and vegetables. These were a departure from his work at Milan Cathedral, where he designed stained-glass windows, but they evidently appealed to Rudolf II, who made him a Count in 1592. He is sometimes pointed out as a proto-Surrealist; Salvador Dali recognized in him a kindred spirit.

**arcosolium** A recess in a crypt, used as a tomb.

**arena** The open space in the centre of an amphitheatre.

**armature** The skeletal structure on which a sculptor builds up his work when using clay, wax or plaster.

**Armory Show** The name accorded to the International Exhibition of Modern Art held in the Armory Building, New York City, in 1913, which the organizers claimed as the birth of the modern spirit in American art. It consisted of an American section with examples by radical painters who felt unfairly treated by the gallery world, and a European section which introduced the public to the work of Cézanne, Matisse, Braque, Picasso, Kandinsky and Marcel Duchamp, whose *Nude Descending a Staircase* was a sensation. Reaction was hostile, but the seed had been sown.

**Arp, Jean or Hans** (1887–1966) French sculptor. Associated with the **Dada** group from its beginnings in 1916, he turned to three-dimensional sculpture after working in reliefs, constructions and collage. He belongs with the Abstract artists of his time whose creative springs were organic rather than analytical, based on his belief that 'art is a fruit that grows in man'. He resisted the term 'abstract' as applied to his work: in his terms, totally non-representational sculpture was more properly called 'concrete'.

**arriccio** A name for the second of the layers of plaster that constitute the support for a fresco.

**arris** The sharp edge at the intersection of two straight or curved surfaces.

**Art Brut** A phrase coined by the French artist Jean Dubuffet to describe the intense visual expression of the untutored – children, psychotics, graffiti writers and so-called primitive painters. Dubuffet has a large collection of such art which he first exhibited in Paris in 1947, and he has founded a society for its promotion. By incorporating the motifs and characteristics of Art Brut into his own work, Dubuffet did much to create the aesthetic climate that was to give rise to Junk art and Pop art in the 1960s.

**Art Nouveau** Literally, the 'new art' of the 1890s. Its origins were the linear tradition of Celtic art, the Rococo, and Japanese art and architecture. In England it manifested itself in the art of Aubrey Beardsley, in the writhing forms of floreate interior decor and domestic

**Art Nouveau** Alphons Mucha's poster for
*Medée*, 1898.

design, and in the Arts and Crafts movement
led by William Morris. It also took root in
Belgium, where the architect Victor Horta
(1861–1947) introduced it into his Hôtel Solvay
and Maison de Peuple, and in Spain, most
notably in the architectural masterpieces of
Gaudi. In Germany, where the style is known
as *Jugendstil*, its leading practitioners were the
sculptor Herman Obrist (1863–1927) and the
illustrator Otto Eckmann (1865–1902).

During the last years of the Austro-
Hungarian empire, architecture and design
were directly influenced by the British example, in particular the work of Charles Rennie
Mackintosh and Charles Annesley Voysey
(1857–1941). The Art Nouveau manner persisted longest in graphic design and in commercial art. The Czech artist, Alphons Mucha,
achieved prominence with his poster designs, in
which the decorative possibilities of the style are
carried to brilliant heights.

Art Nouveau has enjoyed a revival in recent
years, having re-emerged as an adjunct of Pop
art.

**artist's proof** In print making, a proof pulled
by the artist for his own purposes, separately
from an edition, and usually marked as such.
Artist's proofs may be taken from a plate or
block in addition to those printed for a numbered and limited edition.

**Arts and Crafts movement** A term describing the revival of interest in and regard for
hand-made crafts and objects, in a reaction
against the increasing industrialization of life
in late 19th-century Britain. The movement
was headed by William Morris, whose efforts
to turn people's thoughts away from mech-
anization to the standards and virtues of the
medieval guilds attempted to put the somewhat
woolly-minded preachings of John Ruskin into
practice. The Arts and Crafts ethic was rooted
in idealistic socialism and attracted to Morris's
side such socially committed artists as Walter
Crane and the architects Charles Robert Ash-
bee (1863–1942) and William Richard Lethaby
(1857–1931).

The movement's legacy has been a wealth
of hand-woven textiles and fabrics, numerous
finely printed books, and a lasting awareness
of the qualities of good design, including pottery, furniture, domestic utensils, prints and

private presses. Its concept of an alliance between art and industry was absorbed into the doctrines of the **Bauhaus**, where it continued to influence attitudes to design throughout the 1930s.

**Ashcan School** The somewhat dismissive title conferred on the group of American painters known as The Eight, who banded together in 1907 in oppositon to the negativism of the National Academy of Design in New York. They included Robert Henri (1865–1929), John Sloan, William Glackens (1870–1938), George Luks (1867–1933), Everett Shinn (1876–1953), Arthur Davies (1862–1928), Maurice Prendergast (1859–1924) and Ernest Lawson (1873–1939). A joint exhibition in 1908 drew large crowds, and helped prepare the way for the arrival of modern European art at the Armory Show in 1913. The School's more lasting contribution was in consolidating American Scene painting as a valid, indigenous genre.

**ashlar** Masonry of large blocks, accurately cut and with smooth surfaces, and laid in regular courses.

**Asplund, Gunnar** (1885–1940) Swedish architect. He was largely responsible for the lightening of forms and restraint in design that characterizes the best Scandinavian building in this century. His Stockholm City Library, of the 1920s, and Göteborg Town Hall, a decade later, are among his typical works. His Crematorium at Stockholm has been called the most perfect example of 20th-century monument design and religious architecture in existence.

**assemblage** The technique of building up a three-dimensional work using any number of transposed objects, sometimes in combination, with elements painted, carved or modelled by the artist. Picasso's *Glass of Absinthe* (1914) is the first such composition. The technique is an extension of **collage**.

**astragal** A small semicircular moulding, usually applied to the top of the shaft of a column and to its base, and often decorated with bead and reel. It is also called a **baguette**.

**astylar** A building face without columns or pillars.

**atelier** An artist's studio or workshop. The *atelier libre*, a studio which for a small entrance fee provided a nude model but no tuition, was common in 19th-century Paris.

**Atkinson, John Augustus** (*c.* 1775–1833) English painter and illustrator best known for his Russian subjects. He was taken to Russia as a boy, an experience which provided him with material for both exhibition and illustration in later years. He also painted battle pieces and a series of watercolour drawings for an edition of *Don Quixote*.

**atlantes** Columns in the form of carved male figures. See also **caryatid** for female figures.

**atrium** The central open court of a Roman house around which the rooms were built. The word also refers to the enclosed courtyard of an early Christian church.

**attic** A small architectural storey introduced above the main cornice of a building, apparently suggested by the treatment of the upper portion of the Roman triumphal arches.

**attic base** A form of base to a Classical column, consisting of two convex members with a concave one between them, separated by fillets.

**attribution** The ascribing of a work to an artist in the belief that it is of his execution on the grounds either of style or of **provenance**.

**aureole** A holy radiance depicted around a divine or sacred person, usually found in medieval and Renaissance art. Unlike a halo or nimbus which surrounds only the head, an aureole is often stylized as in a mandorla – an almond-shaped radiance which in medieval art is often shown to enclose the figure of the resurrected Christ.

**autograph** A work is said to be autograph when it is, or is thought to be, executed entirely by the artist to whom it is attributed, rather than carried out partly by pupils or assistants under their master's instructions.

**automatism** Non-structured drawing or doodling, with eyes and (as far as possible) the mind closed, was believed by the Surrealists to be a means of tapping the creative powers of the subconscious.

**avant garde** The vanguard, spearhead or fore-runners of a movement. The term has held good in the present century, in which avant-garde ideas and initiatives have dominated the course of art. However, the breakdown of con-ventional aesthetic values over the past two decades has made the term meaningless.

**Avercamp, Hendrick** (1585–1634) Dutch painter, pioneer of the Dutch landscape genre in which village streets, town squares or fields are peopled with busy figures. His winter scenes are especially successful, with their bus-tle of sporting activity: skaters, tobogganists, and children sliding.

**Avignon, School of** A term, no longer much used, to describe the painters who worked in Avignon during and after the 70-year exile there of the Papal court (1309–77). Simone Martini was in Avignon briefly (1340–1), and his style was widely copied. In subsequent years a school of painting flourished in the city, combining Italian and Flemish traditions. Chief among its members were Enguerrand Charonton (b. 1410), whose masterpiece is the *Pietà* of Villeneuve-lès-Avignon, and Nicolas Froment (*c.* 1450–90), whose *Altarpiece of the Burning Bush* is in the cathedral of Aix-en-Provence.

**axonometric projection** A geometric three-dimensional drawing of a building.

**Ayrton, Michael** (1921–75) English artist, illustrator, sculptor and writer, whose graphic style links classical draughtsmanship with modern usages. Many of his themes are based on mythological sources, such as the Minotaur and Daedalus, and on the work of Archilochos, the Greek poet of the 7th century BC whose sur-viving fragments provided him with the theme of a posthumously published suite of etchings and aquatints.

**Baburen, Dirck van** (*c.* 1590–1624) He was a member of the Utrecht School, with Hon-thorst and Terbrugghen.

**Backhuysen, Ludolf** (1631–1708) Dutch marine painter. In his time he was next in popularity only to Willem van de Velde II. His studies of ships tossed in stormy waters set a fashion in marine painting in opposition to the more typical Dutch calms.

**Bacon, Francis** (b. 1909) Self-taught English painter whose original sources of influence, notably Picasso, have long since been absorbed into his own singular and isolated vision. The starting point of a typical Bacon image may lie outside the painter's personal experience, as in his treatment of Velazquez's *Pope Innocent X* or the face of the screaming nurse from Sergei Eisenstein's classic film, *The Battleship Potemkin*, but the projection of these images in terms of outrage and violence is a fiercely personal state-ment. Art, for Bacon, is 'a method of opening up areas of feeling'. The resultant explosions reflect his conviction that man is 'an accident, a completely futile being'.

**baguette** (or bagnette) A small moulding, semicircular, and often decorated with bead and reel. See **astragal**.

**bailey** An open court in a medieval fortified castle.

**Bakst, Léon** (1866–1925) Russian painter and theatrical designer. Born in St Petersburg, he studied in Moscow and Paris before returning to St Petersburg to join Diaghilev, then at the beginning of his career, in the Mir Iskusstva (World of Art) group. He designed ballet sets for Michel Fokine, and subsequently for a series of Diaghilev productions with the Rus-sian ballet, including *Cléopatra, Schéhérazade* and *L'Aprèsmidi d'un Faune*.

Bakst's feeling for folk costume and his vivid sense of colour were well suited to his work for the Russian ballet. Many of his designs, for both costumes and stage sets, have become classics.

**baldachin, baldacchino** A canopy supported on poles or an ornamental roof constructed over an altar, font or tomb to add importance to a sacred object.

**Baldung, Hans** (1484–1545) German painter, follower and pupil of Dürer, whose influence is apparent in his engravings. He became an illustrator for books printed by Ulrich Pinder, and was commissioned to make designs for stained-glass windows. His altarpiece for Freiburg Cathedral (*c.*1512) is his finest surviving work, revealing the influence of Grünewald's recently completed Isenheim altar. With Grünewald he also shared a penchant for distortion and the macabre. His woodcuts are among the most original of his time, comparable in quality to Dürer's.

**Balla, Giacomo** (1871–1958) Italian painter and sculptor. He was born in Turin but worked in Rome. A short period in Paris in 1900 introduced him to Neo-Impressionism, which he passed on to his pupils, Umberto Boccioni and Gino Severini. In 1910 Balla embraced the ideas of Marinetti, leader of the Futurists, and though he painted some dashing futuristic pictures he subsequently returned to a naturalistic style.

**ballflower** An enrichment of mouldings in early medieval architecture consisting of leaf motifs impressed on to semispherical globes.

**ballistraria** Medieval military-cross-shaped opening for firing crossbows through battlements.

**Balthus,** originally named Balthasar Klossowski de Rola (b.1908) French painter, the son of a Polish artist and writer. With the encouragement of Bonnard, Derain and the poet Rilke, he dedicated himself to painting at an early age. He has led a reclusive life, painting in a figurative style reminiscent of Seurat. His later subjects have been adolescent girls closeted in silent rooms, in an atmosphere of innocent eroticism.

**baluster** A miniature column with a capital and base, but with the shaft generally designed with a swell in it, either at the base or in the centre, instead of being straight as in the column proper. It is most frequently used round the roofs of buildings.

**balustrade** A continuous decorative railing of stone, wood or metal.

**bambocciate** A term derived from 'Il Bamboccio', the nickname of the Dutch painter

Pieter van Laer (1592–1642), who was deformed. It refers to scenes of low life of the kind made popular by Dutch and Flemish artists in the 17th century.

**Bandinelli, Baccio** (1493–1560) Florentine sculptor. He was the contemporary and rival of Benvenuto Cellini, who harshly attacked his *Hercules and Cacus*, in Florence (1534). He secured the favours of Cosimo I, carved the reliefs in the choir of Florence Cathedral, and left unfinished his tombs for Pope Leo X and Clement VII.

**Banks, Thomas** (1735–1803) English Neoclassical sculptor. He spent seven years working and studying the Antique in Rome, and was greatly influenced by the art-historical writings of Winckelmann. When he finally settled in England he turned to making busts and monuments in the Neoclassical style, sugared by the prevailing taste for noble sentiments. The great reputation he earned in his lifetime has not stood the test of time.

**barbican** Outer defence structure, commonly in the form of an overhanging battlement designed to protect the gatehouse.

**Barbizon School** The name given to a group of French landscape painters who worked together in the region of the Forest of Fontainebleau in the second half of the 19th century. They included Théodore Rousseau, who was their acknowledged leader, Charles-François Daubigny, Narcisse-Virgil Diaz (1807–76), Jules Dupré (1811–89), Charles-Émile Jacque (1813–94) and Constant Tryon (1810–65). The group shared a belief that country life and direct exposure to natural scenery were prerequisites of honest landscape painting. Millet is sometimes included among them, since he lived near by and was a close friend of Rousseau. But his aims were different from theirs, which owed to Corot and to the example of Constable a feeling for painting from nature for its own sake.

Their work was instrumental in introducing to the British public the naturalism that distinguishes the paintings of Constable, which led to his subsequent rediscovery as an English master.

**bargeboards** Projecting carved and decorated boards covering the incline of a gable to prevent damp penetration.

**Barlach, Ernst** (1870–1938) German Expressionist sculptor and illustrator. Trained in Hamburg, Dresden and Paris, he was a pioneer of the **Jugendstil** (Art Nouveau) movement and sculptor of monuments for Cracow and Magdeburg Cathedrals in the 1920s. In 1933, despite his numerous public honours, his work was proscribed by the Nazis and confiscated. His work in all media, including woodcarving, has a strong sense of ethnic continuity, bypassing modernist tastes and trends.

**Barlow, Francis** (c. 1626–1704) English sporting artist and illustrator. He is among the first in a long succession of English artists who have taken the countryside and its creatures as his subject matter, and his draughtsmanship establishes the pastoral theme that has persisted in English art into modern times. His

masterpiece is his edition of *Aesop's Fables*, which he began to publish as a private press venture in 1666. Many copies were lost in the Fire of London, and the work is now rare.

**Barocci, Federico** (c. 1535–1612) Italian painter. He trained in Urbino and went as a young man to Rome, where he received a commission from Pope Pius IV to decorate a ceiling in the Vatican gardens. Eventually he returned to Urbino to work for the Duke. His style owes its qualities variously to Correggio and Raphael. He was a fine draughtsman, often in the medium of pastel.

**Baroque** A style in art and architecture, originating in Italy, which according to an 18th-century definition is 'the ultimate in the bizarre, the ridiculous carried to extremes'. This view has been tempered by time and scholarship, in acknowledgement of the dynamic and often sublime effects of which the Baroque proved capable from its inception at the end of the 16th century to its merging into the Rococo early in the 18th.

The Italian Baroque is in three periods: Early (Domenichino, Carracci and the young

**Baroque** An 18th-century design for a stage set by Joseph Galli Bibiena.

# 16 barrel vault

Rubens); High (Bernini, Lanfranco, and Cortona); and Late. Rubens was the greatest non-Italian artist to practise the Baroque outside Italy, where it drew much of its force from a return to Classical grandeur. It is apparent in Velazquez and Rembrandt, and more dimly in the work of some English painters and architects such as Van Dyck, Thornhill, Vanbrugh and Grinling Gibbons. It is to be seen at its most opulent in Germany and Austria, where flourished Bernini's pupil, Andreas Schlüter (1660–1714).

The term 'Baroque' remained charged with pejorative overtones until the publication in 1888 of Heinrich Wölfflin's *Renaissance und Barock*, which gave it academic respectability. The modern taste for the theatrical and daring in art has brought it a new generation of admirers.

**barrel vault** A half-cylindrical stone or brick roof built in one continuous arch. It can be semicircular or pointed and is usually over a rectangular space. It is also known as a tunnel vault.

**Barret, George** (1732–84) Dublin-born landscape painter and drawing master. In 1762 he came to London where he prospered, and became a founder member of the Royal Academy. His watercolours are normally ambitious and devoted to subjects of some dignity, such as lakeland scenery, mountain pools and similar Romantic landscape themes.

**Barry, Sir Charles** (1795–1860) English architect, best known for his Houses of Parliament, begun in 1839 and opened in 1852. Other buildings by him, usually in styles reminiscent of the Roman and Florentine Renaissance, include the Manchester Athenaeum, the Travellers' Club and Reform Club, both in Pall Mall, and Cliveden.

His son, Edward M. Barry (1830–80) built the hotel at Charing Cross station.

**Bartlett, William Henry** (1809–54) English topographical artist and illustrator. His travels took him to the Continent, the Near East, Palestine, Egypt and North America. Original works by him are in the careful, pedestrian style of the professional recorder of scenes intended for use as engravings in picture books and annuals.

**Bartolommeo, Fra Baccio della Porta** (*c.*1473–1517) Italian painter of the Florentine school. He joined the Dominican order in 1499, then proceeded, with his close contemporary Raphael, along the broadening path to the Italian High Renaissance. His important commissioned works tend to be solemn and static. When he imitates Raphael, as in the *Salvator Mundi* in Florence, he comes closer to achieving sublime effects. His drawings are noted for their mystical grace: *A Head of the Dead Christ*, in the Ashmolean Museum, Oxford, is a particularly fine example.

**Bartolozzi, Francesco** (1727–1815) Italian engraver. Born in Florence, he worked for most of his life in England and was an original member of the Royal Academy (1769). He was much in demand as an engraver of drawings by Italian masters and was himself a master of stipple engraving, which enjoyed a vogue in the late 18th century.

**bas-relief** Architectural sculptural decoration in low relief. See also **relief**.

**basilica** A Roman building, generally open on one of its longer sides. The interior had a range of columns carrying galleries, with columns in the upper storey supporting a raised roof to the centre portion.

**basilica church** The name given to the typical form of an early Christian church, usually with three aisles and an apse at one end and looking something like a Roman original.

**Bassano** Family of Italian painters named after their native village near Venice, of whom Jacopo or Giacomo (1510–92) is the most prominent. He moved to Venice, where Titian, Lotto and Palma Vecchio were working, in about 1534 and by the 1560s had developed his own low-key style.

His son, Francesco the Younger (1549–92), painted on a smaller scale and chose more domestic subjects, which helps to account for his wider popularity.

**Bastien-Lepage, Jules** (1848–84) French painter. He studied at the École des Beaux-Arts and quickly made his name with Salon paintings of peasants in their natural environment, in his case the uncompromising countryside of his native north east. His *Poor Fauvette*, 1881 (Glasgow Art Gallery), is a characteristic study of the pathos with which he invests his rustic figures, in response to what he recognized as 'the poetry in nature'. His work was influential among the Post-Impressionists, among them the British painter Sir George Clausen.

**Batoni, Pompeo Girolama** (1708–87) Italian painter. He worked in the academic Roman manner which he learned from his master, Sebastiano Conca (1680–1764). It served him well in carrying out numerous commissions, from portraits of royalty to altarpieces and big, mythological set-pieces. His habit of placing his sitters against classical backgrounds, sometimes in fancy dress, made him popular with patrons. With Mengs, he dominated the art scene in Rome, receiving various public honours including a knighthood from the Pope.

**Bauhaus** A modern school of building, craftsmanship and design which was founded in 1919 at Weimar by Walter Gropius. In 1925 it moved to Dessau and in 1932 to Berlin, where it was forced by the Nazis to close down. Its importance lies in its continuing influence on the function of design in industry and technology through the contributions of a succession of brilliant minds from Kandinsky and Klee to Laszlo Maholy-Nagy, who became Director of the New Bauhaus when the school was re-established in Chicago.

The Bauhaus concept was that an artist or architect should at the same time be a craftsman, capable of working with different materials and with a knowledge of the principles of industrial design. By the same token, a building or industrial product should be a collective entity, with all the parts designed and fashioned with regard to the whole. Bauhaus teaching put these principles into practice, with results that have kept its name alive into modern times. See also **Gropius**.

**bay** In Gothic architecture, the longitudinal space occupied by one arch and the adjoining piers of the arcade, and one main compartment of the vaulting, forming the element of the architectural design. The term is not applied to colonnaded architecture, probably because the portion above the colonnade is continuous and not divisible into sections.

**bay leaf** In architecture, a garland of bay-tree leaves used to decorate torus mouldings.

**bay window** An angular window projection. If curved, it is called a bow window; if on an upper floor, an oriel window.

**Baynes, James** (1766–1837) English landscape painter and drawing master. He went on a sketching tour of Wales with the young John Varley, and exhibited watercolours in a subdued, Girtinesque palette that achieves atmospheric effects of true distinction.

**Bazille, Jean-Frédéric** (1841–70) French painter, born into a professional family who wanted him to become a doctor. He broke off his medical studies to embark on a career as a painter in 1862, entering Charles Gleyre's studio where he met Monet, Renoir and Alfred Sisley. He shared lodgings with Renoir, whom he subsidized from his allowance, and returned to his native Montpelier every summer to paint. The most obvious influence on his style is Manet. In 1827 he bought a painting from Monet's studio, *Women in the Garden*, for which he gave 2500 francs, payable in monthly instalments.

A popular member of the Impressionist circle, he appears in Manet's *Déjeuner sur l'herbe* and in Henri Fantin-Latour's *The Studio at Batignolles*. At the outbreak of the Franco-Prussian War he enlisted in the Zouaves and was killed in action within a few weeks, his potential unfulfilled.

**bead and reel** A pattern of circular and elliptical shapes used on classical mouldings. See **astragal**.

**beakhead** In Norman architecture, a carved ornament of a grotesque beaked animal or bird.

**Beardsley, Aubrey** (1872–98) English illustrator identified with the languors of the *fin de siècle*, expressed in the Art Nouveau manner of the 1890s. He first began drawing in the manner of the **Pre-Raphaelites** before finding his own line in his illustrations for Oscar

Wilde's *Salome* and the newly published *Yellow Book*, which captured to perfection the flavour of a rank-scented aestheticism. His achievement was to liberate black-and-white illustration from its naturalistic convention, creating a weirdly beautiful world out of white space and an immaculate line.

**bearing** An architectural term describing the distance between the limits of the points of support, that is, the total unsupported length. The word is also used of the portion which rests upon the supports.

**bearing wall** A wall which supports a vertical load in addition to its own weight.

**Beatus** The name generally applied to copies of a commentary on the Apocalypse by the 8th-century Spanish monk, Beatus of Liébana. The finest is an illuminated version now in the Bibliothèque nationale, Paris.

**beaux-arts** French for fine arts, but also descriptive of the academic tradition embodied in the École des Beaux-Arts in Paris.

**Beccafumi, Domenico** (1484–1551) Italian painter, born in Siena. He discovered the High Renaissance in Rome on his first visit between 1510 and 1512 and on returning to Siena evolved a style which combines Sienese colouring with early Mannerist flourishes. There are three examples in the National Gallery, London: an unidentified street scene, formerly called *Esther and Ahasuerus, Tanaquil*, and *Marcia*. The two last subjects are from a series of famous women of antiquity.

**Beckmann, Max** (1884–1950) German Expressionist painter, prominent in the **Neue Sachlichkeit** movement. He lived in Berlin from 1904, where he became a member of the Sezession, and for a while opposed the artistic trends of the time. His war experiences brought about a nervous breakdown. After his discharge from hospital he moved to Frankfurt, where he began painting the violent and emotional themes on which his reputation rests, and which were vilified by the Nazis. He left Germany for Holland in 1937, and in 1947 emigrated to the United States. He lived to see his work rehabilitated, having once had the distinction of hanging in the Nazis' famous exhibition of Degenerate Art.

**bed moulding** In classical entablature, the small moulding between the corona and the frieze.

**Bell, Vanessa** (1879–1961) English painter, wife of the critic Clive Bell and elder sister of Virginia Woolf. She produced work in the English Art Club manner until the impact of the first Post-Impressionist exhibition in London in 1910. After this her colours brightened and her work broadened into a genteel form of Abstraction. In later years she returned to more figurative forms. She collaborated with Duncan Grant on interior decorating commissions, including designs for rugs and furnishings, and also designed printed fabrics and tableware as part of the general involvement by artists of the 1930s in commercial and industrial design.

**Bellini** Family of Italian Renaissance painters, notably Jacopo (*c*.1400–70) and his sons Gentile (*c*.1429–1507) and Giovanni (*c*.1430–1516). Between them they exerted a decisive influence on the development of Venetian painting. Jacopo, the father, built up his practice with the help of commissions from the Church, and his sons joined him as studio assistants. His working drawings and sketches have survived, revealing his lifelong interest in the effects of perspective. Among his many Madonnas is the *Virgin and Child* at the Accademia, Venice.

Gentile Bellini was appointed offical portrait painter, and was subsequently posted to the court of Constantinople. There he was exposed to Eastern influences which found their way into his painting.

Giovanni Bellini, presumed to be the younger brother, was much influenced by his brother-in-law, Mantegna, though the young Bellini soon demonstrated the lyrical feeling for space and colour which set his works apart. His *Madonna with Saints* (Church of the Frari, Venice) marks the arrival of the true Venetian style, in which light and palette become indivisible.

**Bellotto, Bernardo** (1720–89) Italian painter. He was a nephew and pupil of Canaletto and is sometimes mistaken for him. He travelled much more widely, particularly to Dresden and to Warsaw, where he joined the court of Stanislas II. His records of the city are as detailed and comprehensive as are Canaletto's of Venice.

**Bellows, George** (1882–1925) American illustrator, etcher and painter. His New York cityscapes evoke the grimness and glamour of urban existence: street scenes, slum life, barrooms, prayer meetings and prize fights – all depicted with more exuberance than sorrow.

**belvedere** A structure on top of a building, open on one or more sides and either used as a lookout or else largely ornamental.

**bema** In a basilica church, an open space between the termination of the arcade and the eastern wall and apse. In early Christian churches it is a raised platform for the clergy.

**Benois, Alexandre** (1870–1960) Russian painter and stage designer. He was a near-contemporary of Bakst and a founder of *Mir Iskusstva*, the journal of the Russian avant-garde. He designed sets for Diaghilev, including the classic *Petrushka* (1911). After the Russian Revolution he was appointed a keeper at the Hermitage. His last work in the theatre was for La Scala, Milan.

**Berchem, Nicolaes** or Claesz (1620–83) Dutch painter, the son of Pieter Claesz and a pupil of Jan van Goyen. His small pastoral scenes, usually painted on wood, appealed to a public which liked rustic landscape to be seen through an Italianate haze. He remains popular, and features as a figure painter in the work of contemporaries such as Ruisdael and Hobbema.

**Bernard, Emile** (1868–1941) French painter, writer and critic. He was an early friend of Toulouse-Lautrec, Gauguin and Van Gogh, also of Cézanne and Odilon Redon. Bernard's own work during the years of close contact with Gauguin reaches a high level of originality and verve. Later, he was to spend more time writing than painting. His correspondence with the great painters is a mine of valuable information, reinforced by insights, criticisms and explanations dealing with the formative years of the Modern Movement.

**Bernini, Gian Lorenzo** or Giovanni Lorenzo (1598–1680) Italian painter, sculptor and architect, working in the Baroque style during the Counter-Reformation. He was principal artist in the Papal court of Urban VIII and architect for St Peter's, Rome, to which he also contributed the baldacchino – canopy on twisted columns – over the high altar and some sculptures. He later decorated the apse of St Peter's by order of a new pope, Alexander II, and in 1665 was invited by Louis XIV to make plans for the Louvre, though they were not the ones eventually chosen. He is the embodiment of the Italian Baroque at the height of its confidence and pomp.

**Berruguete, Alonso** (*c.*1489–1561) Spanish sculptor and painter. He is thought to have been the pupil of his father, Pedro Berruguete (died *c.*1503), who was Court Painter to Ferdinand and Isabella. Alonso completed Filippino Lippi's *Coronation of the Virgin*, now in the Louvre, in the style of Michelangelo, whose influence, and that of Leonardo and Raphael, can be traced in most of his work. His commissions as Court Painter to Charles V included a quantity of reliefs, architectural statuary, and carvings for Toledo Cathedral.

**Bertoldo di Giovanni** (*c.*1420–91) Italian sculptor. He was the pupil and assistant of Donatello and teacher of Michelangelo. Later he was employed by Lorenzo de' Medici as Keeper of the Academy of Art in the Medici gardens.

**Besnard, Paul Albert** (1849–1934) French painter. He trained at the École des Beaux-Arts, winning the Prix de Rome in 1874, and became highly regarded as a portrait painter in an Impressionist mode, in which natural settings and fragmented light combine to vivacious effect.

**Bestiary** A pictorial representation of natural history in which real or mythical birds and beasts are used for moral or moralizing ends. It has ancient roots, and entered medieval art through translations from the Latin. It has survived into modern times, for example in the

Apollinaire/Sutherland aquatints published in 1979.

**Bevan, Robert** (1865–1925) English painter. Trained in London and Paris, he was a member of the Camden Town Group and of the London Group. He knew Gauguin at Pont-Aven, and adopted a painting style akin to Pointillism with his clear, linear studies of rural landscape, figures and horses.

**Bewick, Thomas** (1755–1828) English animal artist and wood engraver, credited with the single-handed revival of woodblock engraving as a means of illustration. His illustrations to *A General History of Quadrupeds* (1790) and *A History of British Birds* (1797–1804) are based on the observations of a countryman who regarded his native landscape – the countryside around Newcastle upon Tyne – with an affectionate and observant eye. The small vignettes which he used as tailpieces to fill half-empty pages are masterpieces of English rustic art.

Bewick used the end grain of the block, working it with a burin instead of a knife, lowering those parts which would be background or which he meant to print as silvery grey. By this means he was able to achieve unprecedented subtlety of tone, akin to colour in its range and texture.

**billet** Norman architectural decoration consisting of bands of raised, short, cylindrical or square pieces, or billets, placed at regular intervals.

**Bingham, George Caleb** (1811–79) American painter, born in Virginia. He received virtually no academic training, but turned his eye on everyday scenes in the days of the frontiersmen, fur traders and trappers. These have an authentic force and value; unlike his later work, following a fatal exposure to German Romanticism during a spell in Düsseldorf.

For the last two years of his life he was Professor of Art at the University of Missouri.

**bistre** A brown pigment made by burning beech wood. It was widely used in watercolours and wash drawings until the early 19th century, when it was largely replaced by sepia.

Less reddish in colour than sepia, it is prone to fade on exposure to light.

**bite** In etching, the mordant which corrodes the plate when it is immersed in an acid bath is said to bite it. The temperature and concentration of the mordant determine the extent of the bite, and correspondingly the depth, width and evenness of the etched lines. When a mordant bites through or undercuts the etching ground, the process is described as foul biting. Crevé is the name given to defects which result from over-biting. The extent to which a plate is bitten depends also on the length of time it is left in the acid bath. It may be removed after only a short immersion and the lines which are to be the faintest **stopped out** to prevent them being further bitten. By repeating the procedure, increasingly deeper lines can be selectively produced.

**Blake, William** (1757–1827) English visionary artist, poet, seer and philosopher. He served a seven-year apprenticeship as an engraver before enrolling at the Royal Academy Schools, where he was a contemporary of Henry Fuseli, John Flaxman and Thomas Stothard. Blake then set up as a printer in partnership with a former fellow student, James Parker. The famous illuminated books followed. Text and illustrations were etched on to a copper plate so as to leave words and pictures in relief; colours were applied in ink and wash, and particular passages finished in watercolour. The succession of six major books, handmade and hand printed by Blake – *Songs of Innocence, Songs of Experience, America, a Prophecy, Vision of the Daughters of Albion, The Book of Thel* and *The Marriage of Heaven and Hell* – are a combination of poetry, craft and art unique in publishing.

In wood engraving Blake created a series of illustrations for a schoolbook, Thornton's *Vergil*, which bring his view of pastoral landscape to its highest level of poetic intensity. These small engravings were the first intimations of Blake's genius that inspired the young Samuel Palmer, who inherited much of Blake's highly charged romanticism in his Shoreham days. Blake's *Milton, Jerusalen* and *Book of Job* are now numbered among his most important works. The paintings and watercolours, and pictures in mixed media, show Blake as a Neoclassicist with a wholly individual, non-academic technique which is the despair of orthodox scholars. His influence is still felt in the work of the inheritors of the English pastoral tradition such as Graham Sutherland and Robin Tanner.

**Blaue Reiter** An association of German artists formed in 1911 when the New Artists Association rejected a painting of Wassily Kandinsky's, *The Last Judgement*, for their annual exhibition. He, Franz Marc and Gabriele Münter (1877–1962) seceded and organized their own exhibition, which they called *Der Blaue Reiter* (The Blue Rider), after another picture of Kandinsky's. August Macke and Paul Klee were also connected with the group. It amounted to a loose association of individuals, internationalist in outlook, who proposed no particular programme but were held together by a shared belief in freedom of experiment and the need to embody spiritual perceptions in their painting.

The breadth of their interest is reflected in the works they chose for their exhibitions. Canvases by the Douanier Rousseau and Robert Delaunay were hung at their first show. The second includes those of Braque, André Derain, Picasso and members of Die Brücke. Kandinsky, the dominating force, was interested in discovering an intellectual and artistic synthesis that would establish a spiritual basis for all the arts, particularly the relationship between music and painting. Their magazine, the *Blaue Reiter Almanac*, was dominated by these ideas. In its pages Kandinsky developed his observation that there are two main paths in art, the 'great realism' (as embodied by Rousseau) and the 'great abstraction', both leading to the same goal: the subordination of formal concerns to the artist's need to express his inner meaning.

When the war began in 1914, the *Blaue Reiter* was disbanded. The group represents the high-water mark of pre-war modernism in Germany.

**blind printing** The technique of printing an uninked plate so that the design is embossed on to the paper, giving a three-dimensional form. Japanese print makers use this method, which they call *karazuri*. Its white-on-white image and subtly textured relief appeal to many contemporary print makers.

**block book** A form of illustrated book, printed entirely from wood blocks, both text and illustration being cut from the same block. Block books enjoyed a heyday shortly before the invention of printing, when popular prayer books were often reproduced by this method.

**Bloemaert, Abraham** (1564–1651) Dutch painter who is thought to have been a pupil of Gerrit Splinter and Joos de Beer, and was himself the master of Andries Both, Aelbert Cuyp, Hornthorst and others of their generation. Bloemaert was influenced by the Italian Mannerist, Caravaggio, whose admirers in Holland became known as the Utrecht School.

**blot drawing** A practice described by Alexander Cozens in *A New Method for Assisting the Invention in Drawing Original Compositions of Landscape*, 1786. The artist allows accidental blots or stains to stimulate the imagination into working them into a finished composition. Leonardo da Vinci anticipated the technique, suggesting that blemishes on a stucco wall might serve the same function, and the Surrealists later exploited its random nature as a means of tapping subconscious imagery. Ernst's **frottages** and Dubuffet's **empreintes** are instances of the same principle of taking advantage of chance forms.

**boast** To give rough shape to a sculptor's block before more careful work begins.

**Boccioni, Umberto** (1882–1916) Italian painter. He worked in Rome from 1900, with visits to Paris and Russia, and later in Milan, where he met Gaetano Previati (1852–1920), author of treatises on **Divisionism**. Already influenced by Giacomo Balla's enthusiasm for Neo-Impressionism, he became active in the Futurist movement in both painting and sculpture. He set out to capture in his art the 'absolute movement' of the subject, its inner dynamism and constantly changing relationship with its surroundings. His *Horse* series and his *Iridescent Interpenetrations* explore his notion of 'force forms' and the continuity of movement as described in paint.

**Böcklin, Arnold** (1827–1901) Swiss painter. He trained in Germany, Belgium and Paris, returning to Basel before making for Rome, where he spent seven years painting the Roman Campagna, embellished with mythological figures. He turned to portraiture to make a living, obtained a teaching post at Weimar, and revisited Italy with his confidence renewed. His later landscapes are infused with a poetic romanticism which is matched by his craftsmanlike technique.

**Body art** The concept of creating art through bodily action rather than through the agency of a conventional medium. It has taken sado-masochistic forms, especially in California, involving deliberate mutilation, floating in a bath of dirty water, and getting shot.

**bodycolour** An opaque pigment, as opposed to a transparent or glazing colour.

**Boldini, Giovanni** (1842–1931) Italian painter. He met members of the Impressionist group on a visit to Paris in 1867, which helped to set the style of his highly successful portraits of the *haute monde*. He worked fast, with a deftness and sense of style that put him alongside Sargent and Whistler as a society painter.

**bolection moulding** A wooden convex moulding, used in Renaissance panelling, which projects beyond the face of the frame.

**Bologna, Giovanni de,** otherwise Jean Boulogne (1529–1608) Mannerist sculptor. A Fleming by birth, he spent most of his life in Italy where his marbles and bronzes include the *Fountain of Neptune* (Bologna), the fountains in gardens of the Medici, *Hercules and the Centaur* (Loggia dei Lanzi, Florence), the Grimaldi Chapel at Genoa, numerous equestrian statues and the doors of Pisa Cathedral. His *Flying Mercury* and *Rape of the Sabines*, both in Florence, are examples of Mannerism in the round.

**Bolognese School** Painting and drawings originating in Bologna, particularly from the end of the 16th century under the impetus of the Carracci family (Agostino, Annibale and Ludovic) and the generation of Bolognese artists that included Domenichino, Reni and Guercino. Characteristics of the School are a departure from Mannerism in favour of a style that prefigures the Baroque, and an elegance acquired from High Renaissance sources.

**Bomberg, David** (1890–1957) British painter. He trained as a lithographer, studied at evening classes and at the Slade School, and in 1914 became a founder member of the **London Group**. He exhibited with the Vorticists in the following year. His figure studies were reduced to simplified, semi-abstract forms, often suggesting bodily movement.

A retrospective exhibition at the Tate Gallery in 1967 helped to re-establish him as one of the most single-minded and individual members of the Modern Movement in Britain. His brush-stroke paintings, infused with energetic colour, have an expressionist intensity.

**Bonington, Richard Parkes** (1802–28) English painter, mostly of landscape and coastal marine subjects. He is one of the early 19th-century links between English and French painting which helped to introduce an English concept of landscape into the more academic world of French romantic painting.

Born near Nottingham, he spent most of his short life in France, his family having moved to Calais in 1817. Some outdoor sketching and lessons from Louis Francia (1772–1839) prepared him for the École des Beaux-Arts, Paris. On leaving, aged about 18, he became a pupil of Baron Gros (1771–1835), the painter of Napoleon's epic victories, and travelled in Italy. He exhibited watercolour landscapes at the Salon of 1822 and again in 1824, in company with Constable. In the following year he and Delacroix, whom he had met in Paris, were in England, and worked together – a contact which the French painter was to value all his life.

Bonington's mastery of watercolour, with its capacity to catch elusive effects of light and tone, and the brilliant clarity of his sketches in oils, earned him a high reputation in the short time he was alive. He ranks among the European masters.

**Bonnard, Pierre** (1867–1947) French painter, regarded as a late Impressionist in the line of Monet and Renoir. He worked closely with Maurice Denis and with Edouard Vuillard and exhibited at the Salon des Indépendants. He was active as a print maker and in the theatre at the turn of the century, and subsequently adopted a decorative Post-Impressionist style. The style for which he is best known is a return to the semi-abstraction of Monet, though with an underlying feeling for structure. His favourite subject, nudes in bath scenes, gave him the opportunity to use the reflecting surface of water as a formal component of 'pure painting'.

**bonnet tile** The curved tile used for joining plain tiles along the hips of the roof.

**Borromini, Francesco** (1599–1667) Architect of the High Baroque, he ranks with Pietro da Cortona and Bernini. He started as a stonemason, moved from Lugano to Rome as a young man, and worked as a stone carver at St Peter's. He became chief assistant to Bernini, of whom he was professionally jealous, until 1633, when he received a commission for S. Carlo alle Quattro Fontane, Rome, which he completed in 1646.

He was brilliantly successful in breaking away from orthodox solutions, culminating in the ziggurat splendour of his S. Ivo della Sapienza. The sculptural character of his style, with its voluptuous rhythms, was unique in his time.

**Bosch, Hieronymus** (*c.* 1450–1516) Flemish artist, descendant of two generations of painters, whose aptitude for grotesque imagery sets him apart from such contemporaries as Jan van Eyck and Rogier van der Weyden. Only a handful of his paintings is signed, and fewer than 40 of the ones ascribed to him may genuinely be his work. His macabre fantasy, seemingly–but not necessarily–out of keeping with religious subjects, proved highly popular, and encouraged copyists and imitators. Philip II of Spain formed a collection of his works, now mostly in the Prado, Madrid. Bosch's combination of cruelty, inventiveness and wit endeared him to the Surrealists, who helped to re-establish his reputation in modern times.

**boss** In Gothic architecture, a small projecting block of stone, commonly carved into a foliage design, which is placed either to mask the junction of vaulting ribs, or as the lower termination of a hood mould, or to finish off an interrupted string-course.

**Both, Jan** (*c.* 1618–52) Dutch painter, a pupil of Bloemaert, and predominantly Italianate in style. His landscapes are nevertheless enlivened with authentic touches, as opposed to mythological figures in the style of Claude Lorraine. He shared with Nicolaes Berchem a yearning for golden southern light, which following a visit to Italy in the late 1630s he introduced into the more workaday scenes of his native landscape.

His brother Andries (1612–41), who accompanied him to Italy, collaborated in some of his work, and painted rustic scenes with figures.

**Botticelli, Alessandro di Mariano Filipepi,** called Sandro (1445–1510) Florentine painter, and one of the great innovators of the Renaissance, whose achievement was given its due only in the latter half of the 19th century in the wake of the Pre-Raphaelites. His linear evocations of womanly beauty in such paintings as the *Primavera* (1478) and *The Birth of Venus* (*c.* 1485) look back to Gothic origins, while expressing a contemporary ideal. The recognition of beauty as divinity imparts a devotional quality to Botticelli's religious themes and paintings, in which the Madonna is given the innocent sensuality of a living woman. The *Mystic Divinity* (National Gallery, London), painted when he was 65, bears an inscription implying that the painter was shortly expecting the Apocalypse.

**Boucher, François** (1703–70) French painter. His main subject matter was the languid and frivolous life of the pre-Revolutionary upper class. He was a favourite of Mme de Pompadour, to whom he gave lessons, and was in great demand as a decorator of châteaux, theatrical sets and tapestries. In some of his work there are suggestions of a more substantial talent than was required of him by the voluptuous society in which he lived.

**Boudin, Eugène-Louis** (1824–98) French painter. He was born at Honfleur, the son of a ship's captain, and was awarded a grant to study in Paris. Strongly influenced by Corot, he exhibited at the Paris Salon of 1859. His encounter with the youthful Monet encouraged the boy to start painting open-air scenes. Like Monet, he also learned from Johan Jongkind, who painted in Normandy and along the Channel coast.

Boudin's bright palette and breezy style bring him close to the Impressionists, with whom he exhibited as a token of support at their first exhibition in 1874. His beach scenes at the French seaside resorts remain popular.

**Bourdon, Sebastien** (1616–71) French painter, noted for his use of a variety of other painters' styles. In Rome (1634) he imitated Poussin, Claude, Castiglione, Van Laer and the Netherlands genre painters. In 1652 he became Court Painter to Queen Christina of Sweden. Two years later in Paris he built up a prosperous business in portraiture. His late paintings, lyrical in the manner of Poussin, establish him at last as a painter of charm and intelligence. The National Gallery, London, has his *Return of the Ark* which was once in the collection of the English connoisseur, Sir George Beaumont (1753–1827).

**Bouts, Dirk** (*c.* 1415–75) Flemish painter. He was a follower of Van Eyck and of Rogier van der Weyden, who might have been his master. He left Haarlem, his birthplace, some time after 1448 to work in Louvain, where he prospered for the remainder of his career. His works there include the *Martydom of Erasmus* and *The Last Supper*, both in the church of St-Pierre. His *Justice of the Emperor Otto*, painted for the Louvain town hall and now in Brussels (Musée Royaux des Beaux-Arts), is a characteristically eventful, though undramatic, composition. The *Portrait of a Man* (National Gallery, London), his earliest dated work (1462), is also said to be the earliest example of a portrait in a room with a view through the window.

**bow window** A projecting curved or semicircular window.

**bowstring truss frame** A 19th-century cast-iron roof construction used mainly in railway terminals and enabling the roof to span great widths without using tie beams.

**box frame** A form of frame construction used in the building of flats and offices where the rooms are of uniform size. The load is carried by cross-walls of strengthened girders and vertical stanchions.

**Boyd, Arthur** (b. 1920) Australian painter. He is a member of a dynasty of artists, ranging from sculptors to potters, whose work combines Australian imagery with a richly sensuous use of colour. He has produced paintings and suites of prints on specific themes – *Nebuchadnezzar, The Half-Caste Bride, Europa and the Bull* – enhanced by a sensitive awareness of analogies to the modern world. His brother David (b. 1924) shares many of the same attributes, drawing on native Australian landscape, legends and myths in paintings remarkable for their impassioned, yet immaculate, use of colour.

**Boys, Thomas Shotter** (1803–74) English watercolour painter and engraver of architectural subjects. Apprenticed to an engraver as a youth, he went to Paris in 1823, where he came into contact with Richard Bonington. He returned to London in 1837 to embark on his well-known series of lithographic plates, *Picturesque Views in Paris, Ghent, Antwerp, Rouen etc.* (1839) and *Original Views of London As It Is* (1842). These, and his highly accomplished watercolours rather in the manner of – and often comparable to – Bonington, have secured his place among the most admired English draughtsmen of his time.

**bozzetto** A sculptor's model or maquette which serves as a rough sketch for the final design.

**Brabazon, Hercules Brabazon** (1821–1906) English amateur painter. He was securely financed by his estates in Ireland and spent his life travelling in exotic places, from North Africa to India, amusing himself with his paints. It was not until 1891, when he was 70, that his watercolours, pastels and gouaches were exhibited, and thus brought him to light. They were extravagantly praised, by Ruskin among others, and have remained popular ever since. Many are in the style of late Turner, or of Cox, Muller and De Wint; others are tributes to old masters, notably Velazquez.

**bracket capital** A capital with a bracket projecting from it at each side so as to shorten the bearing of the architrave or lintel from one column to another.

**Bramante, Donato** (1444–1514) Italian architect of the High Renaissance, born at Urbino. He was employed by Duke Ludovico Sforza as a church painter and architect, but was forced to flee to Rome during the French invasion of Lombardy in 1499. His first Roman buildings have a gravity typical of the new respect for antique forms. Under Pope Julius II, who was elected in 1503, he drew plans for the Vatican and St Peter's that would transform them in scale and appearance. Though never brought to fruition, they established a plan that was followed in part by Michelangelo. Raphael, who trained under him, took over his role as the leading architect of Rome, and with it the essence of his bold ideas.

**Brancuşi, Constantin** (1876–1957) Romanian sculptor. He spent most of his life in Paris and was a friend of Modigliani, Henri Rousseau and other members of the Montparnasse set in the early years of the century. He embarked on a process of stripping away superfluous elements in sculpture, to arrive at hidden, embryonic forms. His work consisted, typically, of highly polished materials, from metal to stone, burnished as if rubbing alone might yield the inner secret he was looking for. This led him to forms and structures which, while abstract in appearance, are nevertheless physical and expressive.

**Brangwyn, Sir Frank** (1867–1956) British painter and designer. After working for William Morris as a tapestry designer he turned to painting, chiefly as a muralist, and achieved an international reputation with his grandly conceived designs, which include murals for the Rockefeller Center, New York. A Brangwyn Museum was opened in Bruges, his birthplace, in 1936. He was knighted in 1941.

**Braque, Georges** (1882–1963) French painter, one of the great artists of the century. With Picasso, he was the discoverer of **Cubism** at a time when the two worked together, in Braque's phrase, 'like climbers roped together on a mountain'. After a brief Fauvist period, Braque absorbed the example of Cézanne, which in turn led to the Cubist reworking of forms and the beginnings of Abstraction.

He parted company with Picasso at the beginning of the Great War, during which he was severely wounded in the head. In the 1920s he entered on his period of richest achievement, replacing the deliberately ephemeral or banal ingredients of 'Synthetic' Cubism with more painterly techniques. His palette, in deep, strong tones, moves towards effects which hold out, as he put it, against the colours and tones of nature. Objects are re-created for a new purpose, confined within the frame: they constantly change positions, obeying no logic but the scheme which the artist has created for them. The sequence of *gueridon* compositions – tabletops crowded with objects – illustrate this process most vividly, with their visual distinctions between pictorial and tactile space and their deliberate 'rhymes'. In the late 1930s, these subjects become monumental in scale and feeling.

In a late series, Braque asserts the primacy of painting as a universe in itself by taking the artist's studio as a subject, summing up all that he has discovered about space, volume and the illusory nature of form.

**brattishing** Miniature battlements or ornamental foliage cresting on the top of a screen or cornice.

**brickwork** A brick laid end on so that only the end is visible is known as a header. A brick laid sideways so that its side forms the face of the wall is called a stretcher.

**Bright, Henry** (1810–73) English painter. He was born in Suffolk, took lessons from Norwich School painters and exhibited in London from 1836 and with the Norwich Society from 1848. He was a highly successful teacher and drawing master in a seductively easy style, often mixing media with adventurous results.

**Bril, Paul** (1554–1626) Flemish painter and engraver, mostly active in Rome. He painted several buildings in the city, and was also commissioned by Pope Sixtus V to paint landscape views of the Roman countryside. His pastoral approach to landscape, after the manner of Elsheimer, made its way into the art of Claude Lorraine via Claude's Roman master, Agostino Tassi (1580–1644).

**Bristol School** A designation, loosely applied, to a group of artists resident in Bristol between 1820 and 1840. As at Norwich, large private collections, local patronage and opportunities to exhibit together existed in Bristol, and there was a nucleus of professional painters around whom a company of part-time or amateur artists could form. Their subjects were mostly landscape, often features of the local countryside such as Leigh Woods or scenes along the Avon.

The senior members of the School were Francis Danby (1792–1861), born in Ireland, a respected exhibitor at the Royal Academy; Samuel Jackson (1794-1869), an Associate of the Water Colour Society; James Baker Pyne (1800–75), a drawing master and follower of Turner; the Rev. John Eagles (1783-1855); Edward Villiers Rippingille (1798–1859); James Johnson (1803–34); Edward Bird (1772–1819), who was elected RA in 1815; and William James Muller (1812–45). To these may be added Harry John Johnson (1826–84), a pupil of Muller's; George Fripp (1813–96), who studied under J. B. Pyne (as did Muller); John Harrison (1810–96), Muller's doctor and close friend, an accomplished watercolourist; John Skinner Prout (1806–76), nephew of Samuel Prout; James Chisholm Gooden (active 1835–75); and Edward Dighton (1822–53), another of Muller's inner circle. A link with the Norwich School is provided by Muller's tour of East Anglia in 1830, accompanied by the Rev. James Bulwer (1794–1879), a patron and pupil of John Sell Cotman.

**broach** In Gothic architecture, a sloping, triangular piece of masonry built up from the angle of a tower against the adjacent face of an octagonal spire, serving to fill up the angle and connect the lines of tower and spire. It occurs most often in 13th-century work.

**Broad Manner** During the second half of the 15th century, Florentine engraving was classified as either Broad Manner or Fine Manner. The Fine Manner uses delicate lines and light cross-hatching, whereas an engraving in the Broad Manner is made by lines which are comparatively bold.

**bronze** An alloy of copper and tin, bronze has been the most popular metal used for cast sculpture since antiquity. Bronzes are either sand cast or more commonly made by the lost-wax method. Sand casting involves packing a special sand round the original plaster model to make a mould, inserting a core, baking them both, then pouring molten bronze into the gap between the mould and the core. The lost-wax method uses less bronze. From a plaster cast of the original, a mould is made which is then lined inside with molten wax to form a hollow wax model. Once cool and extracted from the mould the surface of this wax model can be worked on by the sculptor until perfect. A new mould is then made around the finished model, the wax melted out and molten bronze poured into the thin cavity. Any number of such casts can be taken this way. Depending on what final effect is desired, casts made by either method must be finished by filing if they are to have a perfect surface.

**Bronzino, Agnolo Torri** (1503–72) Italian Mannerist painter, a pupil of Jacopo Pontormo, whose style his resembles. He became official portraitist to the ducal court of Florence, and in that capacity was a considerable artist, combining mastery of design with an aloof refinement which detaches him from his subjects. The religious paintings are not so convincing, but in works such as the well-known allegory, *Venus, Cupid, Folly and Time*, c. 1545 (National Gallery, London), his qualities seem well matched. This particular painting, in which an erotic image is brazenly disguised, may well be his masterpiece. It marks the end of the great epoch of Florentine painting.

**Brower, Adriaen** (1605–38) Flemish painter, follower of Franz Hals and of Pieter Bruegel. His bucolic scenes of peasant life are largely set in hovels and taverns. They are enhanced by the painter's skilful handling of colour, and by a delicacy of touch that often brings dignity or pathos to his subjects.

**Brown, Ford Madox** (1821–93) English painter. He was born in Calais and studied at Antwerp, Paris and Rome. He came to England in 1845 and met Dante Gabriel Rossetti, who took some instruction from him. Brown's work then assumed a Pre-Raphaelite aspect, though he never formally joined the Brotherhood. His paintings include a number of well-executed and strongly coloured landscapes, and the well-known *The Last of England* (1855), at Birmingham.

**Brown, Lancelot,** known as Capability Brown (1716–83) English architect and landscape gardener. His houses were in the Palladian style, such as Croome Court and Claremont House. But his true achievement was as a designer of park-like settings for gentlemen's country seats, in which he created pastoral landscapes that could be taken for works of nature. Among them are the grounds and lake at Blenheim Palace, the park at Chatsworth, and the gardens at Audley End and Longleat. In 1764 he was appointed Master Gardener to George III at Hampton Court.

**Browne, Hablot Knight,** known as 'Phiz' (1815–82) His fame rests on his illustrations to Dickens, including the *Pickwick Papers*, but he was also an exhibitor in both oils and watercolour and illustrated Surtees, Le Fanu, Defoe, Swift, Fielding and Smollett with an eye for social caricature and occasional pathos.

**Bruegel,** Brueghel or Breughel A family of Flemish painters who span two centuries, originating in Pieter Bruegel the Elder (*c.*1525–69), the first and greatest. He stands with Rubens and Van Eyck, but unlike them he did not take as his subjects the big set-pieces of the day. He preferred to record the life and troubled times he lived in, with a skill and vigour recognized at the time as surpassing Hieronymus Bosch.

From early folklore subjects with an ironic flavour he moved on to bigger, more ambitious compositions, packing his canvas with explicitly detailed human activity. The *Tower of Babel* (1563), with its technical knowledge of engineering processes, has allegorical overtones. *The Procession to Calvary* (1566), his largest work, makes sombre comments on the indifference of humankind to a tragic event. *The Massacre of the Innocents*, of the same date, shows a biblical scene as an event in his own time, the drama personified in recognizably modern figures.

In the popular series of landscapes month by month, from which only five of the twelve presumed originals have survived, Bruegel's dexterity and command of composition are masterly, his colours glowing with life. *The Magpie on the Gallows* (1568) reputedly has a darker significance than the burgeoning landscape and dancing peasants seem to suggest. If so, the allusion may not be too sinister: Bruegel left that particular picture to his wife.

His son Jan Brueghel (1568–1625) – he restored the 'h' to the family name – was also known as 'Velvet' Brueghel, after the softness of his brushwork. He was a friend of Rubens, and worked with him on some of his paintings. His own specialities were flower studies and still life but he is no less distinctive as a painter of idyllic landscapes in which birds, beasts and humans co-habit in perfect harmony. His sons Jan Brueghel II (1602–78) and Ambrosius (1617–75) painted in much the same style, though with less distinction, and their work, sometimes wrongly attributed, has tended to obscure the merits of their father's.

Copies of Pieter Bruegel's work were made by his son, Pieter Brueghel the Younger, called Hell Brueghel (1564–1638), and by Pieter Brueghel III (1589 – *c.* 1640), who was able to make a living by trading on the famous family name.

**Brunelleschi,** or Filippo di Ser Brunellesco (1377–1446) Italian Florentine architect. He studied in Rome, where he mastered the principles of perspective, and proceeded to apply mathematical and engineering systems to architecture. His studies of Roman architectural construction helped him solve the problem of raising a dome on Florence Cathedral, which he had offered to finish, without the use of supports. The dome, the largest in the world, is his greatest single feat and served as Michelangelo's model for St Peter's, Rome. His churches, built with mathematical proportions, include S. Lorenzo, Spirito Santo, the Pazzi Chapel, S. Croce, and the S. Maria degli Angeli, in which his geometric concept, carried to extreme limits, was never finished.

**brushwork** The term applies to the particular character with which the paint is applied. Every major painter's brushwork is unique, and virtually inimitable. The term applies to the particular character with which the paint is applied. Brushwork is admired independently of its function in representing form. As an extreme manifestation, the quality of the applied paint can become the sole end of a painting, as it did for some of the American Expressionist painters of the 1950s.

**Brutalism** A term dating from the mid-1950s to describe the puritanical style of architecture, beloved by civic authorities, that has over-run large parts of urban Britain in the past 20 years. It originated as the architectural equivalent of **Art Brut** and Musique Concrète, but its possibilities fell short of its ambition. It is responsible for the residential barracks at Park Hill, Sheffield, numerous pedestrian precincts and shopping centres, and the Hayward complex on London's South Bank.

**Buck, Samuel** (1696–1779) English engraver and topographical draughtsman. His specialities were abbeys, castles and picturesque ruins, which he and his brother Nathaniel engraved in a series, eventually brought together as *Buck's Antiquities*, 1774.

**bucrane** A sculptured, garlanded ox skull found in classical friezes.

**Buffet, Bernard** (b. 1928) French painter. He studied at the École des Beaux-Arts and after a Post-Impressionist phase he turned to a more figurative realism. This gives his work a spiky, energetic character which has many admirers and is widely reproduced.

**bull's eye** An oval or circular window.

**burin** An alternative name for a graver, the principal tool used in engraving to cut into the surface of the plate or block. It consists of a steel shaft, usually with a rectangular or lozenge-shaped cross-section cut obliquely to form the point, bedded in a rounded wooden handle which fits into the palm of the hand.

**Burne-Jones, Sir Edward Coley** (1833–98) English Pre-Raphaelite painter. An early friend of William Morris, he attached himself to Dante Gabriel Rossetti while still an undergraduate at Oxford, and left the University to become a painter. Travels in Italy, including a visit to Venice with Ruskin, gave him a taste for 15th-century painting, especially that of Botticelli. This, combined with a sentimental-

ized notion of medieval styles and graces, gives his work a dreamlike sweetness that was much to the Victorians' taste. His works are respected museum pieces. He was made a baronet in 1894.

**burnisher** A tool used in intaglio engraving, made of smooth, rounded, polished metal. Its purpose is to remove unwanted lines, reduce the depth of the lines, and smooth out areas of the plate. See **répoussage**.

**burr** In engraving, this term refers to the rough edge of the furrows cut by the burin in the surface of a metal plate. Where a sharp, clean line is desired, burr may be removed with a scraper. It is, however, considered an attractive feature in **drypoint**, as it softens and blurs the printed lines.

**Burra, Edward** (1905–76) English painter. He was influenced by George Grosz, Giorgio de Chirico and the popular art of Latin America, but retained an individuality that puts him among the most distinctive English painters of his time. He exhibited with the English Surrealists in 1936 and 1938. He worked mainly in watercolour, bringing to the medium an expressive force well suited to the intensity of his style.

**Butler, Reg** (b. 1913) English sculptor and architect, formerly an assistant to Henry Moore. His entry for an international competition, the Unknown Political Prisoner (1953), won him instant renown. His work in metal owes much to Constructivist ideas, which continue to play a part in his more figurative subjects of recent years.

**Butterfield, William** (1814–1900) English architect, prominent in the 19th-century Gothic Revival. He was less interested in building in authentic Gothic forms than in enlivening the high Victorian style with chromatic materials such as coloured bricks and tiles. His most famous monument is Keble College, Oxford, which as time passes assumes the dignity of a classic Victorian design.

**buttress** A substantial projection from the face of a wall to resist outward thrust. In Gothic architecture it is an important element of design.

**Byzantine art** Art and architecture from the foundation of Constantinople in 330 AD to the capture of the city by the Turks in 1453. The term also applies to work done in the Byzantine tradition in the epoch that followed under the patronage or influence of the Greek Orthodox Church. Its origins are religious and theological, its purposes sacramental and didactic. As part of faith and ritual, it is also anonymous: the identity of the artist is as irrelevant as figurative imagery from the real world. Its enduring beauties are of an ornate, otherworldly kind, with a devout attention to stylized form and gesture.

Historically, the Byzantine manner links East and West, its oriental qualities having

impressed themselves on the imagery of European art and architecture, partly through the pillaging activities of the Crusaders. As well as devotional painting and architecture, Byzantine art embraces tapestry, embroidery, jewellery, enamelling and illuminated manuscripts, which carried the beauty of the tradition from hand to hand.

**cable** A twisted rope design, used as a moulding decoration in Norman and Romanesque architecture.

**Caillebotte, Gustave** (1848–94) French painter, a member of the Impressionist circle. He exhibited in five Impressionist exhibitions between 1876 and 1882, and in addition collected his friends' pictures with the intention of passing them to the French state on his death. The bequest eventually consisted of 65 works, including eight by Renoir, sixteen by Monet, five by Cézanne, and seven by Degas. After his death they were rejected by the authorities and Renoir, executor of the will, was obliged to weed out the paintings which were regarded as the most objectionable. Well over half the Caillebotte bequest came into this category. Only in 1928 was the entire collection admitted to the Louvre.

**caisson** A sunken panel in a flat or vaulted ceiling.

**Caldecott, Randolph** (1846–86) English draughtsman and illustrator. His first drawings were published in local newspapers in Manchester. He went to London in 1872, had work accepted by magazines, and achieved success with his illustrations for Washington Irving's *Old Christmas* and *Bracebridge Hall*. His subsequent career as illustrator of children's books, such as *The House that Jack Built* and *John Gilpin's Ride*, puts him alongside the popular illustrators of his time, such as Walter Crane, Phil May and Helen Allingham.

**Calder, Alexander** (b. 1898) American sculptor and Abstract painter. Before taking to art he was trained as an engineer, an interest which emerges in his mobiles and stabiles made of painted wires and metal discs which he produced in the 1930s. His paintings are in the line of Joan Miró and Jean Arp.

**Byzantine art** Detail from the 6th-century Barberini ivory, the *Triumph of an Emperor* (Louvre, Paris).

**Callcott, Sir Augustus Wall** (1779–1844) English painter. He started as a portrait artist, was an associate of Girtin and his circle, and travelled widely in Europe in search of Romantic subjects, mostly landscape and coastal scenery. He was a friend of Turner, and for a short time his rival in critical esteem. He was elected RA in 1810 and knighted in 1837.

**calligraphic** In painting and drawing, a term describing a fluid and rhythmic line or brush-stroke, expressive of an original hand.

**Callot, Jacques** (1592–1635) French draughtsman and etcher. He visited Rome and Florence as a young man, recording daily life in all its picaresque variety, etching with great spirit and directness on to copper plates prepared with a hard ground of his own devising – an innovation which opened up new possibilities in the medium. His most important work is the series of plates done in his last years describing the horrors and atrocities of the times: the *Miseries of War* (1633) and the *Tortures* (1634).

**Callow, William** (1812–1908) English watercolour artist. His long life covered the rise of watercolour painting as a popular and relatively lucrative activity, and its eventual decline into late Victorian picture making. He studied under Copley Fielding, lived for a time in Paris, and shared a studio there with Thomas Shotter Boys. The Bonington influence is strong in his early work.

In 1841 he left Paris to become a drawing master in London, with a variety of well-connected pupils. His work in the latter part of his life lacks the verve and clarity of his Paris years, but he stands among the major watercolourists of the 19th century in popularity. His brother John (1822–79) took lessons from him, and ultimately inherited his practice.

**Calvert, Edward** (1790–1883) English artist and etcher. He joined the circle of Blake's admirers around 1825, and became a close friend of Samuel Palmer with whom he was associated at Shoreham, Kent, as one of the self-styled 'Ancients'. His paintings are less widely admired than his etchings, which were done under the influence of Palmer and the Valley of Vision. They are infused with a dreamy classicism which puts them among the greatest achievements of the English pastoral style.

**camaieu** A painting, drawing or engraving in two or three tones of the same colour. It is distinct from a monochrome, which may use all the tones of one particular colour, and from a grisaille, which is in various shades of grey.

**Camden Town Group** A coterie of English artists who, influenced by Sickert, broke away from the New English Art Club in 1911, in a shared enthusiasm for the work of Gauguin and Van Gogh. The original group, including Harold Gilman (1876–1919), Spencer Gore (1879–1914), Lucien Pissarro (1863–1944) Augustus John and Henry Lamb (1883–1960), were joined by Walter Bayes (1889–1956), Robert Bevan (1865–1925), Duncan Grant, Charles Ginner (1879–1952), Wyndham Lewis, James Dickson Innes (1887–1914) and J. B. Manson (1874–1945). They exhibited together four times before merging with Lewis's set in 1914 to form the London Group. They represent Post-Impressionism in England before it lapsed into art-school pastiche over the next 30 years.

**camera obscura** A device for obtaining accurate drawings by an arrangement of mirrors and lenses in a darkened box which project an image on to a sheet of paper so that it can be traced. Probably invented in the 16th century, it was in use until the 19th century, when the *camera lucida* became widely available. This was more accurate than the *camera obscura*, as it incorporated a prism which allowed variations in the size of the reflected image.

**Camoin, Charles** (1879–1965) French painter. He was an early companion of Matisse in Paris and later a friend of Cézanne at Aix. His work is Fauvist, though not as adventurous as that of Matisse or Derain. In 1905 he published some of Cézanne's sayings on art.

**campanile** The name given to the medieval and Renaissance form of Italian bell tower. The essential character of the campanile is that it is built on entirely vertical lines, with openings increasing in number in the upper stages.

**Camera obscura** A 17th-century engraving
illustrating the principal of the 'dark chamber'
(Kodak Museum).

**Campin, Robert** (*c.*1378–1444) Flemish
painter. He is also identified as the Master of
Flémalle after an abbey of that name supposedly at Liège. He was active in Tournai from
1406, and though none of his works is documented he is known to have been the master
of Rogier van der Weyden and of Jacques Daret
(*c.*1404 – after 1468). Campin's generally
acknowledged works include the *Virgin and
Child before a Firescreen* (National Gallery, London), the *St Barbara*, from the Werl altarpiece
(Prado, Madrid), and the *Annunciation*, from
the Merode altarpiece (Metropolitan Museum
of Art, New York).

**Canaletto,** originally named Antonio Canale
(1697–1768) Venetian painter. Having
worked as a scene painter with his father, who
was a theatrical designer, he went to Rome to
make a living by painting city views. In 1720
he returned to Venice and became a member
of the Guild, painting the city, the canals and
scenes of daily life, for the most part on the
spot. The Grand Tour brought an increasing
number of gentlemanly English travellers to
the city, and these became Canaletto's
bread-and-butter clients. Through these connections he was persuaded to visit England,
where he had difficulty in adjusting his method
to a totally different landscape and light.

His work shows little development from the
successful formula of his middle years, in which
the subject matter is treated with discipline
and restraint, and the city is shown overcast

as often as it is bathed in light. Canaletto's
attention to architecture never slackens, and
his figures are always lively and natural.

A great many of his pictures passed into the
Royal Collection from the collection of Joseph
Smith, English consul in Venice, who, as an
enthusiast for Canaletto's work, did much to
make it popular and widely admired.

**cancelled plate** When an artist has an edition
printed, he may cancel the plate when he is no
longer satisfied with its quality or wishes to
restrict the numbers. This is commonly done
by scoring through the plate. Sometimes, however, further impressions will be taken from a
cancelled or worn-out plate. These are known
as restrikes.

**cancelli** Railings dividing off the semicircular
court in the pagan basilica. They were later
adopted in the basilica form of church; hence
the word 'chancel'.

**Cano, Alonso** (1601–67) Spanish Baroque
sculptor and painter. He trained in Seville,
where his father had a workshop, and under
Francisco Pacheco (1564–1654), one of whose
pupils was the young Velazquez. He left for
Madrid in 1638, possibly at Velazquez's
suggestion, was arrested on suspicion of mur-
dering his wife, released, and eventually
engaged as a prebendary at Granada Cathedral. His designs for the façade of the Cathedral
were carried out after his death.

His paintings, often showing the influence
of Zurbaran or of Velazquez, have the flamboyant religiosity of the Spanish Baroque.

**canopy** A projecting hood construction over
such features as doors, windows and altars.

**Canova, Antonio** (1757–1822) Italian Neoclassical sculptor. Visits to Naples and Pompeii
in 1780 confirmed him in his admiration of the
Antique. A year later, settled in Rome, he
received a commission to design a monument
to Pope Clement XIV in the church of SS
Apostoli. A tomb figure *Genius of Death*, for the
sarcophagus of Clement XIII, followed in
1792. He was appointed to the Academy of St
Luke in 1800. There followed various busts
and statues of Napoleon including two, a
bronze and a marble, showing the great man

in the nude. The bronze version stands in the courtyard of the Brera, Milan; the marble was borne to London as war booty, and is now in the Wellington Museum, Apsley House.

Canova came to London in 1816 to view the Elgin marbles, and in 1819 was commissioned by George III to make a monument to the Stuarts for St Peter's, Rome. His marble *Cupid and Psyche*, in the Louvre, is one of the numerous fine works on which his reputation rests.

**cantilever** In architecture, a supporting beam projecting from a wall and so secured by the weight of the structure along part of its length that it can support the weight of the rest without the use of columns.

**capital** The crowning member of a column or pier, on which the superstructure rests. Capitals are often given decorative treatment, especially in Roman, Byzantine and Gothic architecture.

**Cappelle, Jan van de** (*c.* 1624–79) Dutch painter. As a wealthy Amsterdam dyer he had the means to build an important collection, including works by Rembrandt and other Dutch masters. He amused himself by painting undramatic seascapes somewhat in the manner of one of his favourite artists, Simon de Vlieger (*c.* 1600–53), who was well represented in his collection. These, and his pearly-grey winter landscapes, have secured him an honourable place among the marine painters of his time.

**capriccio** Italian for caprice. In art, the term is applied to any fantasy, but usually means that of a topographical nature. Veduta, when they contain anomalous juxtapositions (as in William Marlow's *St Paul's, London, with the Grand Canal, Venice*) are also called capriccio.

**Caravaggio, Michelangelo Merisi da** (1573–1610) Italian painter. His concept of light and realism made a resounding impact on his contemporaries, from the Netherlands to Spain. As a youth he served a four-year apprenticeship under Simone Peterzano, who may have been a pupil of Titian.

His first important commission, to decorate a chapel in the French church in Rome, reached completion only after a dispute with his patrons, who found his proposed altarpiece objectionable. Other church commissions brought him into disputes with the orthodox, who were offended by his representation of biblical figures as all-too-human flesh and blood. His insistence that 'everything in art is trifling that is not taken from life' brooked of no compromise.

Stylistically, however, as 17th-century critics remarked, he was not successful in showing figures in movement. The violent subject matter, involving outflung limbs and contorted faces, might create the image of action, but did not solve the problem of movement, which required an ability to relate figures in space to each other within an acquired system of pictorial conventions. As Caravaggio despised such conventions, his figures appear curiously still, despite their vigorous actions. However, he succeeds on another level: fidelity to the physical and psychological facts of a situation. There is an emphasis on incidental detail, of the kind the eye picks out at a moment of crisis. He has been called 'the inventor of the anti-hero in religious art' because his Bible figures (including the saints) are shown simply as ordinary working-class people, often with dirty feet.

The influence of his work lasted longest in Spain and the Spanish colony of Naples, where his style was turned into a tough, heavily loaded manner bordering on the theatrical, as in the work of Jusepe Ribera. In Spain, it nourished the imagination of the young Velazquez.

**caricature** The pictorial exaggeration of personal traits and features for jocular, scurrilous or satirical effect. The practice goes back to Greek and Roman times, although the term did not come into English usage until the time of Hogarth.

**Caro, Anthony** (b. 1924) British sculptor, who trained at the Royal Academy Schools and from 1951–3 as an assistant to Henry Moore. A visit to America in 1959 brought about a change in his work from figurative subjects to abstract compositions making use of painted metal.

**Carolean** The red-brick, hipped-roof architectural style common during the reigns of

Charles I (1625–49) and Charles II (1660–85).

**Carolingian art** Art of the reign of Charlemagne, 768–814, and subsequently up to around 900. It flourished alongside the Carolingian revival of culture and learning, which was the glory of the monarch's reign. Artists were encouraged to find their subjects in the origins of Christianity, much as Byzantine artists and craftsmen were directed to religious imagery glorifying the faith. Most paintings would have been decorations in churches, but few traces of these survive. Art treasures of the Carolingian era are most commonly illuminated missals, jewelled caskets, carved ivories and goldsmiths' work, all of consummate beauty. The *Gospel Book of Godescale*, commanded by Charlemagne in 781, is written in gold and silver on purple parchment. The *Utrecht Psalter*, *c.*820, showing realistically drawn figures against a background of mountains, looks back to early Christian models but also anticipates the more secular imagery of the early Middle Ages. A feature of Carolingian art, indeed, is the extent to which it incorporates and refines the themes and styles of ancient times, infusing them with Christian temperance and grace. The school of Tours produced a series of codices – gospels and religious texts – which are among the great achievements of the age. Metz and Reims were other important centres where the intellectual energy and devout craftsmanship of Carolingian artists laid the foundations of early medieval culture.

**Carpaccio, Vittore** (1450–1526) Italian painter. He was of the Venetian School, a follower of Gentile Bellini and studio assistant of Giovanni Bellini. The *Arrival of St Ursula in Cologne* (1490), in the Accademia in Venice, is the best known of his earlier works. His series of paintings in the Scuola di S. Giorgio degli Schiavoni, celebrating the Dalmation patron saints, is renowned for its combination of realistic detail and imaginative fancy.

**Carpeaux, Jean Baptiste** (1827–75) French sculptor and painter of the Second Empire. He studied at the École des Beaux-Arts, won the Prix de Rome (1854) and while still in Rome came to prominence with his *Ugolini*, now in the Louvre. On his return to Paris he was kept busy with portrait busts. Of his large sculptures, the *Flora* reliefs at the Tuileries, and the group *La Danse*, made for the Opéra and thought shocking in its time, are the most familiar.

**Carra, Carlo** (1881–1966) Italian painter, an early member of the Italian Futurists circle. He was author of a manifesto advocating an art that embraced the painting of tones, noises and smells, and in 1917 became co-founder with Chirico of the **Pittura Metafisica**. The subdued tones of his simple motifs eventually gave place to a heightened interest in colour. In later life he became professor of art at the Brera, Milan.

**Carracci** Italian family of painters of the Bolognese School. The most important of them, Annibale (1560–1609), is noted for his decoration of the Farnese Palace Gallery, Rome, which historically has been held in as high regard as the great Renaissance decorations on the same scale. The austerity of Michelangelo's Sistine Chapel ceiling is replaced by a new lightness of conception and touch, with such accessories as painted shells, masks, swags of

**Caricature** *Stock jobbers* by William Hogarth, character studies showing the application of the art to portraiture (Guildhall Art Gallery, London).

fruit and other ornaments covering the feigned architectural framework. Annibale painted some altarpieces in Rome which succeed in liberating a stylized tradition in church decoration by means of warmth and colour. As a history painter, also, he displayed a naturalness and power of composition which were to prove influential in the full flowering of the Baroque. He was buried near Raphael, in the Pantheon.

Agostino Carracci (1557–1602) was more an academic than a professional painter: the designation of Academy conferred on the Carracci studio is probably a tribute to Agostino and his careful teachings.

Ludovico Carracci (1555–1619), more volatile in style than his two cousins, veered from late Mannerism to an almost Expressionist fluidity.

**carrell** A small room in a cloister, for the private devotions of a monk.

**Carriera, Rosalba Giovanna** (1675–1758) Venetian painter, the sister-in-law of Pellegrini. Her portraits in pastel were immensely popular, and she became a celebrity throughout Europe. She made triumphal visits to Paris and Vienna and was elected to the Academies of France and Rome. She painted Watteau, amongst many others, and charged high prices for her pastels of English ladies and gentlemen who visited Venice especially to be drawn by her.

**cartoon** A full-sized drawing made in preparation for a painting, originally done on heavy paper called *cartone* from which the name derives. These drawings were worked out in detail and often in full colour as models for murals, tapestries and easel paintings. The transfer to the wall or canvas was often achieved by 'pouncing', pressing a fine charcoal dust through holes pricked in the main lines of the cartoon to reproduce its outline on the surface beneath, or alternatively by squaring. Sometimes a **spolvero** or duplicate cartoon was made for pouncing, so that the original could be preserved as a reference for the artist or a guide to his assistants.

**cartouche** In architecture, an ornamental tablet in a frame or scroll, often with an inscription or heraldic design.

**carving** see **wood carving, stone carving**

**caryatid** Sculptural female figure used as an architectural support in place of a column. The most celebrated examples are those of the Erechtheum in Athens.

**casein** A milk protein used as a binder in secco (mural) and tempera painting. It cannot be applied to canvas because it becomes very brittle when dry, but it is quick to harden and gives an even matt finish.

**casement** A frame for glass that forms a window. A casement window is a side-hinged window that opens outwards.

**Cassatt, Mary** (1845–1926) American painter who was working in Paris at the time of the Impressionists. The daughter of a banker, she spent her schooldays in France and later travelled in Europe before settling in Paris, where she exhibited in the Salons of 1872 and 1886. She figures in several works by Degas, with whom she had a close relationship. Through her contacts with well-to-do Americans she was instrumental in securing recognition for the Impressionists in the United States. Her own work is graced by tender colouring and a sensitive line, especially in her studies of mothers and children.

**Castagno, Andrea del,** originally named Andrea di Bartolo di Bargilla (c. 1421–57) Italian painter, called after his birthplace. Active mainly in Florence, he was the most vigorous of Florentine painters immediately following Masaccio, both in portraiture and in church decoration. His *David* and the sequence from the *Passion*, at the monastery of S. Apollonia, are typical of his animated style. His series of *Famous Men and Women*, now in the museum at Castagno, is a *tour de force* of statuesque painting.

**castellated** Designed with turrets and battlements like a Gothic castle.

**casting** see **bronze**.

**catacomb** Subterranean burial place outside Rome which was used by the early Christians and consists of tunnels with niches cut out of

**Caryatid** Greek examples in the Erechtheum at
Athens.

the rock face and occasional recesses used as
burial chambers.

**Catalogue Raisonné** A catalogue listing all
the known work of an artist, usually in
scholarly detail, and to that extent an authoritative aid to attribution, dating and so on.

**Cavallini, Pietro** (active 1273–1308) Italian
painter. His cycle of biblical scenes in S. Maria,
Trestevere, a mosaic on the life of the Virgin,
is his first dated work (1291) and shows him
in full command of the medium. At about the
same date he decorated S. Cecilia, also in Tras-
tevere, with scenes of which only *The Last Judgement* survives. Such remains are sufficient to

establish Cavallini as a major influence on
Giotto, investing Byzantine prototypes with
breadth, movement and colour.

**Cavallino, Bernardo** (1616–56) Italian
painter. He was active in Naples, where he
specialized in small biblical pictures, executed
in a dashing manner reminiscent of Caravaggio
but with a decorative Venetian touch. His
*Christ Driving the Traders from the Temple*
(National Gallery, London) is a typically
animated example.

**Cave art** The earliest Western art is to be
found in the caves and rock refuges of the
Dordogne region of France and northern
Spain, known together as Franco-Cantabrian.
It dates from the end of the third Ice Age, the
Aurignacian period (30,000–25,000 BC), when
hunting tribes shared the steppe-like terrain
with herds of animals, many of them species

now extinct. These animals, from the mammoth and woolly rhinoceros to the pony and reindeer, are the principal subjects of European cave art. Animals, and an occasional fish or bird, have also been found incised on stone or bone implements.

The earliest images are scratched or carved, but modelled relief also appears in places where the figuration of the cave surface appeared suitable. During the Solutrean (20,000–15,000 BC) and Magdalenian periods (15,000–10,000 BC) more developed outlines are to be found, sometimes with colours made from natural pigments, either laid on with finger or stick or applied through a blowpipe. At its most developed, cave painting from the Aurignacian period onwards shows a command of form and movement and a sensibility of design unsurpassed in the art of our own time. Its purpose remains obscure, though it is generally assumed to have had a magic, shamanist significance. Lascaux, in the Dordogne, and Altamira, in northern Spain, contain the finest examples of cave art. Both are now closed to the public. There is evidence

that such caves as these, used for ceremonial observances rather than as habitations, were visited over several thousands of years, during which time the original outlines were reworked, and other images added.

**cavetto** A concave quarter-circle moulding found in Renaissance architecture.

**cella** The central portion of a Greek or Roman temple, enclosed within solid walls.

**Celtic art** A generic term applied to the metalwork, ornaments and other artifacts of the tribal peoples of western and central Europe, *c.* 500 BC to 650 AD. A characteristic of Celtic art is its linear patterning which, with the stylization of figurative themes, gives it considerable energy and drama. The earlier period of Celtic art is sometimes referred to as the La Tène style, after the site in Switzerland where important examples have been found. The later period produced art in the British Isles of a quality which has been undervalued, perhaps, until modern times. The curvilinear Celtic style persisted in early Irish art for a further 500 years.

**centering** A temporary construction on which to build an arch and hold it in position till the keystone has been inserted.

**Cave art** Horses and bison, painted in manganese and ochre on the ceiling of Altamira, Spain.

**Cézanne, Paul** (1839–1906) French painter. As a student in Paris he met Pissarro, Monet, Sisley and Renoir, after whose example he took to painting in the open air. A particularly close relationship with Pissarro followed, though he exhibited only twice with the Impressionist group. He became more interested in the structural nature of painting, which he saw as the strength of the old masters. His efforts in that direction separated him from all his contemporaries, and he worked on alone. When they were eventually shown, his paintings changed the course of art. He became an old master in a modern age.

His tightly woven brush strokes and balanced use of colour were taken up by the Fauves, and carried to revolutionary extremes by Picasso and Braque in their explorations of Cubism. His work was first shown in England at the Post-Impressionist exhibition of 1910, organized by Roger Fry.

**Chagall, Marc** (b. 1887) Russian-Jewish painter. He trained in St Petersburg, then joined the studio of Léon Bakst, the stage designer. In Paris in 1910 he made his way into the circle of Apollinaire. Wholly receptive to the new movements in art, he preferred to interpret their ideas in his own way, creating a universe out of his own memories of Russian folk life. He became a brilliant colourist, with a gift of fantasy that impressed the Surrealists. Early in World War II he went to the United States at the invitation of the Museum of Modern Art, eventually returning in 1949 to settle in Venice.

Apart from his paintings, which have continued to draw on Russian folklore, legends and religious beliefs, he has executed stained-glass windows in Jerusalem, a new ceiling for the Paris Opéra, and murals for the Lincoln Center, New York.

**Champaigne, Philippe de** (1602–74) Flemish-born painter, active in Paris from 1621. He worked on the gallery of the Luxembourg Palace with the young Poussin, and was appointed Court Painter to the Queen Mother, Marie de' Medici in 1628. He was a particular favourite of Cardinal Richelieu, whose full-length portrait he painted (Louvre, Paris) as well as doing work for him at the Palais Royal and on the Sorbonne building.

Louis XIII commissioned him to paint historical pieces, and himself makes an appearance in the *Vow of Louis XIII* (Museum and Art Gallery, Caen).

At Port Royal, where his paralysed daughter was a nun, he came under the influence of the Jansenists, and in the fervour of a new-found faith marked the recovery of his daughter by painting his ex-voto *Mère Agnes and Soeur Catherine Praying* (Louvre, Paris) in 1662. His portraits, in particular, mark him as a painter of rational and acute sensibility.

**chancel** A section at the east end of a church between the altar and the nave, used by the clergy and the choir.

**chancel arch** The arch at the west end of a chancel.

**charcoal** A charred wooden twig, usually willow or vine, used for drawing. When used by itself it is generally applied to rough paper. It can be easily smudged, so it is customary to spray the finished drawing with a fixative. In modern times its principal use is for making the first drawing on an oil-painting ground.

**Chardin, Jean-Baptiste-Siméon** (1699–1779) French still-life painter. He trained at the Académie Royale, Paris, and exhibited at the Salon from 1737. His work proved so popular that it invariably sold at once, obliging him to make copies to satisfy his public. His still lifes are made of the simplest ingredients: kitchen tools, fruit, bread, fish, common vegetables, set down with uncompromising bluntness. His less typical genre scenes have a similar honesty, neither coarsened nor prettified. In his last years he abandoned oils for pastel, producing three portraits – two of himself and one of Madame Chardin – which are acknowledged masterpieces.

**Chassériau, Théodore** (1819–56) French painter. He was a pupil of Ingres while still a child, and submitted his first *Susannah at her Bath* (Louvre, Paris) to the Salon while still only 19. In 1840 he went to Rome to re-join Ingres, but his own style was deeply influenced by the exoticism of Delacroix, which he sought to bring within a classical discipline and technique. His *Sleeping Bather* (Musée Calvet, Avignon) and the *Two Sisters* (Louvre) show how close he came to success.

**chequerwork** The use of stone and brick laid in a chequerboard arrangement.

**chevet** The term for the east end of French cathedrals and churches, typified by a series of chapels radiating out from the apse.

**chevron** Moulding in zigzag shapes, common as decoration around stone doorways in Norman architecture.

**chiaroscuro** An Italian word meaning light and dark. It is used specifically to refer to the balance of light and shadow in a painting, as developed during the Renaissance. Leonardo, Caravaggio and Rembrandt are among the masters of chiaroscuro.

A chiaroscuro woodcut is a type of print in monochrome printed from several blocks, each linked with a different tone of the same colour.

**chine appliqué** China paper backed with a stiffer sheet which adheres to it as both sheets, when damp, pass through the printing press.

**Chinese art** With an unbroken culture since *c.* 1000 BC, China has exerted an artistic influence in Asia far beyond her own borders. Bronze vessels and jade were the earliest forms and predominant at the time of Confucius (551–479 BC). With the political stabilization of China under the Han dynasty (206 BC–220 AD) pottery and the fine arts flourished, followed by further advances, both technical and aesthetic, during the Sui dynasty (581–618) and that of T'ang (618–906), acknowledged as the golden age. Thereafter the sequence of dynasties, each with its own achievements in making bronzes, sculpture and pottery, is as follows: The Five Dynasties (907–960); Sung (960–1278); Yüan (1260–1368); Ming (1368–1644); Ch'ing or Manchu (1644–1912).

Landscape painting, one of the earliest Chinese arts, disregards Western ideas of perspective while holding foreground and distant objects in harmonious balance. Painting of the Sung era, in particular, is charged with contemplative intensity, with man reduced to relative insignificance in the sublime natural order. In the 16th century the names of prominent artists emerge with the growth of professionalism in their ranks, culminating in a 17th-century group known as The Individualists. These, with the so-called Eight Eccentrics of Yang-chou (18th century), helped to liberate Chinese art from its time-honoured conventions and bring it, though with mixed success, into the modern age.

**Chinnery, George** (1774–1852) English topographical artist and portrait painter. He started by reactivating a society of artists in Dublin, but suddenly set off for India, China and the Far East, leaving his family and professional affairs to look after themselves. His name as a portrait artist has been overtaken by the numerous drawings, watercolours and paintings which were the records of his travels. He is much admired as a draughtsman, with a particular flair for figures.

**Chinoiserie** Strictly, art or wares emanating from China. However, the term is more usually applied to Chinese-looking objects made by Europeans, to Chinese motifs in Western art, and especially to 18th-century European imitations of Chinese art.

Trade with China from the 14th century onwards brought Chinese goods and styles to the attention of the West, where they were extravagantly valued. Chinese blue and white porcelain was the original of Delft, and the craze for Chinese decoration went well with the French Rococo. This lasted until the early years of the 19th century, as can be seen from the example of the Royal Pavilion at Brighton, a *jeu d'esprit* of the Prince Regent.

**Chirico, Giorgio de** (1888–1978) Greek-born Italian artist. He was identified with the Metaphysical movement (Ferrara, 1917) and was subsequently taken up by the Surrealists. His early work reflects their fascination with dreams and the unconscious, and with the fetishes of the modern age. He later embarked on a career as designer of ballets, including Diaghilev's Ballets Russes de Monte-Carlo, before reverting to a warmed-up classicism.

**chroma** The hue and saturation or degree of vividness of a colour other than white, black or grey. It is the distinguishing element between those and the chromatic colours.

**chromatic colours** All the colours except black, white and grey, which are called achromatic colours.

**chromolithograph** An out-dated term for a colour lithograph.

**chryselephantine** Gold and ivory decoration used for ceremonial statues in ancient Greece.

**churn moulding** The zigzag or chevron moulding used in Norman architecture.

**Cimabue** (*c.* 1240–1302) A mysterious master, perhaps the teacher of Giotto, with whom the history of modern art conventionally begins. His known works are few. Among them are part of the mosaic in the apse at Pisa Cathedral, a large *Maestà* in the Uffizi Gallery, Florence and the S. Croce Crucifix in Florence, which was all but ruined by floods in 1966. What is new in Cimabue is a sense of realism that breaks away from Byzantine models and points the way forward to the Renaissance. But there are doubts as to his true identity; his work might be that of several masters rather than one.

**cincture** The small convex moulding round the shaft of a column.

**cinquecento** The 1500s, that is, the 16th century.

**circus** A circular or oval crescent of houses, typically dating from the 18th century. In modern town planning the term denotes a circular road or junction.

**Classical Revival** The early 19th-century trend of English and Continental architecture which revived the classical forms and decoration.

**Classicism** As an historical tradition, the art and architecture of ancient Greece and Rome, and the revival of those values in later times. As a term descriptive of aesthetic values, it means the predominance of discipline, construction and balance. To these qualities Winckelmann, in his *Reflections on the Imitation of Greek Art*, 1755, added 'noble simplicity and calm grandeur'.

Classical values in art have persistently reasserted themselves from the Carolingian revival in the late 8th to 9th century to the draughtsmanship of Picasso. A bastardized form of Classicism emerges from time to time in the public art and sculpture of authoritarian regimes, such as Nazi Germany and Fascist Italy. But as an aesthetic force it has little relevance in modern times.

**Claude** , known as Claude Lorraine, originally named Claude Gellée (1600–82) French landscape painter. With Poussin he was the originator of a classical-romantic style of landscape painting and drawing which persisted into the 19th century. His compositions were inspired largely by the countryside around Naples and Rome, where he spent much of his working life, and by such Mannerist painters as Bril and Elsheimer with their picturesque approach to architecture and ruins. He developed a poetic serenity which gives his typical work a glowing beauty, with pastoral figures of a Virgilian kind. His popularity spread widely, prompted by the publication of his *Liber Veritatis*, a collection of etched plates recording his own original work. His influence on English landscape painting, from Wilson to Turner, has been profound.

**Clausen, Sir George** (1852–1944) English painter born in London, the son of a painter of Danish descent. At first a devoted follower of Bastien-Lepage, he later came under Post-Impressionist influence, to become a founder member of the **New English Art Club**. The change in his painting style was much to his advantage: his borrowings from Bastien-Lepage border on plagiarism, whereas his debts to Degas and Monet are less blatantly apparent. He developed a distinctive way with misty English lanes and fields, and a wet, free touch with watercolour.

**clay** see **modelling**

**Clennell, Luke** (1781–1840) English landscape painter. He began as a wood engraver working for Thomas Bewick and is reckoned among the best artist-craftsmen of that golden age. His watercolours have an honest, chunky quality. He was a frequent exhibitor, but was handicapped by mental instability and spent his last years in an asylum.

**clerestory** In Gothic architecture, the upper portion of the nave walls in a cathedral or three-aisled church. Being above the aisle roofs and pierced with windows, it constitutes a 'clear' storey in contrast to the dark arches of the triforium arcade below.

**Cleveley, John** (1747–86) and **Robert** (1747–1809) English marine painters. They were born at Deptford into a family of ship-wrights and are noted for the nautical accuracy of their work. This is frequently in pale washes over fine pencil, rather in the manner of Paul Sandby, who first noticed John Cleveley and gave him lessons.

**cliché-verre** A print from a design drawn on glass on photographic paper. The glass is covered with an opaque ground and the design drawn on this with a fine needle, exposing the glass along its lines. The photographic paper is then laid behind the glass and exposed to light, causing the outline of the design to print black.

**Clodion,** originally named Claude Michel (1738–1814) French sculptor. He made a promising start by winning the Prix de Rome in 1759, then spent his time working for Catherine II of Russia. He was kept waiting for official honours, but flourished in the market for small, domestic pieces showing nymphs and goddesses in provocative poses. He survived the Revolution, and adapted his style to suit the more rigorous morality of the Republic by turning from the Rococo to Neoclassicism.

**cloissonism** The separation from one another of strong, flat colours by means of dark outlines, as practised by Emile Bernard and introduced through him to Gauguin in 1888.

**cloister** A covered passageway around an inner quadrangle or courtyard.

**Clouet, François** (c.1522–72) French painter, the son of Jean Clouet (1486–c. 1540), whom he succeeded as Court Painter in 1541. He became a highly successful painter of royal portraits, serving four monarchs in succession. His studies of women have a touch of Bronzino, as in the *Lady in her Bath* (National Gallery of Art, Washington), the model for which might have been either Diane de Poitiers or a royal mistress. His portrait of *François I*, in the Louvre, is as potent an image of kingship as Holbein's *Henry VIII*. His drawings, which were collected by Queen Catherine de' Medici, continue to be admired for their detailed sophistication and grace.

**COBRA** A group of artists existing between 1948 and 1951. The name combines the initial letters of Copenhagen, Brussels and Amsterdam, the cities in which the founding members were living at the time. They synthesized and developed the ideas of three previous groups – the Belgian Bureau International de Surréalisme Revolutionaire, the Dutch Experimentele Groep, and the Danish Spiralen group – into a philosophy based on the liberation of repressed desires through revolutionary struggle and experiment. Their art sought to express unconscious psychic forces through violent, painterly action, often by means of primitive or fantastic imagery.

The most prominent of the COBRA painters was Karel Appel. Other leading members of the group were Asger Jorn (1914–73), Corneille (Cornelius van Beverloo, b.1922), and Pierre Alechinsky (b.1927).

**Cocteau, Jean** (1889–1963) French writer, poet, critic and draughtsman. His association with leading artists and *literati* makes him, in some ways, the Guillaume Apollinaire of his time. He was creator and choreographer of *Parade* (1917), the proto-Surrealist ballet for which the costumes and sets were designed by Picasso, who greatly influenced Cocteau's painting and drawing. An altarpiece by him hangs, somewhat unexpectedly, in the French Church near Leicester Square.

**codex** Latin for book; specifically, a religious text.

**coffering** Decoration consisting of sunken squares or polygonal ornamental panels in a ceiling, vault, or arch.

**cold colours** Colours in which blue is dominant are said to be cold or cool, the opposite of hot or warm colours in which red is the dominant factor.

**Cole, Thomas** (1801–48) American landscape painter. He was born in England, but the family emigrated when he was 17. He began to make headway as a painter on settling in New York in 1825. He favoured Romantic subjects appropriate to the untamed character of America, which became the stock-in-trade of the Hudson River School.

Cole returned to England in 1829, visited Italy in 1832, and made another visit to Europe in 1841.

**collage** The technique of building up a picture in two dimensions or low relief by pasting various materials such as paper, cloth and card to the canvas or panel. The whole work may be completed in this way, or the technique may be used in conjunction with painting. The method was pioneered by Picasso and Braque, the first collage being Picasso's *Still Life with Chair Caning* of 1912. It became a favourite device of the Cubists, Surrealists and Dadaists. See also **montage**, **frottage** and **assemblage**.

**collograph** A form of relief printing in which proofs are pulled from a block on which the design has been made up with collage techniques. A great variety of objects may be placed or stuck on the block, which is then inked, wiped and printed in an etching press. The technique can be used in conjunction with others – for instance, etched or photogravured plates may provide an element in the composition. Collograph blocks may also be used to make embossed prints, with or without ink.

**collotype** A technique of reproduction employing water-soluble gelatines. When laid on a sensitized glass plate these result in a lithographic image with no half-tones. The evenness of the resultant print can come close to that of the original.

**colonnade** A walkway lined with columns, usually found in Baroque or Neoclassical architecture.

**colonnette** A miniature column, sometimes used in monuments or in the parapets of build-

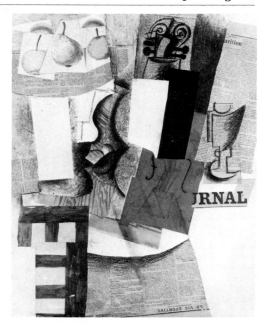

**Collage** *The Violin* (1913) by Pablo Picasso, who was a pioneer of the technique (Philadelphia Museum of Art).

ings. It is more often found in Classical architecture than in Gothic.

**Colour Field painting** A style of painting in which large fields of saturated colour are used. It emerged in the late 1950s in America, and is seen both as a development of and a reaction against Abstract Expressionism. It was encouraged by the dominant New York art theorist of the time, Clement Greenberg, who held that the thrust of the modernist tradition was towards a quintessential 'purity', a concern with what is irreducible in the nature of the medium itself. The Colour Field concept rejected the painterly, gestural expression of Action Painting because it denied the essential flatness which Greenberg saw as integral to the medium.

Under the influence of Still, Mark Rothko, and Barnett Newman, Kenneth Noland (b. 1924) developed a style which consisted of staining large canvases with flat areas of colour in such a way as to remove all expressive qualities in favour of a depersonalized objectivity. Morris Lewis treated colour as a wholly optical phenomenon, using it neither as the vehicle of emotion nor as a property of form. Noland found structure less easy to abandon, and developed what he called 'self-cancelling' compositions, which included symmetrical, unobtrusive shapes like targets or stripes. See also **Post-Painterly Abstraction**.

**colour prints, coloured prints** 'Colour print' is a generic term for any of the processes of engraving which are adapted for printing in colour. The most frequently used method is to prepare a separate block, plate, stone or silk-screen stencil for each colour and print them successively on a single sheet of paper. Coloured prints, by contrast, go through only one impression on the press, and the colour is added by another method, usually by hand or stencil. This has been a popular practice since the earliest woodcuts, and has never been eradicated by colour printing. During the 19th century, for example, a great many hand-tinted aquatints and lithographs were produced, and some artists have revived the technique in this century.

Colour printing from several woodcut blocks was first developed in the 15th century. In essence, the process has hardly changed at all. In all modern methods except silk screen the separate blocks, plates or stones from which each coloured impression is pulled are prepared from the key or master block, plate or stone made from the original drawing. Its outlines are offset on to the other blocks so that the various colours can be placed correctly in register. Where two colours overlap a third colour will, of course, result. Occasionally artists have chosen to ink separate parts of a single plate with different colours to avoid having to make several impressions. However, colour printing *à la poupée*, as this method is called, is as cumbersome as the multiple-plate method because of the careful inking that must be done before each impression is pulled.

All engraving techniques can be used for colour printing, though some are less suitable than others. Woodcut and silk-screen processes are among the most direct. The tonal intaglio engraving techniques – mezzotint and aquatint – lend themselves to the use of colour. But the greatest advance in colour print making came with the invention of **lithography** at the beginning of the 19th century. Manet was the first

major artist to exhibit a colour lithograph, anticipating the work of such artists as Lautrec, Redon, Bonnard, Vuillard and Steinlen in the 1890s.

**colourist** A painter whose outstanding talent is his use of colour is often approvingly described as a 'colourist'. However, the term may also be used to damn with faint praise.

**columbarium** A small recess in the wall of a catacomb or burial vault which will hold an urn with the ashes of the deceased.

**complementary colour** Any one of two colours considered to be the other's opposite. Each of the three primary colours has a complementary which is formed by mixing the other two. The juxtaposition of complementary colours gives the greatest possible contrasts within a painting, and was a favourite technique of the Impressionists. Complementary colours can be depicted on a colour circle which, reading clockwise, goes red, red-violet, violet, blue-violet, blue, green-blue, green, yellow-green, yellow, orange-yellow, orange, red-orange.

**composition** The arranging of all the different elements of a picture into a visually unified and aesthetically satisfying whole. The principles governing composition change from age to age, but good composition is always a highly individual matter, dependent on the skill of the artist. He will decide when the rules of composition should be followed and when they can be successfully broken.

**Conceptual art** A radical artistic mode of the late 1960s and 1970s which abolishes the art object altogether. Conceptual artists have taken the notion of art as commodity (as evinced by the ironic images of the Pop artists) on the one hand, and its ambivalence toward artifice (shared by such dissimilar groups as Performance artists and Minimalists) on the other, to a supposedly logical conclusion. They seek to direct attention away from 'finished' art towards the processes by which it is made, by exhibiting documents suggestive of the actual work – texts, notes, photographs, films and maps – rather than the end product. Thus the idea is elevated above the work itself.

**conch** In architecture, the top of a semicircular niche shaped like a conch shell.

**Concrete Poetry** An artistic and literary form launched in the mid-1950s. It marries poetic expression with the use of words as a graphic medium, along lines anticipated by Mallarmé and Guillaume Apollinaire. The most internationally renowned practitioner is the Scottish poet/artist Ian Hamilton Finlay (b.1925).

**Conder, Charles** (1868–1909) English painter. He started painting in Australia, but returned to Europe in 1890 to study in Paris, where he knew Anquetin, Toulouse-Lautrec and William Rothenstein. He painted in France as well as England – *Blossoms at Dennemont* is in the Ashmolean collection – and exhibited with the New English Art Club. His late paintings, done in watercolour on silk, are out of fashion.

**Coninxloo, Gillis van** (1544–1607) The most prominent member of a family of Belgian painters active in the 16th and 17th centuries, forming a link between the manner of Bruegel and such 17th-century Dutch landscape painters as Van de Velde and Van Goyen. He left Belgium in 1585 and ten years later settled in Amsterdam, where he gained a reputation with landscapes in which literal detail is balanced by a naturalistic treatment of trees, fields and skies.

**conservation** The preservation and restoration of works of art. The term covers everything from the repair of damaged work to a concern for proper lighting, temperature and humidity levels during exhibition and storage.

**console** In architecture, an ornamental, scrolled bracket.

**Constable, John** (1776–1837) English landscape painter. With Turner, he ranks as the greatest and most influential English artist of the 19th century. Born in Suffolk, and steeped in Suffolk ways, he drew on his boyhood experiences all his life, working and re-working the country scenes which, he said, made him a painter. His early instruction was rudimentary.

In 1795 he left for London to take lessons from J. T. ('Antiquity') Smith, and was encouraged by Joseph Farington. He was still showing only mediocre talent when he entered the Royal Academy Schools, where he exhibited his student work in 1802 and 1803. At about this time he was also sketching in Suffolk, sometimes with George Frost, (1744–1821) a follower of Gainsborough and part-time drawing master at Ipswich. An inheritance in 1816 enabled him to marry, and his wife, Maria Bicknell, herself came into money some years later.

His ambitions to be elected a full Royal Academician were disappointed year after year, largely owing to a prejudice against landscape painting; he eventually had to wait until 1829. He made a brief splash in Paris, at the Salon of 1824, and he found loyal patrons among a new breed of collectors. His reputation grew slowly after his death, until his notion of the 'natural painter' became universally accepted.

The Bicentenary exhibition in London in 1976 helped to re-establish the grandeur and beauty of his large exhibition pieces, for which his more generally admired oil sketches were preliminary studies.

**construction** In sculpture, a work that is built out of different pieces rather than modelled, cast or carved.

**Constructivism** A departure from sculptural form, in which man-made materials such as wire and plastic are used to create three-dimensional, usually abstract, structures. The first Constructivists were the group of post-Revolution Russian artists headed by Vladimir Tatlin (1885–1953) and Alexander Rodchenko (1891–1956). The term is applied equally to painting, architecture and design.

**content** The subject matter or motif in a work of art. This is sometimes independent of its form, although the two are not always divisible.

**contour** The boundary delineating one form or area from another in a picture. It is not always a mere outline, for in skilful hands contour can suggest the textural properties of the form it encloses.

**contrafforte** The Italian word for buttress.

**contrapposto** A figure posed with the upper half of the body turned in a direction opposite to that of the lower half.

**Contrefort** The French word for buttress.

**Cooke, Edward William** (1811–80) English marine painter, the son of an engraver, George Cooke (1781–1834). As a boy he met and was encouraged by Clarkson Stanfield. A precocious draughtsman, with a sharp eye for detail, he travelled widely, prospered, and was made RA in 1851.

**Cooper, Samuel** (1609–72) English miniature painter. He was trained by an uncle, John Hoskins, travelled on the Continent, and became the most sought-after miniaturist of the Restoration period. His portraits, in the English tradition of Hilliard and Oliver, are more than mere likenesses, often revealing the artist's response to the sitter's character, and his drawings are similarly highly prized.

**Cooper, Thomas Sidney** (1803–1902) English landscape and cattle painter. The Dutch rural painters made a lasting impression on his style and also determined his speciality, cattle on grassy banks, irreverently known as 'cowscapes'. From his home at Canterbury he painted these subjects for some 70 years. He had several aristocratic pupils and numerous imitators. He was made RA in 1867.

**coping** A flat or sloping protective capping or covering to a wall.

**Copley, John Singleton** (1738–1815) American painter. He began as a portrait painter in Boston, and was urged to visit London by Sir Benjamin West on the strength of a work which he had sent over for submission to the Society of Artists. In 1774 Copley arrived in Europe, visiting Italy, Austria, France, Germany and the Netherlands. His first important commission, *Brook Watson and the Shark* (1778), of which there are versions in Boston and London, and his *Death of Major Peirson* (Tate Gallery, London) 1783, are typical of the blend of Romanticism and Neoclassical influence that give his large history paintings their narrative power.

**Coptic art** Art of the Christian people living in Egypt from the 5th to the 18th century. The earliest period, until the late 8th century, combines the naivety of folk art with a brilliant sense of colour, applied in flat areas rather in the manner of ancient Egyptian wall painting. It was affected, though not overwhelmed, by subsequent Arab and Turkish incursions, and finally succumbed when Napoleon's armies destroyed the Coptic ghettos outside Cairo at the end of the 18th century. Its influence on neighbouring and converging cultures over such a long period may have been more far-reaching than is generally assumed.

**corbel** A stone tailed into a wall and projecting from it in order to carry another weight. Largely used in Gothic architecture, corbels are generally carved in a decorative manner.

**corbel table** In Gothic architecture, a series of supporting corbels, often placed at the base of a spire or under the eaves of a roof. The term also refers to a slab of stone which is supported by a row of corbels.

**corbelled arch** A dome-shaped span of stonework in which each course is projected to overhang in successive steps on either side till the top ones almost meet. A capstone is then put in the centre to close the gap.

**Corinth, Lovis** (1858–1925) German painter, trained in Munich, Antwerp and Paris. He was a founder member of the Munich Sezession and an exhibitor with the Berlin Sezession, of which he became president in 1915. His early period is made up largely of figure compositions, genre and biblical scenes, which gave way to landscape on his move to Berlin in 1900. On the advice of Max Liebermann he released himself from his academic training and broadened his subject matter, attacking the canvas with little or no preparation in a manner that parallels German Expressionism.

**Corinthian** see **order** (of architecture).

**cornice** The upper portion of the entablature in a Classical building. It is divided into three main portions: the bed moulding, the corona, and the cymatium or crown moulding, which springs from the upper edge of the face of the corona. The term is often applied to the mouldings which form the crowning finish to a wall. The Classical cornice represents the decorative treatment of the projection of the roof.

**Corot, Jean-Baptiste Camille** (1796–1875) French painter, a pioneer of plein-air landscape painting. After training as a conventional landscape painter he took to sketching out of doors, direct from nature, in his own style of lyrical romanticism. The freshness and directness of his work put him alongside Constable, whose *Haywain* he might have seen at the Salon of 1824, where Richard Bonington also exhibited. He travelled in Italy and widely in France, filling pocket-books with studies and impressions which catch the tones and colour of his subjects with the accuracy of direct observation.

He was a regular exhibitor at the Salon, though not with the kind of work which influenced Boudin and the young Impressionists: his exhibition pictures tended to be in a vague and stylized 'poetic' manner which suited contemporary taste, and which was to have its admirers into modern times.

**Cortona, Pietro Berrettini da** (1596–1669) Italian painter and architect, a founder of the Roman High Baroque. His main patrons were the family of Pope Urban VII, for whom he painted the frescoes at S. Bibiena and the ceiling of the Barberini Palace, *An Allegory of Divine Providence and Barberini Power*. In Florence he painted two frescoes for the Pitti Palace and seven ceilings depicting *Allegories of Virtues and Planets*, which were completed by his pupil Ciro Ferri (1634–89). His architectural works in Rome include the church of the Academy of St Luke and the S. Maria della Pace. He was one of the architects invited to submit designs for the Louvre, the commission being awarded to Bernini.

**Costruzione Legittima** A strict system of linear **perspective** developed in the 15th century by Leon Battista Alberti and based on the earlier thinking of **Brunelleschi**. It required that, as far as possible, all the objects depicted should appear parallel to the **picture plane**, and employed three mathematically determined receding zones to suggest distance. The

effect, however, was to reduce perspective from a continuum to a series of disconnected planes, giving a stilted and artificial look to pictures painted according to these principles.

**Cosway, Richard** (1742–1821) English miniature painter. He studied under Thomas Hudson (1701–79) and at the Royal Academy Schools, was made ARA in 1770 and a full member a year later. With just the touch for the Regency, he was as elegant, witty and fashionable as his clients and a crony of the Prince of Wales. His wife Maria (*nee* Hadfield) was also a miniaturist, and collaborated with Cosway in his soft-ground etchings.

**Cotman, John Sell** (1782–1824) English landscape and watercolour painter. Like John Crome, he was a dominant member of the Norwich School. He went to work in London as a youth, and joined the circle of young painters patronized by Dr Thomas Monro. In the early 1800s visits to Wales and Yorkshire on sketching tours produced some of his finest work, with flat, schematized designs which strike a modern eye as far ahead of their time.

In 1806 he returned to Norwich and became vice president of the Norwich Society of Artists, earning his living by teaching. His ambitions later took him back to London, where he was appointed professor of drawing at King's College. He never achieved the recognition he longed for, and suffered the humiliation of seeing his most treasured works knocked down at auction for paltry sums. His staunchest patron was the antiquarian and banker, Dawson Turner, on whose behalf he travelled in Normandy to make etchings. His graphic work is highly regarded, especially a series of soft-ground etchings, the *Liber Studiorum*, which was not published until 1838.

His elder son Miles Edmund Cotman (1810–58) succeeded him at King's College. His watercolours, stiffer in style than his father's, are nevertheless of some quality. His younger brother, John Joseph Cotman (1814–78), a somewhat excitable artist given to using strong, vibrant colours, also inherited the father's lyrical touch.

**Cottet, Charles** (1863–1924) French painter, a pupil of Puvis de Chavannes. With Lucien Simon (1861–1945) and André Dauchez

(1870–1943) he was identified with the Bande Noire, so called for the distinctively dark palette used for his melancholy Breton subjects and harbour scenes.

**coulisse** A compositional device in a landscape painting, often a tree placed so as to frame the view. Coulisse and repoussoir are the two main devices used by painters of ideal or classical landscapes.

**counter proof** A reverse impression taken from a wet proof by passing it back through the press facing another sheet of paper. The resulting image will be the same way round as the plate, and is a useful reference for the engraver when making corrections to the plate.

**Courbet, Gustave** (1819–77) French painter. He taught himself to paint mainly by copying in the Louvre. His admiration for Caravaggio and Velazquez, among other masters, led him to an individual brand of realism which was at odds with the polite standards of the Salon, and with public taste. He took his themes from everyday life, including such sombre subjects as the *Stonebeakers* (1849) and the *Burial at Ornans* (his birthplace near the Swiss border), which attracted the enthusiastic attention of Emile Zola. The *Painter in his Studio* (1855), subtitled 'An Allegory of Realism' expresses the confidence, even arrogance, of a painter who made up his own rules of decorum.

His socialist beliefs did nothing to help his career: he was heavily fined for taking part in the destruction of Napoleon's column in the Place Vendôme during the Commune, and eventually took refuge in Switzerland, where he died. Several of his young contemporaries were influenced by him, though he is not a true precursor of Impressionism.

**Couture, Thomas** (1815–79) French historical and portrait painter. A pupil of Gros, he owes his place in art history more to the fact that he gave lessons in their early years to Manet, Fantin-Latour and Puvis de Chavannes. His own speciality was languorous nudes, including *La Romain de la Decadence*, 1847 (Louvre), an orgy in moralistic guise.

**cowl** A metal hood fixed over a chimney or vent to improve ventilation.

**Cox, David** (1783–1859) English watercolour artist and drawing master. He studied briefly under John Varley, then kept himself by taking pupils. This remained a major part of his livelihood even when he had achieved fame and popularity with his distinctively clean, fresh and spirited watercolour drawings.

His subjects are predominantly Welsh – he discovered Betws-y-Coed, his favourite centre for working in Wales – but they also include scenes in Herefordshire, Lancaster and the north French coast. Late in life he took lessons in oil painting from William Muller, and produced paintings similar in mood and subject to his more widely admired work in watercolour.

His son, David Cox Jnr (1809–85), helped him in his teaching practice and inherited some of his father's easily imitated mannerisms. Of Cox's pupils, Edward Webb (1805–54) and David Hall McKewan (1817–73) are among the most able. The Cox style, however, was carried into the present century by a succession of distinguished watercolourists, including Edmund Morison Wimperis (1835–1900), Thomas Collier (1840–91), and Claude Hayes (1852–1922).

**Cozens, Alexander** (*c.* 1717–86) English painter, a pioneer of landscape drawing. By 1763 he was drawing master at Eton College, and began to establish a reputation as a draughtsman in the 1770s. In a classic treatise on landscape drawing he describes his method of starting by means of random blots, which he worked up with the brush into beautifully constructed landscapes. His more conventional drawings, executed in a broad, romantic style, have an impressive dignity and form.

**Cozens, John Robert** (1752–97) English landscape painter, son of Alexander Cozens. He travelled to Italy and Switzerland, where he discovered the grandeur of Alpine scenery. Continental subjects predominate in his work, which is mostly in subdued tones of blue-grey or green, suffused with a poetic light. Constable called him 'the greatest genius who ever touched landscape' – a mark of the profound effect he had on the following generation of English landscape artists, including the young Turner and Thomas Girtin.

**cramp** A thin piece of metal with both ends turned back at right angles. It is used to bind together blocks of masonry or timber.

**Cranach, Lucas** (1472–1553) German painter and engraver. He first makes an appearance in Vienna in about 1503 with two double portraits and a dramatic *Crucifixion*, now in Munich. He later served three successive Electors of Wittenberg, becoming a courtly painter in an original mould. His female figures have a mannered, erotic nudity which is most telling in such works as the *Judgement of Paris* (1529). His engraved works are mostly woodcuts done from his drawings, and are commonly compared with those of Albrecht Dürer.

His son, known as Lucas Cranach the Younger (1515–86), took over the workshop after his father's death.

**Crane, Walter** (1845–1915) English painter, illustrator and designer. He began illustrating children's books while still in his teens, and went on to become a designer of textiles, tiles, stained glass and ceramics. An early socialist, he was active in the Arts and Crafts movement and in the Art Workers Guild. His paintings range from romantic medieval subjects of a Pre-Raphaelite kind, to large allegorical works and grandiose tableaux. His fastidious pencil drawings, studies for more ambitious compositions, and his early watercolours are among his most accessible works.

**craquelure** The hairline mosaic of cracks that develop when oil paintings age as a result of the varying degrees of shrinkage in the ground, pigments and varnish. Craquelure is more common on canvas than on panel.

**crayon engraving** A print-making technique popular in the 18th century. When used in combination with stipple engraving it produces an effect close to the texture of a crayon or chalk drawing. A copper plate is coated with an etching ground and the design drawn with a variety of roulettes and mattoirs, tools which create closely dotted lines and areas in imitation of crayon. The 'crayon manner', as it is often called, was sometimes combined with soft-ground etching. In France, a number of engravers made reproductions of Boucher's and Fragonard's drawings. Prints were frequently taken in a reddish or bistre tone, to imitate the appearance of red chalk. The development of lithography during the 19th century rendered the process obsolete.

**crenel** Section in a military parapet through which soldiers fired their weapons.

**crenellated** Having an indented or notched surface. Crenellation was used as an architectural feature on parapets and the tops of castle walls.

**Crespi, Giovanni Battista,** otherwise called 'Il Cerano' (*c.*1575–1632) Italian Mannerist painter. After studies in Rome he settled in Milan and in 1621 was appointed head of the art academy newly established there by Cardinal Federigo Borromeo. In 1629 he was put in charge of the sculpture workshops at Milan Cathedral. This led to numerous commissions for churches in and around Milan, where most of his work is to be seen.

Daniele Crespi (*c.*1598–1630), also a Milanese painter of the time, may be a relative.

**Crespi, Giuseppe Maria** (1665–1747) Italian painter born in Bologna where he worked for most of his life. He acquired a **chiaroscuro** technique in the tradition of Caravaggio. His church paintings combine bright colours on dark grounds with an almost photographic attention to detail. He was noted as a teacher and left a mark on Venetian painting of the 18th century.

**cresting** A continuous carved or pierced ornament surmounting a screen, cornice or canopy.

**crevé** In etching, a flaw caused by over-biting of the plate, which is a consequence of too concentrated a mordant being used or of the plate being immersed in the acid bath for too long. Lines may be too deeply bitten or fused together, and the only way the plate can be repaired is by resurfacing the affected areas and re-etching.

**criblé** A print-making technique, particularly popular in the 15th century, which used dotted areas for backgrounds and textural effects, often in combination with line engraving. The dots are made with a special punch and the plate is printed as a relief so that the dots and lines show as white in the proof.

**Crivelli, Carlo** (*c.* 1430–95) Italian painter. He was born in Venice, but is associated with the painters of The Marches, where he worked for 30 years. His pictures have an ornate, stylized gravity which was rather behind the times. The Gothic treatment of religious themes and his attention to luscious detail tend to isolate him from his contemporaries. But the beauty and unforced pathos of his *St Mary Magdalen* (Brera, Milan) and of his several versions of the *Virgin and Child* set him among the most accomplished of the Marches painters. His later work, in which he relapsed into a leaden gloom, is not of the same order.

**crocket** In Gothic architecture a decorative projection, generally of carved foliage, on the outer moulding of a gable or on the angle moulding of a spire.

**Crome, John** (1768–1821) English landscape painter, founder of the **Norwich School**. His earliest jobs were sign painting and decorating coaches for the local gentry. He saw his first paintings in the collection of Thomas Harvey of Catton, who encouraged him to copy his Gainsboroughs, Hobbemas and Ruysdaels. In 1814 he founded the Norwich Society of Artists, and remained at the centre of the Norwich group of painters for the rest of his life.

His work is remarkable for its dignity and breadth, an unaffected nobility which marks a departure from the picturesque. His drawings and watercolours are first thoughts towards compositions in oil, a medium in which his effects are achieved by unity of mood and technique. His etchings, published after his death, are typical of his devotion to the quiet places which delighted him in the countryside around his native city.

**Cross, Henri Edmond** (1856–1910) French painter. He was variously influenced by Bastien-Lepage, Manet and the Impressionists, and by the Pointillists, with whom he exhibited. He subsequently worked on the Mediterranean coast, sketching out of doors in watercolours which he then developed in his studio. His experiments in pure colour won him the respect of Maurice Denis, who preferred his sun-soaked landscapes to the more garish palette of the Fauves.

**cross vault** A roof formed by two vaults intersecting at right angles.

**cross window** A window with one mullion and one transom.

**cross-hatching** A means of obtaining depths of tone through line alone. Parallel lines are drawn or etched first one way, and then across the original lines in the opposite direction.

**crossing** In a medieval church, the central space at the intersection of the nave and the transept. The four piers at its angles are called the 'crossing piers', and the main arches which spring from them the 'crossing arches'. The expression 'the crossing' is sometimes used with reference to the whole architectural treatment at this point.

**cruciform** In the shape of a cross. The word is often used to describe churches of such a design.

**cruck** A carved or shaped beam forming the main support at either end of a wood-framed dwelling.

**Cruikshank, George** (1792–1878) English caricaturist and illustrator. He was the second son of Isaac Cruikshank (1756–1811), a Scottish painter and cartoonist, and brother of Isaac Robert Cruikshank (1789–1856), also an illustrator, with whom he sometimes collaborated. George Cruikshank is one of the greatest of his kind, energetic, observant, compassionate, and seemingly always at the top of his form.

After a lifetime illustrating for authors of his day, including Dickens, he took up the Temperance cause, and campaigned for it with unflagging zeal.

**cryptoporticus** A concealed or partially hidden colonnade or portico.

**Cubism** One of the most far-reaching movements in 20th-century art. Between 1907 and

**Cubism** Georges Braque: *Houses at L'Estaque*, 1908 (Berner Kunstmuseum).

1914, Picasso and Braque led painting away from the heady sensuousness of Impressionism towards a literalness based on a new conception of form, inherited from Cézanne. The first phase, known as Analytical Cubism, concentrated on the fragmentation of the subject matter into component parts. The second phase, Synthetic Cubism, introduced forms and materials so arranged as to take painting a further step away from the purely figurative. Picasso declared that he painted forms as he thought of them, not as he saw them: reality, for the Cubists, was what happened in the mind. Picasso's *Demoiselles d'Avignon*, painted in 1907 and shown only to his intimates, stands as the first Cubist painting, with its deliberate dislocations and flattening out of the picture space.

The assault on conventional ideas of perspective and painterly technique was continued by Gleizes, Léger, Kupka, Picabia, Gris and others, leading to the **Section d'Or**, **Orphism**, and the development of **collage** and relief painting over the next 30 years.

**cupola** A small dome-covered erection rising above the general line of a building.

**curtail step** The bottom step of a staircase, with a curved end which projects beyond the newel.

**curtain wall** A non-weight-bearing wall. Historically, this term refers to the outer wall surrounding a castle or fortified dwelling.

**cusps** The pointed ends arising from the subsidiary arches formed on the inner side of Gothic tracery, which give a Gothic window its characteristic appearance.

**cutwater** The wedge-shaped end of a bridge or pier which is constructed to break the flow of the water.

**Cuyp, Aelbert** (1620–91) Netherlands painter. His subjects were most commonly landscapes with animals. Taught by his father, Jacob Gerritsz (1594–1651), and influenced by such predecessors as Jan van Goyen, he became a prolific painter of townscapes, portraits, still-life and genre subjects as well as his familiar cattle grouped on river banks.

**Cupola**

He introduced an Italianate glow into his pictures, which gives them a quality akin to that of Claude Lorraine. They were much to the liking of English collectors, helping to set a standard of taste which lasted 200 years.

**Cycladic** (Cyclades) Belonging to the Bronze Age culture of the Aegean islands.

**cyclopean** In architecture, a term applied to ancient walls built of large blocks of stone of irregular shape.

**cyma** In the vocabulary of Renaissance architects, a moulding composed of a double curve – a convex line and a concave line combined. Where the concave part is uppermost it is called cyma recta; where the convex is uppermost it is cyma reversa. The cyma recta was the favourite crown moulding for a cornice with both Roman and Renaissance architects. A cyma curve is an s-shaped curve.

**cymatium** A cyma moulding which forms the topmost section of a cornice.

**Dada** An international movement propounding nihilism and 'anti-art' which originated in Zurich and New York at the beginning of the First World War. Its heyday was 1916–23, though its influence has persisted to the present day.

The name, which means 'hobbyhorse' in French, was apparently picked from a dictionary by the German writer Hugo Ball in 1916, and was never intended to mean anything. 'Da-da,' declared the movement's leader, the Romanian poet Tristan Tzara, in 1918, 'signifies nothing.' It was born of the stupidities of the war, and was also a reaction against the smugness that supposedly afflicted the institutions of fine art. Dada sought, through burlesque and outrage, to shatter the complacency of bourgeois culture and to contradict established notions of what art should consist of.

Initially, the European wing of the movement was mostly literary in its concerns, focused on the Cabaret Voltaire in Zurich, the scene of increasingly anarchic and absurd entertainments which were forerunners of the Happenings of the 1960s. The only major artist involved at this stage was Hans Arp, who developed the Cubist techniques of **collage** and

**montage** by experimenting with random arrangements of cut-out, coloured paper. In New York, Marcel Duchamp, Man Ray, Francis Picabia and others were working on similar lines, cultivating a reputation as ironists and pranksters. The two factions were united in 1918 when Picabia went to work in Switzerland. The influence of Dada spread to Germany, attracting Max Ernst, Georg Grosz and Kurt Schwitters, and more importantly to Paris, where its principles were embodied in the emergent Surrealist philosophy.

**dado** In Classical architecture, the word refers to the centre cube of the pedestal of a column. In modern terms it can also mean the lower part of an interior wall from floor level up to the dado rail at a height of 2 to 3 ft. It can be panelled or painted.

A dado cap is the crown moulding of a dado.

**Daedalian** The term used to describe the stone sculpture of the 7th century BC which pertains to Daedalus, the mythical first sculptor of Greece.

**Dali, Salvador** (b. 1904) Spanish painter, the most spectacular of the Surrealists. His early work is in the manner, if not the mood, of such admired contempories as Picasso and Braque. In the late 1920s he began to move towards hallucinatory themes which made him a favourite of the Surrealists.

His films *Un Chien Andalou* and *L'Age d'Or*, made with his compatriot Luis Buñuel, embody many of the themes and images which were to become familiar in his paintings, turning paranoia into the stock-in-trade of his art. He went on to create a succession of brilliant, disturbing and scandalous works for which he secured maximum publicity by his own comprehensively Surrealist behaviour. These include *The Great Masturbator, The Enigma of Desire* (both in private collections); *The Persistence of Memory* (Museum of Modern Art, New York), which introduced the famous limp watches, and the *Metamorphosis of Narcissus* (Tate Gallery, London), in which paranoic thought processes are described in a dazzling display of illusionism.

In his later work Dali has experimented with optical wizardry, though still with the technical skills which have enabled his images to penetrate the collective imagination of his time.

**Dalziel, Edward** (1817–1905) English engraver and illustrator. Born in Northumberland, he was brother of George and Thomas Bolton Dalziel and for 50 years a partner in the famous firm of engravers founded by his brother George. He was a fellow pupil of Charles Keene and John Tenniel at the Clipstone Street Academy and an admirable draughtsman in his own right. His son Edward (1849–89) was also an illustrator.

Thomas Bolton Dalziel (1823–1906), illustrator and wood engraver, joined his brothers in the family engraving business in 1860. He was also in the front rank as an illustrator, sharing the illustrations for the Dalziels' edition of the *Arabian Nights* with Arthur Boyd Houghton and contributing 14 plates to the Dalziel Brothers' *Bible Gallery*, 1881.

**Dance, George** (1741–1825) English architect. He was the son of George Dance Snr (d. 1768), who designed the Mansion House. After studying in Italy for seven years he returned to London and quickly made his name with his All Hallows, London Wall and with a strikingly original Newgate Prison, since demolished. His Council Chamber in the Guildhall, also lost, was much admired. His later work includes the College of Surgeons, London, and the south front of the Guildhall.

**dancette** The zigzag decoration in Norman architecture. See **chevron**.

**Danube School** A collective description of Austro-Bavarian artists of the 16th century who shared a common style derived from Lucas Cranach. The most prominent of them was Albrecht Altdorfer. Historically, they are seen to be instrumental in the development of landscape as a genre in its own right.

**Daubigny, Charles-François** (1817–78) French painter. He was the son of a landscape painter, a friend of Corot and like him held in high regard by the younger generation of French painters who were to follow. His subject was landscape, especially the quiet reaches of the rivers Seine and Oise. He showed regularly at the Salon, and was influenced by the Barbizon painters, with whose methods he sympathized. He visited England in 1866 and again in 1870–1, when he met Monet and Pissarro during their exile in London. He like to paint from a boat, made especially for the purpose, an example which Monet followed.

**Daumier, Honoré** (1810–79) French painter and caricaturist. His lithographed cartoons for *Charivari*, which he regarded as drudgery, have become classics of the genre. They cost him his sight, and hampered him in pursuing his ambitions as a painter. His watercolours and occasional oils nevertheless have a highly individual realism. His staunchest friends were fellow artists, among them Delacroix and Corot, who helped him in his destitute old age.

**David, Jacques-Louis** (1748–1825) French Neoclassicist painter. He achieved national celebrity with his republican set-pieces on classical themes, such as the *Oath of the Horatii* (1785). He was appointed a Deputy during the Revolution and became in effect Minister for the Arts, abolishing the Academy (of which he was a member) and helping to found the Institute which took its place. He managed to survive the ensuing power struggles to become a fervent supporter of Buonaparte, whose exploits he celebrated in a succession of large pictures. With the defeat of Napoleon he fled to Switzerland, where he died. He handled big themes with consummate skill, and was held in great esteem by his contemporaries all over Europe. His pupils included François Gérard, Antoine Gros and Jean Ingres.

**De Stijl** The name of the magazine founded by Piet Mondrian and Theo van Doesburg in Leiden, Holland, in 1917. It was edited by Van Doesburg until 1928, and his wife produced a final issue in 1931 in commemoration of his death. Initially it was the vehicle through which the concept of **Neo-Plasticism** was expounded, very much under Mondrian's influence. However, Van Doesburg became increasingly absorbed in Constructivist ideas, and in subsequent issues he initiated a more catholic editorial policy. In 1924 Mondrian dissociated himself from the magazine's new stance. Van Doesburg's modification of Neo-Plasticism became known as Elementarism.

*De Stijl* was perhaps the most influential of avant-garde periodicals between the wars, and its name is often applied to the group of artists and architects who were associated with it.

Besides Mondrian and Van Doesburg, the principal painters in the group, were Vilmos Huszar (1884–1960), Georges Vantongerloo (1886–1965), and Bart van der Leck (1876–1958). The architects included Gerrit Rietveld (1888–1965), Jacobus Oud (1890–1963), and Jan Wils (b. 1891).

**De Wint, Peter** (1784–1849) English water-colour painter. Of Dutch descent, he is regarded as one of the masters of the classic English watercolour manner. He lived for some time in Lincoln, the subject of some of his best-known work, and revelled in the lush, level countryside of the region. His style is distinguished by his broad, mossy greens and untroubled washes. He had several pupils, and was married to the sister of William Hilton (1786–1839), the history painter.

**dead colour** In the traditional method of painting in oils, the first drawing is laid in dead colour, usually monochrome, as a guide to the tonal quality of the picture. The artist then proceeds to work with more attention to detail and colour value.

**decalcomania** A transfer; decalcomania or decal is the process of transferring an image from one surface to another such as a design on to ceramic or glass. The Surrealists, notably Max Ernst, exploited the effects of lifting a mirror image from one sheet of paper to another. Decals have been widely used in Psychedelic art.

**décollage** A form resulting from taking apart, stripping or tearing off layers of material to uncover parts of what might be found underneath. It is a variant of New Realism; its opposite is **collage**.

**Decorated** Gothic architecture in England roughly corresponding to that of the 14th century, but with more flowing tracery and decorative mouldings than in the Early English period. Characteristics of the style include the ogee (serpentine) designs in arches and windows and the profusion of decoration, much of it highly stylized, on stone surfaces. Bristol, Wells, the Lady Chapel and Octagon at Ely and the screen at Lincoln are typical examples.

**Decorated** Entrance to the Chapter House at Southwell Minster, Nottingham, showing the detailed decoration of the mouldings and pilasters typical of the style.

**deep etching** The exceptionally deep biting of an intaglio plate, usually for the purpose of achieving an effect of density or dramatic **chiaroscuro**.

**Degas, Hilaire Germain Edgar** (1834–1917) French painter. He enrolled at the École des Beaux-Arts in 1855 and learned the qualities of draughtsmanship from Jean Ingres. A feeling for realism of the kind introduced by the camera and an eye for quick, journalistic compositions give his work a startling modernity. An early friend of the Impressionists, and a co-exhibitor, he moved away from them as his career progressed. His drawings, pastels, paintings and sculptures show a keen eye for natural movement and gesture. His studies of women at their toilette, in particular, convey an intimate sympathy unequalled in modern art.

**Degenerate art** A term used in Hitler's Germany to denigrate modern artists of whom the Third Reich disapproved. 'Degenerate' was held to be the antithesis of 'German art', which was the Nazi equivalent of the equally hollow and sycophantic Socialist Realism. Degenerate art meant everything that had been produced by Cubism, Fauvism, Dada, Expressionism, Constructivism, Surrealism and other movements of the 20th century. Between 1933 and 1939 nearly 20,000 examples of Degenerate art were confiscated from German collections; many were sold abroad and the rest were burned. In 1937 an exhibiton of Degenerate art was held in Munich concurrently with one of 'German art'. It contained paintings by the mentally sick as well as works by virtually all the German masters of the Modern Movement.

**Delacroix, Eugène** (1798–1863) French painter, and a leading figure in the Romantic movement. He copied Rubens, Veronese and the Venetian colourists in the Louvre, where he met Richard Bonington, a contact with English landscape painting that was developed further after seeing Constable's *Hay Wain* in the Salon of 1824. This was followed by a visit to England in which he acquainted himself with the work of contemporary English painters.

He acquired a taste for exotic imagery while visiting Morocco, and developed the Divisionist technique of achieving vivid effects by the careful placing of adjacent tones. His blatant use of paint as subject matter in its own right was a revolutionary innovation, though he refused to regard himself as a revolutionary, simply as a rebel.

**Delaroche, Hippolyte,** called Paul (1797–1856) French history painter and a pupil of Gros, who painted Romantic subjects in an earnest, academic manner. His skills and limitations are evident in *Lady Jane Grey Executed at the Tower of London*, painted in 1834 (National Gallery, London) and a typical example of his immaculate mediocrity.

**Delaunay, Robert** (1885–1941) French painter. His 'circular cosmic forms', exercises in rhythmical colour effects, were an original contribution to Abstract painting in the 1920s. His insistence on the indivisibility of light and colour led to the concept of Orphic Cubism, in which colour is manipulated in the same way as the notes in a fugue; as Delaunay put it, 'in coloured phrases, contrapuntally'.

His wife Sonia Delaunay, née Terk (1885–1979), who shared in his investigations, applied Orphism over a range of textile and costume designs, ceramics and domestic objects.

**Delvaux, Paul** (b. 1897) Belgian Surrealist painter. Originally a follower of Chirico and Magritte, he developed his own hallucinatory references, such as nude female figures in nocturnal settings, exerting a dreamy eroticism. His watercolour landscapes, less familiar than his paintings, are equally remarkable.

**demi-column** A column set into a wall or pier for half its diameter.

**dentil** One of a line of small projecting rectangular blocks in a cornice. It appears in Ionic, Corinthian and Composite cornices. A dentil course consists of a series of dentils in a row.

**deposition** The representation of the lowering of Christ's body from the Cross.

**Derain, André** (1890–1954) French painter, an early member of the Fauves and one of the first Cubists. He shared with Picasso and his

**Deposition** Fresco by Giotto in the Arena Chapel, Padua (1305–8).

circle the discovery of Negro art but his later work reverts to a more conventional Romanticism.

**design** A preliminary drawing, or a synonym for composition. The term tends to refer chiefly to the linear and graphic elements of a work.

**Desportes, Alexandre-François** (1661–1740) French painter of animals and the chase. Louis XV made him painter of the royal hunt and kennels. His landscape passages, taken from nature, were considered daring in his day, belonging as they did in the Netherlands tradition.

**Devis, Arthur** (1711–87) English painter of portraits and conversation pieces. Lately he has been restored to critical favour. His brother Anthony (1729–1816) is known for his wash drawings and pale watercolour landscapes which have an engaging daintiness though little depth.

**diaglyph** A piece of carving or sculpture executed as an **intaglio**, in which all the forms lie below the level of the surface. It is the opposite of an anaglyph, which is executed in **relief**.

**diagonal rib** In Gothic vaulting, the ribs which cross diagonally from corner to corner of one bay of the vaulting.

**diamond point** An etching tool with a diamond tip used in drypoint.

**diaper ornament** A small carved, painted or inlaid ornament, usually of square or lozenge shape, which is repeated over a considerable surface area.

**dichroism** A term referring to the property of a substance which exhibits different hues when seen under different circumstances. Some oil colours, for example, seem to take on a different appearance when brushed on vertically or horizontally.

**Die Brücke** A loose assocation of German artists formed in Dresden in 1905 by Ernst Ludwig Kirchner, Erich Heckel, and Karl Schmidt-Rottluff (1884–1976). The following year they were joined by Emile Nolde and Max Pechstein, with Nolde remaining a peripheral member of the group. They devised a bold, deliberately archaic style of working based on their interest in early German woodcuts, primitive art, and the work of Van Gogh, Gauguin and Munch. The name (German for 'bridge') symbolized both the bond which held them together and their view of their work as a link with the art of the future. They never managed to formulate what that art might be but instead found unity in energetic revolt against 'long-established older forces'. One of their aims, said Schmidt-Rottluff, was 'to attract all the revolutionary and surging elements of the time'.

Compared with the Blaue Reiter they were a relatively nationalistic association, but no less intense in their convictions, which exerted an influence on public taste. They turned against Impressionism to work in the Expressionist style, favouring large areas of vivid colour. Their most successful medium was the woodcut, which they used to create bold and simplified forms. In 1910 they allied themselves to the Neue Sezession and the group finally broke up in 1913.

**diluent** The liquid used to thin paint to the fluidity an artist desires. Turpentine is the usual diluent used with oil paint, and water with watercolour.

**Dine, Jim** (b. 1935) American painter. He and Claes Oldenburg are considered the pioneers of the **Happening**. In much of his work he introduces everyday objects into paintings, with quasi-comic effect.

**diptych** see **altarpiece**

**Dipylon** A cemetery in Athens which has yielded large vases decorated with figure scenes.

**direct metal sculpture** The technique of shaping or assembling a piece of metal sculpture, as opposed to casting it in a mould. Alexander Calder was one of the originators of the method.

**direct sculpture** The technique of executing a **glyptic** sculpture by carving it directly out of the original material, usually wood or stone as distinct from modelling wax or clay, into the shape of the finished work.

**discharging arch** An arch set in the wall to relieve a lintel, or any of the masonry below, from the weight above.

**disegno** An Italian term which carries a number of meanings. Usually it applies to drawing and design, although the *arti del disegno* means all the visual arts. The notion of the *disegno interno* is a Mannerist invention, standing for the idealized image in the artist's imagination as opposed to the less perfect counterpart in the natural world. This Neo-Platonism underlies all theories of Ideal art. It was used by the proponents of Poussin in contesting the merits of Rubens in the 17th century.

**distyle** A portico with two columns at one or both ends.

**Divisionism** A term coined by the French art critic Félix Fénéon in 1886 to describe the Neo-Impressionist technique of Seurat and Signac. It was based on the careful placing of tiny dots of pure colour in such a way as to mix in the eye of the spectator rather than on the palette or the canvas. Its appeal was intellectual as well as aesthetic, since it satisfied the modern need to find scientific solutions for non-scientific problems. It was championed by those who sought a less spontaneous way of painting than Impressionism, by advocates of chromatic theory, and by the Symbolists. Signac referred to practitioners of Divisionism as

**Divisionism** Paul Signac: *Le pin parasol aux Canoubiers* (1897), an example of the Divisionist technique (Musée de l'Annonciade, St Tropez).

Chromo-luminarists. The more usual synonyms are **Neo-Impressionism** and Pointillism. See also **Seurat**.

**Dix, Otto** (1891–1969) German painter. In 1924 he exhibited with the **Neue Sachlichkeit** group at Mannheim. He continued to paint in the social **Verism** mode of the German realists, finding his subjects in the lame, the oppressed and the victims of war. These works led to his inclusion, with other German painters of his time, in the Nazi regime's exhibition of Degenerate Art in 1937. His later work is broader, less socially committed, painting in the Expressionist manner.

**Dobson, William** (1610–46) English painter of society portraits. He succeeded Van Dyck, but in a manner more robustly English, as in the portrait of *Endymion Porter* in the Tate Gallery, London and his *Charles II as Prince of Wales* (Scottish National Portrait Gallery). He bridges the gap between the imported graces of Van Dyck and the thoroughgoing naturalism of Hogarth's portraits, particularly the *Captain Coram* in the Foundling Hospital, London.

**Doesburg, Theo van** (1883–1931) Dutch painter and architect. With Modrian he founded the **de Stijl** movement in 1916, with a magazine of the same name. He was subsequently associated with Gropius and the Bauhaus, took part in the Dada movement and preached his own brand of **Neo-Plasticism**, which he called Elementalism. In the 1930s he was a leading light in **Abstraction-Création** and co-editor of the journal *Art Concret*. His writings and ideas have proved more interesting than his art.

**dogtooth** Early English ornamentation with a row of toothlike projections, each carved into four leaves and raised like a pyramid.

**Dolci, Carlo** (1616–86) Italian painter. He was born and worked in Florence. He painted portraits, but is best known for his religious subjects, in which his Late Baroque style is distinguished by smooth technique and attention to detail.

**dome** A large, hemispherical vault or curved roof. The essential structural character of a dome lies in the fact that its masonry is in arch form horizontally as well as vertically. An octagonal dome, like that of Florence Cathedral, is not a true dome in a structural sense and its static conditions are not the same as those of a circular dome. Domed roofs have been constructed in timber and iron, but in these the dome form has only been adopted for the sake of appearance and performs no structural function.

**Domenichino** (1581–1641) Italian painter. Born in Bologna, he was a pupil of the brothers Carracci. He went to Rome in 1602, and spent most of the next 30 years there, rivalling Guido Reni as the capital's leading painter, before being overtaken by Lanfranco and Cortona.

In 1631 he went to Naples with a commission to decorate the chapel of S. Gennaro in the Cathedral but, like other Roman painters before him, he was forced to flee the city in face of hostility towards a non-Neapolitan artist. He is remembered for his landscapes, which link the Bolognese School with Poussin and Claude.

**Domenico Veneziano** (c. 1400–61) Italian painter. He worked first in Venice and Umbria, and in Florence from about 1438. For his fresco cycle in Florence, *Scenes from the Life of the Virgin*, now lost, he had the assistance of Piero della Francesca. The *St Lucy Altarpiece* of about 1440 is an early example of the **sacra conversazione**.

**Donatello, Donato di Niccolo** (1386–1466) Italian sculptor, the most important Florentine master of the 15th century. He trained in the workshop of Ghiberti, worked with Nanni di Banco on Florence Cathedral from 1406 and carved his marble *David* in 1408–9 and the classical bronze *David* for the court of the Medici Palace in 1430–2. In Padua between 1443 and 1453 he designed the high altar for the church of S. Antonio, with its numerous statues and reliefs which exploit the dramatic possibilities of perspective.

His concept of sculpture as a means of expressive rather than generalized humanity, from the standing figures made for Or San Michele and Florence Cathedral to the *Mary Magdalene* in the Baptistery, Florence (c. 1456), made a powerful impact on artists of his generation and on Michelangelo, who was taught by Donatello's pupil and assistant, Bertoldo di Giovanni.

**Dongen, Kees van** (1877–1968) Dutch painter, sculptor and potter. He worked mainly in Paris, first as a Fauve and later as a mordant recordist of the 'high life' of the city in the 1920s and 1930s.

**Doré, Gustave** (1832–83) French draughtsman, best known for his illustrations to Balzac's *Contes Drolatiques* (1856) and to such classics as Dante's *Inferno* (1861), *Don Quixote* (1862) and *Paradise Lost* (1866), in a style that combines wiry draughtsmanship with melodramatic grandeur. His plates done in London (1869–71) have a force and dignity which made an impression on the young Van Gogh.

**Doric** see **order** (of architecture)

**dormer window** A window that projects from the sloping roof of a house.

**dosseret** A small block, larger at the top than at the bottom, which was placed above the main capital in Byzantine architecture. It probably originated from the endeavour to level up the unequal heights of columns and capitals brought from older buildings.

**Dou, Gerard** (1613–75) Dutch painter, an early pupil of Rembrandt. His style has little in common with his master's, consisting of highly finished pictures, on a small scale, of humdrum scenes from daily life. He was a founder, with Jan Steen, of the Guild of St Luke at Leiden in 1648. His widely admired style attracted several close followers and imitators. Until the change in taste that followed Impressionism, he was a much more sought-after painter than Rembrandt.

**Doyle, Richard** (1824–83) English cartoonist and illustrator. Born in London, he was the son of John Doyle (1797–1868), the Dublin-born portrait lithographer and political illustrator. He was introduced to *Punch* in 1843 and designed the famous cover that lasted until 1954. He made a popular name with his 'Manners and Customs of Ye Englishe' and with 'Bird's Eye Views of Society', but broke with *Punch* when its anti-Papacy views became too

much for him, and took to illustrating books in his highly individual vein of fairy frolics, of which *The Story of Jack and the Giants* (1851) and *In Fairyland* (1871) are among the best examples of his quirky genius.

**dripstone** A projecting moulding over a door or window arch. It protects the window or door from the elements.

**drop tracery** A tracery design which appears dropped or hung from the intrados of an arch, like a kind of inner ornamental border to it. It is found occasionally in late Gothic architecture.

**drybrush** A means of applying colour so as to achieve a textural effect. The brush is dragged across the surface with little or no paint on it.

**drypoint** A method of **intaglio** engraving in which the design is scratched directly on to a copper plate with a sharp tool, sometimes tipped with a diamond. Drypoint is the least complicated of all the intaglio processes, though its subtleties are amongst the hardest to master. Its particular quality lies in the burr that the needle throws up along each side of furrow as it cuts into the metal. This holds the ink when the plate is wiped and gives to the printed line a furry softness that is much valued. The deeper the line, the blacker it will print. This makes drypoint a very direct and sensitive medium, in which tonality can be achieved by touch alone.

A drypoint plate can produce only a few satisfactory impressions because the pressure of the press flattens the burr. Its life can, however, be extended by electrolytic steel facing. Drypoint may be used for putting the finishing touches to etchings, or for lightly marking out the design for a line engraving before setting to work with the more cumbersome burin.

**Du Maurier, George** (1834–96) English illustrator and novelist. He was born in Paris and studied there under Gleyre. He knew Whistler and his circle, and later drew on their bohemian life style in *Trilby* (1894). In the 1860s he was drawn into the publishing and magazine world and became a contributor to *Punch*, taking over the role of good-humoured social satirist that had belonged to Leech. His languid but observant studies of Victorian bourgeois society have made him famous.

Typically, for a man who did not take his talents too seriously, he turned to writing novels late in life, and produced three successes: *Trilby, Peter Ibbetson* (1894) and *The Martian* (1896), all with his own illustrations. Some of his best work for *Punch* is collected in *English Society at Home* (1880).

**Dubuffet, Jean** (b. 1901) French painter, the originator of **Art Brut**. His typical manner is a tough, versatile expressionism, employing such materials as glass, plaster, gravel and sand, re-worked in figurative forms.

**Duccio di Buoninsegna** (*c.* 1255–*c.* 1318) Italian painter, active in Florence and Siena. His *Virgin in Majesty* (*Maestà*), painted to replace an older version at Siena Cathedral, is a legendary masterpiece, now partly dismembered (large parts of it are in the Cathedral museum). He introduced a feeling of humanity into the austere Byzantine convention, with a narrative content comparable to that of Giotto.

**Duchamp, Marcel** (1887–1968) French painter. He was the brother of Jacques Villon and Suzanne Duchamp, both prominent painters in their day, and of the sculptor Duchamp-Villon. In 1911 he joined the Section d'Or group and in the following year exhibited his first notable work, *Nude Descending a Staircase*, which caused a furore in New York when it was shown there in the following year. He carried the art of the **Ready-made** to new heights, promoting the commonplace to the status of art.

With Francis Picabia, he was prominent in **Dada** and **Surrealism**, which culminated in his most famous work, *The Bride Stripped Bare by her Bachelors Even*, made of wire and glass (Philadelphia Museum of Art).

**Duchamp-Villon, Raymond** (1876–1918) French sculptor, the brother of Marcel Duchamp and of Jacques Villon. He lived in Paris from 1901 and took part in the movements of the time, from Cubism to the Section d'Or. His bronze *Horse* series, 1914 (Museum of Modern Art, New York), has a stylized

Futurist energy. He died in a military hospital after being gassed in the First World War.

**Dufy, Raoul** (1877–1953) French painter. His early work is in the Impressionist manner, followed by a Fauve period. His characteristically sunny Mediterranean pieces date from the 1920s. They deal with regattas, race meetings and the sparkling life of the French Riviera, painted in a quick, light, calligraphic style.

**dugento** The 1200s, that is, the 13th century.

**Durand, Jean-Nicholas-Louis** (1760–1834) French architect and theorist. He was author of *Précis et Leçons d'Architecture* (1802–5), putting a rationalist's case for utilitarian values in building. His ideas were influential in both France and Germany, though they are not apparent in much of his own work.

**Dürer, Albrecht** (1471–1528) German painter and engraver. He was a Renaissance artist equal in stature to the great Italians. Son of a Hungarian goldsmith who settled in Nuremberg, and apprenticed to the painter-engraver Michael Wolgemut (1434–1519) as a youth, Dürer showed prodigious powers of draughtsmanship. In 1494 he embarked on a journey to Italy, which he recorded in a series of remarkable watercolours. His skills as an engraver emerge in his woodcuts for the *Apocalypse* (1498) and in his copperplates, which he executed with ecstatic speed.

Like Leonardo, his intellectual curiosity involved him in the science, literature, mathematics and philosophy which was burgeoning at the time. He absorbed the Italian tradition, while remaining essentially North European in style and temperament. His graphic work, easily transportable across continents, spread his name, his subjects and his methods throughout Europe.

**dust box** A container in which an aquatint plate is coated with finely powdered resin. There are various designs, all of which work on the principle of stirring up the resin so that it floats in a cloud inside the box, and settles evenly on the plate. This is achieved either by a vigorous shaking, or by an arrangement of bellows. Artists usually wait for the heavier particles of resin to settle before inserting the plate.

**Dutch mordant** A carefully mixed solution of potassium chlorate and hydrochloric acid used as a mordant in etching, particularly when delicate lines are to be produced.

**Dyce, William** (1806–64) Scottish painter, born in Aberdeen. On visits to Italy he came into contact with the **Nazarenes** and returned as an early Pre-Raphaelite. His reputation as a painter has been somewhat overshadowed by his distinctions as a scientist and art educationalist – he was appointed director of the Government School of Design in 1840.

Among his most striking works are the well-known *Pegwell Bay* (National Gallery, London), the *Francesca da Rimini* (National Gallery of Scotland), and *Titian's First Essay in Colour* (Aberdeen).

**Dyck, Sir Anthony van** (1599–1641) Portrait painter. Born in Antwerp, he trained in Rubens's workshop as a youth, and made a brief visit to England in 1620 at the invitation of James I. He then spent four years in Italy, where his aristocratic style of portraiture, in the Baroque manner, brought him numerous commissions. After a spell of four years in Antwerp he came to England (1632) as Court Painter to Charles I, who knighted him.

He became prodigiously successful, setting standards in courtly portraiture which had no equal in England until Sir Thomas Lawrence's more than a century later, though many of the paintings bearing his name are largely the work of studio assistants. His most important works include the group of portraits done at Genoa before his move to London, and the studies of Charles, his family and members of the court from which the image of an age has been passed down in vivid, if romanticized, form.

**Eagles, Rev. John** (1783–1855) Amateur sketcher and watercolour artist, a member of the Bristol School. He was steeped in the Classical qualities of Poussin and Claude, but was equally enthusiastic in the cause of open-air sketching, leading parties of friends on sorties into the Bristol countryside, particularly Leigh Woods. He was a regular reviewer of exhibitions for *Blackwoods Magazine*.

It was his attack on Turner in the October 1836 issue that prompted the young Ruskin, then an Oxford undergraduate, to embark on his defence of Turner, which grew into *Modern Painters*.

**Eakins, Thomas** (1844–1916) American painter. Apart from spending four years in Europe in his youth studying under Gérôme and travelling in Spain, he stayed all his life in Philadelphia, where he became a pioneer of the **Social Realism** movement. The impact of Velazquez, Courbet and Manet is apparent in his work. The huge *Gross Clinic* (Jefferson Medical College, Philadelphia), rejected in its day, is now acknowledged as a key painting in the development of the American Social Realist tradition.

Eakins was also influential as a teacher, insisting on students of both sexes drawing from the nude model.

**Early Christian art** The four centuries from *c.*300 AD saw the emergence of Christian art in western Europe, as opposed to that of Byzantium in the East. The oldest examples are mural decorations in the subterranean burial chambers or catacombs in Rome, where the Christians, though oppressed, were able to lay out their dead. The painted figures, somewhat crudely executed in the late Roman manner, show Christ, boyish and unbearded, as the Good Shepherd or as a worker of miracles. The Crucifixion does not occur in Christian art until the early 5th century, by which time the degradation had been turned into symbolic triumph.

As the Christian Church grew, the Gospel stories were told in pictorial form, as frescoes and in mosaic. The new churches drew on the classical temple design, adapted in basilica form to accommodate worshippers. Some of the finest surviving examples of early Christian church decoration are in the S. Maria Maggiore, Rome, and in the mosaics at Ravenna, where the style shows obvious signs of eastern influences. From the middle of the 7th century the Byzantine style becomes dominant.

**Early English** The 13th-century phase of English Gothic architecture. The cathedrals at Wells and Lincoln are examples, with their

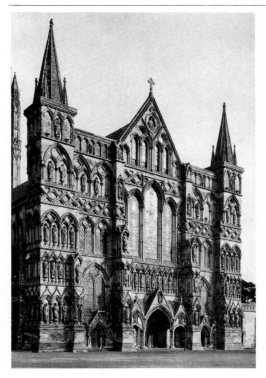

**Early English** The west front of Salisbury
Cathedral, built between 1258 and 1266.

straight walls, absence of chapels leading off
the main area, figured vaults, and simple lancet
windows.

**Earth art** Natural elements, such as soil and
rocks, or entire stretches of land, co-opted as
both media and subject.

**earth colours** Natural pigments, mostly reds,
ochres and umbers, which occur in soil that
has been coloured by metal oxides. They have
been used since primitive times. See **Cave art**.

**easel painting** A generalized term for painting done in studio conditions and by traditional
methods, such as applying paint to canvas by
means of a brush. The distinction has become
necessary as a result of the proliferation, and
acceptance, of other methods which dispense
with conventional painting procedures.

**Ecce Homo** Latin for 'Behold the Man': in
painting, the representation of Christ after the
scourging, presented to the people for
crucifixion.

**echinus** The oval or circular moulding
beneath the abacus of a Doric capital. It was
sometimes decorated with an egg and dart
pattern.

**échoppe** A tool used in etching and engraving
which has an oval, bevelled point. It is used
to cut lines in the plate or ground of a varying
width, that swell or taper along their length.

**École de Paris** see **Paris, School of**

**egg and dart, egg and tongue** An ovolo
moulding decorated with a pattern of alternate
eggs and arrowheads.

**egg tempera** A paint medium in which the
pigments are ground with pure egg yoke.
Usually applied to a **gesso** ground, it gives a
quick-drying matt finish which will never
crack, though it dries a few tones lighter. Tempera colours do not blend, but must be hatched
and cross-hatched to obtain gradations of colour and to allow modelling. For this reason the
technique invites a linear style, and was the
dominant method of easel painting until the
late 15th century. Oil glazes and colours began
to be used on a tempera base as a more versatile
painterly medium was sought. Out of this
period of 'mixed method' came the development of oil painting.

**Eiffel, Gustave** (1832–1923) French engineer. He has been immortalized by his 1010-
foot Tower in the heart of Paris, begun in 1877
and finished two years later. It introduced new
techniques based on Eiffel's experience with
lattice beam building as far afield as Russia,
Portugal and Peru. The Tower, built for the
Paris Exhibition of 1889, was a confident
announcement of a new age in which art and
technology would join hands. Its massive joints
and fields of force were to make a powerful
impression on such artists as Delaunay and
Léger. It is related in kind to Eiffel's two other
masterpieces, the Maria Pia Bridge over the
river Douro, near Oporto (1887–8) and the

Truyère Bridge near Garabit in the Massif Central (1880–4).

**Eight, The** see **Ashcan School**

**Elementarism** An art movement founded by the Dutch painter Theo van Doesburg arising from, though in opposition to, the Neo-Plasticism of Mondrian. Its other principal members were César Domela (b. 1900) and Friedrich Vordemberge-Gildewart (1899–1963).

**elevation** A method of drawing a building or part of a building as if there were no distortion by perspective and as if every part were opposite to the eye at the same time. In an elevation drawing the side or flank of the object is ignored altogether: it must be shown on another elevation at right angles to the front one. The usefulness of an elevation drawing is that the size of a building and that of its components can be exactly represented to scale. An elevation drawing shows one face of an object only, but shows it as it actually is; a perspective drawing shows two or more faces, but as they appear to the eye.

**Elsheimer, Adam** (1578–1610) German landscape painter. He lived mostly in Italy and was influenced by Tintoretto and Caravaggio, though he worked on a much smaller scale, usually on copper. Rubens had such a high opinion of his works that he offered to sell them, after Elsheimer's death, to enrich his widow. Their quality lies in their narrative charm, and in the soft, glowing lights with which the subjects are suffused.

**empaquetage** A word coined by the New Realists referring to the wrapping of huge objects in plastic sheets, as demonstrated by the Bulgarian artist Cristo.

**Empire style** A description applied to French and other European art and decorative styles from the French First Empire (1804–14) into the 1840s. Its essential characteristic is **Neo-classicism**, a concept dear to the heart of Napoleon and developed with much energy by the painter Jacques-Louis David and his disciples, notably Antoine-Jean Gros and Baron François Gérard, the distinguished Empire portrait painter.

Architecture, as well as painting, became imbued with the Empire spirit, from urban reconstruction on the grand scale to the restoration of great houses such as the Louvre, the Tuileries and Fontainebleau, particularly by the architects Charles Percier (1762–1838), Pierre-François Fontaine (1762–1853), Alexandre Théodore Brongniart (1739–1818), Pierre-Alexandre Vignon (1763–1828) and Jean-François Chalgrin (1739–1811). In sculpture, the Empire style is represented in works by Joseph Chinard (1756–1813), Denis Antoine Chaudet (1763–1810) and Pierre Cartellier (1757–1831). The furniture makers and the Sèvres porcelain factory also took the opportunity to create work which combined the dignity of a romanticized past with an opulence appropriate to France's new imperial glory.

**empreinte** A technique developed in modern times by the French painter, Jean Dubuffet. Empreintes are random images taken on wet paper from a sheet of glass or celluloid which has first been covered with ink and then sprinkled with various bits of debris such as leaves, dust, grass, sand, or even tapioca. The paper is pressed on to the 'display' with the hands. Successive impressions may differ widely, depending on how wet or dry the ink and paper are, the placing and pressure of the hands, the disturbance of the surface, and so on. Anything can find its way on to the plate, in search, as the artist put it, of 'the aspect of an image produced by the elements themselves, inscribing themselves directly, without the intervention of any other medium'.

**encaustic painting** A method of painting which dates from Greek and Roman times. Colours were applied to a wall with wax, which had to be kept hot if the mixture was to remain pliable. The last stage of the process was to bed the finished painting into the wall with hot irons. Few encaustic paintings survive from antiquity, but there are many accounts of the process, notably Pliny's, which Leonardo probably used in his abortive attempt to revive the process in 1503, when he began to work on the *Battle of Anghiari*. Only in this century has the technique been mastered.

**encaustic tiles** Glazed and decorated earthenware tiles used in the Middle Ages and for floors in Victorian churches.

**enceinte wall** The outer enclosing wall of a temple or forecourt, or of a collection of temples or other buildings grouped together. In military buildings, the main enclosure of a fortress, surrounded by a ditch or moat.

**enfilading** A system of aligning internal doors so that, when open, they offer a view through a series of rooms. It was introduced in France in the mid-17th century, as an adjunct of Baroque design.

**engraving** The term applies to all the processes of incising a design or an inscription on a hard surface, such as wood or metal, whether for decoration, illustration, or making a plate for a print. In metalwork, sculpture or glasswork surface ornamentation is frequently engraved. In the graphic arts, engraving is used in both **intaglio** and **relief** methods of printing, such as wood engraving, line engraving, drypoint or stipple engraving. Technically, the term only covers techniques where the plate is directly incised and not bitten by acid as in etching and aquatint. Until the beginning of this century it was used as a generic term for all the processes in the graphic arts, and it is still not uncommon to find it applied even to planographic or surface printing, though cutting into a plate or block plays no part in these techniques.

Like all the methods of multiplying prints, engravings can be executed either for purely reproductive purposes, or as original prints, independent works of art. For a classification of all types of graphic reproduction see **print making**.

**Ensor, James** (1860–1949) Belgian painter, born of an English father. An Expressionist before his time, he has much in common with the ironic, often macabre imagination of Bosch or Bruegel. This is most marked in his etchings, in which his fantasies are given full rein. His best work is all comparatively early.

**entablature** In Classical architecture, the whole superstructure resting on the columns, consisting of architrave, frieze and cornice.

**entasis** A slight outward curvature or swelling of what would otherwise be the straight lines of a Classical column, incorporated to correct the optical illusion that the sides of a column curve inwards. For the same reason, entasis is often used on spires.

**Environmental art** A form of art related to assemblage, usually designed to provoke a degree of participation or involvement by the spectator. Environmental art emerged in the 1960s in America out of the general desire to deformalize and declassify the arts, and was an amalgam of sculpture, painting and architecture.

Environments can take many forms. A sculpture which invites the spectator to walk through or climb over it is environmentally conceived. Entire rooms might fuse sculptural, architectural and painted forms into an integrated whole. Or it may take such forms as the life-size tableaux of the Pop and New Realist schools, which the spectator can enter. Some Environments are close to being Happenings, more in the nature of events than fixed and finished pieces of work.

**epistyle** A beam that spans the space between two columns or piers. It is also called an architrave.

**Epstein, Sir Jacob** (1880–1959) Sculptor, born in New York but he lived most of his life in England. He was a founder member of the **London Group**. His monumental carvings such as the *Christ* (1919) and the *Rima* (1925) were shocking in their time, and he remained a controversial artist all his life. His work is a direct development from Rodin, with an energy and primitivism hitherto unknown in such public places as Hyde Park and St James's Park Underground Station.

**Ernst, Max** (1891–1976) German-French painter. He was one of the pioneers of **Surrealism**. His work is infused with childhood fears and memories, and he has shown interest in the art of deranged minds. He joined the **Blaue Reiter** group, and after the war became prominent in **Dada**, dubbing himself 'Dadamax'. He was a master of collage, which has proved a more enduring technique than was

**Engraving** Albrecht Dürer: *The Knight, Death and the Devil* (1513),
an engraving which demonstrates the silvery yet mellow tone that
distinguishes the work of a master.

envisaged by its pioneers, and invented **frottage**. He was awarded first prize at the Venice Biennale in 1954, and at his death was one of the acknowledged masters of the Modern Movement.

**esquisse** The French word for a sketch, used of an initial study for a larger work. An *esquisse en sculpture* is the small model made by a sculptor to help work out the form of the finished piece.

**estampe** The French word for a print, specifically intaglio, and also – confusingly – an impression run off from a copy of a print. An *estampe de tirage limité* is a limited edition not necessarily printed by the artist, though each proof may be signed by him.

**Etchells, Frederick** (1886–1973) English painter, born in Newcastle. He studied at the Royal College of Art, then went to work in Paris and was included in Roger Fry's second Post-Impressionist exhibition, 1912. He joined the Omega Workshops with Wyndham Lewis, then left to found the Rebel Art Centre and throw in his lot with Vorticism. He was represented in the Vorticist exhibitions in London, 1915, and New York, 1917. He spent the rest of his working life as an architect.

**etching** Traditionally the pre-eminent printmaking process, etching relies on acid rather than manual force to bite the design into the plate. A copper, zinc or steel plate is first coated with a 'resist' or etching ground made of an impermeable and acid-resistant substance. The artist draws his design on the grounded plate using a sharp etching needle, the point cutting through the dark ground to the metal beneath as he does so. Once the design is complete, the back and edges of the plate are coated with an acid-resistant varnish and the whole is then immersed in an acid bath containing a mordant (usually dilute nitric acid) which bites into the metal wherever the ground has been pierced by the needle. The deeper a line is bitten or etched in this way the darker it will print, but the process can be halted at any time on selected parts of the design by removing the plate temporarily from the bath and using a stopping-out varnish to cover and protect those lines or parts which the etcher wishes to remain faint.

This procedure of stopping out and re-biting can be repeated many times to create progressively deeper lines, thus allowing considerable tonal variation in the final print. Once the plate is bitten to the etcher's satisfaction it is cleaned, polished and inked before being wiped so as to leave the ink, as with all intaglio processes, in the etched lines only. Depending on how the first proofs look, the plate may well be touched up with **drypoint** technique, which does not involve re-laying the ground and is a means of adding further tonal and textural elements to the design.

There are many variations on each step of this process, although the principle remains the same in each case. Combinations with other techniques, such as **aquatint**, allow the etcher a multiplicity of effects. It is further valued for the fluidity and spontaneity of line, for unlike line engraving or even drypoint there is minimal resistance to the movement of the tool

**Etching** *The Great Jewish Bride* (1635) by Rembrandt, whose mastery helped to establish the potential of etching as equal to any of the graphic arts (British Museum, London).

across the plate, as it is not having to penetrate the metal. An etcher can work on his plate with virtually the same fluency and freedom as he enjoys on paper.

Etching was first developed to save labour in the production of line engravings, using skills developed in the embellishment of suits of armour. The medium remained clumsy and secondary to line engraving until the 17th century when, in the hands of Rembrandt in particular, it came into its own. In the 18th century Piranesi used it triumphantly for his series of architectural fantasies and Goya – perhaps the greatest master of etching combined with aquatint – turned to it for his *Disasters of War* series. During the 19th century Millet, Corot, Pissarro, Degas, Whistler and many others used etching as a graphic extension of their painting. In modern times the majority of major artists have done significant work in the medium, among them Picasso, Braque, Matisse, Sutherland and Moore.

**etching ground** In etching and aquatint, this is the term for the thin acid-resistant ground, sometimes called the 'resist', that is applied to the face of the plate and through which the drawing is incised in etching or grained in aquatint. The ground must resist the mordant for as long as it is immersed, offer minimal resistance to the etching needle, yet be sufficiently adhesive and tough to withstand a certain amount of handling. Usually it is a compound of beeswax, bitumen and resin and is applied by being melted on a heated plate and rolled flat. To blacken the ground in order to make the design stand out more starkly, it may be smoked with burning tapers. Grounds for soft-ground etching are usually made by adding tallow.

**Etty, William** (1787–1849) English artist noted for his paintings of the nude. He studied at the Royal Academy Schools and with Sir Thomas Lawrence, from whom he probably acquired his liking for opulent colour. His figures are somewhat academic, but sensuous. He sometimes brought them together in an ambitious subject-picture such as *Youth at the Prow and Pleasure at the Helm* (Tate Gallery, London).

**Euston Road School** A group of like-minded teachers and pupils who in 1937 came together under Sir William Coldstream (b.1908) in opposition to what they saw as the silliness and perversity of the School of Paris. Their aim was to re-assert the superiority of structural and representational painting, which they themselves practised, in a direct line from Cézanne. The group's leading members were Claude Rogers (b.1907), Graham Bell (1910–43) and Victor Pasmore (b.1908), whose subsequent progress was to be towards Abstraction.

**Evenepoel, Henri** (1872–99) Belgian painter. He trained in Brussels, then moved to Paris to become a pupil of Gustave Moreau. He was attracted by the everyday urban scene that he found reflected in works by Manet, and lightened his palette in the Impressionist mode. He admired the Nabis, though from a distance, and produced a number of lithographs in their style. A visit to Algeria for reasons of ill health brought him close to the intense colour values of Matisse. At the age of 27, before arriving at a style distinctively his own, he died.

**Everdingen, Allart van** (1621–75) Dutch landscape painter and etcher. Born in Alkmaar, he worked in Utrecht and Haarlem, visiting Scandinavia in the 1640s, and returning with a fancy for dramatic waterfalls. His brother Caesar (1617–87) painted portraits and historical subjects, and was a notable painter of the nude.

**ex voto** Latin for 'Out of thankfulness'. This refers to an offering for blessings received in the form of a commissioned work that might include the donor's likeness in an appropriately subservient role.

**exedra** Semicircular or rectangular recess or alcove. The word is also used of a small apse or niche.

**Expressionism** A 20th-century term to describe works of art infused with emotional or intellectual passion, usually associated with nervous turmoil, melancholy or revolt. It gained general currency during the 1914–18 war in a reaction against the strictly visual, ingratiating nature of Impressionism.

The first group to exhibit as Expressionists, at the Neue Sezession in Berlin in 1911, included Braque, André Derain, Picasso, Kees van Dongen and Maurice de Vlaminck. Herwarth Walden, editor of the newspaper *Der Sturm*, used the term in 1912 as the banner for a new art movement – which it never was, since it consisted of virtually any painter who could claim to be breaking new ground. Today the term is applied to German literature and painting between about 1905 and 1918, and by extension – and hindsight – to individual works by masters of the past, such as Grünewald, Rembrandt and Goya. The two pre-war groups, Die Brücke and the Blaue Reiter, include the leading German Expressionist painters. Other artists to whom the term applies are Karel Appel (b. 1921), Francis Bacon (b. 1909), Max Beckmann (1884–1950), Chagall, Munch, Nolde, Rouault, and Chaim Soutine (1893–1944).

**extrados** The outer line or back of an arch, formed by the upper edges of the voussoirs.

**Eyck, Van** Family name of two painters, Jan and Hubert van Eyck, who are regarded as the founders of the Flemish School. Hubert, presumed to be the older brother, died in 1426. Little is known about his career, except that he designed a couple of altarpieces in the 1420s. Jan's life is better documented. He was Court Painter to Philip the Good, Duke of Burgundy, who sent him on diplomatic missions to Spain and Portugal. Some signed pieces indicate an extraordinary skill in painting the textures of stuffs and metals, as in *Arnolfini and his Wife* (1434) in the National Gallery, London. The novelty of his composition, the realistic sense of a living presence, and his use of the oil-painting medium, make him the forerunner of a new epoch.

**eye-catcher** An artificial feature or folly, such as a sham ruin or tower, built on a conspicuous site in an English country estate as a focal point in the landscape.

**Fabritius, Carel** (1622–54) Dutch painter, a member of Rembrandt's circle and his most distinguished pupil. He might also have been the master of Vermeer, who succeeded him as syndic of the Guild of St Luke in Delft. He was killed in the powder factory explosion there, in which most of his work was also destroyed.

His placing of dark figures against a light background – a reversal of Rembrandt's practice – and the delicacy of his finish, are features of his style. His younger brother, Barent Fabritius (1624–73), may also have been a pupil of Rembrandt's. He was the most industrious of the Rembrandt imitators.

**façade** The principal front of a large or imposing building.

**fan vault** In English Gothic, the form of vaulting in which all the ribs radiate, fanlike, from the same point and at an equal angular distance from each other. In this form of vault the ribs are decorative, not structural, each 'fan' being a solid concave-sided semicone.

**Fantin-Latour, Henri** (1836–1904) French painter and lithographer. He studied at the École des Beaux-Arts and at the studio of Gleyre, where he made his first contacts with Degas, Whistler and the Impressionist circle. He became friendly with them all, but did not embrace their methods or ideas. His figure studies and flower paintings, essentially studio pieces, are considered his best work. His lithographs, in a mood of stylized romanticism, are now out of fashion.

**Farington, Joseph** (1747–1821) English topographic draughtsman. His influential role in the art world kept him at the centre of affairs as manipulator and pundit. A pupil of Richard Wilson, he trained at the Royal Academy Schools and became an RA in 1785. His *Diaries* are valuable records of conversations and meetings with the prominent personalities of his time.

**fast colours** Colours that will not fade.

**fat** Colour mixed as a thick **impasto**, rich in oil, is sometimes referred to as 'fat'. It is an adage of oil painting that fat colour should be applied on top of lean, that is, colour which has been thinned with turpentine.

**Fauvism** A term coined by the French critic Louis Vauxcelles, when he used the word *fauves* (wild beasts) to describe a group of young painters whose strikingly coloured compositions were the most provocative works at the

Salon d'Automne in 1905. The term was immediately adopted, though it covers a disparate group of painters whose aims and styles did not all coincide. Chief among them were Matisse, leader of the movement, who first hit upon the Fauvist manner in 1899; several others who had been pupils of Gustav Moreau, including Rouault; Henri Charles Manguin (1874–1943); Charles Camoin (1879–1965); Jean Puy (1876–1960); Maurice de Vlaminck; André Derain; Braque and Dufy. They all shared an enthusiasm for primitive arts, but were more immediately influenced by the major Post-Impressionists, Van Gogh, Gauguin, Cézanne and Seurat.

The typical Fauve painting uses flat areas of colour to describe familiar forms, the background often as vividly coloured as the foreground. The Fauvists' flat compositions and painterly concern with line and colour have had a lasting influence, most noticeably on the Abstract-Expressionist painters.

**Feininger, Lyonel** (1871–1956) American painter of German origin. He was born in New York but worked mostly in Europe, including an association with the Section d'Or, Delaunay's brand of Cubism, and with Gropius at the Bauhaus.

**Fernley, John** (1782–1860) English painter of sporting subjects. Born at Thrussington in the Quorn country, he was at home with horses and hunting scenes, which provided him with a steady living throughout a long career.

**festoon** In architecture, a carved frieze decoration consisting of a garland of fruit, flowers and leaves tied with ribbons and suspended at both ends to form a loop.

**Fetti, Domenico** (1589–1623) Italian painter, born in Rome. His biblical subjects combine the influences of both Caravaggio and Elsheimer. His later work, as one of a group of non-Venetians active in Venice, is distinguished for its vivacity and colour.

**Feuerbach, Anselm** (1829–80) German Romantic painter. He trained in Germany, Antwerp, and in Paris, where he was influenced by Courbet and Delacroix. He was inspired by

humanist ideals, as expressed in early Italian painting. His own work falls short of his ambitions.

**Fielding, Anthony Vandyke Copley** (1787–1855) English watercolour artist. He was the son of a landscape painter, Nathan Theodore Fielding (exhib. 1775–1814) and brother of Thales Fielding (1793–1837), the friend of Delacroix. A member of Dr Monro's circle, he was taught by John Varley, and found his most popular subjects in misty hill country, tranquil lakes and lyrical skies.

**Figurative art** Representational as opposed to abstract art; that is, art which draws its subject matter from nature. 'Figurative' and 'representational' are often used interchangeably, though the latter carries connotations of a greater degree of realism.

**figurine** A small statue.

**Filiger, Charles** (1863–1928) French painter. He was born in Alsace but spent most of his working life in Brittany. His work combines Byzantine art, the Quattrocento and the Cloisonnisme of Anquetin and Bernard, in subjects steeped in Breton mysticism. He is said to have been both alcoholic and mentally unstable, though with a romanticized view of Christianity that is the source of his most impressive work.

**fillet** In a series of parallel mouldings, a narrow strip dividing, where necessary, one moulding from another, or used to define or accentuate the limit of a moulding.

**Fine Manner** see **Broad Manner**

**finial** The topmost ornament on a post, gable or pinnacle.

**Fischer von Erlach, Johann Bernhard** (1656–1723) Austrian architect. He and Hildebrandt were the leading Baroque architects in Austria; he was Court Architect in Vienna from 1704. After building three Italianate churches in Salzburg he was commissioned to build the Karlskirche in Vienna (1716–20), which is regarded as his masterpiece. His son Joseph Emmanuel (1693–1742) finished the great Library in the Hofburg, Vienna, which he started the year before he died.

**flamboyant** Term for the late Gothic style in French architecture. Flamboyant tracery is the wavy stonework in church windows of the period.

**Flaxman, John** (1755–1826) English sculptor. He first worked with the Wedgwood potteries as a designer. A seven-year stay in Rome introduced him to classical sculpture and to Greek vase paintings, which helped to set his style as an illustrator. Back in England he led a busy career as a sculptor and monument maker, including the *Lord Nelson* group in St Paul's. He was elected an RA in 1800, and became the Academy's first Professor of Sculpture ten years later. He stands high among the Neoclassical artists, especially as a draughtsman.

**flèche** A small, light spire planted on a Gothic roof. It is generally constructed of wood and sometimes covered with lead treated in a decorative manner.

**floriated** A word used to describe the flowing lines of the floral and leaf designs in Gothic tracery.

**flushwork** The use of knapped flint in conjunction with dressed stone to produce decorative wall patterns.

**fluting** The vertical channelling on the shaft of a Classical column or pilaster. Its principal use is to give expression to the column by emphasizing its verticality.

**Fluxus** The Latin word for flux, adopted in 1962 to describe an iconoclastic troupe of artists, mostly German and American, who achieved a short-lived Dada revival. The central Fluxus event was the **Happening**. The group described themselves as opposed to serious art and culture and their institutions, to Europeanism, and to 'every form of art which promotes the artistic ego'.

**flying buttress** An arched buttress used in Gothic building to transmit the thrust of the nave vault across the aisle roof to the outer buttress.

**Flying buttress** Part of the supporting structure of Chartres Cathedral.

**foils** Small arcs or leaf-shaped curves. The number of foils used is indicated by the prefix in such adjectives as 'trefoil' or 'multifoil'.

**font** or **fount** In typography, a complete set of type in a particular face and size.

**Fontainebleau, School of** A branch of Mannerism, originated when François I commissioned a group of Italian Mannerist artists to restyle the château of Fontainebleau in 1526. Their work shows influences not only from their native tradition but also from the French environment in which, for 10 years and more, most of them were to work. The result was a distinctive blend of voluptuousness (French) and mannered elegance (Italian) which set a decorative style that spread throughout France. The principal artists of the School are Giovanni Battista Rosso, who came to France in 1531; Primaticcio, a follower of Giulio Romano, who arrived a year later, and Niccolò dell' Abbate.

The so-called Second School of Fontaine-bleau flourished briefly at the end of the century under the patronage of Henri IV, but with nothing like the same inventiveness and spirit.

**Forain, Jean Louis** (1852–1931) French painter and illustrator. He was influenced by Rembrandt and Goya and by Daumier. He exhibited with the Impressionists four times, though his own style as a painter tends to quieter tones.

**fore-edge painting** The painted decoration on the fore edge (that furthest from the spine) of the leaves of a book. In the 18th century a technique was used by which the fanned-out pages, held fast, could be painted with views or conversation pieces which were concealed when the edges were then gilded in the ordinary way. To see the pictures, the reader would fan out the edges, whereupon they reappeared.

---

**Foreshortening** The effectiveness of skilful perspective treatment of the outstretched arms is evident in Caravaggio's *The Supper at Emmaus* (National Gallery, London).

**foreshortening** The effect of applying the principles of perspective when depicting an object or figure.

**forgery** A work done in imitation of another artist's manner so that it may be passed off as being by him. A convincing forgery will deceive not only on aesthetic grounds, but be executed in materials of the appropriate period, bear evidence of the effects of ageing such as **craquelure** and **patina**, and be supplied with a **provenance**. Should any work give cause for suspicion on stylistic or other grounds, museums have recourse to scientific tests to determine beyond any doubt its true age and composition.

Works done in the manner of a master by his pupils and followers may be hard to distinguish from those by his own hand, and wishful thinking can lead dealers and collectors, and even keepers and curators, to upgrade the attribution. In such cases authenticity can only be decided through the eye of the connoisseur and a consensus of the most informed opinion.

**formalism** Conformity to established, traditional and academic principles. However, the term is not specific for it also implies concern with the formal properties of art rather than content. The two meanings can be opposed: for instance, Soviet art that departs from the tenets of Soviet Realism often does so in favour of concern with form over subject matter, and so is called formalist although it rejects the established doctrine.

**Foster, Myles Birket** (1825–99) English watercolour artist and illustrator. Born into a Quaker family, he was apprenticed as an engraver at 16, and at 21 embarked on a highly productive career as an illustrator of editions of the poets, popular classics, and books of English landscape, in a dainty and meticulous style that made his name. His watercolours, in much the same manner, are the epitome of Victorian decorative sentiment. He was a travelling companion of the artist and illustrator Fred Walker (1840–75), with whose work his has much in common, and a friend of the Pre-Raphaelite painters.

**foul biting** In etching, a defect in the plate or in the preparation which produces unwanted marks on the proof. It is usually caused by a faulty etching ground, too strong a mordant, or by leaving the plate too long in the acid bath.

**found object** An everyday object incorporated in a work of art, or itself transformed into art simply by the artist declaring it to be so, and exhibiting it as such. If it is a manufactured item, it is called a **Ready-made** (see also **Duchamp**). Found objects are often subtly modified, or used as parts of larger constructions and assemblages. They were first employed by Kurt Schwitters, who incorporated everyday detritus such as tram tickets and jam-jar lids in his collages, and they were used widely by the Dada and Surrealist artists in accordance with their doctrine that anything can constitute art. Notable examples by Picasso include his *Venus du Gaz*, an iron gas pipe and ring up-ended to become a female form, and his *Bull's Head*, made out of a discarded bicycle seat and handlebars.

**Fouquet, Jean** (*c.* 1425–81) The leading figure in French 15th-century painting. Born at

Tours, he visited Rome as a young man, travelled in Italy, and on his return became a member of the French court, where he was engaged on illustrating manuscripts. In 1475 he was appointed the royal painter, and his work broadened to take in monumental Church commissions such as the *Descent from the Cross* at Nouans. The few works which can be attributed to him with certainty suggest the breadth and intelligence of a master.

**Fragonard, Jean Honoré** (1732–1806) French painter of the Louis XV epoch. He was the epitome of pre-Revolutionary grace and frolic. A pupil of Chardin and of Boudin, he caused a sensation with his famous painting, *The Swing*, commissioned by a French nobleman in 1766, with its deliberately suggestive overtones. It is typical of the frilly, uncaring spirit of his work. He was ruined by the Revolution, and died in poverty.

**Francesco di Giorgio** (1439–*c.* 1511) Italian painter, sculptor and architect. Born in Siena, where he shared a studio with Donatello, he was later employed by Federigo, Duke of Urbino, as a military engineer. He knew Leonardo, whom he encouraged to make notebook drawings of his thoughts and observations. His own paintings have a winsome naturalism, as in the *St Dorothy and the Infant Christ* (National Gallery, London), based on the legend of the

**Found object** Pablo Picasso: *Bull's Head* (1943), a bronze cast from a bicycle seat and handlebars.

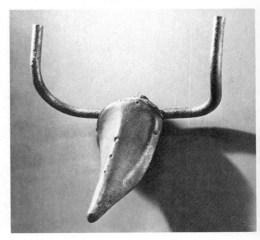

Child appearing to St Dorothy on her way to martyrdom, bearing a basket of roses.

**Francia, Francesco** (*c.*1450–1517) Italian goldsmith and painter. The delicacy and lyricism of his work in partnership with Lorenzo Costa (*c.*1460–1536) in Bologna anticipates the Carracci brothers and Guercino.

**Francia, Louis Thomas** (1772–1839) French-born artist who came to England in 1795, exhibited at the Royal Academy, studied at Dr Monro's, and was a leading figure in the sketching club founded by Thomas Girtin, known as The Brothers. In 1805 he set up as a drawing master in London, but in 1817 returned to Calais, where he gave lessons to Richard Bonington. His watercolours are often of a noble simplicity that he learned from Girtin.

**free-standing**  A description referring to a sculpture or construction that is not attached to a fixed surface, and which may therefore be viewed from all sides.

**fresco**  A method of wall painting in which pigments ground in water are painted on to freshly laid lime plaster. The technique was developed by Minoan and other early Mediterranean civilizations, and has been in use ever since. The Mexican muralists José Clemente Orozco and Diego Rivera are among its great exponents. True fresco (or buon fresco as it is called to distinguish it from fresco secco, which uses a dry plaster ground) is one of the most permanent techniques known, for the pigment dries as an integral part of the wall's surface. The masters of the Italian Renaissance were its supreme practitioners.

Typically, the wall is first given two or three layers of plaster, the rough trullisatio, the arriccio and the arenato. When the last of these is dry, the **cartoon** is traced on to it. Sometimes the working sketch of the whole composition is executed directly on to the plaster in a red-brown colour called sinopia, a term also applied to the resultant underpainting. The last layer of plaster, the intonaco, is confined to an area sufficient for only one day's painting at a time. The relevant section of the cartoon is redrawn over this, and the paint is applied. If any of the intonaco remains unpainted at the end of the session it must be cut away and relaid before the start of the next, so that the working surface is always damp.

**fret**  In architecture, a geometrical pattern of horizontal and vertical straight lines repeated to form a band.

**Friedrich, Caspar David** (1774–1840) German painter, chief exponent of German Romanticism. His imagination was essentially North European, and his work owes little if anything to the Italian-inspired landscapes of his contemporaries. A brooding melancholy in his Pomeranian landscapes, with their mirror-like waters and mysterious distances, suggests a spiritual kinship with his Bavarian predecessor, Altdorfer.

**frieze**  In the Ionic and Corinthian orders, the band left between the architrave and the cornice. It is generally decorated with sculpture in relief, either of figures or ornament, as a result of which the term is sometimes applied to any horizontal band of sculpture in relief.

**Frith, William Powell** (1819–1909) English painter. He was a specialist in large, crowded scenes of contemporary life, such as *Derby Day* (1858) and *The Railway Station* (1862). These were immensely popular, drawing large crowds to the Royal Academy, and sold for spectacular prices.

**frontality**  A term usually applied to sculpture, meaning the head-on depiction of a figure or object: a characteristic of the art of early civilizations, where the front, sides and back of a figure were often conceived as four separate silhouettes, each with a frontal orientation towards the viewer. The result, consisting of four planes independently realized, shows no understanding of three-dimensional spatial organization. However, as early as Roman times the monumental nature of frontal sculpture was useful in conveying an air of **hieratic** authority.

**frottage**  The technique of taking a rubbing from any textured surface by placing a piece of paper over it, and shading with a soft crayon or pencil so that an impression appears on the surface. The practice was first introduced into fine art by Max Ernst, who often employed impressions of wooden surfaces in his collages.

**fugitive** Pigments that fade or change colour with time, or which fail to hold their true tones, are said to be fugitive.

**Fuller, Richard Buckminster** (b. 1895) American architect of the machine age. He designed the 'Dymaxion House' – dynamic plus maximum efficiency – in 1927, which was a realization in literal terms of Le Corbusier's famous definition of a house as 'a machine for living in '. He subsequently developed a motorized version, the 'Dymaxion Three Wheeled Auto'. His Geodesic Domes, based on octa-hedrons or tetrahedrons and built with cheap, light materials, were attempts to enclose maximum space relative to the area of the encompassing form. His biggest, built for the Union Tank Car Company, Louisiana, in 1958, achieved a diameter of 384 feet.

**Functionalism** The dictum that 'form follows function'. It has assumed a modern signifi-cance, but in fact is as old as Man and is instinctively followed by such fellow humans as Eskimos and African hut dwellers. The prin-ciple was made intellectually fashionable by the 19th-century theoretician Eugène Viollet-le-Duc (1814–79), a restorer of medieval castles. His thesis that architecture could be rationalized influenced the young Corbusier. Functionalism has spread far beyond architec-ture to become a powerful force in commercial and industrial design. The converse of the func-tionalist idea – that practicality or efficiency will itself produce a beautiful object – has also taken root in modern times.

**Funk art** An offshoot of Pop art, drawing on the same sources. It flourished briefly in the 1960s, mainly in California.

**Fuseli, Henry** (1741–1825) Swiss painter. The son of a portraitist, he first studied in Berlin then came to London, where Reynolds encouraged him to become a painter. He went to Rome, studying and copying there for eight years, and on his return to London opened the Milton Gallery with an exhibition of his own work. He was promptly made an RA, and soon afterwards Professor of Painting, becoming

Keeper in 1804. His extravagant style and fantastic subject matter, often erotic, are more successful in his drawings than in his oils.

**Futurism** A movement founded by the Italian poet Marinetti in Milan, 1909. In his first Futurist Manifesto of that year, he called for a new art that would free Italy from the dead weight of her cultural past and reflect the mod-ern world with aesthetic criteria based on speed, machinery and violence. He wrote: 'We declare that the splendour of the world has been enriched with a new form of beauty, the beauty of speed. We will glorify war – the only true hygiene of the world – militarism, patri-otism, the destructive gesture of the anarch-ist . . . We will destroy museums, libraries, and fight against moralism, feminism, and all util-itarian cowardice.'

In 1910 the painters Umberto Boccioni, Carlo Carrà, Luigi Russolo, Giacomo Balla and Gino Severini proclaimed their adherence to the new movement, and declared in their manifesto that 'all subjects previously used (in art) must be swept aside in order to express our whirling life of steel, pride, fever, and speed.' They demanded a ten-year ban on the portrayal of the nude in painting, to emphasize their break with tradition. They turned to the use of vibrant colour and Pointillist techniques and later, under the growing influence of Cub-ism, to the simultaneous representation of sub-jective and objective perceptions, held together by interpenetrating planes and 'lines of force'. In 1912 Boccioni turned to sculpture and the following year produced his *Forms of Continuity in Space*, a striding figure in which he found 'not pure form, but pure plastic rhythm, not the construction of the body, but the construc-tion of the *action* of the body'.

Futurism continued as a movement until the mid-1930s, becoming increasingly intermixed with emergent Italian fascism. As an effective artistic force it did not survive the death of Boccioni in 1916. However, it has exerted an influence out of all proportion to its achieve-ments. In France, Apollinaire, Léger, Delau-nay, Duchamp and the Dada artists all assimi-lated some of its ideas. In Russia the Rayonists and Constructivists made use of its principles in different ways, while in England it played an integral part in the development of Vorticism.

**gable** The triangular space of wall, generally with a coping on its sloping sides, which forms the enclosure at the end of a high-pitched roof. It is to Gothic architecture what the pediment is to Classical architecture.

**gablet** A miniature gable, often used as a decoration in a Gothic buttress or in woodwork.

**Gabo, Naum,** originally called Pevsner (b. 1890) American sculptor, born in Russia. A visit to Paris in 1913 introduced him to Cubism. He returned to Russia in 1917 and took up the Constructivist cause, but left for Berlin in 1922, where he continued to propagate Constructivist ideas. Moving to Paris, he was prominent in Abstraction-Création in the 1930s, when he first visited the United States, where he has lived since the end of World War II.

His work has moved from figurative beginnings through kinetic sculptures to constructions using advanced modern materials, including transparent plastic sheeting to achieve the effect of weightlessness.

**Gabriel, Jacques-Ange** (1698–1782) French architect. He is credited with some of the finest achievements in the French classical tradition. He trained under his father, Jacques Gabriel (1667–1742), whom he succeeded as Chief Royal Architect to Louis XV. His big civic commissions included the École Militaire and the Place de la Concorde, both in Paris, and at Versailles the Pavillon Français. Of his smaller buildings, all fine of their kind, the Petit Trianon, Versailles, is perhaps the most admirable for its originality and grace.

**Gaddi, Taddeo** (d. 1366) Italian painter, a pupil of Giotto. His murals in the Baroncelli Chapel at S. Croce, Florence (1338), and altarpiece for S. Giovanni Fuorcivitas, Pistoia (1353), carry the narrative genius of Giotto into the following generation.

**gadrooned** Decorated with a pattern of convex ridges, as opposed to being fluted. See **fluting**.

**Gainsborough, Thomas** (1727–88) English painter born in Sudbury, Suffolk. His first landscapes owe much to the 17th-century Dutch masters, whose work was popular among English collectors. His portraits typically include a glimpse of English landscape, as in the *Mr and Mrs Robert Andrews* (National Gallery, London), painted in a more naturalistic manner than was customary.

Portrait painting had to be his living, and he ranks with Van Dyck, whose work he was able to see in Bath, the fashionable watering-place where he prospered in the 1760s. He was one of the original members of the Royal Academy, but stopped showing there after several squabbles with the Council.

His great rival was Reynolds, whose notice after Gainsborough's death is a worthy tribute to an English master. Gainsborough's brushwork and colour sense put him ahead of Reynolds, and laid the basis for the achievements of Constable and the Romantic landscape school that was to follow.

**galleting** Inserting chips of flint and small pieces of stone into mortar courses for decoration.

**gambrel roof** A gable type of roof with two slopes, the lower much steeper than the upper one. See **mansard roof**.

**gargoyle** A decoratively carved human or animal head which forms a rainspout on the top of a parapet or roof.

**Gaudi, Antoni** (1852–1926) Catalonian architect. He worked mainly in Barcelona where his ideas were influenced by the nationalist culture of the region, with its emphasis on folk crafts and its attachment to indigenous themes. At the same time he sought to establish a Gothic style in a modern, Mediterranean idiom. In 1878 he designed the quasi-Islamic Casa Vicens, making use of stepped prismatic blocks and polychrome tiles.

In 1884 he was appointed to take over work on the huge Neo-Gothic church of the Sagrada family, which occupied him, on and off, for the rest of his life. It is a monument to his inventive constructivism, with mouldings and details drawn from natural forms. Other commissions, including the Casa Mila and the Palau Güell, in the early 1900s, helped to set his individual seal on the city's architectural appearance. His most distinctive work combines all the visual arts in exuberant profusion, embracing modern modes from Art Nouveau to Surrealism.

**Gaudier-Brzeska, Henri** (1891–1915) French sculptor. He studied and settled in England, where he became a member of the literary coterie headed by Ezra Pound, Wyndham Lewis and Roger Fry, and of the Vorticists. From an early style that stemmed from Rodin he moved towards a form of Abstraction in which the materials used play a part in determining subject and form.

**gauged arch** An arch made of masonry or brick of definite shapes and sizes.

**Gauguin, Paul** (1848–1903) French painter. He exhibited with the Impressionists between 1881 and 1886, though without moving far in their direction. He left his family to devote his whole time to painting, first at Pont-Aven in Britanny, then to Martinique, then in Arles with Van Gogh. In 1891 he returned to the South Seas, where he remained, but for a single visit to Paris, until he died.

The Pont-Aven period led him towards a quasi-religious primitivism which found expression in his South Seas paintings. The Symbolist ideas which are present in his work, and his truculent rejection of naturalism, exerted a powerful spell which is still at work.

**Gavarni,** pen-name of Sulpice Guillaume Chevalier (1804–66) French caricaturist and illustrator. He was a contributor to *Charivari* in the 1830s, when he developed his talent for social commentary. In London from 1847 to 1851 he found subjects of a less frivolous kind, which he contributed to *L'Illustration*. His lithographs, under the influence of Honoré Daumier, are among the most accomplished of their time. The Goncourt brothers rated him the equal of Balzac, whose works he illustrated.

**gazebo** An ornamental summerhouse with a turret on the top.

**genre** The term applied to the portrayal of daily life, particularly of the humbler kind. Though always popular, genre has received scant support from academic establishments, where it has not fitted in with traditional ideas of High Art and the Grand Manner. Painters who have specialized in genre include Bruegel, Vermeer, Murillo, Hogarth, Wilkie and Millet, which gives an indication of the depth and permanence of the tradition. The term has a less specific meaning when used to denote a kind or category of painting, such as still life, portraiture or the nude.

**Gentile da Fabriano** (*c.*1370–1427) Italian painter, called after his birthplace in the Marches. His first work, now destroyed, was a series of frescoes for the Ducal Palace in Venice. He subsequently worked in Florence and in Siena, and died in Rome. So much of his work has been lost that he remains a somewhat shadowy figure. His importance was in bringing the International Gothic style to the Marches, where it became widespread. His influence can also be seen in the development of Venetian painting. His best-known work is the polyptych commissioned by the Quararesi family for the church of S. Nicolo d'Oltarno in Venice, now dispersed.

**Geometrical style** Late 13th-century phase of Gothic ornamentation, characterized by bar tracery designed strictly in geometrical forms in which circles and triangles predominate.

**Georgian** English Renaissance architecture practised from the time of George I to George IV (1714–1830). It is distinguished by a Neo-classical concern for symmetry and for such embellishments as spiders-web fanlights over doorways, slender windows, and balconies of finely worked wrought iron. The bowed shop window is also characteristic of the style.

**Gérard, Baron François** (1770–1837) French portrait painter. He was a pupil of Jacques-Louis David, through whom he was made a judge on the Revolutionary tribunal, and at one time was held in equal esteem. He survived the political mayhem of the times, to become a favourite of the Bourbons: his title was conferred by Louis XVIII. His *Madame Recamier*, 1802, in the Musée Carnavalet, Paris, is typical of his diplomatic handling of court portraiture.

**Gericault, Théodore** (1791–1824) French painter, and one of the founders of the Romantic movement in France. He studied with Carl Vernet (1758–1836) and was later a fellow pupil with Delacroix. He was particularly skilled at drawing and painting horses, which he invested with an animal vitality. Equestrian subjects helped to make his name as a young man, and in 1819 he achieved notoriety with *The Raft of the 'Medusa'*, a shipwreck scene with a political message. He was an admirer of Bonington and Constable, and was instrumental in bringing English landscape painting to the notice of French artists.

**Gérôme, Jean Léon** (1824–1904) French painter and sculptor. As a pupil of Delaroche and himself an accomplished draughtsman, he was a lifelong advocate of academic standards. Among his pupils were Edouard Vuillard and the Douanier Rousseau.

**gesso** The ground used in **egg tempera**, and sometimes oil painting, made by mixing chalk and gypsum with glue. During the Renaissance it was usual to prepare a panel (gesso is too brittle to be used on canvas) with two different grades, an undercoat of the coarse gesso grosso, and several top coats of gesso sottile. This is a much finer mixture which dries to a smooth, absorbent white finish.

**Ghiberti, Lorenzo** (1378–1455) Florentine sculptor, originally trained as a goldsmith and painter. In 1402 he competed for a commission to make a pair of bronze doors for the Baptistery, an involvement that was to keep him busy for more than 25 years. Meanwhile, he was appointed to the committee supervising work on Florence Cathedral and had a hand in designing the famous dome built by Brunelleschi. His *Commentarii* contains a wealth of documentation of early classical and Italian art, as well as autobiographical material. His bronze doors, recently cleaned and restored, reveal his skills as a goldsmith.

**Ghirlandaio, Domenico Bigordi** (1449–94) Italian fresco painter, in whose Florence workshop Michelangelo served as an apprentice. He and his brother Davide (1452–1525) headed a family workshop, which was engaged in making altarpieces for the churches of Florence. His most outstanding works include the fresco *The Last Supper* (Ognissanti, Florence),

of 1480, the *Scenes from the Lives of the Virgin and St John* in the church of S. Maria Novella (1486–90), and the *Visitation* (1491), now in the Louvre in Paris.

**Giacometti, Alberto** (1901–66) Swiss sculptor. His father, Augusto Giacometti (1877–1947), was a colourist who was an early member of the Modern Movement. Alberto worked in Paris, joined the Surrealists, and in the late 1930s turned to his own realizations of the human figure, in which the thin, tortured forms are embedded in block-like feet. These in turn grew into the spectral figures of the post-war period, when Giacometti used plaster of Paris over wire frames to create powerful effects of loneliness and disintegration. His drawings can stand on their own as the work of a disciplined imagination.

**giant order** Columns or pilasters which are two or more storeys high.

**Gibbons, Grinling** (1648–1721) English sculptor and woodcarver, born in Holland of English parents. Recommended to Charles II by John Evelyn, the diarist, and by Sir Peter Lely, he was appointed as the royal woodcarver. He worked in the Royal Chapel at Windsor, at St Paul's, London, and in many of the great English houses, including Petworth, where one of the ceilings is regarded as his masterpiece. He maintained a studio, staffed with assistants, for commissions in statuary. These, however, do not compare with his achievements as a woodcarver, which paved the way for the English Baroque.

**Gibbs, James** (1682–1754) English church architect. A Scot, he studied painting in Rome before turning to architecture. His first London church, St Mary-le-Strand, shows his debt to Wren, along with Mannerist and Baroque influences. The church for which he is best known, St Martin-in-the-Fields, Trafalgar Square, was built between 1722 and 1726. It features what became known as the Gibbs Surround: windows with triple-keystoned heads, set in the side elevations. Other notable buildings by Gibbs include the Octagon, Twickenham; Ditchley Park, Oxon; the Fellows' Building at King's College, Cambridge, and the Radcliffe Library, Oxford.

**Gill, Eric** (1882–1940) English sculptor, typographer and engraver. His carvings include the *Prospero and Ariel* on Broadcasting House and the *Stations of the Cross* at Westminster Cathedral. His lasting contribution is in typography: he designed the faces known as Gill Sans-serif and Perpetua. His wood engravings express the socio-religious beliefs on which much of his life and work were built.

**Gillray, James** (1757–1815) English caricaturist. His caustic lampoons on political and royal affairs during the Napoleonic Wars were all the rage at the time. He carried Hogarth's satire to new heights of vilification and wit. He became insane in 1811.

**Gilman, Harold** (1876–1919) English painter. He studied at the Slade School, became a member of Sickert's circle and of the **Camden Town Group**, and in 1912 exhibited in Paris. In 1914 he shared an exhibition with Charles Ginner as a Neo-Realist. He was a Post-Impressionist in his use of pigment and a solid painter of the nude.

**Gilpin, Sawrey** (1733–1807) English animal and sporting painter. Apprenticed to Samuel Scott (1702–72), a marine painter, he imbued his studies of horses with a Romantic energy, as in *Horses Frightened in a Thunderstorm*, 1798 (Royal Academy, London). His portraits of racehorses are more naturalistic.

**Ginner, Charles** (1878–1952) English painter. He was born in France, where he trained at the École des Beaux-Arts and at the Academie Vitti. On coming to England he met Spencer Gore and Harold Gilman, becoming a founder member of the **Camden Town Group** and of the **London Group**. In 1914 he exhibited with Gilman as a Neo-Realist, for which he published a credo in the *New Age* setting out its anti-synthetic, anti-imitative aims.

**Giordano, Luca** (1634–1705) Italian decorative painter, nicknamed 'Luca Fa Presto' on account of his astonishing speed. He is reputed to have turned out some 5000 oil paintings, demonstrating his versatility as copyist and imitator as well as a brightness and exuberance which anticipate Tiepolo. He became Master of the painters' guild in Naples, worked for Charles II of Spain, and on his return after ten years painted one of his finest ceilings, at the Treasury of S. Martino, Naples.

**Giorgione,** otherwise Giorgio Barbarelli or Giorgio del Castelfranco (1475–1510) Venetian painter. His work is so unreliably documented that much of it remains the subject of conjecture. Nevertheless he is an important master, regarded by Vasari as the equal of Leonardo da Vinci and as such one of the definitive artists of his time. His work for the Doge's Palace has long since vanished, but his smaller pictures, painted for private patrons, announce the arrival of the 'landscape of mood' which was to play a leading part in the development of modern art. The most famous example, the *Tempesta*, in the Accademia, Venice, is typical of his fusion of mood and place, enhanced by a painterly sense of nature. His *Concert Champêtre* (Louvre) may include passages by Titian, whom Giorgione could have met while working in the studio of Bellini in the 1490s. The subject was to form the starting point of Manet's *Déjeuner sur l'herbe*, which caused a furore at the Salon des Refusés in 1863.

**Giotto** (*c*. 1267–1337) Early Florentine artist, regarded as the founder of modern painting. He was, perhaps, a pupil of Cimabue, and a follower of the energetic naturalism of the sculptors Nicola and Giovanni Pisano.

In Giotto, feelings and spiritual aspirations are personified in human beings, who become the vehicle of thought and emotion. The Christian idea, and the dramas of the gospels, are seen as belonging to a physical world in which ordinary people are given a sometimes monumental dignity. Giotto's frescoes in the Arena Chapel, Padua (1313), are early examples of this humanizing power. It is also present in the frescoes of S. Maria Annunziata del l'Arena, in Padua, where the west wall ,is covered with a *Last Judgement*. Two sets of frescoes in S. Croce, Florence, represent Giotto's late style. In his last years, revered and famous, he supervised work on Florence Cathedral.

**Giovanni di Paolo** (1403–82) Italian painter. He was born in Siena, a contemporary of Sassetta, and with him was one of the most distinctive masters of the Sienese School. Bernhard Berenson dubbed him 'the El Greco of the Quattrocento', in recognition of his passionate Mannerism. The *Baptism of Christ*, a predella panel from an altarpiece, and *St John the Baptist Retiring to the Desert*, both in the

National Gallery, London, are typical of his weirdly imaginative smaller works.

**Girodet-Trioson,** otherwise Anne-Louis Girodet de Roucy (1767–1824) French painter. He trained under Jacques-Louis David, whose manner he followed, but his choice of subjects belonged to the Romanticism favoured by younger painters. His *Danäe* (Leipzig Museum) caused a sensation at the Salon of 1799. His later work, on more literary themes, includes the *Entombment of Atala* (Louvre) and illustrations of Virgil and Racine.

**Girtin, Thomas** (1775–1802) English water-colour painter. In the space of a short career he elevated the art of watercolour to heights equalled only by his early friend and rival, J. M. W. Turner. He took lessons from Edward Dayes (1763–1804), produced drawings for Dr Thomas Monro, worked briefly in Paris, and in 1802 exhibited a huge panorama of London, now lost. The essence of his manner, which had many imitators, is a combination of breadth and naturalism. Colour is used, for the first time in English watercolour painting, to achieve uniformity of mood and form, the total effect depending on his dignified sense of space rather than graphic line.

**Glasgow School** A group of Scottish artists, many of whom had trained on the Continent, who during the latter part of the 19th century exhibited together in Glasgow. Their common bond was a romanticized view of nature, influenced by the Barbizon School. The group's principal members were William York Mac-Gregor (1855–1923), whose studio became their headquarters; James Guthrie (1859–1930), Ernest Atkinson Hornell (1864–1933), John Lavery (1856–1941: subsequently knighted); Arthur Melville (1858–1904), James Paterson (1854–1932), David Gauld (1865–1936), David Young Cameron (1865–1945), Edward Arthur Walton (1860–1923) and Robert Macaulay Stevenson (1854–1923).

**Glasgow style** Art Nouveau by a group of Scottish artists in the 1890s, notably Charles Rennie Mackintosh.

---

**Glasgow style** *The Peacock*, decoration for the Buchanan Street Tea-Room, a pencil and watercolour study for a mural by Charles Rennie Mackintosh (University of Glasgow).

**glass print** see **cliché-verre**

**glaze** A transparent film of colour applied over a previously painted surface so that its colour is modified. The technique was widely used in traditional oil painting, along with **scumbling**, but has largely died out since the advent of **alla prima**, or direct painting. The use of glazes involves a painstaking and crafts-manlike approach in which later stages of a painting must be exactly anticipated at the time when earlier ones are being executed. It can achieve effects of special depth and luminosity.

**Gleizes, Albert** (1881–1953) French painter. He exhibited with the Cubists in 1911, and was an articulate propagandist for their ideas. He was one of the founders of the **Section d'Or** group, and was among the first to carry their ideas to New York. His talents as a painter were less influential than his writings, notably his essay, *Du Cubisme*, written in 1912.

**Gleyre, Marc Gabriel Charles** (1808–74) Swiss-born history and genre painter. He studied in Paris and in Italy, exhibited with modest success, and is noted for his work as a teacher. His Paris studio was popular with aspiring painters, including some of the Impressionists at the outset of their careers.

**glyph** A shallow, vertical groove cut into a flat or carved surface. Glyphs are found in classic Doric architecture.

**glyptic** Carved, as opposed to modelled.

**Goes, Hugo van der** (active 1467–82) Flemish painter. He is best known for the *Portinari Altarpiece* (Uffizi Gallery, Florence), originally commissioned for the church of S. Maria Nuova in Florence, a work of impressive scale and composition, which includes the figures of the donors in what is essentially a treatment of the Nativity and Adoration. Other works following the example of Jan van Eyck include the *Monforte Altarpiece* (Berlin City Museum) and the *Death of the Virgin* (S. Sauveur, Bruges).

**Gogh, Vincent Willem van** (1853–90) Dutch Post-Impressionist master who carried Impressionism into a uniquely expressive dis-covery of innate power. For the most part self-taught, he made a late start as a painter, and after some agonizing joined his brother Théo in Paris. There he met Pissarro, Degas, Seurat, Toulouse-Lautrec, and also Gauguin, who in 1888 joined him at Arles. His work in the last 18 months of his life before his suicide has no equal for its far-reaching intensity and passion.

**golden section** A principle of **proportion** based on Euclidean geometric theory and cal-culated by Vitruvius, who used it in his *De Architectura* in the first century BC. The prin-cipal states, in strict geometrical terms, that 'ideal' proportion is to divide a line in such a way that the smaller part of it is to the larger in the same ratio as the larger is to the whole. The golden section has often been thought to be the most harmonious of proportions, with an almost mystical perfection. Luca Pacioli's *De Divina Proportione* (1509), for instance, illus-trated by Leonardo da Vinci, defines it as the 'divine' proportion of the title.

**Gore, Spencer** (1878–1914) English painter. He studied at the Slade School, went to Spain with Wyndham Lewis and became a member of the **Camden Town Group** in 1911 and pres-ident of the **London Group** two years later. He exhibited in Paris and was represented in the second Post-Impressionist exhibition in Lon-don, 1912. His *Gauguins and Connoisseurs at the Stafford Gallery* is a record of an exhibition of work by Gauguin and Cézanne, attended by notable English artists of the day, conceived as a paraphrase of Gauguin's *Vision After the Sermon*, now in the National Gallery of Scotland.

**Gorky, Arshile** (1904–48) American painter. Born a Turkish Armenian, he fled to the United States with his family as a boy, to become a prime mover in the establishment of the New York School. His work owes much to his sensitive response to European painting, most noticeably Picasso, Miró, Kandinsky and Matisse. The work of the last few years of his life, before he committed suicide, takes Abstract Expressionism to a high pitch of col-our, form and original light.

**Gothic** A descriptive term for the art and architecture of northern Europe from the mid-12th to the 16th century. The term is also applied to work which lies outside the Gothic period, done in imitation of it or in the same spirit.

In painting, Gothic art begins with the introduction of the third dimension in the work of Duccio, followed by a highly developed sense of decoration, extending to illuminated manuscripts and precious objects. In sculpture, statues expressive of humanity and spiritual peace were carved as intrinsic monuments in Gothic cathedrals and churches.

Distinctive features of Gothic architecture are rib vaulting, the flying buttress, the impression of inner space conveyed by galleries and large windows. The pointed Gothic arch is a survival from the Romanesque. Examples in the British Isles of early Gothic include the Cistertian abbeys, such as Rievaulx and Tintern. Canterbury Cathedral, built largely by a French architect, helped to spread Early English designs, as at Lincoln and Wells. English Gothic finally asserts itself with the gradual

merging of imported styles with the Perpendicular.

In general, Gothic as a descriptive term has come to signify the romantic and ornate as opposed to the Classical in art.

**Gothic Revival** The return to Gothic grandeur and decoration in English architecture which began in the latter half of the 18th century and continued into the 20th. It was most conspicuous in civic buildings and church architecture. Its origins lie in the notion of 'Gothick' beauty propagated by, among others, Horace Walpole, whose house at Strawberry Hill (*c.* 1750–70) was, with William Beckford's Fonthill Abbey, the most famous monument to the style. As the fashion spread it was taken more seriously, until Gothic became the accepted style for public buildings such as railway termini, town halls and the rebuilt Houses of Parliament, as well as for schools, colleges and the homes of the well-to-do.

**gouache** A watercolour technique, also known as bodycolour, in which the paint is opaque rather than transparent due to the binding of the pigment with glue and the addition of

**Gothic Revival** The Library at Strawberry Hill (1753).

white. It has been extensively used by artists of the English watercolour school, from Paul Sandby onwards, both as a means of strengthening certain passages or details in an otherwise 'pure' watercolour drawing or as a medium in its own right, often combined with tinted paper, as in Turner's interiors of Petworth.

**Goya y Lucientes, Francisco José** (1746–1828) Spanish painter and etcher. The son of a master gilder, he settled in Madrid in about 1775 and executed a series of tapestry cartoons on rustic and idyllic themes. He became an academician in 1780 and in 1789 was appointed a court painter to the newly crowned Charles IV. He prospered as a portraitist until in 1792 he was stricken with an illness that left him stone deaf. He continued to paint, gaining in mastery, and became Premier Court Painter in 1799.

His portrait group, *The Family of Charles IV*, (Prado, Madrid) is remarkable for its unflattering candour. The political upheavals and sufferings caused by the changes of regime first under Joseph Buonaparte and subsequently under Ferdinand II, prompted the two paintings known as *The Second of May* and *The Third of May*. Atrocities of which he could have been a witness also inspired his series of etchings *The Disasters of War*, which he made no attempt to publish in his lifetime. His so-called *Black Paintings*, a series of 14 murals which express a nightmarish imagination (now in the Prado) are steeped in morbid pessimism.

Goya's reputation has never stood higher than at the present time: he is seen as the first truly modern painter. In his greatest works such as the *Naked Maja*, *The Third of May*, and in the pitiless scenes recorded in the *Disasters of War* he announces the arrival of a new age, in which the drama of life and death has nothing to do either with compassion or with divine redress.

**Goyen, Jan van** (1596–1656) Dutch landscape painter. After spending a year in France he settled in The Hague, and developed a style of low-key landscape painting close to that of Salomon van Ruysdael. His sense of atmosphere, sometimes with a silvery light, gives his work a distinction that puts him in the same rank as Hobbema and Jacob van Ruysdael.

**gradation** The imperceptible blending of one colour into another, or of a series of tones of the same colour.

**Graff, Anton** (1736–1813) Portrait painter. Born in Switzerland, he became the most prominent portrait painter in Germany, like Reynolds in England. By his own account, he painted over 1200 portraits in his lifetime, including many of the grandees and *literati* of his day.

**graffito, sgraffito** The technique of scratching a design in paint or plaster to reveal a different ground underneath. Medieval panel painters used to paint over a layer of gold leaf, so that by scratching the paint away the gold would show through. During the Renaissance the method was put to decorative use with different plasters on murals and façades. In modern times the textural qualities of graffito have been exploited by Dubuffet, among others.

In architecture, wall decoration is produced by laying a thin layer of light-coloured plaster over a dark one, then removing portions of the thin upper layer so as to produce a design in black and white, or in light and dark tints. It can be done either by removing the upper layer of plaster in the interspaces, leaving the design light on a dark ground; or by removing portions of the top layer forming the design, so as to show it in dark with light interspaces.

**Grand Manner** The elevated style of history painting, with an emphasis on the **Ideal**, as advocated by the academies of the 17th and 18th centuries. In English art Sir Joshua Reynolds, the first President of the Royal Academy, was its most persuasive theorist.

**Grant, Duncan** (1885–1978) Scottish-born painter. He trained at the Slade School and was a member of the Bloomsbury set, the New English Art Club, and the London Group. He was a prominent member of the English avant-garde, much influenced by Cézanne and the Fauves. Roger Fry included him in his second Post-Impressionist exhibition at the Grafton Galleries in 1912. The rest of his long career was spent in the afterglow of his Bloomsbury period, in which he was closely associated with Clive and Vanessa Bell.

**granulation** Decoration consisting of small granules of gold.

**graphic arts** Of the fine arts, those which depend primarily on line work rather than colour, that is drawing and engraving.

**Gravelot, Hubert** (1699–1773) French illustrator and engraver who worked in London from 1730 to 1745. His style brought a fresh quality to 18th-century book illustration in Britain. He gave lessons to the young Gainsborough, and was responsible for the cross-fertilization discernible in the English painter's Watteau-like flights of fancy.

**graver** see **burin**

**Greco, El,** originally named Domenikos Theotocopoulos (1541–1614) Spanish Mannerist painter. Born in Crete, he went to Italy in about 1560, where he joined the circle of Titian and Tintoretto. He remained there until 1577, by which date he was in Toledo, where he lived for the rest of his life, painting works which, for rapturous mysticism and tortured piety, have no equal in his time. His strident use of colour is distinctive. It combines with his ascetic, elongated forms to create energetic tension, as in his numerous subjects from the Passion. The *Assumption*, in the church of S. Vicente, Toledo, finished a year before he died, brings his life's work to a spiritually moving end.

**Greek art** The description refers specifically to the expression of the Platonic culture and ideal of ancient Greece in sculpture, architecture and pottery. Its predominant theme is the place of man in relation to his environment and to his gods expressed in plastic, figurative imagery of unequalled grace and power. Art entered the home as well as the public place, and the names of artists were for the first time attached to their works. Of these, Polycletus, a sculptor and citizen of Argos, was perhaps the most influential. His most famous works, the Doryphoros, *c.*445 BC, and the Diadumenos, *c.*460 BC, break away from the stiffness of the traditional **kouros** in a style which was inherited and developed by such followers as Lysippus, Praxiteles, Phidias, Scopas and Cephisodotus. The survival of examples of work by these and other masters is largely due to the practice of making copies of popular or important pieces, such as the Venus de Milo, *c.*100 BC.

**Greek Revival** A term close to Neoclassicism referring to the rediscovery of Classical Greek architecture which took place in the middle to late 18th century and terminated in about 1840. It was particularly fashionable in the 1780s, when architects such as Sir John Soane and Claude-Nicolas Ledoux incorporated in their buildings the plain, vigorous qualities, previously regarded as barbaric, which have been admired ever since.

**Greuze, Jean-Baptiste** (1725–1805) French painter of genre subjects and portraits. His reputation was made with narrative genre subjects, such as *A Grandfather Reading the Bible to his Family*, which he showed at the Salon of 1755, *The Village Bride* and the *Return of the Prodigal Son*, both in the Louvre. He liked to introduce moral sentiment into his work, as a means of elevating it above mere story telling. It brought him popularity, but has not worn well. His portraits have a thoughtful realism not often found in the work that made his name.

**griffin** A decorative monster with the body of a lion and the head and wings of an eagle. The griffin represents wisdom and watchfulness and was popular in Gothic architecture.

**Gris, Juan** (1887–1927) Spanish painter. Of the **School of Paris**, he was an early associate of his compatriot Picasso and a practitioner of Synthetic Cubism. He wrote: 'I work with the elements of the intellect, to try to make concrete that which is abstract. I compose with abstractions—colours—and make my adjustments when these assume the form of objects.' His distinctively rhythmic, richly coloured works are among the most formative in abstract art.

**grisaille** Decorative painting in grey tones to simulate relief. It was also used in early stained glass.

**groin** The edge formed by the junction of two surfaces of a vault. A groin rib is an exposed rib which follows the line of the groin on a vaulted surface. A groin vault is a roof formed by the intersection of two barrel vaults at right angles.

**Gropius, Walter** (1883–1969) German architect, one of the most influential teachers of the 20th century. His name is inseparable from the **Bauhaus**, the name he gave to the two art and design institutions at Weimar, where he took up the post of Director in 1919.

He left in 1928 in order to devote himself to projects such as the Bauhaus buildings at Dessau, the Municipal Theatre at Jena, and the Total Theatre, for which a model was exhibited in 1930. His urge to improve standards of building for needy urban populations led to the Dammerstock housing project near Karlsruhe, and to the Siemensstadt complex outside Berlin. He moved from Germany in 1933 and came to London, and in 1937 left for the United States, having accepted the Chair of Architecture at Harvard University.

Both as a teacher and as an innovator, Gropius was instrumental in raising standards of public and domestic architecture in the West. He was a pioneer of prefabrication, and made adventurous use of such modern materials as concrete, glass and steel.

**Gros, Antoine-Jean** (1771–1835) French painter. He trained under Jacques-Louis David, studied Rubens and Van Dyck on a visit to Italy, and was an accredited war artist under Napoleon. His celebrations of Napoleon's campaigns, packed with action and glory, earned him fame and favour. Charles X made him a Baron, but his reputation faded in the post-Napoleonic era, when the younger faction deserted him. His battle-pieces remain among the most accomplished works of their kind in European art.

**Grosz, George** (1893–1959) German-born illustrator, painter and graphic artist. From the start of his career he was obsessed by the immorality and cynicism of militarist politics. His sardonic caricatures have become the accepted image of a bestialized and ridiculous society, the Germany of the post-war epoch. From 1932 he lived and worked in America, where he found less embittered topics for his satire. His late works have an apocalyptic pessimism akin to that of Goya.

**grotesque** Descriptive term for fanciful decoration in paint or stucco, consisting of such items as animal and human forms, fruit, flowers, foliage, sphinxes and medallions.

**Grünewald, Matthias** (c. 1460–1528) German painter, formerly mistaken for Mathis Neithart or Gothart. Grünewald was a contemporary of Dürer, and to an extent shared that master's North European tradition. But his work is essentially Gothic. The famous *Isenheim* altarpiece at Colmar, with its gruesome but moving image of the suffering Christ, stands for both Grünewald's style and his faith.

**Guardi, Francesco** (1712–93) and **Gianantonio** (1699–1760) Venetian painters, the sons of Giacomo Guardi (1678–1716) who founded a family workshop. Francesco is the better known, through his animated views and scenes of Venice. These have suffered in the past by comparison with the work of his contemporary Canaletto, but Guardi's spirited brushwork and feeling for mood and atmosphere have brought him more supporters in modern times.

His brother Gianantonio sometimes worked with him on a painting, but his speciality seems to have been altarpieces and similar public commissions. Gianantonio was elected to the Venetian Academy in 1756, the year in which Tiepolo, his brother-in-law, became president.

**Guercino, Giovanni Francesco Barbieri** (1591–1666) Italian painter of the Bolognese School, born at Cento. He was a pupil of Ludovico Carracci, whose influence he absorbed into an individual naturalism that gives his earlier work a spirited grace. In 1621 he was called to Rome, where he established his name with a succession of large works including an altarpiece at St Peter's. In Rome he was increasingly influenced by the more sober classicism of Guido Reni, and lost some of the Baroque airiness of his early days. Guercino returned to Bologna in 1642, and set up his own workshop. His *Aurora*, on the ceiling of the Casino Ludovisi in Rome, is one of his most dazzling achievements.

Guercino's drawings were eagerly sought after by English collectors, and remain highly prized. There is a particularly fine group in the Royal Collection.

**Guilio Romano** (c.1495–1546) Italian painter and architect. He is best known for his work in the service of Federigo Gonzaga at Mantua, combining ancient Roman motifs with daring misuses of classical details and deliberate rusticity. His liberties with traditional form and lack of architectural reticence bring him close to Mannerism. His most grandiose design was for Mantua Cathedral (1545).

**guilloche** A pattern of interlacing bands forming a plait which is used for the decoration of moulding.

**Haden, Sir Francis Seymour** (1818–1910) English etcher. He practised as a surgeon, but devoted much of his time to promoting the resurgence of the etcher's craft in an age when his brother-in-law Whistler, and other leading artists, were giving some of their best talents to it. He produced some 250 etchings, in a line that begins with Rembrandt, including mezzotints and drypoints. He liked to work in the open with a prepared plate, to which he added little or nothing in the studio.

**Hague School** A group of Dutch artists, roughly contemporary with the Impressionists in France, who worked in The Hague. They painted realistic pictures of the surrounding towns, landscapes, seascapes and scenes of everyday life in a manner reminiscent of 17th-century Dutch painting, particularly sensitive to the nuances of light and atmosphere. Leading members of the group included Hendrik Weissenbruch (1824–1903), Johannes Bosboom (1817–91), Jozef Israels (1824–1911), Jacob Maris (1837–99) and his brother Willem (1844–1910), Antoine Mauve (1838–88), and Hendrik Mesdag (1831–1915).

**half-column** A rounded pilaster or column partially involved in the structure of the wall.

**half-timbering** A Gothic style of timber house construction where the heavy beams and posts form the visible skeleton on the interior as well as the exterior of the building. The spaces between the woodwork were filled with wattle and daub, plaster, stone or brick.

**hammerbeam roof** In late Gothic architecture, a timber roof built up on the principle of a series of framed brackets, each carried by and projecting beyond the one below it and with the lowest one resting on the wall. The hammer brace is the curved vertical timber which supports the hammerbeam, the horizontal timber taking the place of a tie beam. A hammerbeam truss is a Tudor arch form in wood, each end of which rests on a large wooden bracket which is usually carved.

**Happening** An event, whether provocative or banal, in which the Happening is offered as an artistic experience, often attacking or satirizing popular attitudes to modern life. Happenings were first staged in New York in the 1960s, and have subsequently taken the form of one-man performances, often of a sado-masochistic nature.

**Hard-Edge painting** Term denoting a type of Abstract painting in which flat areas of colour are marked by the sharp edges of brush strokes, separating each passage from its neighbours. The technique owes its success to the use of acrylic paints rather than conventional oils.

**Harding, James Duffield** (1797–1863) English watercolour artist and draughtsman. He took lessons from Samuel Prout and was apprenticed to an engraver, Charles Pye, before embarking on a career as professional exhibitor and teacher of art. His instructional books were widely influential, and included immaculate examples of his own elegant and well-observed draughtsmanship, particularly of trees and tree forms, reproduced in soft-ground or lithography, in which he was something of a pioneer. He differed from most other drawing masters of the time in encouraging students not simply to copy but to use their eyes. His manuals were intended 'not so much to supply examples for imitation, as through them to make the pupil capable of observing nature truly for himself.' He had numerous successful pupils, among them John Ruskin, who called him 'after Turner, unquestionably the greatest master of foliage in Europe.'

**harmonic proportions** In the early Renaissance, a system of proportion that related architecture to music by comparing its measurements to the ratios of octave and pitch.

**Harpignies, Henri** (1819–1916) French painter and engraver. He was originally influenced by Corot, whose stylized romantic manner is to be seen in his work. His etchings and drawings are popular with collectors.

**Hartung, Hans** (b.1904) French painter, born in Leipzig. He is noted for calligraphic Abstracts painted with strong brushstrokes of dark colour, to which he gives cryptic numbers instead of titles.

**hatching** The shading of a picture by means of parallel lines. By varying their density, different tones and patterns of light and shade can be suggested by linear means alone. Hatching is therefore mostly used in drawing and engraving. In egg tempera painting, where the colours do not blend, it is also employed to achieve effects of modelling. **Cross-hatching** is shading in two directions, one set of parallel lines criss-crossing another.

**Hawksmoor, Nicholas** (1661–1736) English architect of the Baroque. He worked closely with Wren and with Vanbrugh, with whom he had a hand in building Greenwich Hospital, where he succeeded Wren as surveyor. In 1711 he was appointed surveyor in charge of 50 new churches to be built in London. The six that he designed himself are regarded as his finest work: St Alphege, Greenwich; St Anne, Limehouse; St George-in-the-East, Stepney; St Mary Woolnoth, Lombard Street; Christchurch, Spitalfields; and St George's, Bloomsbury. In Oxford he is responsible for All Soul's College and the Clarendon Building.

**Haydon, Benjamin Robert** (1786–1846) English painter. He aspired to history painting on the elevated planes advocated by Reynolds, but fell tragically short. He was a Romantic, a friend of Wordsworth and Keats, and author of an autobiography, published in 1853, which is a more lasting monument to his frustrated gifts than any of his works as a painter.

**Hayman, Francis** (1708–76) Painter and illustrator. His best-known work was the decorations for Vauxhall Gardens; two of his studies for these are in the Victoria and Albert Museum, London. He was also a book illustrator, a friend of Hubert Gravelot, and a painter of conversation pieces. He became a founder member of the Royal Academy and was its first Librarian.

**Heartfield, John** (1891–1968) German painter and designer. With George Grosz he founded the subversive journal *Neue Jugend* (1917). A founder of **Dada** in Berlin, he extended his satiric range in a series of photo-montages attacking the evils and vulgarities of political regimes, of which the most hateful, in his view, was Nazism.

**Heckel, Erich** (1883–1970) German architect. He was a founder of **Die Brücke** with Kirchner and Schmidt-Rottluff in 1905. He came in contact with Macke and Marc shortly before the outbreak of the 1914–18 war, survived four years in the army medical corps and was among the German artists whose works were vilified by the Nazis. He escaped to Switzerland in 1944.

**helix** A spiral motif.

**Helladic** A term applied to the culture of mainland Greece during the Bronze Age, that is, from 2600 to 1100 BC.

**Hellenic** The culture of Greece and lands under Greek influence between 1100 and about 323 BC, sometimes extended to include the Hellenistic period.

**Hellenistic** The term applied to Greek culture during the period between Alexander and Augustus, that is, about 323 to 27 BC.

**Helleu, Paul** (1859–1927) French painter and print maker. He was trained in ceramics before studying at the École des Beaux-Arts. He was an intimate of Marcel Proust and a friend of Sargent and Monet, both of whom held him in high regard as a colourist and portrait artist. His most characteristic subjects are boats and the seaside, decorated by elegant women.

**helm roof** A roof made up of four inclining sides which meet at a central point at the top and form four gables at the bottom.

**Henri, Robert** (1865–1929) American painter and teacher. He led the break from American academism in the early 1900s by starting his own school, which was attended by Edward Hopper, Rockwell Kent, George Bellows and Yasuo Kuniyoshi. Henri and his group, rejected by the Academy in 1908, staged the independent exhibition at the Macbeth Gallery, New York, known as The Eight.

**Hepworth, Barbara** (1903–1975) British sculptress. She trained at the Royal College of Art and in Florence and Rome, where she began carving. She subsequently established herself among the leading sculptors of modern times, in company with Henry Moore and Brancuşi, both of whom influenced her to a certain degree. In the 1930s her work consisted mainly of free organic forms and geometric constructions. Later she turned to 'pierced' masses and figurations which make use of strings and wires. From 1931 to 1951 she was married to Ben Nicholson.

**herm** A pillar surmounted by a sculptured human head or bust.

**Herring, John** (1795–1865) English sporting painter. He started life driving a stage coach, turned to painting portraits of racehorses and became a popular practitioner of his trade. His patrons included George IV and Queen Victoria. His son, John Frederick Jnr, followed in his father's tradition and comes close to him in style.

**herringbone work** Stone, brick or tile decoration, for floors or walls, in which the materials are laid diagonally to form a zigzag pattern.

**hetimasis** Representation of Christ's throne.

**Heyden, Jan van der** (1637–1712) Dutch painter, chiefly of townscapes, which he brought to an unprecedented pitch of accuracy while animating walls, roofs and architectural detail by means of sympathetic colour. He made his fortune in Amsterdam as the inventor of street lighting and the pumping principle used in fire fighting.

**hieratic** Pertaining to art produced to conventionally fixed criteria, based on long tradition and usually used for religious purposes.

The term generally applies to Byzantine or ancient Egyptian art, though it is sometimes extended to cover painting or sculpture which makes use of a rigid **frontality** in composition–as, for example, in Gaudier-Brzeska's *Hieratic Head of Ezra Pound*.

**Highmore, Joseph** (1692–1780) English portrait and narrative painter. Trained at Kneller's Academy, he became a competent illustrator, doing 12 paintings for Richardson's *Pamela*. There is also a history painting of his, originally prompted by Hogarth, in the Foundling Hospital, London.

**Hildebrandt, Johann Lukas von** (1668–1745) Austrian architect of the Baroque. Born in Genoa, he settled in Vienna, where he was appointed Court Architect in 1700. In 1723 he succeeded Fischer von Erlach as Chief Court Architect, having just completed one of his finest works, the Belvedere, built for Prince Eugene. His secular buildings are admired for the shapes of their rooms and for their vivacious decorations. He was knighted by the emperor in 1720.

**Hilliard, Nicholas** (*c.*1547–1619) English miniature painter. Son of a goldsmith and trained in the craft of jewellery, he became the leading miniaturist of the Elizabethan age, rivalled only by his pupil Isaac Oliver in later years. He painted the young Queen Elizabeth, and such figures as Drake, Sidney and Raleigh at the height of their glory. His portraits of less exalted Elizabethans support his belief in the graces of the English race, 'not for the face only, but every part, for even the hand and foot excelleth all pictures that yet I ever saw'. His treatise *The Art of Limning*, from which this quotation is taken, is an exposition of miniature painting as an art for gentlemen, not for the common man.

**hip** The external angle formed when two sloping roof surfaces meet.

**hip tile** A saddle-shaped tile placed where two sloping roof surfaces meet.

**hipped roof** A roof with the ends and sides at the same slope or pitch.

**History painting** Benjamin West's *The Death of Wolfe* (1771), in which the figures are shown in contemporary dress, an innovation at the time (Royal Ontario Museum, Canada).

**history painting** A term which embraces narrative painting based on classical, mythological and historical themes. As religious painting gave way to secular subject matter, painters turned to scenes of equivalent high-mindedness; such as moral allegories and uplifting memorials of great deeds. With portraiture, history painting was regarded as a prime function of art from the 17th century until well into the 19th, by which time genre and landscape painting had begun to break the monopoly.

**Hobbema, Meindert** (1638–1709) Dutch landscape painter. He was a pupil of Jacob van Ruisdael, with whose work he has much in common. His paintings mostly belong to the earlier part of his life: at the age of 30 Hobbema secured a job in the municipal offices at Amsterdam, and seems to have painted only part-time thereafter. He was much admired by English collectors for his tranquil, rustic scenes, and by early English landscape painters, especially John Crome, founder of the **Norwich School**.

**Hockney, David** (b. 1937) English painter and etcher. After studying at the Bradford School of Art and at the Royal College he was awarded a succession of prizes and honours, including one at the Paris Biennale, 1963. In that year he held his first one-man exhibition. A retrospective was held at the Whitechapel Gallery, London, as early as 1970.

His sense of the present, combined with a light, unfailingly skilful touch, as in his graphic work and his swimming-pool subjects, have made him the most prominent English artist of his generation.

**Hodler, Ferdinand** (1853–1918) Swiss painter. He trained in Geneva, where he held his first exhibition in 1885. He became a member of the Berlin and Vienna Sezessions, exhibited with Klimt in 1905, and in 1916 was awarded an honorary professorship at the École des Beaux-Arts in Geneva. He developed a structural theory, known as Parallelism, reflecting what he saw as the order and repetition inherent in nature. In his landscapes this takes the form of a simple, symmetrical design and the repetition of horizontal themes in the composition.

**Hogarth, William** (1697–1764) English painter and engraver. His first paintings were small conversation pieces. Following a success with his *Scene from the Beggar's Opera* (1729), he went on to deal with subjects which he could invest with a moral message, notably *A Harlot's Progress*, *A Rake's Progress* and *Marriage à la Mode*, all in a succession of scenes, which subsequently enjoyed great popularity as engravings. The numerous pirated versions of these are still apt to confuse the collector. He turned his satire to social and political issues, as in his *Election* (1754), and became identified with John Bull-ish antagonism towards foppery and the French.

His portraits are among his finest work: he regarded his *Captain Coram* (1740), which still hangs in the Foundling Hospital, London, as the best he ever did. His success in persuading other artists to join with him in presenting paintings to the Hospital, which drew large crowds, was instrumental in encouraging the idea of a Royal Academy of Arts.

The vigour, honesty and directness of his work, and his choice of subjects, did much to redirect English taste away from imported classicism towards narrative painting and genre.

**Holbein, Hans** (1497–1543) Painter, the son of Hans Holbein the Elder (*c.* 1465–1524), who trained him and his brother Ambrosius in his workshop at Augsburg. Hans Holbein the Younger, as he is known, left to work in Basel, where he was soon engaged in illustration for publishers. For one of these, Johann Froben, he designed the title page for Froben's edition of Sir Thomas More's *Utopia*. He prospered in Basel, both with his paintings and his woodcuts, chief among which is *The Dance of Death* (1523–26), which went into ten editions in as many years.

With introductions furnished by his friend Erasmus, he went to England in 1526 and stayed for eighteen months, during which time he painted a group portrait of the entire More family in their own home. After a return visit to Basel he went back to England and entered

on his career as portrait painter of the Tudor hierarchy. His image of Henry VIII has made him one of the most famous painters in history.

**Holl, Elias** (1573–1646) German architect of the Renaissance. He studied under Palladio in Venice, and on returning to his native Augsburg was appointed City Architect in 1602. The Town Hall of 1615–20, rebuilt after war damage suffered in 1944, ranks as one of his most distinctive works.

**Hollar, Wenceslaus** (1607–77) Artist and engraver. He was born in Prague, but spent much of his career in the service of English patrons, notably the Earl of Arundel, who took him on a tour of Europe as recorder and illustrator of the journey. His series of views of London before the Great Fire, and his finely etched plates of the people, buildings and events of his time, are valued for their historical rarity no less than for their craftsmanship.

**Homer, Winslow** (1836–1910) American painter. His early work as an illustrator, especially of the American Civil War, was a preparation for the clear-sighted naturalism that distinguishes his painting. His subjects, drawn from the great American outdoors, strike a responsive chord to this day. His style is clean and clear, impressionist in feeling but based on linear design. His use of watercolour shows the same lucid command of the medium as his oils.

**Honthorst, Gerard van** (1590–1656) Dutch painter, one of the three major figures of the Utrecht School. A pupil of Bloemart in Rome, he was much influenced by Caravaggio, and is identified by his device of using a sole candle as a source of light. He visited England in 1628 and painted *Charles II and Henrietta Maria with the Liberal Arts*, now at Hampton Court. On his return to Holland he was appointed Court Painter at The Hague.

**Hooch, Pieter de** (1629–83) Dutch painter. He was born in Rotterdam but is commonly regarded as belonging to the school of Delft. His calm interiors, with domestic figures, are akin to those of Vermeer. Both painters were masters of the subtle play of light on planes and surfaces in the tradition of the Utrecht

School. De Hooch went to work in Amsterdam in about 1667 and his paintings after this date forsake their earlier modesty and charm for more grandiose effects.

**hood mould** In Gothic architecture, a projecting moulding above the arch of a window or door or, in English Gothic, above an internal arch. See **dripstone**.

**Hopper, Edward** (1882–1967) American painter, a pupil of Robert Henri, whose observant realism brought him to the fore in the 1930s. His paintings of urban life have an angular melancholy that evokes the America of lonely rooms and vacant lives.

**Hoppner, John** (1758–1810) Portrait painter, born in London of German parents. He studied at the Royal Academy Schools, and was appointed Portrait Painter to the Prince of Wales in 1793. Although he shared in the esteem enjoyed by such portrait painters as Sir Thomas Lawrence and Sir Joshua Reynolds, he fell well short of their achievements.

**hot colour** A colour in which red is dominant is said to be hot, the opposite of a cold or blue colour. The term can also be used critically of a picture to mean that it tends too far towards the red end of the spectrum.

**Houdon, Jean-Antoine** (1741–1828) French sculptor. He was unrivalled throughout Europe for the brilliance of his portrait busts. His *Voltaire*, of which there are several versions, is perhaps the best known. He was invited to the United States to make a statue of George Washington, which he completed in 1791. A bronze copy stands outside the National Gallery, London.

**Houghton, Arthur Boyd** (1836–75) English painter and illustrator. He was born in Madras, trained at the Royal Academy Schools, and soon afterwards turned to book illustration. His drawings for Dalziel's edition of the *Arabian Nights*, 1865, are among the finest of the time. He was also a successful illustrator for *Good Words*, *The Graphic* and other magazines flourishing in the 1860s.

In 1869–70 a commission to visit the United States for the *Graphic* gave him the chance to produce some of his most important documentary drawings, which appeared simultaneously in London and New York. He stands with Keene, Leech, Tenniel, Du Maurier and F. W. Walker as one of the foremost draughtsmen of the 'golden age' of English illustration.

**Hoyland, John** (b. 1934) British painter. He studied in Sheffield and at the Royal College of Art. A visit to New York in 1964 acquainted him with the Abstract Expressionists, whose aims and methods he pursues in a personal idiom, dominated by colour, and on a heroic scale.

**Hudson River School** A school of American landscape painting, based in New York, which flourished in the mid-19th century. Chief among its members were Thomas Cole, an Englishman by birth who admired the painting of Claude and Turner but whose work was more exaggeratedly romantic than theirs, and Asher Durand (1796–1886), who began by working in the tradition of the 17th-century Dutch landscape painters and later turned to painting **plein air** compositions in a more realistic manner than Cole's.

**hue** The specific colour of anything, identified by name. Scientifically, it has been established that there are 150 discernible hues.

**Hunt, William Henry** (1790–1864) English watercolour painter. He was apprenticed to John Varley, then entered the Royal Academy Schools and was employed by Dr Monro before setting up as an architectural and rustic painter. His early work is mainly in pen and ink with coloured washes. Later he turned to a stipple manner which he used with great effect in his numerous still-life and genre figure studies. These were immensely popular and also won him critical acclaim, particularly from Ruskin who hung a 'Bird's-nest Hunt', as he became known, over his bed. Hunt became a cripple and had to be pushed about in a wheelchair, which helps to explain his concentration on the static subject matter that made his name.

**Hunt, William Holman** (1827–1910) English painter. He was a founder of the **Pre-Raphaelite Brotherhood** and perhaps its most loyal adherent. Visits to Egypt and the Holy Land provided him with startlingly realistic settings for his biblical allegories, of which *The Scapegoat* (1856) is a striking example. His painting of Christ knocking at a cottage door, *The Light of the World* (Keble College, Oxford), is a masterpiece of its time.

**hypogeum** An underground tomb or large chamber for devotional gatherings.

**hypostyle** A covered hall, the roof of which rests on pillars or columns.

**icon** A venerated image of Christ, the Virgin or a saint. The sacred personage depicted is believed to be synonymous with, or present within, the effigy. The term is used particularly in the Byzantine, Greek and Roman Orthodox Churches. Icons are most often small tempera paintings on a wooden panel, but they can be mosaics or large double-sided screens for processional purposes. Iconoclasm is image breaking.

**Icon** *St George and the Dragon*, an icon from the second half of the 19th century attributed to M. M. al-Qudsi, at Saida in the Lebanon.

**iconography** The images, symbols and motifs conventionally used in association with particular subject matter, and their descriptive interpretation. Medieval art, for instance, is often rich in Christian and pagan symbols and allegories, and its complex iconography can only be read by a practised scholar.

**iconology** The history of pictorial motifs and their meanings.

**iconostasis** A screen on which icons are placed. It divides the nave from the chancel in Byzantine and Greek and Russian Orthodox churches.

**Ideal art** A recurrent notion that the arts should strive to depict mentally conceived ideal forms rather than the flawed ones of the material world. At the root of such thinking is Plato's *Theory of Ideas*, according to which perceived objects are merely imperfect copies of the pure form they attain in the primary reality, which is available to the imagination but not to the senses. Pliny tells the story of the painter Zeuxis, who combined the most perfect attributes of five different girls to produce a portrait of Helen, and this kind of practice reappeared with the neo-Platonic doctrines of the Italian Renaissance.

During the 17th century the increasing glorification of the artist as the one who alone sees beyond the confines of the material world led to the endorsement of artists such as Poussin by the academies of the time, and to the official approval of the **Grand Manner** over that of the Dutch **genre** painters. This attitude persisted throughout the 18th and 19th centuries. Under changing guises, the impulse towards the Ideal seems always present. Its influence can be detected in Symbolist theory and in many forms of abstract art, especially in that of Mondrian and others of the mystically inclined **De Stijl** group.

**illumination** The ornamentation of handwritten manuscripts with coloured pictures, border designs and elaborate calligraphic initial letters. The term derives from the Latin word *illuminare*, meaning to adorn. Illumination was practised in antiquity in Byzantine and Islamic cultures and in western Europe, where it flourished during the Middle Ages

but went into decline with the advent of printing in the 15th century.

Manuscripts of all kinds were illuminated, but of those produced before 1000 the most splendid tend to be gospels, such as the 8th-century *Book of Kells*, and the earlier *Lindisfarne Gospel*. Later illumination was used for psalters and large bibles, including such 12th-century examples as *Winchester Bibles*. In the 14th century it was extended to *Books of Hours*, small devotional missals such as *Très Riches Belles Heures du Duc de Berry*, painted by the Limburg brothers.

**illusionism**  The capacity of naturalistic art to induce suspension of the spectator's awareness of a work as mere artifice. Less broadly, the term can also refer to an artist's attempt to deceive the eye, so that artifice masquerades as reality. Illusionism of this kind was used in many wall paintings at Pompeii, and was wittily employed by Renaissance and Baroque painters to create architectural decorations, illusions of space, and even illusory wall paintings, complete with frame. At its most extreme this technique becomes **trompe l'oeil**.

**imbricate**  To overlap tiers of tiles to give a fishscale appearance. The technique is used for tile roofs and for walls and columns.

**impasto**  A heavy application of paint, thick enough to stand up noticeably from the canvas. If used extensively it bears the marks of the brush or pallette knife.

**impost**  Any point from which an arch springs, whether defined by a capital or not.

**impression**  The term for print, taken by any method.

**Impressionism**  The word 'Impressionist' was coined by a scoffing critic in 1874 at the first exhibition of the group calling themselves the 'Société anonyme co-operative des artistes peintres' when he applied it to Monet's oil sketch, *Impression: sunrise*, painted at Le Havre. The leading members of the group adopted the

**Illumination** The Incarnation Initial from the *Book of Kells*, the 8th-century Irish manuscript (Trinity College, Dublin).

**Illumination** *The month of April* from the *Très Riches Heures du Duc de Berry*, a 14th-century devotional missal by Pol de Limburg (Musée Condé, Chantilly).

name and exhibited under it seven times in the next 12 years. They included Monet, Renoir, Pissarro, Sisley, Cézanne, Degas, Armand Guillaumin and Berthe Morisot, with Manet in the background as their acknowledged figurehead and leader. Their shared aim was to achieve a new realism by catching what the eye perceives at first glance, a surface view in which shapes and shades appear as fragmentations of light playing or dissolving on the retina. Monet explained his work as trying to imagine what a blind person might see on suddenly regaining his sight. Pissarro urged the need to 'paint generously and unhesitatingly, for it is best not to lose the first impression.' Accordingly, the Impressionist palette was confined to the spectrum – red, orange, yellow, green, blue, indigo and violet – plus white, for directness of effect and speed of execution: an Impressionist painting might take only minutes from start to finish.

The bright colours and high key which are typical of Impressionism have had a lasting effect on painting. The Impressionist idea, however, was overtaken within the lifetime of most of the group by a return to thoughtfulness and structure.

**imprimatura** A thin transparent glaze applied to a white ground or sometimes laid over a preliminary drawing. It was usually in a warm brown or red ochre, or a cool green or grey, depending on the desired result.

**Informal art** A term which has emerged in Europe since the 1950s to describe painting which is based on spontaneous improvisation. The artist abandons all notions of inherited form in favour of untrammelled psychic expression – the term is virtually a synonym for Action Painting. George Mathieu (b. 1921) is the artist who has done most to popularize the concept.

**inglenook** A wide, recessed chimney corner, sometimes with benches at the side.

**Ingres, Jean Auguste Dominique** (1780–1867) French painter, son of a sculptor and miniaturist. He trained in Toulouse and Paris where he studied in the studio of Jacques-Louis David. He won the Prix de Rome in 1801 with *The Ambassadors of Agamemnon*, a Neoclassical work. After a period in which he made a living as a portraitist he settled in Florence, where he worked on *The Vow of Louis XIII*, a commission for the cathedral of Montauban, his native city. Exhibited at the Paris Salon in 1824 it was a great success, establishing him as the leading Classicist at a time when the tide of Romanticism was rising fast.

He was appointed Director of the French School in Rome, and subsequently Professor at the École des Beaux-Arts in Paris. His rigid views, combined with the authority of his position, had a largely stultifying influence. He contained his own emotions and sensuality within the purity and grace of his line.

**Innes, James Dickson** (1887–1914) Welsh landscape painter. He studied at the Slade School, joined the New English Art Club, and painted in Wales with Augustus John, by whom he was influenced. His work, usually on a small scale, is vigorously coloured in the Fauve manner.

**intaglio** Inverted relief, in which the lines and forms are cut out of the surface of a plane, rather than made to stand up from it. In engraving, intaglio techniques are those used on metal such as in line engraving, etching, drypoint, mezzotint, aquatint, soft-ground etching, and crayon and colour engravings. Intaglio prints are made by inking the plate and then wiping its surface clean, so that ink remains only in the engraved lines. The image is transferred to a sheet of dampened paper by rolling it and the plate through a press. The other major types of print making are relief and planographic. See **print making**.

**intercolumniation** The space between columns considered proportionately to the diameter of the columns themselves.

**intermediate ribs** In Gothic vaulting, ribs that are not structurally necessary but are introduced between the main structural ribs for the sake of appearance. They are used more in English than in Continental vaulting. The intermediate ribs are also called 'tiercerons'.

**International Modern** American term for the dominant architectural style of the early 20th century, largely established by Frank Lloyd Wright (1869–1959), Tony Garnier (1869–1948), Adolf Loos (1870–1933), Walter Gropius (1883–1969) and their followers. Its precepts were that architecture should be considered as 'volume rather than mass, and regularity rather than axial symmetry' when ordering design.

**interpenetrations** Mouldings intersecting each other, as in Gothic vaulting.

**intimisme** A form of Post Impressionist painting characterized by a preference for small, domestic scenes of an everyday nature. Vuillard and Bonnard were its main exponents.

**intonaco** The layer of wet plaster on which the **fresco** artist works.

**intrados** The inner curve or surface of an arch.

**Ionic** see **order** (of architecture).

**Isabey, Jean-Baptiste** (1767–1855) French miniaturist painter whose career flourished from the Revolution to the Second Empire. His subjects included Napoleon, Wellington, Louis XVIII and the main participants at the Congress of Vienna. His son Eugène Isabey (1804–86) was a genre and landscape painter.

**Jacobean** English Renaissance architecture during the reign of James I (1603–25). It follows the Elizabethan in structure though with more Classical and Netherlandish touches, as at Hatfield House and Audley End. Large windows, gables, richly carved wood or plaster decoration are also typical of the style.

**Japanese prints** see **Ukiyo-e**

**Japanese School** The main schools of Japanese painting from the 10th century to modern

**Jacobean** The Long Gallery at Aston Hall, Birmingham (1618–35).

**Japonaiserie** A woodcut by Hokusai (1760–1849), typical of the Japanese art imports that were popular in Europe in the second half of the 19th century.

times are Yamato-E (900–1400), Suiboku (1300–1500), Tosa (1400–1800), Kano (1400–1800), Korin (1600–1800), Nanga (1600–1800), Nagasaki (1700–1800), and Maruyama (1700–1800).

**Japonaiserie** Decorative wares exported from Japan to Europe in the latter half of the 19th

century, including woodblock prints, fans, fabrics and household objects. Articles of Japonaiserie appear in several French paintings of the time, for example Manet's portrait of Emile Zola.

**Jawlensky, Alexej von** (1864–1941) Russian painter. He studied at St Petersburg and Munich and evolved his own style of painting in the Fauve manner, plain forms in a bright palette. In the 1920s he embarked on a series of faces, painted in rudimentary strokes to a geometrical design. His later work, though essentially of the same subject, became increasingly Abstract and Expressionist.

**jesting beam** In architecture, a decorative or ornamental beam which is not an essential part of the structure.

**joggle** The groove or the projecting part of pieces of stonework or masonry which fit together to make a joint.

**John, Augustus** (1878–1961) English painter, born in Wales. He trained at the Slade School, where he was hailed as the greatest natural draughtsman since Raphael. As the leader of the young English set, he was much publicized, though more as a colourful bohemian than as a painter. His typical subjects were scenes of life among the Welsh gipsies, with whom he lived for a while. As a portrait painter he enjoyed fashionable success, without necessarily flattering his sitters. His most interesting work is early, in the Post-Impressionist interlude of the New English Art Club, which he joined in 1903.

**John, Gwen** (1876–1939) Sister of Augustus John. She studied at the Slade School and took lessons from Whistler in Paris, where she became deeply attached to Rodin. Hardly less gifted as a draughtsman than Augustus, she achieved a modest fame with her gentle, reserved portraits, usually in a low key of pale greys and brown. She exemplifies the 'positive and disinterestedly passionate state of mind' which is Roger Fry's definition of the Classic spirit in art.

**Johns, Jasper** (b. 1930) American painter. A former Abstract Expressionalist, he turned to

emblematic imagery and subsequently to attaching real objects to his canvases as an extension of collage.

**Johnson** or **Jonson, Cornelius** (1593–1661) Netherlandish portrait painter. He was born in London and was active in England from 1619 to 1643, when he moved to Holland. His small, domestic portraits are some of the best of the age before Van Dyck, whose work influenced him. He was a contemporary of Daniel Mytens, and worked in much the same manner.

**Jones, Allen** (b. 1937) English painter, noted as one of the new generation of Pop artists in the 1960s. His work is largely figurative, often marked by an exploitive sexuality.

**Jones, Inigo** (1573–1652) English architect and stage designer. From 1605 he was involved in the staging of court masques, elaborate spectacles in which his grasp of Italian design in

**Jones, Inigo** A typical drawing by Inigo Jones of a design for scenery for *The Masque of the Queens*, 1640 (The Library, Chatsworth).

the High Renaissance style is apparent from the surviving drawings.

He prospered as an architect of stately homes, including Hatfield House, the seat of the Salisbury family, and of such public buildings as the Queen's House, Greenwich and the Banqueting House in Whitehall, both in the symmetrical manner of Palladio. As Royal Surveyor under Charles I he added a portico to the west front of Old St Paul's Cathedral after restyling the nave in classical form. Virtually single-handed, he redirected the course of English architecture away from the Baroque towards the flexible classicism of Wren.

**Jongkind, Johan Barthold** (1819–91) Dutch painter and etcher. He studied at The Hague and in Paris, exhibited with the Barbizon painters and at the Salon des Refusés (1863). His favourite painting ground was Normandy, where, like Eugène Boudin, he made vivacious sketches along the coast. Again like Boudin, he influenced the young Monet, and is regarded as an important precursor of **Impressionism**.

**Jordaens, Jacob** (1593–1678) Flemish painter, a pupil of Adam van Noort (1526–1641). His first paintings were of religious subjects, including a *Crucifixion* in St Paul's, Antwerp. He later began painting the boisterous genre subjects, usually tavern scenes, for which he is best known.

**Jugendstil** A German term for **Art Nouveau**, after the magazine *Die Jugend* (meaning 'Youth'), founded in 1896.

**Junk art** Works based on the premise that any material is suitable for art, and which incorporates it either as an *objet trouvé* or in modified form. The tradition is rooted in **Collage** and Construction and has surfaced frequently since, for example in the work of Kurt Schwitters and Robert Rauschenberg and the New Realism of the 1960s.

**Juvarra, Filippo** (1678–1736) Italian architect and draughtsman of the Late Baroque. After making a name as a theatrical designer in Rome he was invited to Turin by the King of Savoy, whom he served for 20 years, building palaces, churches and houses and engaging in town planning. His most notable churches at Turin are the Superga, the S. Filippo Neri and the S. Croce. Of his palaces, the Stupinigi and the Venaria Reale are typical of his flair for theatrical effects. A year before he died he went to Spain at the invitation of Philip V to design a new Royal Palace in Madrid, which was brought to completion by his pupil, Giovanni Battista Sacchetti (1700–64).

**Kandinsky, Wassily** (1866–1944) Russian-born painter, a founder of modern Abstract art. After studying law and politics at the University of Moscow he opted for a career in art after seeing Monet's work at an exhibition of Impressionist paintings held in Moscow in 1895. He was a founder of the **Blaue Reiter** group, returned to Russia at the outbreak of war in 1914 and in 1921 went back to Germany, where he taught at the Bauhaus until 1933 when it was closed by the Nazis. He took refuge in Paris, became a French citizen, and worked there for the rest of his life.

He defined three categories in his own work: direct impressions of an 'exterior' nature, unconscious expressions of an 'interior' nature, and pictures arising from long periods of work and gestation, called 'compositions'. His free use of brush or pencil as an involuntary extension of his ideas anticipates **Action painting**.

**Kaprow, Allan** (b. 1927) American painter. He was the creator of the **Happening** and of action collage, in which he makes use of materials ranging from straw and paper to flashing lights. Another motif is involvement of the spectator as part of the 'environment' of a work, in support of his belief that art is inseparable from real life.

**Kauffmann, Angelica** (1741–1807) Neoclassical painter, born in Switzerland. She became fashionable in Venice, Rome and London where she formed a close attachment to Reynolds and became a founder member of the Royal Academy (1768). She was well endowed with talents, including a fine singing voice, and profited from the friendship of Winckelmann, whose portrait she painted in 1764 (Kunsthaus, Zurich). Her *Lady Elizabeth Foster* (Ickworth) and *Lady Cornelia Knight* (Manchester City Art Gallery) are typical of her readily enjoyable manner.

**keel arch** A curved ogee arch that rises to a point.

**keel moulding** An architectural term for a moulding where the decorative outline is shaped like the keel of a ship. See **ogee**.

**Kent, Rockwell** (1882–1971) American painter and illustrator, a pupil of Robert Henri and artistic descendant of Winslow Homer. His book illustrations also reveal his debt to William Blake.

**Kent, William** (1685–1748) English painter, garden designer and architect. His patron was Lord Burlington, whom he met while working as a guide on the Grand Tour and who led him towards the Palladian style, which he adopted in his most important commissions. However, he also displayed a talent for decoration and furnishing, derived from Italian Baroque and from his close acquaintance with the designs of Inigo Jones, whose drawings he edited for an edition published by Burlington in 1727.

His best-known building is probably Holkham Hall, Norfolk, begun in 1734, for the Earl of Leicester. He adapted the same design for the Horse Guards, London, which was finished after his death by his friend and collaborator, John Vardy. His work as a landscape designer included gardens at Rousham, Oxon; Stowe, Bucks; and at Burlington's villa at Chiswick.

**key** The overall effect of a painting's tonal and colour values determine its key. A painting in a high key is one in which bright, pale colours and light tones predominate. Tenebrist paintings are low-keyed, as in the works of Caravaggio and his followers.

**key block, key plate, key stone** In multicoloured prints, the master from which the surfaces used to print the individual colours are made. The key block (woodcuts), key plate (aquatints), or key stone (lithographs) contains the complete design as if for a black and white print, and from this the drawings for each of the blocks, plates, or stones are copied. By making sure that all these print in register with each other, it is possible to reproduce the design on the key exactly in its appointed colours. See **colour prints**.

**keystone** In architecture, the central voussoir in the crown of an arch, the last to be placed in position.

**Kinetic art** Constructions in which movement takes place so that the relationship of forms and the effects of light and shadow are constantly changing. The components may be driven by motors or by natural forces, as in **mobiles**.

**kingpost** In a trussed roof, the vertical post which is gripped between the heads of the main rafters and holds up the centre or the tie beam with iron stirrups or bolts.

**kingpost truss** Roof supports joined together to form a triangular girder which supports the roofing materials and transmits the weight of the roof to the walls or piers.

**Kirchner, Ernst Ludwig** (1880–1938) German painter. He was a founder of **Die Brücke** at Dresden in 1905. His most authoritative work was done in Berlin between 1911 and 1917, when he painted street life in the Expressionist manner.

**kitcat** A canvas measuring 36in by 28in. It was named after the members of the Kit-Cat Club, who had their portraits painted on canvases of this size by Sir Godfrey Kneller between 1702 and 1717.

**kitsch** A German adjective describing self-consciously vulgar, sentimental or pretentious artifacts, whether commercially produced or aspiring to the fine arts.

**Klee, Paul** (1879–1940) German painter, one of the leading Abstract artists of the 20th century. He exhibited with Macke, Kandinsky and Marc in the third Blaue Reiter group exhibition, and made his first reputation as a graphic artist in black and white. In Paris, Delaunay's theories of light introduced him to the mysteries of colour, which at first he exploited in the medium of watercolour. His mature work combines elements of Expressionism, Cubism and Surrealism in a dream-like universe which includes micro-organisms from the natural world. His advice to students at the Bauhaus, where he taught in the 1930s, was to 'dig deep and lay bare'.

**Klimt, Gustav** (1862–1918) Austrian painter and decorative artist. In 1897 he became a founder member of the Austrian Sezession, was its president until 1903 and wrote extensively for its journal, *Ver Sacrum*. His ornate Art Nouveau style (*Jugendstil* in Austria-Germany) was often employed on a considerable scale, as in the panels he painted for the Sezession building in Vienna. His female portraits, often embellished with jewel-like splendour, can be both exotic and symbolic. His drawings show the nervous candour with which he approached such subjects and help to link him with the generation of Expressionists that followed.

**Kline, Franz** (1910–62) American painter. After studying in Boston and London he settled in New York, where he became a prominent exhibitor of Abstracts, consisting typically of bold black strokes on a white canvas.

**knapped flint** Flints cut and laid so that the split black sides make an attractive wall facing. See **flushwork**.

**Kneller, Sir Godfrey** (*c.* 1647–1723). Born in Lübeck, he trained in Amsterdam under Ferdinand Bol (1616–80), a pupil of Rembrandt, and was active in England as a portrait painter from 1675. His output includes many examples which do him less than justice, and which have proved detrimental to his reputation as Principal Painter to William and Mary. At his best he has a vigour and freedom of technique which break free of the constraints of the Dutch manner. Kneller's Academy, which he founded in 1711, was the first attempt to create an academic foundation for English art.

**Kokoschka, Oskar** (1886–1980) Austrian Expressionist painter. His early works were mainly portraits, remarkable for organic insights which give them a tortured force. He served in the 1914–18 war, in which he was wounded, and afterwards took a teaching job at Dresden. He travelled widely, recording town scenes and landscapes on a dynamic scale. Forced to leave Germany in 1934, he moved to London, where he stayed for the rest of his life.

His energetic townscapes and portraits, brilliant drawings and emotional use of colour, mark him as one of the foremost Expressionist painters of his time.

**Kollwitz, Käthe** (1867–1945) German graphic artist and sculptress. Her etchings and carvings express a womanly sympathy with the unfortunates of this world. Her war memorial at Essen (1932) and her *Pyramid of Mothers* (1937), a protest against war on behalf of all women, are typical of her deep concern.

**Kooning, Willem de** (b. 1904) Dutch-born painter and a leading exponent of Abstract Impressionism in America, where he has lived since 1926. An early influence was Arshile Gorky, who helped to lead him towards an airy

**Kouros** Marble kouros from Melos, *c.* 550 BC, showing the characteristic stance with one leg forward (National Museum, Athens).

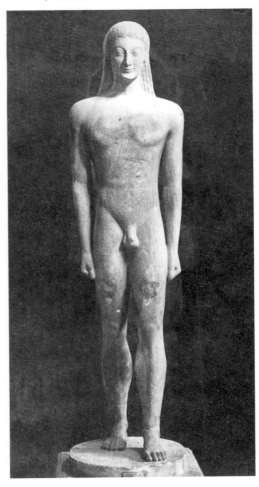

simplification of style. In the 1940s he became preoccupied with the female figure, which he described in passionately monstrous forms. His black-and-white compositions are typical of his contribution to Abstract Expressionism, though he has refused to be labelled as a member of any movement or school.

**kore**  Any statue of the Archaic period of ancient Greece depicting a young girl. The standing stance is formal, with one leg slightly advanced. The figure, usually full size, was carved in marble or cast in bronze, and coloured.

**kouros**  Term for the type of male statuary made in the Archaic period of ancient Greek art.

**Kupka, Frank**  (1871–1957)  Czech painter. He was an originator of Abstraction who worked for most of his life in Paris. He exhibited with the Section d'Or and embraced the concept of Orphic Cubism practised by Delaunay. His later work has a strong verticality, sometimes relieved by decorative themes from his native Bohemia.

**La Touche, Gaston**  (1854–1913)  French painter of costume pieces, genre and Breton subjects. He was much admired in his time as a colourist and master of natural light.

**La Tour, Georges de**  (1593–1652)  French painter of religious and genre subjects. He is renowned for his dramatic use of lighting derived from Caravaggio through the Utrecht School. His use of candle light gives distinction and impressive calm to his interior studies with grouped figures.

**La Tour, Maurice Quentin de**  (1704–88)  French pastel artist. After visiting London as a young man he settled in Paris, where pastel portraiture was enjoying a revival, and was an instant success. His patrons included Louis XV, Rousseau, Voltaire, Madame de Pompadour and a host of lesser celebrities. With Jean Baptiste Perroneau (1715–83) he established pastel as a medium worthy of comparison with oils, capable of a hitherto unsuspected expressiveness and subtlety.

**lacing**  A course, usually of brick, inserted as a bond in a wall constructed of cobble, stone or other material of rough, uneven texture.

**Lady Chapel**  A chapel dedicated to the Virgin.

**laid paper**  Paper in which the impression of the mould wires used in the hand-made process of paper making shows through. Usually it is an indication of age or quality, but it can be easily simulated in machine-made papers.

**Lam, Wilfredo**  (b. 1902)  Cuban painter. He studied in Madrid and Barcelona, and in 1937 went to Paris, where he became a member of the Surrealist group headed by André Breton and Paul Eluard. After a short spell as an Abstract Expressionist he began to find his subjects in the menace and violence of untamed jungles, drawing on his South American origins for themes that link him to the European strain of Abstraction.

**Lamb, Henry**  (1883–1960)  Australian-born painter. He studied in London and Paris, and made visits to Brittany from 1908. He was a member of the Camden Town Group and exhibited with the New English Art Club. He served as a war artist in both world wars, and in later years turned to portraiture with success.

**lancet arch**  An acutely angled arch, resembling a lancet, which is characteristic of the Early English architecture of the 12th and 13th centuries.

**Lancret, Nicolas**  (1690–1743)  French painter. He was a follower and imitator of Watteau, a designer for the theatre and painter of decorative genre subjects.

**Land art**  Also known as Earth art, this is a form of art which emerged in the late 1960s and consisted of modifying the landscape, usually in a deliberately ephemeral sense but sometimes more permanently. Few land artists have much in common with each other: the terrain is simply a newly discovered medium which different artists put to different uses. Some are essentially sculptors, others conceptual artists, or makers of environments, or protestors against the institutionalization of art, 'back to nature' campaigners, and others.

Among the practitioners of Land art are the Americans Dennis Oppenheim (b. 1938) and Michael Heizer (b. 1944); the British artists Richard Long (b. 1945) and Hamish Fulton (b. 1946); and the Bulgarian-born Christo (b. 1935).

**Landseer, Sir Edwin** (1802–73) English painter, especially of animal subjects. Prodigiously talented from childhood, he gathered public honours while still in his youth and became the favourite painter of Queen Victoria, achieving national celebrity with his ingratiating animal pictures, which were widely known through engravings. His anthropomorphized dogs, in particular, were much to the public's taste. *The Old Shepherd's Chief Mourner* (1827), in the Victoria and Albert Museum, is a well-known example. The lions in Trafalgar Square, London, are also his work.

**lantern** A word used in architecture for a windowed turret making a finish to a dome or tower, generally for reasons of effect. The small structure on the top of the dome of St Paul's is a conspicious example.

**lantern cross** A sculptured churchyard cross with a lantern-shaped top.

**Larionov, Mikhail** (1881–1964) Russian painter and designer, the creator of **Rayonism**. In his early work he drew widely on Primitivist themes and collaborations with Diaghilev and the Ballets Russes followed. His designs for the ballet, including make-up, decor and costumes, are probably his most successful achievement. His interest in the popular arts, such as the circus and graffiti, made him an inventive and useful member of Diaghilev's inner circle. With Natalia Goncharova (1881–1962) he propagated the Rayonist ideas of 1911–14.

**Latin cross** A cross with one long arm and three short ones.

**lattice** Openwork crisscross made of thin metal strips or wooden laths.

**lattice girder** A girder with braces diagonally crossing over each other to form a lattice effect.

**lattice window** A window with leaded glazing bars forming a diamond lattice pattern.

**Laurens, Henri** (1885–1954) French sculptor and illustrator. An early friend of Braque and Picasso, he was a specialist in collages, constructions and sculptures in the Cubist mode. He was a designer for Diaghilev and a sculptor whose rounded forms achieved a lyrical naturalism, often based on classic themes. He was awarded the Grand Prix at Sao Paulo in 1953.

**Lavery, Sir John** (1856–1941) Scottish painter. He was born in Belfast and studied in Glasgow and Paris. Primarily a portrait and figure painter, which made his reputation – he was knighted in 1918 – he was a member of the Berlin, Munich and Vienna Sezessions and a close associate of Whistler. *The Tennis Party*, 1885, in the Aberdeen Art Gallery, is typical of his 'real life' subjects, which owe something to Lavery's admiration for Manet.

**Lawrence, Sir Thomas** (1769–1830) English portrait painter. A glittering figure of the Regency, he was appointed Painter in Ordinary to the King at the age of 23. His portraits of royal, rich and aristocratic persons exude glamour and power, and his studies of women and children have a vivacity not often found in his famous contemporary, Reynolds. His reputation has suffered a period of eclipse, possibly the fault of his gifts, which tend to disguise his craftsmanship and hard work. In the bigger canvases there are passages of landscape painting that are reminiscent of Gainsborough.

Lawrence's high earnings enabled him to form an unequalled collection of master drawings, of which some examples may be found in the Ashmolean, Oxford.

**lay figure** A wooden, articulated manikin which can be made to assume any pose. It may be anything from a few inches high to life size. Though clearly not a substitute for a live model, it serves to remind an artist of the proportions and attitudes of the human figure. It may be hung with drapery so that work can continue on that part of a picture without the sitter.

**lay-in** see **dead colour**

**Le Corbusier, Charles-Edouard** (1887–1965) Swiss-French painter and architect, the dominant figure in 20th-century building design and urban planning. His ideas have shaped modern attitudes to all aspects of architecture in a metropolitan environment.

Seizing on Cubism at the outset of his career, he explored its implications through his own painting and with Amadée Ozenfant developed the notion of Purism in a book, *Après le Cubisme* (1918). His *Warning to Architects*, a collection of articles which he brought together in 1923, sets out the main principles for a 20th-century approach to architecture: the exclusion of all stylistic borrowings, reduction of forms to basic geometrical shapes, and the concept of the house as 'a machine for living in'. The garden city, with high-rise dwellings set in open parkland, was seen as a means of saving space and arresting the growth of traffic.

Le Corbusier was able to implement these ideas in the 1920s and 1930s, but it was only after the last war that he was given a chance to demonstrate them on a large scale in the Unités d'Habitation complex at Marseilles, begun in 1947, and at Briey-la-Forêt, near Nancy, in 1960. His Notre-Dame du Haut at Ronchamp (1950–4) is a dazzling example of his mastery of sculptural form in architecture. The design for the United Nations building in New York (1947), for which he was one of the architects, is essentially his.

The growing reaction against his ideas has been less architectural than sociological, as his solutions to the problems of dense urban habitation have been shown to fall short in purely human terms.

**lean colour** see **fat**

**Lebrun, Charles** (1619–90) French painter and administrator. He was supreme in the arts in the age of Louis XIV. He studied under Poussin, whose principles he preached all his life, became a protégé of Richelieu and took a leading part in founding the French Academy (1648) of which he was eventually appointed Director. In 1663 he was made Principal Painter to the King and a year later Director of the Gobelins tapestry company, with responsibility for designs and fabrics for use in the royal residences. His own work, mostly decoration on a grand scale, includes the Apollo Gallery at the Louvre and paintings at Versailles.

**Ledoux, Claude-Nicolas** (1736–1806) French architect in the Louis XVI style. The Pavillon de Louveciennes, 1771, was his first commission from Mme du Barry, his most influential patron. He was appointed Royal Architect two years later, and went on to design some of the most powerful and expressive works of his time. Among them were the theatre at Besançon, the saltworks, Arc-et-Senans and the Hôtel Thelusson, Paris, with a garden landscaped in the English manner. These works, along with others by Ledoux, survive only in ruins, if at all.

**Leech, John** (1817–64) English illustrator and cartoonist. He contributed to the popular magazines of the early Victorian era, illustrated Dickens's *A Christmas Carol* and the popular 'Jorrocks' novels by Surtees in the 1850s. He drew 3000 illustrations and cartoons for *Punch*, and exhibited some of his most popular subjects as hand-coloured enlargements in 1860. His humour is of a gentle, unmalicious kind, though with a sharp eye to the fads and foibles of the time.

**Léger, Fernand** (1881–1955) French painter. He was an early friend of the Cubist group, of the Section d'Or painters, and of Le Corbusier, with whom he exhibited in 1925. He spent the war in America, and on returning to Paris extended his work to stained glass, ceramics and mural painting. He remained true to the Futurists' faith in the machine age: a modern painter whose belief in 20-century civilization produced some of his noblest work.

**Legros, Alphonse** (1837–1911) French painter and etcher. He was originally a follower of Courbet and later a member of the circle of Rodin and Whistler. He exhibited regularly at the Salon and in 1863 at the Salon des Refusés. In 1863, at Whistler's suggestion, he moved to London, and remained in England for the rest of his life.

As a teacher at the Slade School (1876–92) he was instrumental in bringing about a new emphasis on draughtsmanship. His etchings, usually of figurative subjects, are once again being given their due.

**Lely, Sir Peter,** originally named Pieter van der Faes (1618–80) English portrait painter of Dutch descent. He trained at Haarlem and in about 1642 came to England, where he filled the gap left by the death of Van Dyck as a fashionable painter of the aristocracy and court. In 1661 he was appointed Principal Painter to Charles II, who found Lely's languid style much to his taste. His group portrait, *The Greenwich Flagmen* (National Maritime Museum, London), depicts the victorious admirals who had lately overcome the Dutch. His portraits known as the *Windsor Beauties* set a standard of languorous glamour, unsurpassed until the advent of Sir Thomas Lawrence.

**Leonardo da Vinci** (1452–1519) Italian painter. He trained at the studio of Verrocchio in Florence, where his early work includes an *Annunciation* and an *Adoration of the Kings*, both in the Uffizi Gallery. In 1482 he went to Milan under the patronage of the Duke Ludovico Sforza, to whom he recommended himself as an inventor of military machinery. It was in Milan that he painted the *Last Supper* in the S. Maria delle Grazie and the *Madonna of the Rocks* (National Gallery, London).

He returned to Florence in 1499, and eventually, in 1516, settled in France. To his late Florence period belong the *Mona Lisa* (Louvre), the *Virgin and the Child with St Anne and the Infant St John* (Louvre; cartoon in the National Gallery, London) and the *Leda and the Swan* (Wilton House, Salisbury).

Leonardo's paintings, few in number, are among the masterpieces of Western art, with depths and complexities which penetrate to the unconscious mind. His drawings reveal the inexhaustible curiosity of his intellect, which embraced the unknown as well as the physical world.

**letterpress** Relief printing from frames where type and blocks are set at a uniform height – 'type high'. The term also means a commercial printing process, as distinct from offset lithography.

**Lewis, Wyndham** (1884–1957) English painter and writer, the founder of **Vorticism** and editor of *Blast*. His early work is in the Cubist manner, from which the Vorticist style

is derived: a vehement onslaught on contemporary attitudes, both cultural and social, with *Blast* – 'The Battering Ram as a work of Art' – as its public weapon.

Lewis was a brilliant draughtsman, whose spare and strong linear style gives his portraits, in particular, a compelling modernity and force. His *Edith Sitwell* (1923) and *Ezra Pound* (1939), both in the Tate Gallery, London, are characteristic.

**Lichtenstein, Roy** (b. 1923) American painter and sculptor. His paintings based on pulp-magazine imagery are among the most substantial works of **Pop art**. His deliberate choice of mechanical, everyday images from the mass media, magnified to show both the coarseness and the power of the original, have proved to be durable statements on the emotive force of the banal.

**Liebermann, Max** (1847–1935) German painter. His receptivity to modern European art led him to Impressionism, which he discovered in about 1890. He became president of the Berlin Sezession in 1898, and was much respected by the generation of German painters whose careers were affected by the anti-cultural attitude of the Nazis.

**lierne rib** In late Gothic architecture, a short rib connecting two main ribs.

**Lievens, Jan** (1607–74) Dutch painter and etcher. He was born in Leiden, where as a young man he worked with Rembrandt. This association ended in 1632 when Rembrandt left for Amsterdam. Lievens is thought to have visited England at that time, and re-emerges in Antwerp in about 1635. Back in Holland, from 1639 he achieved success as a landscape and portrait painter and held a public position in Amsterdam and The Hague. *Tobias and the Angel, Portrait of Anna Maria Schurman*, and *Self-portrait*, all in the National Gallery, London, are typical of his painterly qualities.

**life drawing** A drawing of the human figure from a live model.

**limited edition** A stipulated number of prints pulled from a block or plate, or sculptures cast from a mould. When the edition is complete

– that is, when the determined number of copies have been made – the plate or mould is destroyed or scratched (see **cancelled plate**), and the edition numbered. Each print is usually numbered in pencil below the impression. Thus a print numbered 10/50 is the tenth to be pulled in an edition of fifty.

The practice of limiting editions developed from etching and drypoint, in which over-use of the plate can result in a deterioration of quality. However, even when there is no technical or practical reason for doing so, editions are often limited to preserve the work's status as an original, and so that rarity may enhance its value.

**line engraving** The earliest and most direct of the **intaglio** methods of engraving. The design is first drawn on the smooth surface of a copper plate, and then incised into the metal with a burin. The engraver pushes the point through the copper, throwing up a continuous spiral of metal and leaving a clean, V-shaped line in the surface of the plate. The greater the pressure, the deeper is the furrow cut by the burin, and so the thicker is the eventual printed line. As with all intaglio methods (see **print making**), the plate is printed by leaving ink only in the engraved furrows, which is then transferred to damp paper in a heavy press. Trial proofs can be repeatedly pulled as the work progresses, so that the engraver can see which lines need further attention. Though it is essentially a linear technique, **hatching**, **cross-hatching** and textural shading can contribute tonal effects.

Line engraving seems to have developed simultaneously in Germany, Italy and the Netherlands during the 15th century, as an extension of **niello** and other metal-working methods. The German artist Martin Schongauer, the son of a goldsmith, was the first to produce important work in the medium. It flourished in the 16th century, reaching a peak in the work of Albrecht Dürer. From the beginning of the 17th century, artists began to be attracted to the more expensive technique of **etching**. Line engraving was subsequently confined to reproduction and book illustration.

**linear** Works of art are said to be linear when their composition depends more on the flow of line than on the arrangement of masses.

Drawing and engraving are both linear techniques, depending on outline rather than compositional effects or tone and colour to delineate form.

**linenfold** Carved wooden decoration resembling the folds of linen and found on panelling of the 15th and 16th centuries.

**Linnell, John** (1792–1882) English landscape painter. As a young man he was close to William Blake and his circle, including Samuel Palmer, who eventually married his daughter. His own early work has a 'Shoreham' quality, later lost in the sugary tones of a run-of-the-mill Victorian landscape painter. His watercolours come closer to the freshness of vision that he shared with The Ancients at the beginning of his career.

**linocut** A form of relief printing developed from the woodcut and employing linoleum as the ground. A variety of chisels and gouges are used to cut away the areas of the surface that are to print white. The remaining upstanding parts of the block are then inked, and the design is printed either by hand or on a press. Linoleum is easier to work than wood and offers a smoother, if less interesting, surface. It is well suited to designs composed of broad masses, conceived and executed boldly.

**Linocut** *The Wrestlers* by Gaudier-Brzeska. The technique is especially suited to the execution of a bold design (Victoria and Albert Museum, London).

**lintel** A horizontal piece of metal, stone or wood which supports the weight over a door or window.

**Lippi, Filippino** (*c*.1457–1504) Italian painter, the son of Fra Filippo Lippi. He entered Botticelli's workshop in about 1472 and was later commissioned to complete the frescoes in the Carmine, Florence. Other fresco work by him includes the cycle in the S. Maria sopra Minerva in Rome, where he acquired a taste for antiquarian remains which find their way into his later work.

**Lippi, Fra Filippo** (*c*.1406–69) Italian painter. He was a member of the Carmelite order from boyhood and became Abbot of S. Quirico at Legnaia, near Florence, in 1442. His early fresco paintings, done in Florence, show the influence of Masaccio. In Prato, where he was Chaplain at S. Margherita, he painted an altarpiece for the convent chapel. There he met Lucrezia Buti, a nun, who bore him the son, Filippino, whom he taught to paint in his manner. He is also thought to have given lessons to Botticelli.

**lipping** Bricks laid so that the top edge is set in from the plane surface of the wall.

**Lissitsky, El** (1890–1941) Russian painter. Originally an architect in Moscow, he was a pioneer of Suprematism and Constructivism. He was influenced by Chagall and by Malevich, a fellow teacher at the Vitebsk Academy of Fine Art after the Revolution. His abstract works in geometric planes, which he called *Prouns*, were exercises in spatial construction, combining painting with relief. He worked mainly in Germany, but in 1928 returned to the Soviet Union, where for the rest of his life he played a part in staging public exhibitions.

**litho press** The press on which lithographs are printed, the proofs being taken from the lithographic stone or plate. The stone is inked and a sheet of wet paper laid over it, which in turn is covered with tympan, a sheet of strong wood or board which protects the paper and ensures an even impression. The stone and paper are cranked underneath the scraper, a padded bar which bears down on the tympan as the bed passes beneath it, causing the trans-

**Lithograph** A poster for *Divan Japonais* by Toulouse-Lautrec (1892), printed by lithographic colour process (Art Institute of Chicago).

fer of ink from stone to paper. See also **transfer lithography** and **offset**.

**lithographic stone** A thick slab of limestone, its face ground to a finely grained surface, used in lithography.

**lithography** The major form of planographic or surface printing. It is distinguished from relief or intaglio methods in that the design is not incised into a plate or block, but drawn on the surface of a lithographic stone. Invented in 1798 by Alois Senefelder, the process is based on the principle that grease and water repel each other. The artist draws his design on a heavy slab of flat, fine-grained limestone, using either tusche or a special lithographic crayon composed of wax, soap and lampblack. The stone is then treated with a variety of chemical solutions which fix the grease in the drawing and enhance the porosity of the blank areas, so that when water is applied it is immediately repelled by the grease but accepted by the bare stone surface. Greasy ink is next spread over the stone with a roller. It, in turn, adheres only to the grease of the drawing. The other areas, being damp, repel it, making it possible to pull prints from the inked stone.

There are a number of variations to the technique. Metal, usually zinc, and plastic plates are often used instead of limestone. A design may be drawn on paper and then transferred to the stone for printing (see **transfer lithography**), possibly by the **offset** method, which means it will not be reversed. But the basic method of lithographic printing has remained unchanged since Senefelder's day. It is well suited to both linear and tonal designs, and will print exactly as it is drawn, thus encouraging a free and gestural quality in the artist. Lithography is also ideally suited to colour printing, when a separate stone or plate is used for each colour (see **colour prints**). It is this, together with the fact that an almost unlimited number of proofs can be pulled from each stone, that has led to its widespread commercial use.

Photolitho offset, in which prepared artwork is photographically transferred to the plate and printed in an offset-litho press so that the image is not reversed, is the dominant commercial printing process in use today.

**local colour** The colour of an object as seen in plain daylight, as distinct from any apparent colour which it might assume under other conditions.

**London Group** A society of British artists, painting in Post-Impressionist styles, who first exhibited together in 1913 and 1914. It consisted of members of the Camden Town Group with the addition of aspiring members of the avant-garde, presided over by Harold Gilman (1886–1919), a member of Sickert's circle. The London Group therefore represented an identifiable opposition to the still-influential academism of the Slade School. Its members included John and Paul Nash, Roger Fry, Duncan Grant, Vanessa Bell, David Bomberg, Jacob Epstein and Wyndham Lewis, all of whom helped to keep the Group active in later years. Its original identity faded with time, though it lives on as a loosely knit exhibiting society with indeterminate aims.

**long and short work** In Saxon masonry, flat horizontal stones alternating with tall vertical stones; often used on the corners of walls.

**Longhi, Pietro** (1702–85) Italian painter. He is noted for his genre and figure paintings depicting social life in Venice, where he lived from about 1730. Allesandro Longhi (1733–1813), his son, became official portrait painter to the Venetian Academy, of which his father was made a member in 1766.

**Lorenzetti, Ambrogio** (c. 1290–1348) Italian painter born in Siena, where most of his surviving work is to be seen. He was probably the pupil of his brother, Pietro Lorenzetti (c. 1280–1348), who is thought to have been taught by Duccio. Both brothers' work continues the broad, naturalistic approach to religious subject painting initiated by Duccio and by Giotto.

The *Birth of the Virgin* (Opera del Duomo, Siena) shows Pietro as a master of both colour and design. Ambrogio's frescos, *Good and Bad Government*, in the Palazzo Pubblico, Siena, are a vivacious record of everyday events in the city, painted with individual freedom and style.

**lost-wax process** see **bronze**

**Lotto, Lorenzo** (c. 1480–1556) Italian portrait painter. He is thought to have been born a Venetian, and to have worked in the studio of Bellini before seeking to make his name in Rome. The palette and style of such contemporaries as Titian, Correggio and Perugino can be seen in his work, which at its best ranks with the most discerning portraiture of the Renaissance.

**Louis XV style** A description synonymous with French Rococo when applied to the decorative arts, especially in furniture, ornamentation and interior design. Essentially it is non-Classical, curvilinear and fantasticated, as seen in the boudoir interiors of such mid-18th century French artists as Fragonard and Boucher.

**Louis XVI style** Late French Rococo, c. 1760–89, marking the swing to Neoclassicism. The return to less frivolous values, based on admiration for the antique, led to rectilinear decorations, chaste colours (white and gold), and columnar motifs in furniture and domestic design.

**louvre** A ventilator or foul-air outlet. It is usually an opening faced with horizontal slats of wood, metal or glass, as in a modern louvre window.

**Lowry, Laurence Stephen** (1887–1976) English painter, born and bred in Manchester. His highly individual versions of the Northern industrial landscape have made him one of the most recognizable artists of his time. His townscapes, usually peopled with gawky figures, are steeped in melancholy charm. His drawings can have an expressionist force rarely apparent in his paintings.

**Lucas van Leyden** (1494–1533) Dutch painter and engraver. He entered the Painters' Guild at Leiden in 1514, travelled to Antwerp and to Middleburg, and through his contact with Dürer in about 1521 developed his skills as an engraver and woodcut artist. His portraiture is notable for psychological insight and his genre subjects such as the *Card Players* (Wilton House, Salisbury), for the unaffected realism that was to become important to the Netherlandish tradition.

**Luce, Maximilien** (1858–1941) French painter. He was a member of the Pointillist circle that included Seurat, Signac and Pissarro whose manner is to be seen in much of his work. He tended towards industrial subjects, in accordance with the anarchist sympathies which he shared with Pissarro. He was jailed for these beliefs in 1894, though not brought to trial. His most ambitious work, *The Iron Foundry* (1899, now in Oslo) is a monument to working-class heroism on the shop floor.

**Luini, Bernardino** (*c.*1481–1532) Milanese painter. He is noted for his sugary treatment of Leonardo's style, which in Victorian times established him, though briefly, among the masters of the Renaissance. His *Christ among the Doctors*, in the National Gallery, London, has in its time been ascribed to Leonardo. The *Virgin and Child with St John*, in the same collection, is a typical exercise in the master's manner.

**luminism** A concern with the depiction of bright, clear light. The name is loosely attached to late 19th-century paintings, particularly Impressionism and Pointillism, referring to a heightened interest in the effects of light and colour.

**luminosity** The quality of brightness. A coloured object is said to be luminous when it is brighter than its surroundings.

**lunette** A painting of semi-circular shape, usually made to fit a space in an architectural design.
In architecture, it is the term for a crescent-shaped or semicircular aperture to admit light, usually in a dome or vaulted ceiling.

**macchia** An Italian word meaning a stain or blot, sometimes used of the underpainting for an oil colour. The Macchiaioli were a group of Florentine Realists of the mid-19th century loosely influenced by the colour theory of the Impressionists, who applied their paint in individual smears or touches.

**Macke, August** (1887–1914) German painter. He was closely associated with Franz Marc, who introduced him to Wassily Kandinsky and his circle. He joined the **Blaue Reiter** group and was also associated with Robert Delaunay, whose **Orphism** influenced his later work. His declared aim was to 'dissolve the spatial energies of colour'. In 1914 he paid a visit to Tunisia with Klee, who held him in high regard. Like Marc, he died on the battlefield, serving in the German army.

**Mackintosh, Charles Rennie** (1868–1928) Scottish architect, designer and watercolour artist. He was the dominant figure in the **Art Nouveau** movement in Glasgow. In 1897 he won a competition for an extension to the Glasgow School of Art, the buildings for which were completed in 1909. They were widely admired for their geometrical, unornamented design and made a name for Mackintosh abroad as well as at home. He carried the same anti-revivalist precepts into his designs for interiors, including furniture and fittings. In 1900 he exhibited with the Vienna Sezession.

His watercolours, among them flower studies, are remarkable for the Japanese-like purity of their design and colour.

**Maes, Nicolaes** (1632–93) Dutch genre and portrait painter. As a young man he worked in Rembrandt's studio, and his early works are in the master's manner. He gradually evolved his own style, which brought him success as a painter of small, Frenchified portraits.

**Maestà** A name for medieval and Renaissance pictures of the Virgin and Child surrounded by angels.

**Magic Realism** A type of painting which evolved in Germany during the 1920s. It was closely related to Neue Sachlichkeit and Surrealism, in which realistic imagery is infused with the weird and incongruous.

**Magnelly, Alberto** (1888–1971) Italian painter. His career began in Paris when he came in contact with the Cubists and the Futurists, and subsequently with the group centred on the poet Guillaume Apollinaire and Picasso. After 1915 he turned briefly to Abstract painting, which he abandoned in the 1920s for a strictly figurative manner. In 1933 he joined the **Abstraction-Création** painters and found his own style within the Concrete Art movement. His work in this manner was particularly influential in Italy.

**Magritte, René** (1898–1967) Belgian painter. A lifelong Surrealist, he did not, however, follow the precepts of automatism laid down by André Breton, preferring to challenge the spectator's imagination by the incongruous juxtaposition of familiar objects. The tension between recognizable, figurative forms and their unexpected presence in relation to one another gives Magritte's work an enduring modernity.

**mahlstick** A stiff wooden rod, three or four feet long, which the painter uses to steady his hand for delicate work. It has a ball-shaped pad at one end which is rested on the canvas.

**Maillol, Aristide** (1861–1944) French sculptor. He studied at the École des Beaux-Arts under Jean Gérôme and Alexandre Cabanel.

His early tapestry designs reflect an interest in Gauguin, whom he met in 1883. He turned to sculpture and woodcarving in 1900, making the female nude the centre of his sense of self-contained form. His sculptures show the nude as devoid of associative meanings, with a powerful feeling for mass in womanly forms.

**malerisch** see **painterly**

**Malevich, Kazimir** (1878–1935) Russian painter, founder of **Suprematism** and a leading figure in the early development of Abstract painting. He was influenced by the Cubists, whose ideas he took back with him to Russia after a stay in Paris. They formed the basis of the Suprematist concept of an art that abandons natural objects in favour of symbols, particularly the square, the circle and the triangle, to express 'the primacy of pure sensation'. He exhibited a *Black on Black* in 1915 and a *White on White* in 1918: works which carried the Abstract idea to lengths which have never been exceeded.

**mandorla** see **aureole**

**Manet, Edouard** (1832–83) French painter and adoptive leader of the Impressionists, though himself a Salon painter whose ambitions were by no means the same as theirs. After studying in the studio of Thomas Couture he embarked on a series of paintings in which his direct method and his dramatic use of black announced him as a follower of the Spanish masters, notably Velazquez and José Ribera.

In 1863 he caused a sensation with his *Déjeuner sur l'Herbe*, exhibited at the Salon des Refusés, and two years later with his *Olympia*, which had been accepted by the Salon. Between them these two paintings (both in the Louvre) heralded the arrival of modern art, in terms which the struggling Impressionists recognized as those of a kindred spirit. Though he never exhibited with them, Manet became the central figure in their bid for acceptance, and shared much of the critical hostility which their work aroused. Manet's use of themes from old masters was provocative to established taste, as was his insistence that the painter's method should be made plain, not disguised by academic finish.

At the end of his life he was awarded the Légion d'Honneur: just in time for him to feel that his work would last.

**manière criblée** or **dotted manner** A 15th-century method of engraving on metal and printing in relief. The lines were engraved with a burin and the remaining areas stippled with a texture of dots made with a punch, which show as white when the plate is printed. The technique was not much used after the Renaissance, though it underwent a brief revival towards the end of the 18th century.

**Mannerism** A style in Italian art, emerging in the second half of the 16th century, in which the classical standards of the High Renaissance gave way to embellishments and figurations of a more virtuoso kind. The term has a faintly pejorative flavour, as if a painter in the wake of Raphael and Michelangelo were necessarily degenerate if he departed from their example. It is, nevertheless, descriptive of an identifiable change in European painting.

The characteristics of Mannerism are an intellectual approach to the subject rather than an essentially visual one; a readiness to break away from the accepted formulae and conventions, and an expressive use of the human figure. At the same time, the Mannerist palette tends to be bright, at times garish, and the lighting somewhat theatrical. Together, these elements make for tension, often of a neurotic kind, and disturbance. Painters who come into this category include Bronzino, Pontormo, Parmigianino, Rosso, Salviati, Vasari, and Giulio Romano.

**mansard roof** A hipped roof with two slopes on each side. The lower slope is much steeper than the upper one. A roof of this style but not hipped is called a 'gambrel' roof.

**Mansart, François** (1598–1666) French architect of the Classical school. He was born in Paris, where he established a reputation at an early age. The unfinished château at Blois, and a country house for the wealthy de Longueil family at Maisons Lafitte, near Paris, are among his best-known works.

**Mantegna, Andrea** (c. 1431–1506) Italian painter. After an apprenticeship with Francesco Squarcione (1394–1468) he was given a commission to decorate the Ovetari Chapel in Padua with frescos including scenes from the life of St James. He left Padua in 1459 to become Court Painter at Mantua. His nine paintings of the *Triumph of Caesar*, intended for a room in the palace, now hang in Hampton Court.

His genius for giving paintings on walls and ceilings more than a purely decorative presence sets him apart from his contemporaries. His reworking of themes from the antique, at a time when relics from the classical world were being rediscovered and revalued, made an impression on other painters, influencing Giovanni Bellini and, outside Italy, Albrecht Dürer.

**maquette** A sculptor's small model made of wax or clay. The Italian equivalent is called bozzetto.

**Marc, Franz** (1880–1916) German painter. Born in Munich, he made two visits to Paris, where he met Wassily Kandinsky, and with him published *Der Blaue Reiter* in 1912. The name also served as the title for an exhibition in which Henri Rousseau and Robert Delaunay were among the painters represented.

Marc's personal vision of an indivisible world, in which nature and animals join with man, is expressed in romantic, mystical works such as his 'horse' pictures and *The Enchanted Mill* (Art Institute, Chicago). He subsequently carried these themes into a purer form of Abstraction, with a developed sense of colour. Marc was killed in action at Verdun.

**Marin, John** (1870–1953) American painter. He started as an architect and lived for a time in Paris, where he was influenced by Whistler, returning to the United States in 1911. He was an exhibitor at the Armory Show (1913) and in the 1920s pointed the way towards Abstraction in an elliptical, allusive watercolour style.

**marine painting** A genre in its own right since the 17th-century Dutch and Flemish painters, many of whom were equally adept in both marine and landscape subjects. English marine painting owes much to the Van de Velde family, father and son, and produced an early master in Charles Brooking (1723–59).

The Dutch influence was dominant until well into the 19th century, by which time many of the leading English painters, including Constable, Bonington and Turner, were painting marine subjects in the Romantic style. The increasing popularity of marine painting helped to keep a large number of specialist artists busy, among them George Chambers (1803–40), Charles Bentley (1806–54), Edward William Cooke (1811–80), Edward Duncan (1803–82) and Clarkson Stanfield (1793–1867). The tradition is still alive in our own times, though the subject matter is usually drawn from the days of sail, as in the work of the most popular of modern marine artists, Montague Dawson (1895–1972).

**Marinetti, Filippo Tomaso** (1876–1944) Italian poet and propagandist for Futurism. His views may be summed up in his declaration that 'a fast car is more beautiful than the Victory of Samothrace'.

**Marini, Marino** (1901–1966) Italian painter and sculptor. His *Horse and Rider* sculptures, by which he is best known, date from the mid-1930s. They have their roots in ancient classic art, but Marini has used the image as

a seemingly inexhaustible metaphor – an ancient theme for modern times.

**marouflage** The process of gluing a canvas to a panel or wall. This was traditionally done with a mixture of white lead and linseed oil, but many adhesives can be used.

**Martin, John** (1798–1854) English painter and engraver. His paintings on grandiose Romantic themes, rich in melodramatic effects, were received with enthusiasm at the Royal Academy. They included such apocalyptic subjects as *Joshua Commanding the Sun to Stand Still* (1816), *The Fall of Babylon* (1819) and *Belshazzar's Feast* (1826), engravings of which carried his name all over Europe. They are once again popular, in the wake of a public appetite for the paranormal on a cinematic scale. Martin's mezzotints in illustration of the Bible and *Paradise Lost*, in the manner that earned him the soubriquet 'Mad' Martin, are also back in favour. His watercolours, in a more conventional strain, are among his most sensitive works.

**Martini, Simone** (*c.*1284–1344) Sienese painter. He was a pupil of Duccio, whose influence is apparent in the *Maestà* fresco in the Palazzo Pubblico at Siena (1315). Martini, however, also included Gothic elements in his work, for example in the altarpiece for a chapel

**Marine painting** Van de Velde (the Younger): *Battle of the Texel* (National Maritime Museum, Greenwich).

in Siena Cathedral, now in the Uffizi Gallery, Florence, and in the *St Louis of Toulouse*, now in Naples. He spent the last years of his life at Avignon, then the seat of the Papacy, where some traces of frescoes by him survive in the Cathedral.

**Masaccio,** born Tommaso di Giovanni di Mone (1401–*c.* 1428) Italian painter, one of the founders of Renaissance painting. Of the only documented work by him, a polyptych for the Carmine at Pisa, one panel is now in the National Gallery, London. It shows the Virgin and Child, with angels, in attitudes which reactivate the naturalism and painterly force of Giotto. Other panels from the same masterpiece are in Berlin, Naples, Pisa and Vienna. He is, with Brunelleschi and Donatello, one of the formative humanists, a link between Giotto and Michelangelo.

**mask stop** A 13th-century decorative ending to a dripstone or a hood mould. It was often carved to resemble a human face.

**masses** Fundamental shapes which, through their relationships and proportions, form the essence of a composition. Masses are therefore a work's most basic structure, and exist before any detail is added.

**Masson, André** (b. 1896) French painter. His studies were interrupted by the First World War, which left an indelible mark on his imagination, leading him towards Surrealism, and to experiments with 'automatic' drawing and painting. In 1940 he went to the United States, where his work and ideas influenced the painters of the New York School. After the war he returned to Paris, where he was active in the theatre.

**Massys, Matsys** or **Metsys** A family of Flemish painters consisting of Quentin (*c.* 1464–1530), Cornelis (*c.* 1510–70) and Jan (*c.* 1509–75). Of these, Quentin, the father, is the most prominent. He seems to have been familiar with Italian art, and certainly with that of Leonardo da Vinci. His paintings on religious themes have a sense of movement uncommon in Northern art, and his portraits combine likeness with a depiction of the sitter's function, as in his *Erasmus* (1517), sometimes with satirical effect.

Cornelis Massys painted landscapes peopled with peasants going about their daily tasks. Jan Massys, his brother, preferred scenes from Bible stories – *Lot and his Daughters, Susannah and the Elders* – with moralizing overtones.

**Master of . . .** The designation given to the works of an artist whose name is unknown, but whose style and quality may be identified in a single painting or place of work. The following are some typical examples: Master of Alkmaar (active 1490–1520), a Dutch artist sometimes identified as Cornelis Buys (d. 1520); Master of the Carnation (late 15th century), Swiss or German painter of altarpieces; Master of Flémalle (1378–1444), perhaps Robert Campin or Rogier van der Weyden; Master of Frankfurt (active 1480–1530), named after a tryptych at Frankfurt; Master of the Life of the Virgin (late 15th century), close to Rogier van der Weyden; Master of the Playing Cards (mid-15th century), engraver of an anonymous set depicting animals, figures and flowers; Master of the Virgin inter Virgines (late 15th century), a Netherlands painter probably working in Delft; Master of Wittingau (late 14th century), the unknown painter of Passion scenes and saints on double-sided panels of an altarpiece at Trebon, Czechoslovakia.

**Mathieu, Georges** (b. 1921) French painter. He was the originator of Abstraction Lyrique, the counter-movement against geometric forms in Abstract art. His own work is calligraphic, based on Eastern methods, in rapidly executed figurations of red, white, blue and black.

**Matisse, Henri** (1869–1954) French painter, the most important and influential of the Fauves. He was introduced to Impressionism in the late 1890s, experimented briefly with Pointillism, and in 1905 emerged as a colourist of unmistakable mastery. His flat planes of colour, often of clashing brilliance, made a sensational impact, not least on other young painters working in Paris, among them Rouault, Vlaminck, Derain, Dufy and Braque.

After 1910 Matisse began introducing the flowing arabesques of Near Eastern art which distinguish his work of the 1920s and which persisted, in decorative forms, into his later years. His achievement lies in his progress from the Fauvist use of colour as a dominant source of light towards a more structured manner, in which natural forms acquire a simplified grandeur akin to a sculptor, as he put it, 'cutting into living colour'.

**matroneum** In early Byzantine churches, a gallery over the aisle of a basilica reserved for women.

**mattoir** An implement used in crayon engraving and mezzotint to give tonal quality to the plate. It has a semi-spherical head on which are mounted a number of small spikes, irregularly arranged.

**meander** A geometric ornament in the form of a Greek key pattern.

**medium** The liquid in which pigment is ground in the manufacture of paint. However, the term is frequently used more broadly to mean the method in which an artist works. Oil painting, watercolour, gouache, pencil and chalk are all media in this sense; so are clay, bronze, stone and other materials. By extension in the same sense, it can also refer to the various forms of art: painting, drawing, or sculpture.

**Memling, Hans** (1435–94) German-born painter and member of the Flemish school. He is thought to have been a pupil of Rogier van der Weyden, in whose manner he worked, and stands comparison with Jan van Eyck for the technical delicacy of his detail and finish. His representation of the Mother and Child go beyond mere piety to a grave, ennobling serenity and grace, as in the *Donne Triptych* (National Gallery, London).

**Mengs, Anton Raffael** (1728–79) German painter. He established himself in Rome at an early age, to become a leading figure in the emergence of Neoclassicism. His father, a court painter at Dresden, prepared him for his career by naming him after Correggio and Raphael. He embraced the theories of Winckelmann, wrote his own treatise on the *Beauties of Painting* (1762), and studied the ruins of Herculaneum at first hand. His *Parnassus* (Villa Albani, Rome), painted in 1761, announces a break with the Baroque version of Illusionism, treating the subject as if viewed at eye level. He spent ten years in Spain as Court Painter,

returning to Rome to work in the Vatican, and in his last years gave way to Jacques-Louis David, with whom Neoclassicism well and truly arrived.

**Menzel, Adolf von** (1815–1905) German painter and illustrator, whose plein-air subjects have been regarded as precursors of Impressionism. He was trained as a lithographer and owed his livelihood to his graphic work, notably for a life of Frederick the Great, published in 1840–2.

**Meryon, Charles** (1821–68) French architectural etcher. His *Views of Paris*, from the 1850s, are among his most typically idiosyncratic work. Its manic, visionary quality sets him apart from all other architectural etchers except Piranesi, who was in some ways a kindred spirit. He died in an asylum.

**metal cut** An engraving made on metal which is nevertheless designed to be printed in relief. **Manière criblée** is one example.

**metope** The plain or decorated square space between two triglyphs in a Doric frieze.

**Metsu, Gabriel** (1629–67) Dutch painter, a 'little master' influenced by Rembrandt, Vermeer and Pieter de Hooch. His intimate studies of figures and interiors, and his still lifes and bourgeois genre scenes, often bear comparison with those of his more famous mentors.

**mezzo rilievo** see **relief**

**mezzotint** An intaglio method of engraving in tone, widely used during the 18th and 19th centuries for reproducing paintings. A copper plate is scored with a rocker, which creates a uniform burr over the whole surface. The design is formed by smoothing and polishing the areas which are to print lighter with a burnisher and scraper. The smoother the surface, the less ink it will take, so that mezzotint is capable of every tonal gradation from black to white. It can be combined with other techniques, particularly etching, and is characterized by a velvety surface richness and a pleasing softness of form. Being an essentially tonal as opposed to linear medium, mezzotint is especially well suited to making colour

**Mezzotint** *Scene in the Campagna*, a mezzotint for Turner's *Liber Studiorum*, which he embarked on in 1809, employing professional engravers.

prints. It shares with **drypoint** the limitation of being able to produce relatively few prints from each plate before the burr is destroyed by the action of the press. Its function was superseded in the 19th century by photoengraving and photogravure.

**Michelangelo,** born Michelangelo Buonarroti (1475–1564) Italian painter and sculptor, a master of the Italian Renaissance. A Florentine by birth, he learned the elements of fresco painting from Domenico Ghirlandaio and the techniques of carving from Bertoldo di Giovanni, who was employed by Lorenzo de' Medici, Michelangelo's first patron. When Lorenzo died in 1492, Michelangelo left Florence to work in Bologna and in Rome, where he created his early masterpiece, the *Pietà* in St Peter's. He returned to Florence in 1501, and in five productive years carved the great *David* (Accademia), painted the *Doni Tondo* (Uffizi

Gallery), and embarked on a series of sculptures of the Twelve Apostles for the Cathedral. His fresco for the Council Hall, commissioned to accompany another by Leonardo da Vinci, was never finished and is known only from copies.

He was entrusted by Pope Julius II with the task of designing and building the pontiff's tomb, which he eventually completed, in diminished form only, in 1545. His greatest painting commission, to decorate the ceiling of the Sistine Chapel, was carried out between 1508 and 1512. His *Last Judgement*, for the wall behind the altar, occupied him from 1536 to 1541. As chief architect of St Peter's from 1546 he was responsible for designing the original dome.

His last works include *Pietàs* which express his despair at man's relationship with God, and drawings of the Crucifixion which have the awesome immediacy of apparently being observed on the spot. Vasari's *Life* is a tribute to his intellect and genius.

**Millais, Sir John Everett** (1829–96) English painter who with Rossetti and Holman Hunt founded the **Pre-Raphaelite Brotherhood**. His prodigious talents as a young man brought early success and subsequent riches, though some of his works, such as *Christ in the Carpenter's Shop* (1850), were roundly disapproved of. His famous exhibition pictures, such as *The Blind Girl* (Birmingham City Museum) and *Autumn Leaves* (Manchester City Art Gallery) are once again admired as expressions of high-minded Victorian sentiment.

**Millet, Jean-François** (1814–75) French painter. A pupil of Antoine Gros and of Paul Delaroche, he joined Théodore Rousseau at Barbizon in 1849 and at once found the theme, peasant life, which was to possess him for the rest of his career. *The Sower*, *The Gleaners* and *The Angelus*, all in the Louvre, laid the basis of a huge popular success, despite the essentially austere nature of his subjects. His pencil drawings and his etchings after his own paintings are of particularly high quality.

**miniature** A term originally applied to pictures in illuminated manuscripts, but subsequently used to describe small, portable portraits, executed on vellum or card and mounted as a locket in a round or oval frame. Elizabethan miniature painting reached its height in the work of Nicholas Hilliard and his pupil Isaac Oliver. Its greatest vogue was during the 17th and 18th centuries, when Samuel Cooper and Richard Cosway were among the English masters of the form. Its legacy can be seen in the oval mounts which are commonly used in formal portrait photography.

**Minimal** or **Minimalist art** A term to describe art in which all expressive elements and all artifice are deliberately minimalized. Like Hard-Edge and Post-Painterly Abstraction, it is a manifestation of the desire for a stringently impersonal quality in art. Minimal art derives from two traditions: that founded by Malevich and the Suprematists, with their *White on White* and similar experiments, descending to the chromatic abstractions of Mark Rothko, Barnett Newman and Clyfford Still; and that of Marcel Duchamp and his **Ready-mades**, which insist on impersonality by denying the artist even the role of maker.

Minimal artists eschew the personal commitment of Abstract Expressionism, while inheriting from it a sense of scale, primacy of colour and all-over composition. Robert Ryman (b. 1930), David Budd (b. 1927), and Frank Stella are among the American artists associated with the Minimalist vein. Others have turned to a kind of perfunctory sculpture in their search for elemental clarity, such as Carl Andre with his *Fire Bricks* at the Tate Gallery. As the formal interest within their work has decreased, they have begun to explore the significant relations between the object and its environment. Thus Minimalist work is often produced with a particular space in mind: artists are as likely to use a gallery to mount an installation as an exhibition.

**Minoan** Belonging to the Bronze Age in Crete. The name is derived from the legendary King Minos.

**Miró, Joan** (b. 1893) Spanish painter. He belongs with his compatriots Picasso and Juan Gris and with Francis Picabia as an activist of the School of Paris. His Surrealist paintings of the 1920s include images from his native Catalonia. Later paintings, ceramics and sculptures make use of amoeba-like forms and dreamlike figurations, in a fastidious range of colours.

**misericord** A small ledge, often carved, found projecting on the underside of a hinged seat in the choir stalls to enable a chorister to rest during long services.

**mixed media** Prints or drawings combining different techniques or materials.

**mixed method** see **egg tempera**

**mobile** A form of Kinetic sculpture which is free-moving. It was invented by Alexander Calder in 1932 after a period of experimentation with manually driven Constructions, and christened by Marcel Duchamp. Most mobiles involve an arrangement of metal or wooden planes of various shapes, connected in delicate balance by rods and wires, the whole structure suspended in such a way that a breath of air or the touch of a finger will set it into motion. A stabile, another invention of Calder's, resembles a mobile in that it is made of metal sheets in abstract, curvilinear shapes, but these are bolted or welded together, and so immobile.

**Mobile** Alexander Calder: *Seven red, seven black, one white.*

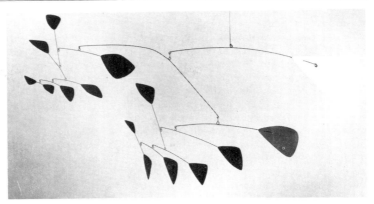

**modelling** In painting, drawing and engraving, modelling is the technique by which three-dimensional form is depicted on the flat surface in such a way that it appears solid. Linear media rely on **hatching** to realize such an effect. In painting it is achieved through the juxtaposition of areas of colour and the representation of light and shade.

In sculpture, modelling is the fashioning of plastic materials such as clay or wax to build up a form, and as such is the opposite of carving.

**modello** An initial version, though often highly finished, of a proposed painting or drawing submitted to a patron in the hope of a commission.

**Modigliani, Amedeo** (1884–1920) Italian painter and sculptor. He left Italy for Paris in 1906, where he spent the rest of his short life. A wonderfully gifted draughtsman, he devised a sinuous, linear style of painting which has associations both with early Mannerism and with African carving. His sculpture, encouraged by Constantin Brancuşi, one of his circle of friends and admirers, is distinguished by the same instinct and expressive form.

**Moholy-Nagy, László** (1895–1946) Hungarian-born artist. He studied in Berlin, spent five years teaching at the Bauhaus, and lived briefly in Amsterdam and London before emigrating to the United States to become head of the 'New Bauhaus' in Chicago. His artistic energies took him into photography, constructions, cinema and theatre as well as painting, in which he was associated with the art movements of the 1920s from **Suprematism** to **Dada**. His precepts and ideas have been more influential than his own works, which were essentially demonstrations of his notions of mobility in art and his lifelong preoccupation with systems of light.

**Mondrian, Piet** (1872–1944) Dutch painter, one of the foremost Abstract painters of the 20th century. He absorbed the Cubist experience before rejecting it for 'not accepting the logical consequences of its own discoveries', which he progressed as a founder of the **De Stijl** group. Within the group he pursued his personal view of pictorial structures as intrinsically real abstractions, needing no figurative elements in support. His Neoplastic paintings confine themselves to geometrical shapes and designs, predominantly right angles in white, black, red and grey. His characteristic grid-based compositions have had a lasting influence on commercial art. See **Neo-Plasticism** and **De Stijl**.

**Monet, Claude** (1840–1926) French painter, a pivotal figure in the Impressionist movement. He was befriended as a youth by Eugène Boudin, who encouraged him to take up plein-air painting. At Charles Gleyre's studio in Paris he met Frédéric Bazille, Renoir and Alfred Sisley, the nucleus of what was to become the Impressionist group.

In 1870 he fled to London to escape the Prussian advance on Paris, and met Camille Pissarro and Charles Daubigny. He discovered Constable and Turner, painted Westminster Bridge and, on returning to France, moved to Argenteuil, outside Paris, where he was joined by Renoir and Manet. His *Impression: sunrise*, shown at the friends' first group exhibition in 1874, gave rise to the term 'Impressionist' flung at them by a scoffing critic.

Monet's persistent attempts to catch on canvas the elusive qualities of light made much of his work incomprehensible to critics and gallery goers, but recognition slowly followed. By the end of the century, established as a modern master, he moved to Giverny, where his garden and lily ponds absorbed his creative energies for the rest of his life. With the Giverny paintings, Monet brought Impressionism to the brink of Abstraction.

**monochrome** A painting or drawing in various shades of a single colour. See **Camaieu**, **Grisaille**.

**monotype** A single print taken by painting a sheet of glass or metal with oil colour or printer's ink and then transferring the image, in reverse, on to paper. If the plate is of glass this has to be done by hand, but when etching plates or lithographic stones are used the impression may be taken on a press. Not all the colour is transferred to the paper during printing, and if further impressions are required the artist can repaint the plate, following the 'ghost' that is left after the first print is taken. However, inevitable variations in repainting and printing mean that no two monotypes will be identical. They are valued for the textural qualities that result from the pressure of printing. The technique has been used by Castiglione, Blake and Degas, among many others.

**Monro, Dr Thomas** (1759–1833) Physician, patron and collector. His collection included a number of Gainsborough drawings and examples of the work of the young artists who enjoyed his hospitality at evening sessions of copying and conversation. Among these were Turner, Thomas Girtin, John Robert Cozens, John Sell Cotman and others whose association under Monro's roof had mutually beneficial results.

Monro's own drawings, usually in black chalk or stump, are similar to those of Gainsborough in style and subject. 'Monro Family' drawings are of this kind, including sketches by his sons Edward, Henry, Robert, John and Alexander.

**montage** A technique in which pre-existing images such as those found in prints, photographs and magazines are cut out and arranged so that they overlap or join. Photomontage uses photographs only. All forms of montage differ from **collage** and **papier collé** in using only illustrative and representational cuttings, though the technique can readily be combined with any other.

**Montagna, Bartolommeo** (*c.* 1450–1523) Italian painter, who trained in Venice and later worked at Vicenza. His biblical subjects are noteworthy for their strongly modelled forms and solid backgrounds, often including rocks or architectural features.

**monumental** Art that is intended to commemorate something – a person, an event, an idea or religion – or which has come to stand for an epoch or civilization is called monumental. Picasso's *Guernica*, Rodin's statue of Balzac, the pyramids, Stonehenge and the Easter Island statues are all, in their degree, monumental works. The term is also used in art criticism to connote properties of dignity, high seriousness and enduring significance.

**Moore, Henry** (b. 1898) English sculptor. He trained at the Leeds school of Art and at the Royal College of Art, London, where he taught until 1932. A number of public commissions advanced his reputation in the 1930s, and he was awarded the international prize for sculpture at the Venice biennale of 1948. By then he had achieved a popular reputation with his *Shelter Drawings*, made during the bombings of London by the Luftwaffe. His reclining figures, semi-abstract forms, and groups in wood, stone and bronze, became familiar features of the open spaces in townscapes or, as with the nobly evocative *King and Queen* (1952), on remote upland sites.

Moore's vision is one in which the natural forms of landscape take on figurative meanings, from which are derived the locking shapes and tensile surfaces of his compositions. His drawings exhibit a corresponding insight into mass and space.

**Morandi, Giorgio** (1890–1964) Italian painter. He was born and worked in Bologna. Though removed from the turmoils of Paris, he nevertheless took an interest in the **Pittura Metafisica** of Chirico and Carrà, which influenced him briefly. His still lifes are in the traditional mode, sufficient for his private expression of the mysteries of form. He is also highly regarded as an etcher.

**mordant** The term in etching for the acid solution in which the plate is immersed in order to bite into those areas of the metal not protected by the etching ground, so creating the design. Dilute solutions of hydrochloric acid or nitric acid are commonly used. The word comes from the French *mordant*, meaning 'biting'.

**Moreau, Gustave** (1826–98) French painter of classical, biblical and literary subjects. His work shows a Symbolist romanticism that gives him a continuing relevance as precursor of Surrealism. Moreau said 'I believe only in what I do not see and solely in what I feel.' He retired from painting in about 1880 and was appointed Professor of Painting at the École des Beaux-Arts, where his pupils included Matisse and Rouault. His watercolour studies have been seen as anticipating Tachism and the Abstract Expressionist movement.

**Morisot, Berthe** (1841–95) French painter. She was a member of the Impressionist circle and a pupil of Corot. She exhibited at the Salon and in all the Impressionists' exhibitions except the fourth (1879). She suffered the same derision as the rest of the group, who defended her devotedly, and her work has a sunny insouciance which makes it often equal to the best of theirs. She was particularly close to Manet, who was her brother-in-law, and later to Renoir.

**Morland, George** (1763–1804) English rustic painter. He began exhibiting at the Royal Academy as a child of ten and achieved early success with his farmyard scenes, but practically ruined himself with unruly behaviour. His work was widely reproduced in softground and mezzotint by his brother-in-law William Ward (1761–1826), brother of James Ward RA. He helped to establish peasant scenes and picturesque squalor as fitting subjects for English taste. Some of his animal drawings have a rugged vigour.

**Morris, William** (1834–96) English artist and craftsman. He was the leading figure in the Arts and Crafts Movement. Originally apprenticed as an architect, he took up painting in sympathy with his friends in the **Pre-Raphaelite Brotherhood**, with whom he worked on the frescoes for the Oxford Union. His interests broadened into industrial design, interior decoration, wallpaper and furniture design, stained glass and printing. His Kelmscott Press (1890) set new standards of ornamental typography and hand-crafted book production, consistent with his devotion to medieval notions of the oneness of art and life. The modern world has proved too harsh a place for such ideas to prosper; but they nevertheless have a particular value in a mechanistic age.

**mosaic** The art of making pictures out of **tesserae** – small pieces of coloured glass, stone, marble, ceramic or wood – set in cement against the wall surface or on a floor, or on the concave surfaces of a dome or vault. Mosaic was first employed by Sumerians around 3000 BC, and later in Greek, Roman and other early civilizations. It was used as a means of decorating Early Christian and Byzantine churches and was widespread until the early 14th century, when it was succeeded by fresco and other forms of pigment decoration.

**Motherwell, Robert** (b. 1915) American painter, at one time a university academic. In the early days of Abstract Expressionism he was one of the founders of 'The Club', which became the forum for experimental artists and writers. He has described his own work as 'an effort to close the gap that modern men feel. Its abstraction is its emphasis.'

**motif** A visual theme, often recurrent.

**moucharaby** A defence balcony with a parapet over the entrance of a gate or medieval building.

**mouchette** A 14th-century curved dagger tracery motif.

**moulding** A modelling of the surface of any material in a profile carried along continuously so as to produce lines of light and shadow. The

finest mouldings have been produced by the Greek and English Gothic architects, for marble and stone respectively, and by the Italian Renaissance architects.

**Mucha, Alfons Marie** (1860–1939) Czech artist and poster designer. He was one of the leading figures in **Art Nouveau**. His designs, typically including women with loose, tendril-like hair, framed in ornate borders, are the epitome of fin-de-siècle decoration. His most ambitious work was a series of large paintings on patriotic Bohemian themes. They hang in Prague, where he worked during the latter part of his life.

**Muller, William James** (1812–45) English watercolour painter and a member of the **Bristol School**. Muller's precocious talents brought him local celebrity, and he was highly regarded by the leading English watercolour painters of the day, notably John Sell Cotman, whose influence is to be seen in much of Muller's earlier work. He made his name with subjects which he brought back from his travels to the Near East. Essentially an open-air sketcher, he ranks with the most adventurous watercolour painters of his time.

**mullion** A vertical bar dividing up a Gothic window into separate lights.

**multifoil** A foil with more than five arches of arc-shaped diversions.

**multiples** Quasi works of art produced by industrial processes in potentially unlimited quantities.

**Munch, Edvard** (1863–1944) Norwegian painter. He studied in Oslo and Paris, where he discovered Seurat, Van Gogh and Gauguin. His melancholic disposition inclined him towards Symbolism and Expressionism as vehicles for his mordant imaginings. These made a particularly strong impression in Germany, where his work was instrumental in fostering a native Expressionism hardly less neurotic than his own.

**Mosaic** *The Emperor Justinian*, detail from the mosaic in the Basilica of San Vitale, Ravenna.

**mural** A painting applied directly on to a wall or ceiling, rather than hung or secured. **Fresco** is the traditional technique used, though **oil painting**, **secco**, **casein**, **tempera** and **acrylic** are cheaper and less laborious methods.

**Murillo, Bartolomé Esteban** (1617–82) Spanish painter. He lived most of his life in Seville, painting religious compositions for churches and monasteries and simple figure subjects such as the *Beggar Boy* (Louvre) and the *Flower Girl* (Dulwich Picture Gallery). His directness and fluency earned him great popularity. The endearing nature of his subjects has concealed his real gifts, which include an unaffected naturalism expressed in softly modelled forms.

**Mytens, Daniel** (c. 1590–c. 1648) Dutch portrait painter, active in England from about 1615. By 1624 he was in the service of Charles I, who awarded him a life pension. A visit to the Low Countries in 1626 helped him towards the mastery evident in such works as the full-length *Duke of Hamilton*, 1629 (on loan to the National Gallery of Scotland).

**Nabis, The** A group of young painters who came together in Paris in 1888, and exhibited together between 1892 and 1899. They were converted to Gauguin's expressive use of colour when one of their number, Paul Sérusier, showed them a small painting he had done under Gauguin's guidance. They adopted their name from a Hebrew word meaning 'prophet', partly in fun and partly because they regarded the new kind of art as a mystical illumination.

Chief among the Nabis were Maurice Denis, Edouard Vuillard, and Pierre Bonnard and the composer Debussy was also a member of their circle. One of Denis's statements expresses a fundamental truth behind most subsequent painting: 'Remember that a picture – before being a war-horse, a nude woman, or some sort of anecdote – is essentially a surface covered with colours arranged in a certain order.' The Nabis found the naturalism in Impressionist painting distasteful (though Bonnard and Vuillard were to cultivate a modified Impressionist style when they turned to Intimisme) and painted in a Symbolist manner using flat, pure colours. They were not above acknowledging the decorative potential of their painting through which they became an influence in the growth of **Art Nouveau**.

**nailhead** Early English architectural decoration of small pyramids repeated as a band.

**Naive art** Unsophisticated, though not necessarily unskilled, modern painting. It is characterized by idealized, child-like and cartooned depictions of everyday scenes, linear composition, bright colour and close attention to detail. Masters of the genre include the Douanier Rousseau and American Grandma Moses.

**Nanni di Banco** (*c.*1384–1421) Florentine sculptor. He worked with his father, Antonio, on the Cathedral in Florence in 1406–7, and contributed a sculpture and a relief (the

*Assumption*) to the façade in 1408. His group of four martyred saints for the Or San Michele are based on antique Roman figures, but possess a fluidity of gesture that evokes his contemporary, Donatello.

**narthex** A shallow porch extending the whole width of the west end of a church. It is a common feature in early Christian churches, arising out of the practice of having an atrium as a forecourt to the church.

**Nash, John** (1752–1835) English architect. His command of the Neoclassical idiom was well suited to the tastes of Georgian England. In partnership with Humphrey Repton, the leading landscape gardener of the age, he designed numerous country houses, including Southgate Grove (1797) and Ravensworth Castle (1808, since demolished), making generous use of stucco. Regent Street and Regent's Park, London, were among his commissions, along with the restyling of the Royal Pavilion,

**Naive art** *Aerial Navigation*, an endearing example of the genre by the Douanier Rousseau.

Brighton, Carlton House Terrace, Trafalgar Square, and the original Buckingham House, later Buckingham Palace. He also conceived the model village at Blaise, near Bristol, an imaginative exercise in the picturesque.

**Nash, John** (1893–1977) English painter and wood engraver. He was the brother of Paul Nash, and a member of the London Group and the New English Art Club.

**Nash, Paul** (1889–1946) English painter. He studied at the Slade School and served in the infantry in World War 1 until being appointed a war artist in 1917, in which capacity he produced some of the most memorable images of the battlefield. After 1928 his work took on poetic and Abstract qualities. These, combined with the essentially English nature of his vision, give him an honoured place in the English pastoral tradition.

**Nasmyth, Alexander** (1758–1840) Scottish portrait painter. A pupil of Allan Ramsay, he later took to landscape painting after visiting Italy in 1782. He is also credited with the layout of Edinburgh's handsome New Town (1790).

**Nasmyth, Patrick** (1787–1831) Scottish landscape painter, the son of Alexander Nasmyth. He left Edinburgh in 1810, exhibited at the Royal Academy from 1812, and achieved popularity with works in the manner of the Dutch masters such as Hobbema and Ruysdael, translated into terms of the English countryside.

**Naturalism** A visual description of the natural world in straightforward and recognizable terms. Sometimes used incorrectly as a synonym for **Realism**.

**nave** The principal part of the interior of the early Latin church. In the medieval church it is the longest section west of the crossing.

**Nazarenes, The** A group of German artists sharing a devotion to primitive Christian art, who in 1810 established themselves as a 'brotherhood' in a deconsecrated monastery in Rome. They were Johann Friedrich Overbeck (1789–1869), Franz Pforr (1788–1812), Lud-

wig Vogel (1788–1879) and Johann Konrad Hottinger (1788–1828). The name 'Nazarenes' was applied to them, somewhat jocularly, when they attempted a revival of **fresco** painting as practised from the time of Giotto to Raphael. Their *Story of Joseph* (1816) and the frescoes in Laterano on themes from Dante and earlier classical writers (1822–32) were much admired. By this time they had been joined by other artists who shared their primitivist aims. The most notable of these was Peter Cornelius (1783–1867), who caught the eye of the future King Ludwig I in Munich, for whom he decorated the Glyptothek, completed in 1830.

The Nazarenes, sometimes referred to as the Lukasbrüder, or Brotherhood of St Luke, were forerunners of the **Pre-Raphaelites**, who knew of their work through the English religious and historical painter, William Dyce.

**nebule ornament** A Norman style of architectural decoration used on mouldings and consisting of a continuous wavy line.

**necking** A narrow moulding round the bottom of a capital and below the main shaft of the column.

**Neo-Attic** Used to describe the work of sculptors in Athens around 100 BC who copied and imitated earlier Greek sculpture for the Roman export market.

**Neo-Dada** A label applied to the work of Jasper Johns, Robert Rauschenberg and other American Pop artists in the early 1960s. Their work included or imitated banal, everyday objects in a way that seemed superficially similar to the travesties of the original Dadaists. But though influenced in formal terms by the Dada tradition, they shared little of its motivation, and the term is now rarely used.

**Neo-Impressionism** A term first used in 1886 by the critic Félix Fénéon to describe the movement initiated by Seurat in the wake of Impressionism, which adopted Divisionist techniques as its technical basis. As well as Seurat and Signac, its supporters included Henri-Esmond Cross (1856–1910), Charles Angrand (1854–1926), Albert Dubois-Pillet (1846–90), and Odilon Redon, all founder members of the Société des Artistes Indépendants in June

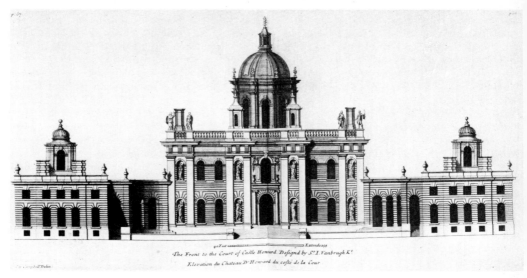

The Front to the Court of Castle Howard Defignd by Sᵗ I Vanbrugh Kᵗ

Elevation du Chateau Dʻ Howard du cofté de la Cour

**Neoclassicism** An elevated drawing of Sir John
Vanbrugh's design for Castle Howard (1699–1726).

1884. Pissarro was briefly a convert, with his
son Lucien. A group of Belgian painters under
the influence of Seurat's masterpiece, *La Grande
Jatte*, exhibited Divisionist works in Brussels
in ̇ 1887. Hippolyte Petitjean (1854–1929),
Maximilien Luce (1858–1941) and Lucie
Cousturier (1870–1925) carried the movement
into relatively modern times. An account of
their aims and ideas was published in Signac's
*From Delacroix to Neo-Impressionism*, 1899. See
**Divisionism**.

**Neo-Plasticism** An essentially Dutch movement that began in 1917, when Piet Mondrian
founded the magazine *De Stijl* with Theo van
Doesburg. Until 1924 the magazine was
devoted to the principles of Neo-Plasticism,
which was an attempt to create Abstract art
without reference to any objective reality.
Mondrian looked forward to a future which
would see 'the end of art as a thing separated
from our surrounding environment, which is
the actual plastic reality'.

The exploration of Neo-Plasticism has had
effects beyond painting: architects and
designers have found universal values in ̇ its
serene structures and impeccable line. See also
**De Stijl** and **Mondrian**.

**Neoclassicism** A generalized term for the
aesthetic movement in art and architecture
that sprang from the late 18th-century craze
for the antique. It was encouraged by exca-
vations of the ancient Greek and Roman world,
and by the writings of Johann Joachim Winckelmann (1717–68), the German art historian,
author of the *History of the Art of the Ancient
Peoples* (1764).

From Rome, Neoclassicism quickly spread
across Europe in the wake of Rococo and
Baroque. In English architecture it is to be
seen in the work of Robert and James Adam;
in France, in that of Jacques-Ange Gabriel
(1698–1782), Jacques-Germain ̇ Soufflot
(1713–80), Jean-François Chalgrin (1739–
1811), who built the Arc de Triomphe in Paris,
Alexandre-Théodore Brongniart (1739–1813)
and Claude-Nicolas Ledoux; and in Germany
in the designs of Carl Gotthard Langhans
(1732–1810), architect of the Brandenburg
Gate, Berlin. Winckelmann's view that in
imitating classical works artists should also
aspire to their high-mindedness and morality
led to the sentimental rhetoric of the Italian
sculptor, Antonio Canova (1757–1822), and to
the sugary allegories of the Swiss artist, Angelica Kauffmann (1740–1807).

In painting and drawing, Neoclassicism
embraces such disparate artists as Anton Raffael Mengs (1728–79), Giovanni Battista Piranesi, William Blake, Sir Benjamin West and

Jacques-Louis David, who carried the style to its ultimate in his glorification of the Revolutionary idea.

**Nervi, Pier Luigi** (b. 1891) Italian architect. His notion of 'static sensibility', combining technology with aesthetic values, distinguishes his most typical work. He is a master of reinforced concrete, which he moulds in sweeping arcs to achieve lightness with strength, as in his Exhibition Hall, Turin (1948–9), consisting of a single roof structure made of undulating units. His rhythmic sense of construction is to be seen in his design for the main railway station in Naples (1954) and in the Palezzetto dello Sport in Rome (1957).

**nervure** A secondary or side rib in a groin vault.

**net vault** A very heavily decorated rib vault used in the late Gothic period in Germany.

**Neue Sachlichkeit** A term coined in 1923 by the director of the Kunsthalle in Mannheim, as the title of an exhibition showing the development of post-war art in Germany. The 'New Objectivity' was distinct from the more abstract work of the **Blaue Reiter** and **Die Brücke** groups, in that it represented a sharp reaction against the dominant modes of Abstraction and Expressionism. Instead it offered a caustically literal, often satirical, image of the moral disintegration of post-war Germany. The leading practitioners of the style were Max Beckmann, Otto Dix and George Grosz.

Although reactionary in figurative terms, the Neue Sachlichkeit was one of the many inheritors of the nihilism of Dada. The leading literary representative of the movement was the playwright Berthold Brecht.

**Neumann, Johann Balthasar** (1687–1753) German Baroque architect. His major work, the Würzburg Residenz, was begun in 1719 and finished in 1750. In addition to a spectacular staircase turning through 180 degrees, it contains a huge fresco by Giambattista Tiepolo, which includes Neumann's portrait. His churches in the duchy of Franconia are among the finest achievements of German Baroque.

**neutral colour** A colour such as medium grey and brown that is neither hot nor cold.

**Nevinson, Christopher** (1889–1946) English painter. He was closely associated with the Futurists and with Vorticism. He trained in Paris, where he shared a studio with Modigliani, and in 1913 became a founding member of the **London Group**. His work as a war artist is interesting for its angular, Neo-Cubist designs.

**New Artists' Association** An association of artists formed in Germany in 1909, headed by Kandinsky, Alexei Jawlensky (1864–1941), and Gabriele Munter (1877–1962). However, the association could not keep up with its leaders and was fraught with internal ructions. Its exhibitions of 1909 and 1910 represented the German avant-garde and also included work by artists such as Picasso, Braque, Rouallt and Derain. But by 1911 its energy was spent. Kandinsky's exploration of Abstraction overwhelmed it and led to the secession of the **Blaue Reiter** group.

**New English Art Club** In 1886 a coterie of English artists, plus Whistler, set up in opposition to the encrusted conservatism of the Royal Academy. Their guiding spirit was Sickert, and their common bond was that they had nearly all worked or studied in Paris. Their

**Neue Sachlichkeit** *Night* (1918) by Max Beckmann, one of the leading exponents of the movement which sought to express a 'new objectivity' in their work (Kunstsammlung Nordrhein-Westfalen, Düsseldorf).

subject matter was unacademic, popular genre, painted in the plein-air manner of the Impressionists. They enjoyed the status of an avant garde, not always deservedly, until about 1912, when some younger members left to form the Camden Town Group, which later merged into the London Group. The New English Art Club did, however, include some distinguished painters at the peak of their careers, among them Sickert, Steer, Whistler and John. Degas, Monet and Berthe Morisot exhibited with them as guests.

**New Realism** The term is applied to two distinct and unconnected movements in post-war art. In France it was used by the critic Pierre Restany in 1960 to describe a number of artists who were rejecting traditional concepts of easel painting. Instead of applying pigment to canvas, they sought to adapt 'real' materials and existing objects, such as making arrangements of industrial artifacts or using hydraulic presses to squeeze scrap metal into sculptural forms.

In the United States, on the other hand, New Realism is the term describing the movement that emerged alongside Pop art in reaction against Abstract Expressionism, in which artists returned to the kind of subjects which characterize American Scene Painting, though in a later age. These show everyday scenes such as city streets, fast-food bars, neon-lighted shop fronts, and cars, sometimes sardonic but also celebratory of small-time affluence. New Realist painters such as Philip Pearlstein (b.1924) and Alex Colville (b.1920) work in a manner close to photographic exactness without, however, making use of photographs to achieve their effects. In this respect they are not to be confused or equated with the Super-Realists who have followed them. The younger generation of New Realist painters in America includes Richard Estes (b.1936), Robert Cottingham (b.1935), Lowell Nesbitt (b.1933) and Chuck Close (b.1940).

**New York School** see **Abstract Expressionism** and **Action Painting**

**newel** A post fixed at the top or bottom of a wooden staircase to carry the handrail. The word also refers to the central shaft of a spiral staircase. In Elizabethan and Jacobean mansions newel posts were often elaborately carved.

**Newman, Barnett** (1905–70) American painter. Together with Baziotes, Rothko and Motherwell he was a founder of 'Subjects of the Artist' and hence of the New York School. He took as his subject matter indigenous American myths and pre-Columbian art, using vibrating planes of colour to create an optical sense of space.

**niche** A recessed space in a wall used to display an ornament.

**Nicholson, Ben** (b.1894) English painter and sculptor, son of Sir William Nicholson who had been a founder member of the National Portrait Society. His work, originally influenced by Mondrian, combines Abstraction with a strong sense of figurative design, including constructions and relief. His *White Reliefs* of the 1930s are derived from Neo-Plasticism. Barbara Hepworth, the sculptor, was his second wife.

**Nicholson, Sir William** (1872–1949) English painter. He studied at Herkomer's School of Art, Bushey, and in Paris. With James Pryde he designed posters under the name The Beggarstaff Brothers. He exhibited at the New English Art Club, was a founder of the National Portrait Society, and was knighted in 1936. He was the father of Ben Nicholson, some of whose themes are reminiscences of objects in his father's still lifes.

**niello** A black compound of metallic alloys used to decorate metal surfaces. Worked into incised lines, it is fused there by heat, and then polished to leave the pattern in black on a burnished ground. The process played an important part in the development of **line engraving**, since goldsmiths would sometimes take a print from the niello so as to examine their design more clearly. During the late 15th century some Italian craftsmen took the logical step of engraving plates solely to take prints on paper.

**nimbus** see **aureole**

**Noguchi, Isamu** (b.1904) Japanese-American sculptor. An early associate of Constantin Brancuşi, he has combined elements of Eastern and Western art in free-standing sculptures conceived as objects in a landscape.

**Nolan, Sidney** (b.1917) Australian painter. Much of his work has been devoted to Australian myths and themes realized in dramatic or poetic terms. It includes his series on *Ned Kelly*, begun in 1946, *Fraser and Bracefell* (1948) and the *Explorer* series (1950) based on the adventures of Burke and Wills.

**Noland, Kenneth** (b.1924) American painter. His point of departure from the Abstract Expressionists is his sense of colour relationships, formalized and geometric, which interact with the angular shapes of the canvas to produce a sense of movement.

---

**Norman** Part of the interior of Durham Cathedral, showing the round-topped arches typical of Norman architecture.

**Nolde, Emil** (1867–1956) German Expressionist painter. He studied in Munich and Paris and eventually found his own way to Expressionism by way of Munch and Van Gogh. Although he was briefly a member of Die Brücke, he preferred to remain ouside formal schools and movements, using his sense of identity with primitive art as a source of creative energy. The violence and coarse emotionalism of his paintings are not so apparent in his watercolours, which may well be considered his true achievment.

**Nollekens, Joseph** (1737–1823) English sculptor. He first worked in Rome, returned to London in 1770 and quickly achieved a following, becoming an RA by 1772. His portrait busts include those of David Garrick, Laurence Sterne, Dr Samuel Johnson, Charles James Fox and Samuel Pitt.

**Norman** English architecture of the late 11th and 12th centuries in the style brought over from France by William the Conqueror. Edward the Confessor's Westminster Abbey

(dismantled in the 13th century) was the first such building. Other early cathedrals on a similar scale show many differences, also signs of different Continental origins than the purely French. The style is notable for solidity and roundness, the square and the circle, the weight of the structure being held by sheer bulk, giving a Norman church its characteristic stockiness. Barrel vaulting and the pointed arch help to open up the inner space. Windows and doors tend to be round topped. Secular carvings, often around outside doors, are strikingly vivacious and well made.

**Norwich School** An association of artists, professional and amateur, which flourished in Norwich during the first decades of the 19th century. The best-known of the English regional schools, it is remarkable for its attachment to East Anglian rural culture and scenery, and for having produced some of the most endearing masterpieces in English landscape painting. Its two leading figures are John Crome and John Sell Cotman, both of whom earned their living chiefly as teachers and drawing masters.

Crome, with Robert Ladbrooke (1770–1842), founded the Norwich Society of Artists in 1803. The first exhibition was held two years later with works by Crome, Robert Dixon (1780–1815), Charles Hodgson (1769–1856), Ladbrooke and John Thirtle (1777–1839), after which exhibitions were held regularly until 1825. They exhibited again in 1828 in a new gallery, part of the Norwich Corn Exchange, and continued until 1833 as the Norfolk and Suffolk Institution for the Promotion of Fine Arts. Under this broader title an increasing number of honorary exhibitors were invited, from prominent Royal Academicians to such well-regarded amateurs as Thomas Churchyard (1798–1865), the lawyer-artist of Woodbridge in Suffolk.

A second generation of Norwich School artists flourished into the 1860s and beyond, among them James Stark; Cotman's sons, Miles Edmund and John Joseph; Crome's sons, John Berney and William Henry; Alfred Stannard (1806–89); Samuel David Colkett (1808–63); David Hodgson (1798–1864); John Berney Ladbrooke (1803–79); Robert Leman (1799–1863); Thomas Lound (1802–61); John

Middleton (1827–56) and Henry Bright (1810–73).

**nymphaeum** Originally a Roman shrine dedicated to the nymphs; in later usage a court or small hall with a fountain.

**obelisk** A square, slightly tapering pillar with the angles rounded or canted inwards at the top to a central, pyramidal apex. An ancient Egyptian form, it is phallic in origin.

**objet trouvé** see **found object**

**O'Conor, Roderic** (1860–1940) Irish painter. He studied in Antwerp and Paris, and spent most of his life in France. At Pont-Aven he met Gauguin and members of his circle. His work bears strong signs of Symbolist influences from these contacts, which formed an important link between French and British artists of the age.

**octastyle** Denoting a structure, especially a portico, with eight frontal columns.

**oculus** A circular opening in the crown of a dome; a round window.

**odalisque** A female slave kept in an Eastern harem, and a favourite subject of 19th-century art.

**Odalisque** Dominique Ingres: *The Turkish Bath* (1862), a variation on the favourite 19th-century theme of the Eastern harem (Louvre, Paris).

**oeillet** A small opening in the wall of a medieval castle, through which missiles could be fired.

**oeuvre** An artist's total body of work.

**offset** The process of transferring a design from one surface to another, as when a counterproof is taken. In print making the term is used for an impression taken from an intermediary surface between the plate and the paper, so that the resulting proof is not reversed, but is identical to the original design. In offset lithography, for instance, a cylindrical rubber roller or blanket passes over the inked stone and picks up its impression, and in the same movement deposits the ink on to paper. Offset presses are almost exclusively used in commercial lithography, though artists also make use of them in pulling original prints.

**ogee** Moulding formed by two curves, the upper concave and the lower convex, forming together an S-shape and ending in a point. In Gothic vaulting the ribs that cross the vault diagonally are known as ogee ribs. See **keel arch**.

**ogival** The French term for a pointed arch and hence a general term, now obsolete, for French Gothic architecture.

**oil painting** The dominant easel-painting technique since the middle of the 16th century. The term refers to a variety of methods, each using different combinations of materials. It consists essentially of applying pigment which has been ground into a smooth paste in a medium of linseed, poppy or walnut oil to a non-absorbent ground, such as primed canvas. The paint can be thinned to a desired degree of fluidity by adding **diluent**, usually turpentine.

The technique of oil painting evolved in Italy during the 15th and 16th centuries. Only in modern times, with the invention of acrylic paints, has its supremacy been challenged. The traditional method of painting in oils is a laborious process, in which the initial drawing, sometimes done on a coloured ground such as **imprimatura**, is built up into a monochrome underpainting in which the picture's tonal values and balances are worked out. Only then is the first colour applied. This is done in glazes of transparent or semi-transparent colour, and by **scumbling**. Each layer modifies those beneath, and is in turn modified by them, as light is reflected up through the glazes from the last opaque layer laid down.

As interest in the textural and expressive properties of paint itself grew, so did the use of **impasto** and the attention to **brushwork**. Titian, Rembrandt, Rubens, and Velazquez all advanced their own styles of oil painting in this direction. However, it was not until the mid-19th century, when technological changes combined with a new spirit of spontaneity to give birth to alla prima, or direct painting, that paint handling and surface texture were accorded the importance they still hold today.

**O'Keeffe, Georgia** (b. 1887) American painter. She exhibited with Alfred Stieglitz (whom she married), at his 291 Gallery from 1916 onwards. Her work is Precisionist, isolating images from their natural context to give them a poetic intensity and drama.

**Oldenburg, Claes** (b. 1929) American painter, a pioneer of **Happenings** and of **Pop art**. His subjects are deliberately mundane, typically made of soft, vulnerable materials.

**oleograph** A simulated oil painting, superficially close to an original but achieved by mechanical means. The process, popular in the 19th century, consisted of printing in oil colours on a cloth board.

**Oliver, Isaac** (before 1568–1617) English miniaturist of Huguenot extraction. He learned his craft under Nicholas Hilliard, and succeeded him in fame and reputation. His manner, more naturalistic than Hilliard's, appealed to Jacobean courtly taste. He was appointed limner to Anne of Denmark in 1604 and later to the household of Henry Frederick, Prince of Wales.

**Oost** A Flemish family of painters active throughout the 17th century. The most prominent members were Jacob van Oost, known as The Elder (1601–71), his brother Frans (1595–1625), from whom he took lessons, and Jacob van Oost The Younger (1639–1713).

**Op art** One of Bridget Riley's creations, *Crest 1964*, bringing movement into a normally static medium (Peter·Stuyvesant Foundation, London).

**Op art** A form of Abstract art which is intrinsically unstable, exploiting geometric patterns and ambiguous effects to create an optical disturbance in the viewer. The artist's hand is not apparent in the means by which this is achieved. The origins of Op art lie in Constructivist techniques and in kinetic imagery of the kind introduced in the 1940s by the French artist Victor Vasarély (b. 1908). The English artist Bridget Riley (b. 1931), following his precepts, has carried Op art to the point where the identity or presence of the artist is obliterated by the picture.

**Opie, John** (1761–1807) English painter of portraits and genre. After a rural upbringing in the West Country he was taken up by a wealthy amateur, Dr John Wolcot, who introduced him to London society. In 1782 George III commissioned a portrait from him, and he was launched on a prosperous career. His 'fancy pictures' were popular, and led him to take up history painting. In 1806 he was elected Professor of Painting at the Royal Academy.

**Orcagna, Andrea di Cione** (*c.* 1308–68) Florentine painter, sculptor and architect. His altarpiece *The Redeemer* for the Strozzi Palace chapel in S. Maria Novella in Florence shows him reverting to the Byzantine manner of the preceding century. His decorations for the tabernacle at Or San Michele, Florence, are partly the work of assistants, including his brother Matteo. Orcagna (a nickname meaning 'archangel') achieved effects of an awesome kind, both as artist and supervisor, in work that is both Byzantine and Gothic.

**order** In Classical architecture, a term applied to the base, shaft, capital and entablature (with architrave, frieze and cornice) of a column. There are three Greek orders: Doric, Ionic and Corinthian. The Doric has no base and a fluted shaft. The Ionic has voluted capitals and canalized column shafts. The Corinthian has a fluted shaft and a bell-shaped capital with an ornamented acanthus. In addition to these three Greek orders there are two Roman ones: Composite, which includes elements of both Ionic and Corinthian; and Tuscan Doric, which is the plainest, most massive and least ornate.

**oriel window** A projecting window supported by a corbelled brick or stone construction and usually built on an upper floor.

**original print** A print made by an artist as an original work, as opposed to a mechanical

**Oriel window** *c* 1460

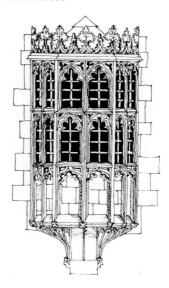

or photographic reproduction. Original prints are made by hand, the artist creating the image on a plate, block, stone, or screen (see **print making**) and often printing it himself.

**Orozco, José Clemente** (1883–1949) Mexican painter. His murals and fresco paintings were inspired by revolutionary fervour, patriotism, and strong humanistic beliefs. They include the *Catharsis* (Palacio de Bellas Artes in Mexico City), the *Allegory of Mexico*, frescoes for the Mexico City university and law courts, and the *Hidalgo and the Liberation of Mexico*, in the Government Palace at Guadalajara.

**Orders:** Corinthian order, Doric order, and Ionic order.

**Orpen, Sir William** (1878–1931) Irish painter. He studied in Dublin and at the Slade School. With Augustus John he supervised the Chelsea Art School. He joined the New English Art Club in 1900 and was a founder of the National Portrait Society in 1921. He served as a war artist in the First World War and was knighted in 1918. He was one of the most accomplished of the English Post-Impressionists, and moved easily in and out of the prevailing styles of the day.

**Orphism** A term coined in 1913 by Guillaume Apollinaire to identify a branch of **Cubism** that was being developed by Marcel Duchamp, Robert Delaunay, Francis Picabia and others. Apollinaire meant by it an art that was more abstract, more lyrical, and more concerned

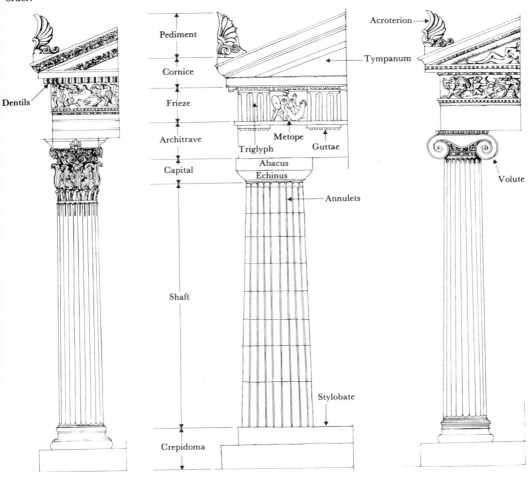

Dentils

Pediment
Cornice
Frieze
Architrave
Capital
Shaft
Crepidoma

Acroterion
Tympanum
Metope
Triglyph
Guttae
Abacus
Echinus
Annulets
Stylobate

Volute

with colour than Analytical Cubism. He described it as 'the art of painting new structures out of elements which have not been borrowed from the visual sphere, but have been created entirely by the artist, and endowed by him with the fullness of reality . . . This is pure art.'

**Os, Van** A Dutch family of painters consisting of Jan (1744–1808), his son Georgius Jacobus Johannes (1782–1861) and his daughter Maria Margrita (1780–1862). They were predominantly fruit and flower painters in the tradition of Van Huysum, for whose work theirs is sometimes mistaken.

**Ostade, Adriaen van** (1610–85) Dutch painter of genre subjects. A pupil of Franz Hals, he first specialized in bucolic low life and murky interiors, painted in sombre tones of brown. In later life his subjects brightened and his palette with them. He belongs to the tradition of Bruegel and Teniers as an observer of the human comedy. His etchings are highly prized.

**ottocento** The 1800s, that is, the 19th century.

**Oudry, Jean Baptiste** (1686–1755) French painter. He treated still life and sporting subjects in the Flemish manner originated by Desportes. He was made Court Painter to Louis XV and worked for the tapestry workshops at Beauvais, where he became Director, and for the Gobelins, for whom he designed an ambitious series of the royal hunt.

**Overbeck, Friedrich** (1789–1869) German painter. With Franz Pforr (1788–1812) and others he founded the *Lukasbrüder*, a fraternity of St Luke, from which emerged the Nazarenes. Their aspirations were similar to those of the English Pre-Raphaelites, who held Overbeck in high regard. His works include *Joseph Sold by his Brothers* (State Museum, East Berlin), the *Miracle of the Roses* (S. Maria degli Angeli, near Assisi), and the *Triumph of Religion in the Arts* (Frankfurt).

**overdoor** A transom architectural design set over a front entrance door. It is usually made of lead or wood mullions and paned with glass.

**overhanging eaves** The lower end of a sloping roof, projecting beyond the top of a wall to form an overhang.

**oversailing** Courses of stone or brick projecting beyond the face of the wall below.

**ovolo moulding** A wide convex moulding, forming in section a quarter of a circle or ellipse.

**Ozenfant, Amédée** (1886–1966) French painter and art theorist. He published his theories on Purism in the periodical *L'Esprit Nouveau*, which he edited jointly with Le Corbusier (then known by his own name, Charles-Edouard Jeanneret). His two volumes on the state of art, *The Balance Sheet of Modern Art* and *The Structure of a New Spirit*, are famous. He opened a school in London in 1935, but transferred to New York in 1938. His works are mostly on an heroic scale. *Life* and *The Four Races*, both in the Musée National d'Art Moderne, Paris, are the most spectacular.

**painterly** A term generally applied to highly competent brushwork and handling. It was given a special meaning by the Swiss art historian Heinrich Wölfflin in 1915, who used it to define painting which expresses form in terms of tonal masses, colour, light and shade. A painterly style is likely to employ the techniques of modelling and gradation rather than linear treatment, and its delineation of form is correspondingly less distinct. Painterly styles evolved with oil painting during the Renaissance. A short list of 'painterly' artists would include the great Venetians, Rembrandt, Fragonard, Constable and de Kooning.

**pala** see **altarpiece**

**palette** A thin oval or oblong board with a thumb hole at one end, on which a painter arranges and mixes the colours. It is usually of light wood, although many artists prefer to use glass, porcelain, enamel or marble slabs in preference to hand-held palettes.

The term can also refer to the spectrum of colours which an artist chooses to work with; thus a 'restricted palette' is one with only a narrow range of pigments arranged upon it.

**palette knife** A flexible metal spatula with a three- or four-inch blade. It is used for handling and mixing the paint on the palette as well as applying it to the canvas, usually as **impasto**.

**Palladian, Palladianism** Descriptive terms derived from Andrea Palladio (1508–80), the Venetian architect whose writings were a decisive influence on subsequent Italian architecture. Modelled on the ancient Roman, the style is distinguished for its monumental dignity. The church of S. Giorgio, in Venice, is an outstanding example.

Palladio's ideas and designs made their way into English architecture in the early 18th century through such admirers as Inigo Jones and Colen Campbell (d. 1729), who built Mereworth Castle, Kent, as an exact replica of Palladio's Villa Rotunda at Vicenza. Wilbury House, Wiltshire (1710) by William Benson

(1682–1754), who succeeded Wren at the Board of Works, is an early example of Palladianism. The third Earl of Burlington was also an enthusiast for the style and was responsible for Chiswick House, Middlesex, built for him by William Kent.

Characteristics of Palladian architecture are a Classical portico, small upper windows, and a severe, unadorned exterior. The style worked its way down into less ambitious dwellings such as the small town or country houses of squires and gentlemen, built for them by such architects as John Carr of York (1723–1807) and John Wood, father and son, of Bath (Wood *père* 1704–54 and John Jnr, 1728–81).

**Palladian window** A window design in three sections consisting of four columns and three windows. The two side windows have a straight cornice over the top and the centre window an arched cornice. It was very common in 18th- and 19th-century architecture in England.

**Palladio, Andrea** (1508–80) Italian architect. He began as a mason, and made visits to

**Palladian** The interior of S. Giorgio Maggiore, Venice, designed by Andrea Palladio and embracing his precepts of Classical form.

Rome from Vicenza, where he grew up, during the 1540s, later publishing a guide to the antiquities there. The Classical style was absorbed into his own, which combined airy symmetry with antique adornment. He built town and country palaces in the Vicenza region, making use of colonnades, loggias and bays to establish the dignity of spatial interiors. Sculptural or stucco decoration was often added, under his supervision, by Alessandro Vittoria (1525–1608) or by Paolo Veronese (1528–88) and his workshop.

Much of his finest work is in Venice. It includes S. Giorgio Maggiore, his most splendid non-secular building, and Il Redentore, which dates from shortly before his death. His precepts lasted into the 18th century, and were further extended by the admiration for Palladianism inherited by such English architects as Inigo Jones, William Kent and Robert Adam.

**palm vaulting** A fan-shaped decoration composed of narrow sections and resembling a palm leaf. See **fan vaulting**.

**Palma Vecchio,** Jacopo Negretti (c. 1480–1528) Italian painter. He was traditionally assumed to have been a pupil of Bellini. He worked in Venice, where the influence of Titian and Giorgione helped him towards a lyrical style of portraiture and figure painting, notably of female subjects. *The Reclining Venus* at Dresden is an elegant example. His grand-nephew, Palma Giovane (1544–1628), was among the artists commissioned to decorate rooms in the Ducal Palace, Venice, damaged in the fire of 1577. He worked in the studio of Titian, and is a representative of Venetian Mannerism.

**Palmer, Samuel** (1805–81) English painter, noted for the visionary landscapes of his Shoreham period. His meetings with Blake at an impressionable age set him on the path to a mystical lyricism in which forms, shapes and creatures from the natural world assume a potent magic.

At Shoreham he was joined by Edward Calvert, George Richmond and others in a community who called themselves 'The Ancients'. The 'Valley of Vision' inspired Palmer's most intensely Romantic work, painted in watercolour and gouache. His later career as a landscape painter obliged to satisfy the Victorian market was an anticlimax, except for a late series of etchings in which he recaptured the Shoreham experience in a dozen plates of mysterious beauty.

Rediscovered in the 1920s, he has remained a powerful influence on painters in the English pastoral tradition, among them Paul Nash and Graham Sutherland.

**palmette** A decoration resembling the fan-shaped palm leaf. A single palmette is often called an **anthemion**.

**panache** The area of a groined vault which lies between two ribs.

**pantile** A roofing tile which has an S-shaped curve enabling it to overlap the next tile.

**Pantocrator** The representation of Christ in Byzantine church paintings as the awesome ruler of the universe. Among the finest examples are the mosaic version in the 11th-century Monastery at Daphni, Greece, and the 12th-century mural in the Church of Panagia Tou Arakou, Cyprus.

**papier collé** A form of collage which employs, literally, pasted paper glued in layers.

**Papworth, John Buonarotti** (1773–1847) English architect. He was a leading exponent of Regency architecture; his monument is the town of Cheltenham. He gave himself the name Buonarotti in acknowledgement of a flattering comparison with Michelangelo.

**parallelism** see **Hodler**

**parapet** A small wall erected for protection at the sides of bridges, or above the cornice of buildings, especially where there is a flat or low-pitched roof. In Renaissance architecture parapets are usually designed with open panels filled up by balusters. Gothic parapets are often richly decorated with open-work tracery or with carving in panels.

**pargeting** Exterior plastering of a timber-framed building modelled in picturesque designs of flowers, leaves, figures or animals.

the *Madonna with the Long Neck*, in the Uffizi Gallery, Florence. This reflects the temperament which, in his last years, made him difficult to deal with. His style became widely known through his etchings and through reproductions of his work as engravings and woodcuts.

**Pasmore, Victor** (b. 1908) English painter. In 1937 he co-founded the Euston Road School whose early figurative work has given way to constructions and paintings which, while essentially Abstract, retain the formal qualities of basic design. His latest work puts the emphasis not on concept or subject but on the inherent nature of the painter's materials.

**pastel** A medium of coloured crayons, consisting of pigment mixed with just enough gum or resin to bind them. No vehicle is used, the colour being applied dry by rubbing. Its main disadvantage is that it sticks precariously to the ground, and must be held with a fixative. The technique is usually referred to as a painting rather than a drawing: although a stick is used, the colours are applied in masses rather than in lines. However, only the softest pastels truly resemble paint, giving a particularly rich and brilliant powdery texture to the picture surface.

Pastel painting was popularized by the Venetian painter Rosalba Carriera, who introduced the technique to France in the 1720s. It has remained a predominantly French medium, from Maurice Quentin de La Tour (1704–88) to Degas.

**pastel manner** An 18th-century engraving technique which developed out of crayon engraving, and to which it is similar in execution. It differs only in that the prints were designed to imitate the appearance of a pastel drawing rather than chalk or crayon, and so had to be multi-coloured. Several plates were made from the key (see **colour prints**) and over-printed. Like crayon engraving, the pastel manner was rendered obsolete early in the 19th century by the development of lithography.

**pasticcio** An imitation of an artist's work which, while not a direct copy, combines characteristics of his style, giving the appearance of an original.

**Pargeting** Decorative plasterwork on houses in Saffron Walden, Essex.

**Paris, School of** Usually taken to mean the entire body of work done in Paris from around 1912 to 1939, when the city was the acknowledged centre of argument and innovation in the arts. The term is sometimes used more narrowly to refer to the semi-abstract styles which were a persistent feature of the period. The description is useful only in a broad and uncritical context: strictly, there is no such thing as a 'School of Paris'.

**Parmigianine,** otherwise Francesco Mazzola (1503–50) Italian Mannerist painter. Born in Parma, he was commissioned while still in his teens to decorate the south transept of the cathedral. He was in Rome a year later, and managed to escape during the Sack of Rome (1527) to Bologna, where he painted his *S. Rocco with a Donor* in the Basilica of S. Petronio.

Returning to Palma in 1531 he was again busy with ecclesiastical commissions. His style was by now highly individual, marked by tapering lines and rhetorical attitudes, as in

**pastiche** A picture made up of borrowings from a superior original.

**pastophory** In early Christian and Byzantine churches, a chamber that served as a secondary room, for use as a vestry or storeroom or for the reception of suppliants.

**patera** In Classical architecture, a small, flat, circular or oval ornamentation, sometimes decorated with rose petals or acanthus leaves.

**patina** An incrustation, usually greenish, which forms on the surface of copper and bronze as it ages. Since the Renaissance, it has been valued for its own sake, and attempts have often been made to encourage patination artificially. By extension, the term has come to mean the enhancing effects on all hand-made objects as they mellow with age.

**Paxton, Sir Joseph** (1803–65) English architect. He began as a gardener, served the sixth Duke of Devonshire, and became a fashionable landscape gardener before turning to architecture. He is best known for the Crystal Palace, built for the Great Exhibition of 1851 and the largest structure ever erected up to that time, which made use of principles he had developed in designing horticultural buildings such as the Great Conservatory at Chatsworth, and which were also used by Decimus Burton (1800–81) for the Palm House in Kew Gardens in 1844.

**Peale, Charles Wilson** (1741–1827) American portrait and still-life painter. After two years in London under his compatriot, Benjamin West, he returned to found the first American art school and subsequently, following the War of Independence, the first art gallery, where he showed his own work.

His sons were given names such as Raphaelle, Rembrandt, Titian and Rubens, and a daughter was christened Angelica Kauffmann. Titian, Rubens and Rembrandt Peale all became painters. Rembrandt's mural, *The Court of Death*, enjoyed a popular success when it went on tour. His portraits, though not as accomplished as his father's, show a genuine talent.

**Pechstein, Max** (1881–1955) German painter. He joined Die Brücke in 1906, travelled in Italy and France, and in 1910 founded the New Secession (see **Sezession**) in Berlin. His paintings are less distorted and agonized than most Expressionist work, and deal with homely subjects, including beach scenes and still lifes. The most persistent influence on him was probably Matisse.

**pediment** The triangular figure or gable formed by the horizontal and the two raking cornices at the end of a Greek or Roman temple. From the time of the Renaissance the pediment came to be regarded as an ornament to be used over doors and windows.

**pele-tower** A small tower or building used as refuge against sudden attack, once common in northern England and Scotland.

**Pellegrini, Giovanni Antonio** (1675–1741) Venetian painter, pupil or follower of Sebastiano Ricci. His travels in Europe, including England, helped to spread the Venetian decorative style with its Rococo sprightliness and Illusionist light.

**pellet ornament** Norman and Gothic architectural decoration which resembles flattened balls or disks.

**pellicle** The film or skin which forms on the surface of oil pigment as it dries.

**pencil** Until the end of the 18th century, the word 'pencil' referred to a small brush, and 'pencilling' to brushwork. Sticks of natural graphite and some crude manufactured 'lead' pencils were also in use, but it was only in the late 1790s when a means was found of varying the hardness of graphite in manufacture that the pencil became the draughtman's universal tool.

**pendant** Either one of a pair of paintings. In architecture, a hanging elongated boss, often suspended from a fan vault.

**pendentive** The triangular section of concave masonry that transmits the weight of a circular dome to four corner supports.

**pent roof** A single-angled roof; lean to.

**pentimento** An Italian word meaning 'a repentance', used of visible evidence of a painter's change of mind, or mistake, in a picture. It sometimes happens that a feature that has been painted out during the execution of the painting begins to make a shadowy reappearance.

**Performance art** The enactment of a Happening before an audience, either by bodily action or by mechanical means. Performance art therefore embraces the function of both Body art and Happenings.

**peristyle** A colonnade inside a courtyard or room or round a temple.

**Perpendicular** The last phase of Gothic architecture in England, following the Decorated period in the 15th and early 16th centuries. It is characterized by vertical lines of tracery, which give an appearance of slenderness to the structure; large windows, elegant carving, rib vaulting carried into the greater delicacy of fan vaulting, and soaring buttresses. The hammer-beam roof is also typical of the period, often standing out as the supreme achievement of a single building. Mouldings, foliage and fancifully decorated battlements add to the good-humoured dignity of the Perpendicular style. It is summed up to perfection in King's College Chapel, Cambridge.

**perspective** A system for representing three-dimensional spatial recession of the two-dimensional **picture plane**. It can also be used in forms which employ a shallow depth, such as relief sculpture. Perspective is a fundamental element in Western representational art, and its development is broadly synonymous with that of geometrical optics from the time of Euclid. It seeks to imitate the photographic image, or that of the **camera obscura**, and in so doing to reproduce the way we see the world, although recent work by psychologists suggests that our visual perception does not conform exactly to the principles of geometric perspective. Most modern methods are versions of **Costruzione Leggitima**, based on the fact that although parallel lines never meet, they appear to do so as they recede to the vanishing point. Early systems were constructed around a single, central vanishing point; later ones employed several in the interests of greater veracity. Most painting of this century either abandons pictorial depth altogether or creates its own internal, independent, spatial relationships.

Aerial perspective has nothing to do with geometry, but with the fact that the atmosphere tends to make distant colours appear cooler or bluer than those in the foreground. Illustration of this atmospheric effect gives an illusion of recession to a painting.

**Perugino,** otherwise Pietro Vannucci (*c.* 1445–1523) Italian painter. Originally from Umbria, he first worked in Florence, where he acquired the new-found skills of oil painting from Verrocchio. By 1481 he was painting frescoes at the Sistine Chapel with Botticelli and Ghirlandaio. His numerous paintings of the Madonna and Child display the prettiness which was to endear him to the Pre-Raphaelites 400 years later. On a grander scale he stands with the masters in the transition from Early to Late Renaissance art.

**Peruzzi, Baldassare** (1481–1536) Italian architect of the High Renaissance. Born in Siena, he went to Rome in 1503 to work with Bramante on his designs for St Peter's. An early masterpiece is the Villa Farnesina, started in 1508, with frescoes by Raphael, Giulio Romano, and Sodoma, as well as his own. He succeeded Raphael as architect of St Peter's, took refuge in Siena after the sack of Rome in 1527, and returned to carry out his last work, the Palazzo Massimo alle Colonne, which he finished in the year of his death.

**photo-engraving** A commercial printing process which uses an etched plate but prints it in relief. A photographic negative of the original design is printed on a sensitized metal plate. This is then coated with a special powder which adheres only to the photographic image, and which when heated forms an acid resist on those parts of the plate which make up the design. This is then etched (see **etching**) in the normal way, the difference being that it is the parts of the plate which will carry the ink that are protected by the resist, instead of the other way round. The plate is then inked and printed

in relief – differing in this respect from photogravure, which is an **intaglio** method of reproduction.

**photogravure** A commercial printing process, noted for high fidelity. The design to be reproduced is photographed through a very fine screen on to a metal plate. The screen divides the image into a series of regular, equal-sized, minute areas, and the plate is then treated in such a way that, when it is etched, the acid will bite to a depth in accordance with the degree of tone that each of the tiny areas is required to print. The process differs from photo-engraving in being an **intaglio**, not a **relief** printing technique.

**Picabia, Francis** (1879–1953) Cuban-Spanish artist, born in Paris. He belonged to the main art movements of the early 20th century, from Cubism to Dada, without establishing himself as an artist with an individual style. His main interest is as a lively participator in avant-garde happenings, and as a catalyst for more single-minded talents.

**Picasso, Pablo Ruiz** (1881–1973) Spanish painter, sculptor, ceramic artist and print maker. Born in Málaga, he spent most of his life in France, where he engaged in a lifelong campaign to reshape art around the human form and psyche as seen through his highly individual, but essentially Catalan, mind. In the process he drew on the achievements and images of artists of all schools and ages, from cave paintings and African carvings to Velazquez, Delacroix and Manet.

Many of his themes, such as the bullfight, the artist and his model, and the lover watching over a sleeping mistress, recur over the full span of his working life, from his earliest days in Paris to the exuberant last decade. After the Blue and Rose periods, tinged with introspective melancholy, he turned the lessons of Cézanne into a new form, **Cubism**, in partnership with Braque. Meanwhile, he was working out the disfigurations of *Les Demoiselles d'Avignon*, with its seemingly destructive energies, only to revert in the 1920s to a variety of Neoclassicism.

His sculptures and prints followed the same zig-zag course, opening up new possibilities from old forms. His isolated masterpieces, such as *Guernica* and the *Vollard Suite* of etchings, both from the 1930s, contain autobiographical elements which are common to all his work. Few painters, in any century, have so dominated their time.

**picture plane** The surface area of a painting. In much modern art, the picture plane is deliberately flattened so as to bring the images and colours right up to the spectator. Recession from the surface is achieved primarily by **perspective**, including diminution of objects placed further back in the composition.

**Picturesque, The** Originally a standard of taste developed during the 18th century, it amounted to an aesthetic category in the appreciation of pictorial experiences, whether in painting, architecture, literature or nature. Its essential quality was the irregularity of unspoiled scenery, as opposed to the orderly, idealized visions of Poussin and Claude. Its propagandists included William Gilpin (1724–1804), Richard Payne Knight (1750–1824) and Uvedale Price (1747–1829), whose *Essay on the Picturesque*, published in 1794–98, helped to advance the concept of romantic rusticity that persisted into the late 19th century. The term has lost its earlier connotations, and now serves as a tag for conventionally paintable – or photographable – scenery.

**pier** In Gothic architecture, the built-up vertical structure from which an arch springs, distinguished from a column by the fact that it is not a cylindrical or octagonal shaft. The term is also used to describe the uninterrupted vertical masses of wall in any building, in contradistinction to the portions of the wall that are pierced with openings.

**pier arches** In a Gothic building, the arches situated between the nave and the aisles.

**Piero della Francesca** (*c.* 1410–92) Italian painter. Born in Tuscany, he worked outside Florence all his life. Works by him are to be found in Rimini, in Rome and in Urbino, where

**Perpendicular** The great cloisters at Gloucester Cathedral, showing the tracery and fan vaulting characteristic of the Perpendicular style.

he is thought to have painted the extraordinary *Flagellation* under the patronage of Duke Federigo da Montefeltro, who had invited him to the city. His biggest project was the decoration of S. Francesco, Arezzo, which occupied him from 1452 to 1459. On a further visit to Urbino he painted the double portrait of Federigo and his wife Battista, a diptych, now in the Uffizi Gallery in Florence. His *Sinigallia Madonna* at Urbino is remarkable for placing the Virgin in a domestic setting, after the manner of the Flemish master, Rogier van der Weyden, whom he may have met in 1449.

His painting has a breadth and intelligence which challenge the mind, posing questions which can only be answered within the mysterious formality which is a feature of his work.

**Piero di Cosimo** (*c*.1462–1521) Italian painter of the Florentine School. He is thought to have assisted Cosimo Rosselli, his master, on the Sistine Chapel frescoes. His religious paintings are often remarkable for their sentiment, as in the *Madonna and Child Reading a Book* (Stockholm) and the *Madonna and Child with a Dove* (Louvre). His other work is rich in mythological fancy and in images from Piero's imagined version of man's primitive past, such as the *Fight between the Lapiths and the Centaurs* (National Gallery, London).

**Pietà** A representation of the Virgin supporting the dead Christ.

**Pietro Berrettini da Vortona** (1596–1669) Italian painter and architect of the High Baroque. He was patronized by the family of Pope Urban VIII, the Barberini, for whom he painted the magnificent ceiling for the Barberini Palace (National Gallery, Rome). He subsequently painted frescoes in the Pitti Palace, Florence, and in the Chiesa Nuova, Rome, as well as providing cartoons for mosaics at St Peter's. As a force in the Roman High Baroque, he stands with Bernini.

**pilaster** An imitation of the Classic column and capital in the form of a flat, rectangular projection from a wall. It is the essential character of a pilaster that it forms part of the wall. Pilasters were often used by Renaissance architects, and are still employed as a means of giving architectural dignity and expression.

**pinnacle** A small, upright structure, usually pyramidal or cone-shaped, forming a decorative finish to buttresses and spires. It is also seen as the angle finish to towers, especially in architecture of the late Gothic period.

**Pinturicchio, Bernardino di Betto** (*c*.1454–1513) Italian painter of the Umbrian School. He worked with Perugino in Siena, and again in Rome, on the Sistine Chapel. Also in Rome, he decorated Pope Innocent's apartments at the Villa of the Belvedere and the Borgia rooms in the Vatican.

**Piper, John** (b.1903) English painter. A modern Romantic, his work has moved from two-dimensional Abstraction to topographical naturalism. As a war artist during the Blitz he revealed his deep sympathy with architecture. It plays a prominent part in his painting and

**Pietà** The *Pietà* of Michelangelo, completed about 1500, a sublime expression of the composite attainment of 15th-century Florentine art (St Peter's, Rome).

print making as a focus for his strong, sometimes theatrical, designs.

**Piranesi, Giovanni Battista** (1720–78) Italian etcher and architect. Born in Venice, he went to Rome to study engraving under Matteo Luccesi (1705–76) and then embarked on a series of topographical etchings of the city. His feeling for the subject enabled him to raise his task to heights of creative brilliance, making dramatic use of light and shade to achieve his effects. In his 'Prisons' series (*Carceri d'Invenzioni*), 1745, he invests the subject with an almost Surrealist fancy. His etchings carried an image of classical Rome far beyond the city, and were influential in forming the English taste for Neoclassicism.

**Pisano, Nicola da** (d. 1280) and **Giovanni** (d. *c.*1314) Italian sculptors and architects. Nicola, with a studio and workshop in Pisa, was influential in carrying the Romanesque style into the early Gothic.

His son Giovanni worked in Siena as master mason of the Cathedral and later in Pisa, where he is thought to have met his namesake Andrea Pisano (*c.*1290–1348), a mason of equal skill who became master of the works at Orvieto Cathedral in 1347. Giovanni, in particular, paved the way for the Gothic splendour of the trecento. Arnolfo di Cambio (d. 1302), the designer of Florence Cathedral, was Nicola Pisano's pupil.

**piscina** A small basin in a niche near the altar in a church, used for washing the sacramental vessels.

**Pissaro, Camille** (1830–1903) French Impressionist painter. Born in the Virgin Islands, he was sent to Paris to study for a business career, but in 1855 he enrolled at the École des Beaux-Arts and at the Académie Suisse, where he was a contemporary of Monet. Lessons from Corot encouraged him to take up plein-air painting. In 1870 he fled to England to escape the Prussian advance on Paris. He met Monet there, and also Durand-Ruel, a young dealer who became a staunch supporter of the Impressionist group.

Back in France he developed the pure Impressionist style for which he is known, though not without a brief flirtation with Pointillism, urged upon him by Seurat and Signac. He was particularly close to Cézanne during that lonely painter's formative years. All the Impressionists honoured him, as both sage and friend.

His son Lucien (1863–1944) exhibited with the Impressionists in 1886 but afterwards settled in England, where he became a member of the Camden Town Group and of the London Group.

**pitched roof** A roof which slopes at an angle of 20 degrees or more from the horizontal.

**Pittura Metafisica** A short-lived movement which flourished during 1917, formed by Giorgio de Chirico and Carlo Carrà (1881–1966) out of dissatisfaction with the functionalism of Cubism and Futurism. The two met while convalescing in Northern Italy, and together started painting in an enigmatic style that paved the way for German Magic Realism and French Surrealism.

**planographic printing** One of the three major print-making methods, the others being **relief** and **intaglio**. Planographic, or surface printing, was a term invented to characterize lithography, a process in which proofs are pulled from a surface which is neither incised nor raised in relief, but perfectly flat.

**plaster cast** Sometimes a finished work of sculpture, but more often an intermediate stage in its production. There are a number of methods of making moulds for plaster casts, but they share the same basic principles. The first step is to divide the initial model, usually of clay, into as few separate sections as possible, allowing for the halves of the mould to be lifted off easily. A thin coating of tinted plaster of Paris is applied to the model, then a thicker one of plain plaster. Once dry, the sections of the mould are removed, – often with some of the clay adhering to them, which has to be cleaned out – and the inside surfaces are then smeared with oil to stop the cast from sticking. After the sections of the mould are reunited, more plaster is poured into the open base, and when this has hardened the mould is chipped away. All casts need a certain amount of finishing, especially along the seams that mark the places where different sections of the mould have been joined.

**plastic** An adjective describing the impression of mass and movement.

**plasticity** The malleable property of certain solid materials, such as clay or wax, that enables them to be modelled into different forms. Oil paint also has plasticity in this sense, and the term is sometimes applied to its capacity for suggesting three-dimensional form.

**plate mark** The impression left by the edge of a block or plate when a print has been put through the press. It is therefore an indication that the print is pulled from an original plate, as opposed to a reproduction. However, a plate mark can be artificially impressed into the paper to simulate an original impression.

**plateresque** In Spanish architecture of the 16th century, an ornate style serving no functional purpose.

**plein air** A term used of painting done out of doors, or which evokes the feeling of the open air. Changing tastes, and the invention of easily portable artists' materials, led to the increasing popularity of outdoor **alla prima** painting from the first quarter of the 19th century. Complete pictures could be finished on the spot, instead of being worked up in the studio from rough sketches. Some of the first to adopt the technique were Constable, Corot and the painters of the Barbizon School. The pleinairistes, as they were sometimes called, were a group of Impressionists of the 1880s and the 1890s, notably Monet, Pissaro, Sisley and Renoir.

**plinth** A plain surface of masonry below the base moulding of a building, pedestal or column, which forms the base of the complete structure and connects it with the ground. Sometimes a plinth is formed, without any moulding, by slightly projecting it beyond the plane of the wall above it.

**plinth block** A small block of wood used at the bottom of a door trim.

**pochade** A quick oil sketch, done out of doors, as a study for a more finished work to be executed in the studio.

**pochoir** French for stencil. The word is also used of a stencilling technique used for making multi-coloured prints, or colouring and tinting black-and-white reproductions and book illustrations.

**podium** A high basement of a temple or other building, having its own plinth, base-mould and small cornice. Roman temples were often elevated on a podium, with a flight of steps leading up to the entrance door. The special character of the podium is that it is a basement with a vertical face, as opposed to the stepped base of a Greek temple.

**Pointillism** Inseparable from **Divisionism** and **Neo-Impressionism**. See also **Seurat** and **Signac**.

**pointing** A method of realizing a three-dimensional model, usually a plaster cast, in stone or some other carving medium. The sculptor takes a series of measurements from three fixed points on his original model, relating the location of all its principal features to them. Masons working from these measurements then reproduce the work in stone, leaving the finishing touches to the sculptor.

Many different systems have been used since the technique was first developed by the ancient Greeks. In the early 19th century a pointing machine was invented which mechanized the whole process. From then until the early years of this century, most stone sculpture was produced in this way. Modern sculptors, however, more concerned with the expressive properties of their chosen medium, prefer direct carving.

**Poliakoff, Serge** (1906–69) Russian Abstract painter. He studied in Paris and London, eventually settling in Paris as an associate of Wassily Kandinsky and Jules Delaunay. After his first one-man show in 1945, he became increasingly prominent in the School of Paris. He brought the explorations of the earlier Abstract painters to a point where colour exists as both form and subject, divorced from any naturalistic origin.

**Pollaiuolo, Antonio** (c. 1432–98) and **Piero** (1441–96) Florentine brothers who worked as painters, sculptors, goldsmiths and engravers.

Antonio worked with Verocchio on the *Silver Altar* of the Cathedral at Florence. His *St Sebastian* (National Gallery, London) and his engraving *Battle of the Nude Men* show a heightened understanding of anatomy.

Piero was a pupil of Andrea del Castagno, whose influence is apparent in both brothers' work. Lorenzo de' Medici declared Antonio to be 'the premier artist of Florence'. The *Tomb of Pope Innocent VIII* and the *Tomb of Pope Sixtus IV*, both in St Peter's, Rome, are the brothers' last works.

**Pollock, Jackson** (1912–56) American painter, one of the leading Abstract Expressionists of the 1950s. Early in his career he was influenced by the colour and passion of contemporary Mexican artists, such as Orozco, to which he added Surrealist elements. Carrying Automatism to unprecedented limits, he then evolved the methods of Action Painting: dripping and splashing and working without brushes on huge canvases lying flat on the ground. The effect, a contrived chaos, can have inadvertent forms and rhythm.

**polymer** see **Acrylic Paint**

**polyptych** see **altarpiece**

**pompier** French for fireman, and also the nickname for a particularly pompous tradition of French Neoclassicism. Its origins lie in the posing of male nude models wearing a fireman's helmet in imitation of ancient Greek warriors, in the style of David.

**Pont-Aven School** A company of painters working in Pont-Aven, Brittany, in the 1880s under the influence of Paul Gauguin. His simplified forms and intense colours set them free, as Maurice Denis put it, from the 'ball and chain' of copying nature. The Pont-Aven artists included Emile Bernard (the true originator of the Pont-Aven style), Francesco Mogens Ballin (1871–1914), Charles Laval (1862–94), Claude-Emile Schuffenecker (1851–1934), Jacob Meyer de Haan (1852–95), Wladyslaw Slewinski (1854–1918), Paul Sérusier (1864–1927), Armand Séguin (1869–1903), Maurice Denis, Charles Filiger (1863–1928), Jan Verkade (1868–1946), Henry

Moret (1856–1913), Henri-Ernest de Chamaillard (1865–1930), Maxime Maufra (1861–1918), Gustave Loiseau (1865–1935), Emile Jourdan (1860–1931), Jens Willumsen (1863–1958) and Roderic O'Conor (1860–1940). Robert Bevan (1865–1925) was the sole British member of this multi-national community, who together shaped a new style in art, Syntheticism.

**Pontormo, Jacopo** (1491–1556) Italian painter, whose elegant and excitable style hastened the growth of Mannerism in Florentine art. A pupil and assistant of Andrea del Sarto, he was also influenced in the course of a fluctuating career by Dürer, Leonardo da Vinci and Michelangelo. He was commissioned to decorate the hall of Lorenzo de' Medici's villa at Poggio a Caiano (1520) and to paint a sequence of frescoes depicting the *Passion* at S. Lorenzo al Monte at Galluzzo. His *Deposition* at S. Felicita, Florence, is regarded as one of his finest and most typical works.

**Pop art** A movement that emerged in the mid 1950s, based on the throwaway imagery of the affluent society. The name covers a wide range of different modes and intentions, with a common interest in the iconography of the mass media and consumer culture. Pop art has been described by the American painter Roy Lichtenstein as 'an involvement with what I think to be the most brazen characteristics of our culture: things we hate, but which are also powerful in their improvement on us.'

Generally speaking, however, painters in America have taken a less respectful view of Pop art than those in Britain, where the term originated. It was coined by the English critic Lawrence Alloway during the course of a series of meetings of the Independent Group at the Institute of Contemporary Arts in London, 1954–5. It was out of these meetings, which were called to discuss fashion, the mass media and commercial design, that the kernel of the British Pop art movement grew. Eduardo Paolozzi (b.1924) and Richard Hamilton (b.1922) were two of the original innovators. Later adherents to the style included David Hockney (b.1937), R. B. Kitaj (b.1932), Allan Jones (b.1937), Peter Blake (b.1932) and Derek Boshier (b.1937). In America Robert

**Pop art** Roy Lichtenstein's *Wham!*, a manifestation of the 'brazen characteristics' of popular culture with its imagery drawn from the mass media (Tate Gallery, London).

Rauschenberg and Jasper Johns set about painting pictures which used abstract techniques to depict everyday objects, setting the scene for the more truly Pop artists who were to follow. In New York, Andy Warhol, Roy Lichtenstein, Claes Oldenburg (b. 1929) and Tom Wesselmann (b. 1931) began using Hard Edge and commercial techniques to reproduce popular images. In California, artists such as Ed Kienholz and Wayne Thiebaud developed a more eclectic style.

Pop art has precedents in Cubist collage, the **found objects** of the Surrealists and Dada **Ready-mades**. It was recognized as a reaction to 'ultra-modern' art and in America to Abstract Expressionism. More recently, critics have been prepared to accept the essential seriousness of the genre, noting its similarities to Minimal and Hard-Edge painting. Nevertheless, the ebullient questioning of the whole notion of art, no less than of a consumer culture, that the movement achieved has probably generated more enjoyment, however short-lived, than any other art movement in this century. Its most memorable images include Rauschenberg's *Coca Cola Plan* (1958), Jasper Johns's *US Flag* (1958), Lichtenstein's *Wham!* (1963), Oldenburg's *Hamburger* (1961), Jones's *Girl Table* (1969), and Hamilton's *Just What Is It That Makes Today's Home So Different, So Appealing?* (1956).

**poppyhead** An ornamental finial of a bench or stall-end carved with figures, animals, flowers or foliage.

**portico** A term properly applied to the colonnaded space in front of the entrance door to a Classical temple or other building in similar style, such as the National Gallery, London.

**Post-Impressionism** A term coined by Roger Fry for an exhibition of modern French art which he mounted at the Grafton Galleries, London, in 1910. It contained works by Manet, including the *Bar at the Folies-Bergère*, now in the Courtauld Institute gallery; Cézanne, Gauguin, Van Gogh, Seurat, Paul Sérusier (1863–1927), Maurice Denis (1870–1943), Vallaton, Odilon Redon, Georges Rouault, Maurice de Vlaminck, Derain, Picasso and Matisse. Not all these painters were subsequently categorized as Post-Impressionists; the term has hardened around Seurat, Gauguin and Van Gogh, with Cézanne, the modern old master, as the progenitor of them all.

But Post-Impressionism is not confined to French artists. As the recent Post-Impressionist exhibition at the Royal Academy in London made clear, the impact of the movement was felt in Germany, Holland, Norway, Switzerland and Italy, as well as in Britain and Ireland. Artists working within the representational, non-abstract tradition, albeit liberated by Impressionism and with their roots in the French achievement, come within the modern meaning of the term.

**Post-Painterly Abstraction** A term formulated by the American critic Clement Greenberg to describe a generation of artists who had developed under the influence of Abstract Expressionism, but who were reacting to it in new ways. He used it of an exhibition which included works by Ellsworth Kelly (b. 1923), Kenneth Noland (b. 1924), Frank Stella (b. 1935), Jules Olitski (b. 1922), Helen Frankenthaler (b. 1928), and Paul Feeley (1910–66). The term is sufficiently general to cover all American artists who during the 1960s began to develop Hard Edge and Colour Field styles.

Greenberg was an influential theorist and critic, as much a catalyst as a commentator in that productive period of American painting. He was also a formalist thinker, who believed that the direction of modern art has been towards a revelation of the technical limitations of art. He argued against the vestiges of illusionistic space that remained in the painterly work of Pollock and De Kooning, because it disguised (he said) the essential flatness of the picture plane. Instead of regarding a canvas as a surface on which to make an image, he proposed an art which integrated its materials into a perceptual whole in which paint was not so much applied to a ground as integrated with it. One response was the stain technique of some **Colour Field** painters, replacing the existential gesture painting of the Abstract Expressionists with cool, objective fields of saturated colour. Another response is typified by Frank Stella, who set out to base painting on the fact that 'only what can be seen there is there . . . What you see is what you see'.

**poster colours** Inexpensive paints made with water-soluble binders, ideal for applications of flat, opaque colour.

**Potter, Paulus** (1625–54) Dutch animal painter. His earliest work is dated 1640. The precocious son of a painter, he achieved mastery in his short life with studies of cows, horses and sheep in tenderly painted landscape settings. He was also a skilled etcher which helped to make his subjects widely known and sought after.

**pouncing** A method of transferring a drawing from one surface to another, used in **fresco** painting to reproduce the original cartoon on the surface of the wall. The lines of the first drawing are perforated, and a fine powder of chalk or charcoal, called pounce, is sifted through the holes, duplicating their pattern on the surface beneath. If the cartoon must be kept intact, it is traced on to tracing paper which can then be pounced instead of the original.

**Poussin, Nicolas** (1594–1665) French painter. He was the founder of the Classical school of European painting. He left his birthplace, Les Andelys, for Paris, then travelled to Rome via Venice and worked in the studio of Domenichino.

He developed a passion for the Antique, coupled with a feeling for the pastoral mythology of the classical poets, occasionally tempering clarity and order with a poetic lyricism. The principles he established in this process were adopted at the Académie as counterweights to the colourists and proto-Romantics. Poussin occupies a complementary position in European art to that of Claude Lorraine.

**Pre-Columbian art** The term embraces all art and art objects in Central and South America dating from before the arrival of Columbus and the subsequent Spanish conquests (1520–42). Though some indigenous arts survived the collapse of the Mexican and Peruvian civilizations and the decimation of entire populations, the period of high achievement was already in the past.

Artistic remains of the early hunters and of the so-called archaic age are rare, but from Mexico's pre-classic or formative years, 1500 BC to AD 200, figurines and vessels are found. In the classic age, from about 300 to 900 AD, the Meso-American cultures flourished: it was the period of Teotihuacan and the Maya. The post-classic period in Mexico, from about AD 1000 to 1521, is rich in ceremonial remains from the Toltec and Aztec dynasties. In Peru, too, the first 900 years AD saw a flowering of crafts, engineering, architecture and road building. The Inca civilization, known as the imperialist period, produced art and architecture of a less malign character than that of the Aztecs.

As occurred with African art, the first objects brought to the West from Central and South America were regarded as barbaric, much as they had seemed to the Spanish marauders. But at least one Pre-Columbian masterpiece has inspired a master in our own century: the alert, half-recumbent figure of Chac Mool, a rain spirit of the Mayans, was the prototype for Henry Moore's Reclining Figure, 1929, 'an essentially sacral art', as he called it, 'in a secularized age'.

**Pre-Columbian art** A ceremonial gold knife, originally inlaid with turquoise, from the Lambayeque Valley in Peru (Museum für Völkerkunde, Berlin-Dahlem).

**Pre-Raphaelite Brotherhood** An association of English artists, led by William Holman Hunt, John Everett Millais and Dante Gabriel Rossetti, who in 1848 set themselves the task of bringing about 'a child-like reversion from existing schools to Nature herself'. By 'Nature' they meant the innocent state of Italian art before it was supposedly overwhelmed by the great men of the Renaissance. They adopted a highly finished quasi-fresco technique, strongly literary in subject, painted with deep seriousness and moral fervour. The first of the Brotherhood's paintings to be labelled 'PRB' was Hunt's *Girlhood of Mary Virgin*, 1849. Millais' *Christ in the House of his Parents*, now in the Tate Gallery, London, stung Dickens to a furious attack.

Though the leaders of the movement held together for some five or six years, the essential differences in their characters and talents gradually separated them. Hunt remained true to the Brotherhood's ideals, and Edward Burne-Jones carried them forward into a stylized, late-Victorian symbolism.

In addition to Hunt, Millais and Rossetti the Brotherhood also included Thomas Woolner (1825–92), the only sculptor to become a member; James Collinson (1825–81), who left the group to become a priest; Frederick Stephens (1828–1907), who combined painting with art criticism; and William Michael Rossetti (1829–1919). Ford Madox Brown (1812–93), though not a member of the Brotherhood, worked for a time in their style. It was also adopted by a number of painters of the following generation, of whom John Melhuish Strudwick (1849–1935) is a prominent example.

**Precisionism** The art practised by a group of American painters (also known as the Immaculates) during the 1920s and early 1930s. Although they were never a unified group they did much to develop the increasingly abstract tendency in American art by applying some of the formal elements of Analytical Cubism to naturalistic subjects. Their work has also been dubbed 'Cubo-Realist', in explanation of the styles they sought to amalgamate. They drew their subjects from American urban and rural life. But the country barns and farm interiors of Charles Sheeler (1883–1965) and Georgia O'Keefe, and the architec-

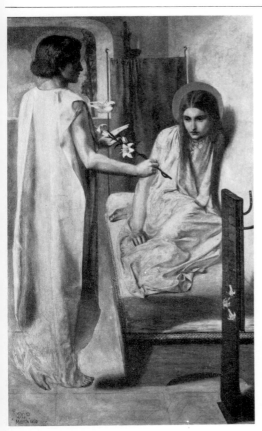

**Pre-Raphaelite** Dante Gabriel Rossetti: *The Annunciation* (Tate Gallery, London).

others can be mixed, though in practice pigments are not pure enough for this to be so. Secondary colours such as green or orange are mixed from two primaries, and tertiary colours, such as brown, from all three.

**Primaticcio, Francesco** (1504–70) Italian painter and architect. He worked under Giulio Romano in Mantua, after which he was called to Paris by Francois I to work at Fontainebleau, where he joined Rosso. Together they were responsible for the distinctively French Mannerism known as the Fontainebleau School.

**priming** In oil painting, a thin coat of white lead applied to the sized canvas to provide a base for the picture that is evenly absorbent. It may constitute a **ground**, though sometimes a further layer is applied.

**Primitive** The art of so-called 'primitive' cultures, which flourish, or have flourished, outside the main centres of civilization. Since the early 1900s it has had a considerable influence on Western art. Gauguin's fascination with Tahiti and Picasso's and Braque's response to African masks began the assimilation of primitive motifs into the modern movement, leading to the more recent interests in Eskimo carving, Australian aboriginal art, Navajo weaving, and the arts of Polynesia.

As an extension of this, Primitive is also used as a synonym for 'Naive', meaning art that is relatively innocent and unschooled.

Though somewhat outmoded, the term is also conventionally applied to painters of the Netherlandish and Italian Schools of the late 14th and 15th centuries, such as Bosch, Van Eyck, Van der Weyden, Giotto, Fra Angelico and Uccello.

**Primitivism** A form of Russian Expressionism, influenced by Fauvism and Cubism but also by Russian folk art, which developed over 15 years from around 1905. Its principle exponents were Natalia Goncharova (1881–1962) and Mikhail Larionov. Goncharova mastered a technique of painting brilliant, decorative compositions, infused with Fauvist colour but with a concern for theme and content, expressed through simplified motifs drawn from Russian icon painting and such peasant

tural and industrial scenes of Charles Demuth (1883–1935) and Morton Schamberg (1881–1918), were chosen largely for the opportunities they presented for painting in geometrical and rectilinear forms. Their work is essentially formal, with a few social references, executed in wide areas of flat colour and neat, precise contours.

**predella** Paintings forming a fringe or strip at the base of an Italian Renaissance altarpiece.

**presbyterium** In church architecture, the section where the clergy sit, to the east of the choir.

**primary colours** The three colours – red, blue and yellow – from which theoretically all crafts as wood carving and embroidery. Larionov was the more dominant figure. He too felt the power of the Russian folk tradition, but was equally absorbed by the crude graffiti he saw around him, and his work, though often lyrical, exploited its banal vulgarity to more powerful effect. However, the Primitivist phase of the movement's two initiators was brief. By 1911 their work was moving away from its ties with the Russian past towards the mainstream of European modernism. In that year Goncharova and Larionov exhibited the early works of Tatlin and Malevich and in 1912 launched the short-lived but influential Rayonist movement. See **Rayonism**.

**principal** Short for principal rafters, the raking rafters which form part of the roof truss, and support the roofing. Sometimes the whole truss is referred to as the principal.

**profile perdu** The term for a head which is turned three-quarters away from the viewer, so that only the contour of the cheek and jaw can be seen.

**progressive proofs** Proofs pulled at successive stages of work towards a final print. They may be taken periodically, so that the artist can see how much work remains to be done on his plate or block, or simply as a record of the work's creation. Such proofs are sometimes taken from each block in the creation of a colour print and at the end of each colour run, showing the progress of the print at each stage.

**proof** An impression of any kind of engraving, taken from the block or plate by the artist or printer, usually while the work is progressing. A 'proof before letters' is one made of the final state but before any inscription is added. An artist's proof, often inscribed as such in the lower margin, is a proof taken outside the numbered limited edition, for the artist's own reference, or for private sale. However, the term is often less specific. It is not uncommon to find the word used as a synonym for print.

**proportion** The mathematical ratio of the parts of a composition to each other, and to the whole. Perfect proportion in a building or in a depiction of the human figure is judged to have been achieved when the constituent parts are in the most pleasing and harmonious relationship. From the time of the Pythagorean philosophers of ancient Greece, who formulated the first theory of proportion, theoreticians and artists have sought to find a rational basis to visual harmony to compare with the mathematical explanation of musical harmony. All the theories of proportion are grounded in a mathematical constant to the ratios. So, although the height of the average human figure is apparently seven and a half times the height of its head and roughly equal to the span of its outspread arms, in **Ideal art** it might be depicted as being eight times the height of its head, and exactly the span of its outspread arms.

Since the Renaissance, concern with rigid theories of proportion have gradually died out. Such formulas were inimical to Mannerism and to the precepts of Romanticism. Nevertheless, exercises in the Classical are still part of an academic art education, since feeling for proportion is felt to be essential to the unity and balance of a work.

**propylaeum** In Greek architecture, the main entrance or portal to an enclosed area such as a temple.

**prostyle** A porch, open on three sides, supported by a row of columns and surmounted by a pediment.

**prothesis** In Byzantine churches, a chamber where the preparation of the Eucharist ceremony takes place.

**prothyrum** A porch or entrance to a Roman house.

**Prout, Samuel** (1783–1852) English watercolour painter. His early work consists mostly of shore scenes with beached fishing boats. His travels on the Continent subsequently produced architectural subjects which he drew with a characteristically crumbled line, catching the picturesque nature of old stone or timber. He was also a teacher, and his methods became popular by means of his published drawing manuals.

**provenance** The pedigree of a work of art, that is, the documented record of its various owners and of information which helps to authenticate its authorship or attribution.

**Prud'hon, Pierre-Paul** (1758–1823) French painter of portraits, mythological and religious subjects. A stay in Rome (1784) introduced him to the work of Correggio and Leonardo da Vinci, which had a marked influence on his subsequent style. He enjoyed favours at the French court, painted the Empress Josephine, and survived the fall of Napoleon to become a member of the Institute Français. His work is essentially 18th century in its elegance and style, but with a Romantic warmth.

**Psychedelic art** A decorative style of the 1960s and early 1970s, characterized by swirling, livid colours in fluid arrangements. It was conceived as a visual analogy for the artificially induced hallucinations of the emergent drug culture. It appeared first in the 'underground' papers that grew up in Britain and America as the Hippy movement burgeoned, and spread to the popular arts such as posters and record sleeves. It often combined visual, aural and kinetic elements, especially at rock concerts. In its concern with sensory perception it can be seen as an adjunct of **Op art**.

**Pugin, Augustus Welby Northmore** (1812–52) English architect and craftsman. His passion for the Gothic helped to accelerate the **Gothic Revival** in England. He shares his monument, the Houses of Parliament, with Charles Barry.

**pull** A printing term – a proof is described as pulled, not printed.

**pulpitum** In church architecture, the stone gallery or rood screen separating the choir from the nave and carrying the crucifix.

**punch** see **stone carving**

**Purism** A movement launched by the painter Ozenfant and the architect Le Corbusier in 1918, when they published *After Cubism*. They regarded Cubism as having become merely ornamental and proposed as an alternative the doctrine of Purism, which would strip art of all that is superfluous to efficient design, in accord with the new era of the machine. Purism

expresses all Le Corbusier's architectural precepts, and through his influence has had a profound impact on the contemporary environment.

**purlin** A beam carried by the roof trusses, which in turn supports the rafters.

**putto** From the Italian: a representation of a small child, usually nude or in swaddling bands. See **amorino**.

**Puvis de Chavannes, Pierre** (1824–98) French mural painter. His attempts to recreate fresco painting on an Italian scale were carried out in a Post-Impressionist manner, the colours flat and pale and the subjects redolent of Symbolism. He was well regarded by Gauguin, Seurat and Lautrec, and by Rodin, with whom, among others, he set up the secessionist Société Nationale des Beaux-Arts. There are murals by him in Paris at the Hôtel de Ville, the Sorbonne, and the Panthéon.

**Pynacker, Adam** (1622–73) Dutch landscape painter. A pupil of Jan Both, his otherwise typically Dutch landscapes are touched with Italianate passages. His strongly vegetative foregrounds and silvery tree trunks seem to have made an impression on the Norwich painter, John Crome.

**quadra** In architectural terms, a moulded frame sometimes used to accent a relief sculpture. It also means the plinth block of a platform or podium.

**quadratura** The illusionist device of painting a wall or ceiling so as to simulate an open space. The effect, commonly found in Italian **Baroque**, is achieved by foreshortening and perspective.

**quadriga** A sculptured chariot drawn by four horses.

**quadripartite** The name given to the most simple form of cross vaulting, with two transverse and two diagonal ribs, dividing the plan of the vault into four triangular spaces.

**quatrefoil** A four-lobed decoration similar to a four-leaved clover. It is often used in Gothic window tracery to symbolize the Cross and the four Evangelists.

**quattrocento** The 1400s, that is, the 15th century.

**Queen Anne** A symmetrical, red-brick style of domestic architecture in the reign of Queen Anne (1702–14), which coincided with the English Baroque. Characteristics include hipped roofs instead of gables, evenly sloping on all four sides to preserve the horizontal line of the eaves, sash windows (newly invented) and canopies over main doorways.

**queen-post roof** Two major vertical supports in a roof truss, instead of the single king support in the centre.

**quoin** Dressed stones at the angle of a building, projecting beyond the main wall plane. They are often rusticated to give them greater emphasis.

**Raeburn, Sir Henry** (1756–1823) Scottish-born portrait painter. After travels in Italy he returned to Edinburgh and set up a studio, becoming the leading portrait painter in the North Country. His bluff and vigorous approach put him on good terms with his sitters.

He became a full Royal Academician in 1815 and was knighted by George IV on a royal visit to Scotland in 1822.

**Raimondi, Marcantonio** (c. 1480–1534) Italian engraver. Born in Bologna, he went to Venice in about 1506 where he first discovered woodcuts by Dürer. His engravings of classical, mythological and religious subjects are based largely on original works by Raphael and Giulio Romano. Many of them became widely known as decorations on Italian majolica dishes.

**Ramsay, Allan** (1713–84) Scottish portrait painter. He was born in Edinburgh and studied in London, Rome and Naples after which he returned to paint in an impressive Italian manner, combining vigorous colouring with classical grace. He even rivalled Reynolds, who was somewhat aggrieved when George III appointed him Painter-in-Ordinary in 1761.

A friend of the philospher David Hume, he enjoyed the company and conversation of prominent writers, politicians and thinkers. His portrait of *Jean-Jacques Rousseau in Armenian Costume* (1766) is one of several works by him in the National Gallery of Scotland, Edinburgh.

**Raphael,** otherwise Raffaello Sanzio (1483–1520) Italian painter. He was born in Urbino, the son and pupil of Giovanni Santi. He came under the influence of Perugino in Perugia while still a youth, and may have worked in his studio. In about 1504 he visited Florence and fell under the spell of Leonardo da Vinci, and his *Entombment* of 1507 (Borghese) suggests a similar admiration for Michelangelo.

In 1508 he was invited by Pope Julius II to undertake new frescoes for the Papal apartments in the Vatican. Other public commissions followed, including the *Madonna di Foligno* for Sigismondo de' Conti and frescoes for the Villa Farnesina for Agostino Chigi, a banker. His cartoons for tapestries for the Sistine Chapel, acquired by Charles I, have remained in England.

His work evokes the High Renaissance at its most sublime, a celebration of the human spirit.

**rasp** A coarse file, used in sculpture for shaping and abrading stone, wood, plaster or clay.

**Rauschenberg, Robert** (b. 1925) American painter. He worked with some of the most prominent Abstract Expressionist painters, including Albers, Motherwell and Kline, but later developed multi-media techniques which have taken him away from easel painting to assemblages and constructions. The most obvious influences on his work are Kurt Schwitters and Marcel Duchamp.

**Ray, Man** (1890–1976) American painter and photographer. With Marcel Duchamp and Francis Picabia he founded the New York **Dada** group and subsequently (1925) exhibited with the Surrealists in Paris. His 'Rayographs', images made by placing solid objects against sensitized paper, were published in albums in the 1930s, accompanied by poems by André Breton, Duchamp and others. In 1923 he anticipated the fashion for Happenings by creating an *Object to be Destroyed*. It was duly smashed up by a group of students when it was shown at a Paris exhibition in 1957.

**Rayonism** A theory of art aesthetics, propagated in Russia between 1911 and 1914 by Mikhail Larionov (1881–1964) and Natalia Goncharova (1881–1962). Strongly influenced by both Impressionism and Cubism, it was energetically promoted by the Italian Futurist, Marinetti (1901–66). According to Larionov's manifesto, the genius of the time was to be found in 'trousers, jackets, shows, tramways, buses, aeroplanes, railways, magnificent ships'. The Rayonists sought to capture modern energy in work based on the depiction of rays of light reflecting from unseen surfaces, which by their intersections and contrasts created novel kinds of spatial form.

**Read, Samuel** (1815–83) English draughtsman and illustrator. He was born in Suffolk, which he frequently revisited during his subsequent travels, mainly for the *Illustrated London News*, to which he was a regular contributor and subsequently art editor. In 1853 he was sent by the journal to the Crimea as the first artist-correspondent. He was trained as a wood engraver, and cut many of his illustrations himself. A collection of these was published in *Leaves from a Sketch-Book*, 1875. He exhibited watercolours at the Old Water-Colour Society, and was a sensitive pencil draughtsman of architectural and landscape subjects.

**Ready-made** A manufactured item or article exhibited as a work of art. The form was first exploited by Marcel Duchamp, who by exhibiting such items as a lavatory bowl sought to express the relative nature of social values. The idea has been widely influential and found particular favour with Pop artists of the 1960s.

**Realism** In general, the term means the depiction of non-aesthetic subject matter without distortion or stylization and in this sense is the opposite of Ideal art. An early champion was Courbet, who organized a Realist Exhibition in 1855. Realist painting of this kind, which prefers the squalid and ugly as its subject matter, is distinct from mere Naturalism – a concern with the accurate representation of

nature – although the two words are often used interchangeably.

'Realistic' is also the term often used to mean the opposite of 'Abstract' though it quickly becomes self-contradictory when applied to artists like Bosch or Dali, whose fastidious attention to detail makes them realistic stylistically, while their subject matter is pure fantasy. See also **trompe l'oeil, Magic Realism, Verism, Social Realism,** and **New Realism**.

**rebate** A recess on the edge of a slab, generally for the purpose of fitting a separate construction into it.

**recession** The apparent gradation into distance of a picture's imaginary depth, achieved among other means by the use of **perspective**.

**Redon, Odilon** (1840–1916) French painter and print maker. A contemporary of the Impressionists and friend of Ignace Fantin-Latour, who taught him lithography, he exhibited at the first Salon des Indépendants (1884) and at the last Impressionist exhibition (1886). He was attracted by the Symbolist movement which helped to infuse his work with an idyllic, quasi-religious quality, at odds with Naturalism. His use of colour, learned from Delacroix, is well suited to his somewhat melancholy imagination, which has much in common with the Surrealists.

**Regency** Architectural style in England at the time of the regency and reign of George IV (1811–30). It is a continuation of the Georgian tradition in domestic architecture, and expresses much the same cultural confidence and ease. The material is brick, sometimes covered with stucco for better protection. The influence of Neoclassicism lingers in the proportions and the interior embellishments. The terraced façades of Regency squares, as in Brighton, Cheltenham and parts of London, achieve a sunny lightness and charm which continue to set a standard for their present-day, debased imitations.

**register** In colour print making, the accurate imposition of separately prepared plates to produce the finished result. Colour prints are made by taking a number of impressions from differently inked plates, blocks, or stencils on

**Regency** Nash's Quadrant in Regent Street, London, a fine example of a Regency façade.

the same piece of paper, each contributing a different colour to the final proof.

**relief** Carving, modelling or sculpture in which the forms stand out from a background. Reliefs may be executed in stone, wood, or metal and are categorized according to their degree of projection. High relief, or alto-rilievo, is when the forms stand out by at least half their true depth from the surface of the block. Bas-relief, or basso-rilievo, means that there is no undercutting, the forms barely projecting above the surface. Half-relief, or mezzo-rilievo, is the intermediary category. The term rilievo-stiacciato is applied to the most minute projections, such as those by Donatello. Cavo-rilievo means **intaglio**.

Relief engraving is the generic term for all print-making techniques in which the areas which have to be left white are cut from the block, and those which are to print are left. See **Print making**.

**relieving arch** An arch built into a wall above a lintel or window-head to take the weight of the upper part of the wall off the lintel, which then only has to support the part of the wall between it and the arch.

**remarque** In etching, a small sketch made on the edge of the plate to work out corrections, or to test the strength of the mordant before immersing the plate. Remarques may be

**Relief** Dancers on an Etruscan sarcophagus at Chiusi (Archaeological Museum, Florence).

removed with a burnisher and scraper before the final version is printed. They are sometimes found on proofs of advanced states; these are known as remarque proofs.

**Rembrandt van Rijn** (1606–69) Dutch painter and engraver. He studied at the university of Leiden, where he was born, served an apprenticeship for three years, then spent six months in Amsterdam with Pieter Lastman (1583–1633). Back in Leiden in 1625 he began working in company with his friend Jan Lievens (1607–74), who was himself to become a successful painter. His work at this period includes several self-portraits and studies of old age, notably *The Artist's Mother as the Prophetess Anna* and *Jeremiah Weeping over the Ruin of Jerusalem*, both in the Rijksmuseum, Amsterdam.

He left Leiden for Amsterdam in 1632 and entered into the prosperous middle period of his life. Marriage, family life, and plentiful commissions, including the *Anatomy Lesson* (1632) and *The Night Watch* (1642), established him among the leading citizens. His portraits and etchings of the next decade have not been surpassed for humanity and spiritual power.

In 1656, overcome by money troubles, he was declared bankrupt and was obliged to sell his expensive collection (part of his misfortune) and his home. The last twelve years of his life produced a succession of masterpieces, among them the *Syndics of the Amsterdam Cloth Hall* (1662) and the penetrating late self-portraits.

Of his pupils and imitators the most prominent are Gerard Dou (1613–75), Gerbrand van den Eeckhout (1621–74), Govaert Flinck (1615–60), Aert de Gelder (1645–1727) and Salomon Koninck (1609–56).

**Renaissance** The emergence in 15th-century European art of Classical aesthetic values. Seen from within a Christian ethic, the ancient world assumed qualities that enabled nature – essentially pagan – to be accommodated within a broadly humanist view of life and its purpose. The concept of beauty was widened to include Platonic theory and more naturalistic forms than those imposed by the Byzantine style. At the same time, the absorption of some aspects of pre-Christian culture could be seen as offering continuity in Man's search for the ideal.

In the first phase, sometimes known as the Early Renaissance and stemming originally from Giotto, the liberation of the human form is a dominant aspect of painting and sculpture, as seen in the work of such artists as Piero della Francesca, Donatello, Dürer and Van Eyck. The High Renaissance, covering the years between 1490 and 1520, saw the aspirations of the previous half-century brought close to fulfilment in the works of Raphael, Leonardo, Michelangelo and Giovanni Bellini, in which Man, freed from the stereotype of Church art, assumes his psychological identity. In the next generation, Titian hastened a revolution in technique by developing the new medium of oil painting in succession to tempera.

In architecture, the term applies to the European revival of Classical architecture from the 15th to 17th centuries, beginning with Brunelleschi and leading in to Mannerism and the Baroque. The humanist characteristics of Rennaissance thought and ideas are less evident in the architecture of the period than in painting and sculpture. Bramante's *Tempetto* at S. Pietro in Montorio, Rome (1502), intended to mark the spot where St Peter was crucified, is typical of the re-use of Antique ideas in a modern building which influenced the design for St Peter's, Rome. In Venice, Jacopo's Library of S. Marco, begun in 1537, the first major Renaissance building in the city, was based on the external wall of a Roman theatre. In Paris, Pierre Lescot's façade for the Louvre, begun in 1546, marks the spread of the style in northern Europe. The original Somerset House, London (1547–52), was in the same mode.

**Reni, Guido** (1575–1642) Italian Baroque painter. He was active in Bologna and in Rome. His style wavers between that of Caravaggio and the Raphaelesque classicism of the Carracci. His *Crucifixion of St Peter*, painted in 1603 (Vatican), has its origins in Caravaggio; the *Martyrdom of St Andrew* of 1609 (S. Gregorio Magno, Rome), and the *Aurora* frescoes of 1614 (Casino Rospigliosi, Rome), belong in the Renaissance tradition. He was highly successful in Rome as a painter of religious subjects, some of which, to a modern eye, show an over-sugary piety.

**Renoir, Pierre Auguste** (1841–1919) French painter, one of the leading Impressionists. He began by painting designs in a porcelain factory but went on to train in Marc Charles Gleyre's studio, where he met Frédéric Bazille, Alfred Sisley and Claude Monet. It was as a close companion of Monet that he embraced Impressionism: in the period around 1872 the two painters' work, sometimes done side by side, is strikingly similar. He took part in the first Impressionist exhibition (1874) and was a popular member of *la bande à Manet*.

During the 1880s he reverted to less Impressionist techniques, while still rejoicing in the liberation of the palette. In the well-known *Umbrellas* (National Gallery, London) there is a more structured sense of design, suggesting that Renoir had taken Impressionism as far as it suited him, and was ready to go another way. His last works, including several monumental nudes, are notable for their plastic values and naturalistic use of colour.

**replica** An exact copy of a work, done in the same medium, in the same size, and – strictly speaking – by the same artist who created the original, or at least under his supervision.

**repoussage** A technique for smoothing out the surface of an etching plate after it has been corrected or repaired. Areas of a plate to be re-etched are usually worn to a flat surface after being rubbed with a burnisher and scraper. This leaves the worked area lower than the surrounding surface of the plate. The term repoussage, from the French *repousser*, to push back, refers to the technique of laying the plate face down on a flat surface, and tapping the back over the depressed spot with a broad hammer until the surface is level again.

**repoussé** Metalwork where the design appears in relief, punched out from the reverse side.

**repoussoir** A figure or other object placed in the immediate foreground of a picture, usually to the left or right. This serves to push back or give depth to the principal subject of the composition.

**Representational art** Art in which recognizable elements of the natural world are depicted; a term often used in contrast to Abstract art.

**reproduction** A copy or likeness of an original work, done by someone other than the artist. Although sculpture has been reproduced since classical times, it was only with the advent of the woodblock in the 15th century that the means was found to reproduce a two-dimensional design. From then until the invention of photography and lithography, book illustrations and reproductions were done by craftsmen copying an original design as an engraving. In this century the engraver's craft has largely been replaced by a variety of photo-mechanical processes such as the half-tone, photogravure, offset photolithography and collotype.

**Repton, Humphrey** (1752–1818) English landscape gardener. He specialized in the laid-out terraced garden, close to the house, that became standard in the 19th century. His writings on the subject, among them his *Theory and Practice of Landscape Gardening in England* (1816) were influential in changing English taste; in fact it was he who coined the term 'landscape gardener'.

**rere-arch** An arch which supports the wall over a door or window.

**reredos** A decorated wooden or stone wall or screen placed behind an altar. See also **altarpiece**.

**resist** In the graphic arts, a general term for substances used to mask out an area so as to make it resistant to chemical action. The two most obvious examples are the etching ground and stopping-out varnish used in **etching** and **aquatint** to prevent the mordant biting into the unexposed parts of the plate. The same principle is sometimes applied in watercolour painting for protecting details intended to remain white, or to be given separate attention after the wash is dry.

**restrike** An impression taken from a plate, block, stone or stencil or from a sculptor's mould after the original edition has been completed.

**retable** A shelf behind an altar, for siting the Cross.

**reticulation** In early architecture, a method of wall decoration in the form of squares set diagonally giving a net-like effect.

**retroussage** The process of wiping ink from the surface of a plate prior to printing, so that it remains only in the etched or engraved furrows. A muslin pad or veil can then be used to draw across a cleanly wiped plate, pulling a little ink out of the furrows and so giving a slightly 'furry' look to the printed lines similar to the burr in drypoint.

**Reynolds, Sir Joshua** (1723–92) English painter, the leading portraitist of his day and first President of the Royal Academy. A pupil of Thomas Hudson (1701–79) and influenced by Hogarth and Ramsay, he was enriched by his exposure to Italian painting during two years spent in Rome (1750–52), particularly that of Raphael, Correggio, Michelangelo and Titian. His *Self-portrait*, painted in 1753 (National Portrait Gallery, London), takes as its model a self-portrait by Rembrandt, which he had also seen in Rome.

His grounding in the European masters made him the best-equipped English painter of the age; his borrowings and references only seemed to strengthen his claims to leadership of what, by the 1750s, could fairly be called the English School. The essential Classicism of his style was tinged with a sympathetic naturalism, best seen in his portraits of women. He had a high-minded view of the function of art, to which he attached a moral significance, and was unsympathetic to the stirrings of Romanticism, for example in the work of Gainsborough. His *Discourses* established a canon of taste which persisted into the 19th century. He was laid to rest in St Paul's, among England's greatest men.

**Ribera, José de** (1591–1652) Spanish painter. He was born near Valencia, and spent most of his working life in Naples. His first paintings were in the Tenebrist manner derived from Caravaggio. Later, working with a brighter palette, he introduced tenderly painted landscape elements into his religious subjects, among which are *Jacob's Dream* (Prado, Madrid) and his altarpiece at the monastery in Salamanca.

**Ricci, Sebastiano** (1659–1734) Italian painter. Trained in Venice, he was a precursor of the style associated with Tiepolo. With his nephew Marco (1676–1730) he visited England in 1712 in hopes of securing the commission to decorate the dome of the new St Paul's Cathedral. This was awarded instead to Sir James Thornhill. He spent the rest of his career in Venice, working in a decorative style owing much to Veronese. A number of his religious subjects, painted jointly with Marco, were commissioned by Joseph Smith, the British Consul in Venice, from whose possession they passed to the Royal Collection in 1762.

**Richards, Ceri** (1903–71) Welsh painter. His early work shows the influence of Picasso, Joan Miró and Max Ernst, and he was associated with Surrealism in the 1930s. His most characteristic work is both abstract and naturalistic, drawing on Welsh themes and on music for romantic, painterly effects.

**ridge** The horizontal edge where the two sloping sides of a roof resting on parallel walls meet at the top.

**ridge rib** In Gothic vaulting, a moulded rib running longitudinally along the central apex of the vault. It was seldom used in French vaulting, but is almost universal in English Gothic.

**ridge tile** The tile which is shaped to fit the ridge of a roof.

**Rigaud, Hyacinthe y Ros** (1659–1743) French portrait painter. In a long career he served both Louis XIV and Louis XV as Court Painter, producing a succession of stately works redolent of the pomp and elegance of the age. He ran a well-organized studio, in which bands of specialist assistants did much of the hand work. He has been called the French Van Dyck, and his images of aristocratic grandees, especially the archetypal *Louis XIV* (1701), have proved no less durable.

**Riley, Bridget** (b. 1931) English painter. She trained in London, and her early work was influenced by George Seurat, whose preconceived ideas of colour and light gave her a point of departure from which she developed what became known as Op art. In this the optical senses both receive and generate incessant surface movement. Her other obvious forbear is Victor Vasarély.

**Riley, John** (1646–91)  English portrait painter. He held the appointment of Principal Painter to the King and Queen jointly with Kneller until his death. His native style, sober and observant, was carried forward by his pupil Jonathan Richardson (1665–74).

**rilievo** see **relief**

**riposo**  Picture of the Holy Family's rest on the flight into Egypt.

**Rivera, Diego** (1886–1957)  Mexican painter. With José Orozco and David Siqueiros, he represents the revolutionary art of modern Mexico. His murals of the 1920s, in such public buildings in Mexico City as the National Palace of Fine Arts and the Ministries of Health and Education, are in a stylized 'popular' manner owing little to his exposure to modern art movements in Europe. His innate belief in Soviet dialectical materialism denied him the greatness that at one time seemed within his grasp.

**Robert, Hubert** (1733–1808)  French painter. His landscapes, based on drawings made on his travels in Italy and Sicily, are in the picturesque taste of the time, making a particular feature of architectural ruins. He survived the French Revolution to become Keeper of the Royal Pictures under Louis XVI and Curator of the Louvre.

**Roberts, William** (1895–1980)  British painter. He studied at the Slade, travelled in France and Italy, and on his return joined the coterie of artists around Wyndham Lewis. He exhibited with the Vorticists and was a signatory of their *Manifesto*, later including himself in the group painting, *Vorticists at the Restaurant de la Tour Eiffel* (Tate Gallery, London) along with Wyndham Lewis, Ezra Pound and Frederick Etchells. His figures, described in clear, rounded forms, are in a style derived from Fernand Léger, which remained typical of his work from the 1930s to the end of his life.

**rocaille**  A French term for the numerous variations of the scallop shell as a motif in the Rococo, occurring more often in German art of the period than in France.

**rocker**  A steel tool with a curved and serrated front edge, used in **mezzotint** engraving to prepare the plate. It is rocked all over the surface until it is completely abraded.

**Rococo**  A term that has come up in the world from being treated with dismissive jocularity to a serious recognition of the exuberant, curvilinear decorations and artifacts associated with French art and architecture of the 18th century. In painting, it reached its summit in the works of Watteau, Boucher and Fragonard, all of whom communicate what the Goncourt brothers described as the charm and coquetry of the Rococo, 'that subtle thing that seems to be the smile of a contour, the soul of a form, the spiritual physiognomy of matter'.
Its beginnings were the ceiling of a room in the Château de la Ménagerie at Versailles, decorated by Claude Audran for the 13-year-old fiancée of Louis XIV's eldest grandson. Audran later gave lessons to Watteau. The playful dispositions of abstract forms, floreate patterns and interwoven figures, all conceived with a lively, flowing line, are the acknowledged forerunners of the style. Under the patronage of Louis XIV and XV it spread into all forms of ornamented art, from the figure sculpture of Étienne Falconet (1716–91) to the mirrors, wall panels, fireplaces and furniture of French mansions in which rooms were styled as a series of tall, slender units, white and gold under blue-painted ceilings. In Italy the impact of the Rococo on Venetian painting, especially that of Tiepolo, has proved one of its enduring pleasures.

**Rodchenko, Alexander** (1891–1956)  Russian painter. His early works were Abstracts, which he exhibited with Vladimir Tatlin in 1916. After the Revolution he was appointed Director of the Museum of Art and Culture, Moscow, and promoted the Constructivist idea

---

**Rococo** The highly ornamented interior of the Pilgrimage Church, Birnau.

that artists should also equip themselves to be designers and engineers. His 'hanging sculptures' carried his spatial ideas beyond easel painting, but all such concepts were erased when in 1932, by Soviet decree, Socialist Realism became the only permissible art.

**Rodin, Auguste** (1840–1917) French sculptor. He worked as a stonemason while studying under the animal sculptor Antoine Bayre (1796–1875), followed by six years in Brussels in the studio of Carrier de Belleuse (1824–87). He went to Italy in 1875, and fell under the spell of Michelangelo. His *Age of bronze* at the Salon of 1877 and his début as an original and non-academic artist caused a sensation.

In 1880 he received a commission for the *Gates of Hell* for the doors of the Musée des Arts Décoratifs, which he worked on for the next 20 years, creating a densely packed design of human bodies, gesturing and writhing. Some of these exist as individual subjects or groups, such as *The Thinker* and *The Kiss*. In 1884 he was invited to produce a monument in honour of the liberation of Calais from the besieging English in 1347: his *Burghers of Calais*, completed in 1886, of which a replica stands at Westminster. His *Victor Hugo* and *Balzac*, both masterpieces, were rejected on their first appearance.

The inherent power in his work, his instinct for physical movement, and his heroic romanticism, have established Rodin among the Titans of 19th-century art.

**roll moulding** Architectural moulding of a semicircular, or more than semicircular, section. With a fillet it is known as a roll and fillet moulding.

**Roman art** This is generally taken to mean the art of the early citizens of Rome and their immediate descendants and the art of the Roman civilization as a whole, extending to the Roman empire and including elements of its Etruscan and Greek forbears. In architecture, Roman innovations included the use of concrete, resulting in larger-scale buildings than are found in Greece, and of marbles and granite for opulent, decorative effect. Domestic architecture was based on a symmetrical ground plan around a central court or hall, with pitched and tiled roofs. In sculpture, the late Hellenistic style prevails, with portraiture

carried to new levels of realism. Roman portrait painting, much of it funerary, evokes individuals rather than mere types. Wall paintings from excavated houses, in particular at Pompeii and Herculanaeum, include lively illustrations of familiar stories such as the Odyssey, with occasional early examples of landscape, genre and still life.

**Romanesque** A term to describe the sculpture and architecture of Europe from the middle of the 11th century until the end of the 12th, between the last remnants of Carolingian culture and the onset of the Gothic. Masons and carvers drew freely on pagan, Gallic, Islamic, classical and oriental models to create fantastic creatures and groups of animated figures as decorations in abbeys and churches. The style took root in such centres as Cluny, Moissac and Provence, to the alarm of such orthodox clerics as St Bernard of Clairvaux, who complained to his abbot that the barbaric marvels of Romanesque sculptors and decorators were distracting worshippers from their proper

**Romanesque** Part of the relief sculpture of the 12th-century tympanum at the church of S. Pierre, Moissac.

devotions. The distortions and stylizations of Romanesque art have an expressionist energy unique in early Christian culture.

In architecture, the style gave rise to stone vaulting in the new, enlarged churches that sprang up in Europe, with their wide naves and ceremonial girth, in the decoration of which Roman forms combine with grotesque and exuberant motifs from less classical sources. The finest examples are the great Cluniac foundations in southern France, notably Moissac and Souillac, where the stone carvings contain a sometimes demonic energy. The solid architecture is relieved by brilliantly active detail, while expressing in the loftiest terms the power and dignity of the Redeemer.

Monuments of the Romanesque outside France include the cathedrals of Modena and Pisa, the shrine to St James at Santiago de Compostela, and in England the cathedrals at Durham, with its early rib vaulting, Ely, Norwich, and Winchester, which exemplify the 'Norman Romanesque' introduced after the Conquest.

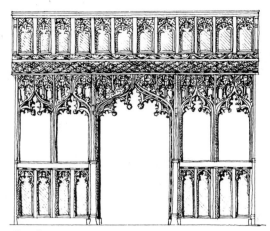

**Rood screen**

**Romano, Giulio** (*c.*1499–1546) Italian painter and architect. He was a pupil of Raphael, with whom he worked in the Vatican, and whose workshop he eventually took over. He completed the Sala di Constantino frescoes and Raphael's unfinished *Transfiguration*, both in the Vatican, in a Raphaelesque style that moves towards Mannerism. His *Fall of the Giants*, in Mantua (1532–4), is a *tour de force* of fresco painting, extending from floor to ceiling. After his death his plans for Mantua Cathedral were used by the architect Giovanni Battista Bertani (1516–76).

**Romanticism** A concept rather than a specific art-historical term (though it is often used as one), Romanticism suggests the difference between what appeals to emotion or sensibility and what satisfies the desire for permanence and order. The concept is older than the word, which first came into use at the beginning of the 19th century. By then, in Western culture, the distinction between the sensuous and the Classical was becoming clear. Winckelmann's view that art 'should aim at noble simplicity and calm grandeur' was at variance with the Picturesque, with its appeal to subjective moods and sensations. The Romantic move-

ment in France, from Delacroix, Courbet and Corot to the Impressionists, Rodin and the School of Paris, is conventionally seen as linking the beginning of the modern era with present-day Abstraction.

But Romanticism has been an equally potent force in North European art. It can be traced in a collateral line from Blake, Friedrich, Palmer, Turner, Van Gogh, Nolde, Mondrian and Sutherland to Pollock and Rothko, all of whom, to a degree, invested their work with Romantic religiosity or mysticism. By the 1970s the Paris-orientated and North European traditions had between them brought European painting to its present point of departure.

**Romney, George** (1734–1802) English portrait painter. He studied in Kendal and York before moving to London in 1762. A year later he set off for Italy, where he acquired the Neoclassical mannerisms of his subsequent work. He developed a fluent and stylized way of painting women which gives them a simplified, poetic grace. He had a passion for Lady Hamilton, whom he painted in various incarnations, such as *Prayer* (Kenwood) and *Ariadne* (Greenwich), and a weakness for literary and historical themes. His talents fell short, on the whole, of his aspirations.

**rood screen** The chancel screen between the nave and the choir.

**Rops, Felicien** (1833–98) Belgian painter, etcher and illustrator. He was born in Brussels and in 1874 settled in Paris, where he forsook painting for print making, illustrating erotic books and works by Symbolist writers such as Baudelaire. His floreate style anticipates Art Nouveau. His more demonic subject matter made an impression on Ensor and Munch.

**Rosa, Salvator** (1615–73) Italian painter and engraver, also poet, actor and musician. He represents the popular stereotype of the wild Romantic: volatile, rich in fanciful imagery, provocative and (according to later legend) a one-time bandit. He became known for landscapes and especially for battle scenes, in appropriately savage settings. He moved from Naples to Rome, then to Florence and finally back to Rome in search of a living, at one stage incurring the wrath of Bernini, whom he made fun of in one of his verses. His pictures appealed to the growing taste for the Picturesque in the late 18th century, when he enjoyed a posthumous fame. His etchings, done in the last decade of his life, have always been well regarded.

**rosette** A carved, painted or moulded architectural decoration resembling a rose.

**Rossetti, Dante Gabriel** (1828–82) English painter, and a founder member of the **Pre-Raphaelite Brotherhood**. Under the eye of Holman Hunt he painted the *Girlhood of Mary Virgin* in 1849 (National Gallery, London). In the following year he met Elizabeth Siddal, whose brooding, romantic looks became the epitome of Pre-Raphaelite womanhood. Rossetti's interests were poetic and literary, and he was a weaker painter than the rest of the Brotherhood. His most enduring pictures are of Elizabeth Siddal, whom he married and who ended her life in tragic fashion in 1862.

**Rosso, Giovanni Battista** (1494–1540) Italian painter. One of the founders of **Mannerism**, he worked under Andrea del Sarto with Jacopo Pontormo. He was summoned to France with Francesco Primaticcio (1504–70) to work at Fontainebleau, and with him devised the curiously fashioned imagery of the Fontainebleau School. His *Pietà*, in the Louvre, is characteristic of work in his original style.

**Rothenstein, Sir William** (1872–1945) English painter. He studied at the Slade School and in Paris, where he joined the circle of Forain, Bernard and Puvis de Chavannes. He returned to London in 1894, when he became a member of the New English Art Club. In 1920 he was appointed Principal of the Royal College of Art, and was knighted in 1931. His early connections with French painters are evident in his work, though he aimed at producing a distinctively English style of painting from the legacy of Impressionism.

**Rothko, Mark** (1903–70) American painter of Russian origin, born in Latvia. With Baziotes, Robert Motherwell and Barnett Newman he founded 'Subjects of the Artist' in New York. His work moved from a figurative Expressionism through Surrealism to the pure Abstraction of his later years, in which broad bands of luminous colour shimmer and float in blocks of suspended space: the irreducible image.

**Rouault, Georges** (1871–1958) French painter. He began as a stained-glass worker, studied at the Ecole des Beaux-Arts and under Gustave Moreau, then turned to the Fauves, with whom he exhibited at the Salon d'Automne in 1905. The dealer Vollard took an interest in him, and with this encouragement Rouault went his own way, using resonant colour to bring theme and imagery together. His work is essentially Expressionist and confined to basic themes, notably the drama of the Passion.

**Roubiliac, Louis François** (*c.*1705–62) French sculptor, who spent most of his life in England. He arrived some time before 1735 and quickly made his name with a bust of Handel for Vauxhall Gardens (now in the Victoria and Albert Museum, London). A vivid sense of character and a lively gift of expression are marks of his work, which had no equal in his time. It ranges from busts of prominent men and women such as *William Hogarth* (National Portrait Gallery, London), *Isaac Newton* (Trinity College, Cambridge) and *Dr Martin Folkes* (Wilton House) to tomb sculpture of considerable vivacity and drama.

**roulette** A tool used in print making to form small dots in the surface of a metal plate. It consists of a spiked, revolving metal cylinder on the end of a handle. It was widely used in the 18th century when mezzotints, crayon engraving and other tonal processes were employed for reproductive work.

**Rousseau, Henri,** known as 'le Douanier' (1844–1910) French painter. The naive or 'Sunday' painter *par excellence*, his imagery derived, he said, from his service as a military bandsman in Mexico in the 1860s: exotic, luxuriant landscapes occupied by wild beasts. He did not begin painting until about 1880, by which time he was a humble functionary in the Customs Service (hence his nickname). He exhibited at the Salon des Indépendants, where his work attracted the attention of the Impressionists and later that of the circle of artists and writers around Picasso, who in 1908 paid him seriocomic homage at a dinner given in his honour.

Rousseau took a perfectly serious view of his art, and did not hesitate to compare himself and Picasso, in the painter's presence, as the two greatest artists of the age – 'you in the Egyptian manner, I in the modern'. His works have influenced later generations of 'primitive' painters, and have been much admired by the Surrealists.

**Rousseau, Théodore** (1812–67) French landscape painter. He was a member of the Barbizon School, where he was closely associated with Jean Millet and Narcisse Diaz. He shared the group's rejections at the Salon, but in 1851 was officially commissioned to paint his *Marshes in the Landes* (Louvre), an undoubted masterpiece. Recognition came in 1855, when a roomful of his work was shown at the Exposition Universelle.

**Rowlandson, Thomas** (1756–1827) English caricaturist and watercolour artist. As a boy he studied in Paris, returning to London to enrol at the Royal Academy Schools when he was nineteen. His gift for humorous drawing began to find expression from about 1780. His large *Vauxhall Gardens* was exhibited in 1784, and for the rest of his life he was kept busy with caricature and illustration in his familiar mode – a lively line, flickering with amuse-ment, with monochrome washes or water-colour. His subjects reflect his own diversions, such as gambling, carousing and wenching. He also, on occasion, treated landscape with a rolling lightness of touch, sensitive and free. His prolific output was largely to meet the bills for a roistering life. Not all his work does him justice, and imitations abound.

**rowlock** Rows of bricks laid on edge, usually used to form the ring of a brick arch.

**rubbing** A reproduction of an incised or carved surface, such as church brasses or iron-work, made by placing a sheet of paper over the object and rubbing over it with a soft, black crayon. Rubbing techniques can be used cre-atively. See **frottage**.

**Rubenism** An aesthetic movement in 17th-century French painting which elevated colour above design. It came into conflict with the Poussinistes, who took the opposing view that colour was merely a decorative adjunct to good composition and drawing, pointing to Raphael and Poussin in support of their argument.

**Rubens, Sir Peter Paul** (1577–1640) Flemish painter. He became a Master of the Antwerp Guild as early as 1598, travelled in Italy and Spain, made copies of paintings by Titian, Tintoretto and Correggio, and of works by Michelangelo, before returning to Antwerp in 1608. The following year he was appointed painter to the Archduke Albert of Austria and his wife Isabella, viceroys for the King of Spain.

There followed 20 intense years of profes-sional engagements, including triptychs, altar-pieces, designs for tapestries and ceiling paint-ings, and a series on the *Life of Maria de' Medici* for the Palais du Luxembourg. His travels were combined with diplomatic missions, which he accomplished with impeccable skill. Charles I of England knighted him in 1629 during a stay in London in which, among other work, he prepared the ceiling decorations for Inigo Jones's Banqueting Hall. His energies over-flowed into a scholarly interest in antiquities and classical literature, and into landscape painting of masterly splendour.

Something of the speed and certainty with which Rubens worked may be seen in his oil sketches and drawings, first thoughts which rarely needed to be modified. Studio assistants would then take over, leaving the master to add the finishing touches. His awesome nudes are a lasting monument to Flemish womanhood.

**rubrication** The practice, common in illuminated manuscripts and fine books, of picking out initial letters and section headings in another colour.

**Ruisdael, Jacob van** (1628–82) Dutch landscape painter, the nephew of Salomon van Ruysdael (1600–70) and the greatest of the 17th-century School. Born in Haarlem, he settled in Amsterdam in about 1665, the date of his *Windmill at Wijk*, in the Rijksmuseum, Amsterdam. His work became increasingly Romantic in character, with a sensitive attention to atmosphere in which skies play a dominant part. The overall mood is a restrained poignancy, expressed in a palette of natural colours, the brighter tones being used with a deliberate and sparing hand. He is said to have painted more than a thousand pictures, yet was not tied to stock subjects or a labour-saving formula. He is the forerunner of Romantic landscape painting, not least of the Norwich School, who knew of him as the master and rival of Meindert Hobbema.

**running dog** Classical decoration used in a frieze, similar to the wave ornamentation.

**Ruskin, John** (1819–1900) English critic, art-intellectual, pundit, prophet and teacher. His *Modern Painters* (1843–60), begun as a defence of Turner, develops his high-minded concept of the artist's role. He was an enthusiast for the Gothic, which he declared had 'a noble hold of nature', and for the virtues of medievalism, which prompted him to give warm support to the Pre-Raphaelites. He tried, single-handed, to impose a uniform aesthetic standard on English art at a time when it was developing in vigorous and contrary directions. His influence on architectural taste was widespread, and led to the debased mock-Italian decoration that disfigures much Victorian building.

In old age, his wits awry, Ruskin launched his notorious attack on Whistler for 'flinging a pot of paint in the public's face', setting in

**Rustication**

train the libel case that forced the painter into bankruptcy.

**rustic stonework** Stonework in which the face is rough although the masonry is carefully levelled and shaped and set in a straight course.

**rustication** A method of producing an effect of ruggedness in a building by emphasizing the joints of masonry and roughening the surface of the stone. It is more common in Renaissance work than in any other period.

**Ryder, Albert Pinkham** (1847–1917) American painter. Born in the whaling port of Bedford, Massachusetts, he was obsessed by the sea, which he painted from memory in his lonely New York studio. His work is the expression of Romantic yearnings, rich in intelligence and feeling. His paintings are mostly in America, where he has the status of an old master. They include *Toilers of the Sea*, 1884 (Metropolitan Museum, New York), the *Flying Dutchman*, c.1890 (National Collection, Washington), and *Race Track*, 1895 (Cleveland Museum of Art).

**Rysselberghe, Theo van** (1862–1926) Belgian painter. Born in Ghent, he studied there and at the Académie in Brussels. He travelled in Spain, Africa and the Near East, and moved to Paris in 1897, where his friends included Maeterlinck, Gide and the critic Félix Fénéon. His work in the Post-Impressionist manner dates from 1887, with stylistic borrowings from Seurat, Signac and Whistler.

**Sacra Conversazione** The representation of the Madonna and Child in the company of saints. The 'holy conversation' refers to the inter-relations of the group of figures. The convention succeeded the earlier one of placing sacred figures in separate panels.

**Sacra Famiglia** The depiction of the Holy Family in a domestic setting. Although scenes of the Nativity and Adoration occur from the early Christian period, the unaccompanied Holy Family does not appear before the 15th century.

**Sacred Monogram** This refers to the Cross, in its various early, cryptic versions, as a symbol of the Christian faith. It occurs in early Christian art as a construction made from a combination of the Greek characters Chi and Rho, or alternatively of Iota and Chi, the first two letters of the Greek word for 'fish', which was also used as a symbol by the early believers. Another version in the 9th century uses the letters Iota, Eta, Sigma, which are the first two letters and the last of the name 'Jesus' in Greek.

**saddleback roof** The roof of a tower which has a ridge and ends in gables.

**salon** Historically, the premier art centre of France. The name is derived from the Salon d'Apollon, a room in the Louvre, where the early Academicians exhibited.

**sand casting** see **bronze**

**sand painting** An aboriginal art form which has been brought to a high level of achievement by the Indians of the south-west United States, especially the Navajo of New Mexico and Arizona and the Hopi along the Rio Grande. Sand painting is the central ritual in ceremonies of healing by magic. The painting is executed by the healer and his assistants, its nature depending upon the ailment. Among Navajo there are 17 healing ceremonies with as many as 25 sand paintings involved in each. They are made of a loose, coloured sand which is poured from the hand on to a level ground of white sand about ten feet square. Each colour has a symbolic significance, and the design is orientated around the cardinal points of the compass. The paintings incorporate stylized depictions of mythical scenes, gods and goddesses, animals, plants and the natural world, as well as symbolic notations. When the painting is finished the sick member of the tribe sits in the middle of it to draw in its magic, and then it is systematically destroyed.

**Sandby, Paul** (1725–1809) English watercolour painter and topographical artist. With his brother Thomas (1721–98) he was first employed as a draughtsman for what became the Ordnance Survey Department. When Thomas was appointed deputy ranger in Windsor Great Park, he shared with him the cottage that went with the job. He exhibited a view of Windsor at the fourth exhibition of the Society of Artists in 1763. His Windsor landscapes and studies of the Castle were frequently exhibited up to 1775. With his brother, he was a foundation member of the Royal Academy. His travels in the British Isles, especially in Wales, produced work which, for delicacy of picturesque effect, was unequalled at that time. His work stands at the beginning of the great age of early English watercolour painting.

**Sandys, Frederick Augustus** (1832–1904) English draughtsman and illustrator. Born in Norwich where he attended the Government School of Design, he began working for wood engravers and exhibited at the Royal Academy in 1851. He joined the circle of Rossetti, and adopted a Pre-Raphaelite sense of ornate mysticism. His plates for *Once a Week*, *The Cornhill*, *Good Words* and other magazines of the period from 1860 to 1880 reveal him as an artist of more quality than his relative obscurity might suggest.

**sanguine** A crayon or chalk, burnt umber in colour, which is used for drawing.

**Sansovino, Andrea** (*c.* 1467–1529) Italian sculptor and architect. A pupil of Antonio Pollaiuolo, his first patron was Lorenzo de' Medici, who sent him to Portugal in 1491. He worked in Florence and in Rome, where he made wall tombs for Cardinals Sforza and Girolamo della Rovere (1505–07) and carved the *Virgin and Child with St Anne* (S. Agostino, 1512). His later years were spent in Loreto, supervising sculptures for the Holy House.

**Sansovino, Jacopo Tatti** (1486–1570) Italian architect and sculptor. He was born in Florence and was a pupil of Andrea Sansovino, from whom he took his name. From 1529 he was the city architect of Venice, where his work includes the Library of St Mark, the loggia of the Campanile and the Palazzo Corner on the Grand Canal. Two statues by him, *Mars* and *Neptune*, stand in the Doge's Palace.

**sarcophagus** Stone or terracotta coffins used in antiquity, often elaborately carved.

**Sargent, John Singer** (1856–1925) Portrait painter. Born in Boston, Massachusetts, and trained in Paris and Florence, he worked in London from 1884, following a furore over his portrait of *Madame X* at the Salon, which obliged him to leave Paris.

His instant success as the favoured portrait painter of the Edwardian rich rests on the brilliance of his technique and the enhanced glamour with which he invested his sitters. He was also capable of psychological insight, and of irony bordering on caricature. His landscape sketches and watercolour figure studies, in the summery French manner, have considerable quality.

**Sassetta, Stefano di Giovanni** (*c.* 1392–1450) Italian painter. Active in Siena between 1425 and 1450, he seems to have been aware of such moderns as Ghiberti, Donatello and Masaccio, but his work is predominantly Gothic in feeling, with naturalistic embellishments. His *St Francis Altarpiece* for Borgo S. Sepolcro, in his liveliest manner, is often compared to the work of Piero della Francesca. Seven panels from this altarpiece are now in the National Gallery, London.

**saturation** A term used to describe the purity of a colour, its vividness and intensity.

**satyrs** In Greek mythology, attendants of Dionysus. They are often portrayed as half men, half goats, to stress their association with male sexuality.

**scagliola** Plaster which has been coloured to simulate marble, used by Georgian interior decorators.

**scaling** A decorative surface finish which resembles the scales of fish.

**scalloped arch** An arch with more than five foils.

**scenae frons** A survival from Roman painting, in which an architectural background is painted on a church wall.

**schema** A simple, generalized diagram or representation used to instruct students in figure drawing, composition or proportion.

**Schiele, Egon** (1890–1918) Austrian painter. Trained at the Vienna Academy of Fine Art, he was influenced by Klimt and by Hodler, and played an active part in the development of Austrian Expressionism. Pain, eroticism and disquiet give his figure subjects a disturbing presence. He was prosecuted for public exposure of indecent drawings in 1911. The Vienna Sezession mounted a comprehensive exhibition of his work in 1918, but he died, with his wife, in the Spanish 'flu epidemic that swept Europe after the war.

**Schildersbent** A group of Dutch or Flemish painters, living in Rome, who formed themselves into a fraternal society in 1623. Their bibulous habits obliged the Pope to suppress them in 1720.

**Schinkel, Karl Friedrich** (1781–1841) German architect and painter. His public buildings are markedly Grecian in character, though with Gothic embellishments that give them a Romantic character appropriate to an artist who in his early years was a successful stage designer. Many have suffered from war damage. He visited England in 1826 in his capacity as a functionary of the Public Works Department of the Prussian government.

**Schmidt-Rottluff, Karl,** otherwise Karl Schmidt (1884–1976) German painter, a leading figure in German Expressionism. It was he who suggested the name Die Brücke for the group that included Ernst Kirchner and Erich Heckel, his fellow students at Dresden Technical School. He was classified as one of the 'degenerate' German artists whose works were removed from public exhibition under the Nazis. He survived the regime and went to live and teach in East Berlin.

**School** A term used to denote a geographical or national category of art. It may be as vague as its country of origin – for example, English School, Italian School – or apply to a specific locality – Norwich School, New York School. It is also sometimes used to identify adherence to a movement, such as Impressionist School, New Realist School. In another sense it may be applied to work executed by an anonymous follower or pupil of a noted painter, for example School of Rubens.

**Schwitters, Kurt** (1887–1948) German painter. A founder of **Dada** in Hanover, he was among the most active of the group in promoting its ideas throughout Europe, and was among the 'degenerate artists' persecuted by the Nazis in the 1930s. He took refuge in England, was interned during the war, and later resumed working in the Lake District, where he died. He coined the term 'Merz', meaningless in itself, as his own term for 'playing off sense against nonsense'; hence Merzbau, Merz-poetry and Merz-theatre. His assemblages, often made from bits of rubbish, have proved influential.

**scorper** or **scooper** A tool used in wood engraving to cut away large areas of the block. It has a bevelled, usually rounded edge.

**scorzo** An Italian term for dramatic foreshortening.

**scotia** In architecture, the small concave moulding between the two torus mouldings in the base of a column.

**Scott, Samuel** (c.1702–72) English topographical and marine painter. He first worked in the style of the Van de Velde family, but revised his approach on seeing Canaletto's work on the latter's arrival in London in 1746. His Thames views are particularly close to the Canaletto model.

Scott has enjoyed a revival of interest in recent years, and is now regarded more highly, perhaps, than at any time since his death.

**Scott, Sir George Gilbert** (1811–78) English architect of the Gothic Revival. To him we owe St Pancras Station (1860) and the Albert Memorial (1862–72), along with cathedrals, parish churches and public buildings either built or 'improved' in the Gothic image.

His grandson Sir Giles Scott (1880–1960) is responsible for Liverpool Cathedral, the New Bodleian Library building, Oxford (opened 1946), and the rebuilt House of Commons chamber (1950).

**Scott, William** (b.1913) British Abstract painter. Born in Greenock, Scotland, he studied in Belfast and at the Royal Academy Schools, lived briefly in Wales with the poet Dylan Thomas, then went to Pont-Aven, in Brittany. He was given a retrospective at the Venice Biennale in 1958.

**scrambled colours** Oil colours which have been lightly mingled on the palette but not fully mixed, so that swirls of the original colours can still be seen. Allowing the constituent colours to remain apparent in this way can add interest and luminosity to the paint surface.

**scraper** A steel tool, used in engraving and etching to remove the burr from the engraved plate. It has a triangular blade with concave sides, forming three sharp edges along its whole length and tapering to a point at its tip.

**scrimshaw** Carved or engraved whalebone, a form of folk art particularly popular among American sailors in the 19th century.

**scroll** Curving or spiralling ornamentation, usually consisting of acanthus leaves, ivy, oak, laurel and wheat.

**scroll moulding** A moulding resembling a curled piece of paper.

**sculpture** The creation of forms in three dimensions by carving, modelling or assembling. See **bronze, modelling, stone carving, wood carving, pointing, plaster cast, relief.**

**scumbling** In oil painting, applying a layer of paint on another in such a way that it modifies without obliterating it. Scumbling differs from glazing in that the colour is either thin enough for some light to show through it from underneath, or it is applied irregularly to leave a broken and uneven effect.

**Seago, Edward** (1910–74) English painter. Largely self-taught, he was encouraged in his early days by Alfred Munnings (1878–1959), the popular horse painter, with whom he shared an enthusiasm for the circus. After leading a gipsy life himself, Seago began to find patrons for his equestrian paintings and East Anglian landscapes. He served as a war artist, then based himself in rural Norfolk, making painting excursions abroad in his ocean-going yacht. His mastery of the traditional English method, both in oils and watercolour, made him the most popular landscape painter of his day.

**seascape, sea-piece** A picture in which the sea is the dominant element. When a seascape includes nautical features it is often called a marine.

**Sebastiano del Piombo,** or Sebastiano Luciani (*c.*1485–1547) Italian painter. He studied first under Bellini, then took Giorgione as his master and painted his Venetian works, such as the *Death of Adonis* (Uffizi Gallery, Florence), under his influence. He moved to Rome in 1511, where his first commission was to paint frescoes for the Villa Farnese. Before long he was painting portraits, of which the *Portrait of a Young Woman* (1512) and the *Portrait of a Young Man* (1514), both in the Uffizi, are outstanding examples.

The encouragement of Michelangelo helped him to extend his work with paintings on the scale of the *Raising of Lazarus* (National Gallery, London) and the *Flagellation* (S. Pietro in Montorio, Rome). In 1531 he was appointed to the post of Keeper of the Papal Seal, a lucrative sinecure from which his nickname (Piombo) is derived.

**secco** Renaissance term for a wall painting done on dry plaster, as opposed to **fresco** which is executed on a wet surface. The pigment must be applied with some binding medium such as tempera emulsion. It is easier to apply than fresco, but lacks both the brilliance and the permanence of the more laborious method. Often the finishing touches to a fresco have been painted *a secco*, and have faded away with time.

**secession** A term used to denote a breakaway by a group of artists from conservative institutions or traditions. See **Sezession**.

**Second Empire style** An American usage, applied to architecture of the French Second Empire (1853–71), with its ornate decoration and pretensions to aristocratic dignity.

**secondary colours** The three colours that result from mixing the three pairs of primary colours: green (blue and yellow), orange (red and yellow), and violet (red and blue).

**Section d'Or** A modern revival of the 16th-century system of perfect proportion. It gave its name to a movement and magazine promoted by Jacques Villon and his circle, including Fernand Léger, Marcel Duchamp, Francis Picabia and Juan Gris. The Section d'Or was part of the reaction against Analytical Cubism. See **Orphism**.

**sectroid** The curved surface between the groins in a vaulted ceiling. See **Panache**.

**Seghers, Hercules** (*c.*1590–1640) Dutch landscape painter and engraver. His paintings are the work of a turbulent mind, which regards nature as an implacable force and man as a forlorn traveller. For romantic grandeur they challenge Rubens, or even Rembrandt, who owned several of his works and was thought to have been the painter of the *Great Mountain View* in the Uffizi Gallery, Florence, until it was re-attributed to Seghers in 1871.

He was an equally impassioned etcher, who experimented with mixed media and pulled proofs on variously coloured paper.

**segmental arch** An elliptical arch with a rounded portion of less than a semicircle in length.

**Seguin, Armand** (1869–1903) French Post-Impressionist painter. He visited Brittany throughout the 1890s and met Gauguin on the latter's return from Tahiti in 1894. He became a member of the Pont-Aven group and earned the respect of the master, who contributed an introduction to his one and only exhibition, in 1895.

**seicento** The 1600s, that is, the 17th century.

**self-portrait** A portrayal by the artist of his own likeness. It has been a recurring subject since the earliest recorded example, Theodorus of Samos, who according to Pliny cast his own portrait in bronze. Dürer, Rembrandt, Velazquez, Goya, Van Gogh and Picasso all at some time used self-portraiture to make statements about themselves and the nature of their art.

**Senefelder, Aloys** (1771–1834) German printer, inventor of lithography. The legend is that Senefelder, writing out a laundry list one day and not having a piece of paper handy, used stone to write on, and so got the idea for a new printing process. In his *Complete Course of Lithography* (1818) he gives a more comprehensive account of what he calls a 'chemical method' by which the ink, 'prepared of a sebaceous matter, adheres only to the lines drawn on the plate, and is repelled from the rest of the wetted surface.'

**sepia** A brown pigment, obtained from the ink sac of the octopus and other celaphods. It was used by the Romans, but was most popular during the early 19th century, when it largely replaced **bistre** in wash drawings. It fades quickly in bright light.

**serigraphy** see **silk screen**

**Sérusier, Paul** (1864–1927) French painter. He is one of the more important followers of Gauguin, whom he met at Pont-Aven in 1888. His painting *The Talisman*, in the same year, caused much excitement in the group for its depiction of what Maurice Denis recognized as 'the passionate equivalent of an experienced sensation'.

In 1889 Sérusier became one of the Nabis, along with Bonnard, Denis, Ibels, Ranson, Roussel and Vuillard, and was involved in their puppet theatres. He was one of many prominent artists of his time to borrow from Japanese art, which he saw as the repository of absolute beauty.

**settecento** The 1700s, that is, the 18th century.

**Seurat, Georges** (1859–1891) French painter. He studied at the École des Beaux-Arts, becoming interested in the theory of colour published by the French chemist Chevreul, and also in Delacroix, whose work he saw as a demonstration of his own half-formulated ideas. These and other contemporary examples led him to his notion of a static light, as opposed to the Impressionists' flickering palette, in which colour is governed by fixed laws, notably Chevreul's law of the 'simultaneous contrast of colours'. In terms of Neo-Impressionist theory, objects close to one another not only exchange reflections of their own colours but also generate complementary colour reactions. Dots of colour, set down with the tip of the brush, were Seurat's method of achieving this scientific simulation, which he called **Divisionism**. He developed the technique in a series of major works, including *La Grande Jatte* (Art Institute of Chicago), which was shown at the eighth and last Impressionist exhibition in 1880.

**Severini, Gino** (1883–1966) Italian painter. Born in Cortona, he settled first in Rome, where he met Boccioni and Balla, and then in 1906 in Paris. There he joined the circle of Picasso and Braque, and in 1910 that of the Futurists. His work during the period of 1912 to 1913 comes close to pure Abstraction, but from 1916 it is dominated by Cubism, in which he uses tones of silvery-grey. His later work, in the **Abstraction-Création** period, is influenced by the decorative values of Juan Gris.

**Sezession** The abandonment of established institutions by groups of 19th-century German artists to form their own organizations less obstructive to radical ideas. Examples are the Munich Sezession in 1892, the Berliner Sezession (led by Max Liebermann) in 1899, and the Vienna Sezession (founded by Gustav Klimt) in 1897. Further sezessions included the Neue Sezession of 1910, led by Max Pechstein, and the Freie Sezession of the Expressionists, Ernst Barlach and Max Beckmann.

**sfregazzi** A delicate, shadowy glaze applied over flesh tones with the fingertips.

**sfumato** An Italian term (*fumo*: smoke) to describe the subtle gradation between areas of paint, the mark of masterly technique.

**sgraffito** see **graffito**

**shade** A term with no precise meaning in art, used of the degree of brightness or quality of hue of a particular colour. One green may be described as a shade darker, lighter, deeper, brighter, or bluer than another. Colour darkened with black is also called a shade. The word is also used of all the darker parts of a picture.

**shading** The gradation of one tone into another. The term can also mean the darkening of areas in a picture by hatching or the use of darker colour to assist in modelling, or to depict shadows and other areas of lower illumination.

**shadow edge** In painting, a technique that consists of placing a fine line of brightness around a painted form to make the edge less abrupt, and to suggest the presence of back lighting. It is especially favoured by portrait painters.

**shaft** The main portion of a Classical column, as distinct from the base and capital. It is also used to characterize the long, thin quasi-columns common in Gothic architecture.

**Shahn, Ben** (1898–1969) American painter, born in Lithuania. He was a specialist in Social Realism, which he used as a medium for public protest, as in the series of works on the Sacco and Vanzetti trial in 1931–2 (Museum of Modern Art, New York). He was commissioned to do murals for the New York Public Works of Art project, and worked with Diego Rivera on the Radio City murals in 1933.

**shouldered arch** An arch with a rectangular lintel supported by shaped corbels. The inner edges of the corbels are shaped to make the arch.

**siccative** A substance which is added to paint to make it dry faster.

**Sickert, Walter Richard** (1860–1942) English painter. He served an apprenticeship with Whistler in Paris, where he also made friends with Degas, who was to prove the dominant influence on his style and subject matter. His genre scenes, interiors, and intimate glimpses of the theatre and music hall have the stamp of Degas on them, though the muted tones and brushwork are more obviously English. In 1911 Sickert founded the **Camden Town Group**. He also supported the New English Art Club, taught at Westminster Art School, and practised etching with a typically observant eye.

**Sienese School** A succession of 14th-century Italian painters who fused Gothic and Byzantine elements into a distinctive and sensitive cultural style. The first of them was Duccio, followed by Simone Martini, who brought French Gothic ideas into Italy. Then came Pietro Lorenzetti (active *c.*1319–*c.*1348), Stefano Sassetta (*c.*1392–1450), Matteo di Giovanni (active 1452–95) and Giovanni di Paolo (*c.*1400–82).

**Signac, Paul** (1863–1935) French painter, Pointillist and Neo-Impressionist. He met Seurat at the Société des Artistes Indépendants in 1884, and together they arrived at the principles which were to divert Impressionism from its course. Signac became the leader of the Neo-Impressionist group after the death of Seurat in 1891. His book *From Delacroix to Neo-Impressionism*, published in 1899, is his monument to the cause, which he gradually abandoned for a more Abstract style in which scientific principles no longer apply.

**significant form** An aesthetic term introduced by Clive Bell in 1914 to describe that property in the visual arts which, by the arrangment of form, line and colour, stirs the aesthetic emotions and so identifies the piece as Art. Bell's contention was that significant form is independent of both technical achievement and narrative or representational qualities, residing purely in the formal properties of a work.

**Signorelli, Luca** (*c.*1445–1523) Italian painter. He was said to be a pupil of Piero della Francesca and his early works show evidence of Piero's style. In 1481 with Raphael, Perugino and others, he was chosen by the Pope to decorate the Sistine Chapel. His contribution was the *Testament and Death of Moses*.

A succession of other important commissions followed, culminating in a cycle of fresco paintings in Orvieto Cathedral which had been left unfinished by Fra Angelico, depicting the *End of the World*, the *Anti-Christ* and *The Last Judgement*. His command of figures, not least the nude, is a striking feature of his Michelangelesque visions.

**silhouette** A name derived from Étienne de Silhouette, an unpopular French minister during the 18th century and maker of paper cutouts. It refers to any image, design or portrait depicted in a single, undifferentiated colour bounded by a sharp outline. A craze for silhouette portraits grew up during the 18th and 19th centuries. They were usually miniatures, painted in black on white paper or card. During the 19th century there was also a vogue for cutting them freehand out of pieces of black paper. They provided a cheap, quick and portable image, but their popularity quickly died out with the advent of photography.

**silk-screen printing** A modern development of stencil printing, also known as serigraphy. Paint is brushed with a squeegee through a fine silk screen, held taut in a wooden frame and masked in places by a stencil or impervious lacquer. By the use of successive stencils, colour prints can be easily made. The process is used commercially, but is also used by artists for producing original prints. The advantages of the process are that the image is not made in reverse, as in most types of printing, and the artist does not have to use ink. Paints can be made to simulate washes, impasto, or the effects of gouache and pastel.

**silver point** A drawing technique popular in the 15th and 16th centuries, which has been virtually obsolete since the advent of the graphite pencil. The drawing is made on a sheet of abrasive paper, prepared with a coating of opaque white pigment. The drawing implement is a piece of silver wire, often embedded in wood like a modern pencil, which deposits minute particles of metal as it is drawn across the surface, leaving an indelible line that darkens as it tarnishes. Copper, lead and gold have also been used.

**Simone Martini** (*c.*1285–1344) Italian painter of the Sienese School. His *Maestà* fresco in the Palazzo Pubblico, painted in 1315, owes a debt to Duccio, his supposed master, though it also shows the beginnings of Gothic influence. By 1333, when he painted the exquisite *Annunciation* altarpiece now in the Uffizi Gallery, Florence, the Gothic element was paramount. This painting is also signed by his brother-in-law, Lippo Memmi.

In 1340 Simone was invited to the Papal court at Avignon, where he painted the *Christ Reproved by his Parents* (Walker Art Gallery, Liverpool). He met Petrarch in Avignon, and illustrated the frontispiece of the poet's copy of Vergil, now in the Ambrosiana, Milan.

**simultaneity** A catchword of the Futurists. It summed up one of their most valued principles: that a single creative act can express the emotions, associations, memories and desires that are present in the mind of the painter and which shape his work. It has been an important notion in the development of 20th-century painting, surfacing in the Abstract Expressionists and persisting in the various modes that have followed.

**simultaneous representation** The depiction of an object or image from more than one angle in the same picture. This technique was first exploited by the Cubists. Picasso's portraits in which a head, for instance, is a stylized synthesis of both front view and profile, or Duchamp's *Nude Descending a Staircase* of 1912, are obvious examples.

**singerie** The depiction of monkeys aping human occupations and behaviour. The origins of the tradition lie in medieval manuscript decoration, and in 18th-century France the singerie became a distinct genre. Juan Berain (1640–1711), Claude Audran (1658–1734),

Watteau, and Claude Gillot (1673–1732) all made use of it.

**sinopia** A red pigment used in fresco painting to execute the initial sketch on the plaster and, by extension, the name for such a sketch.

**Siqueiros, David Alfaro** (1896–1974) Mexican painter. With Rivera and Orozco he represents the modern school of wall painting in post-revolutionary Mexico. His work has been closely bound up with his political activities, which have three times driven him into exile. The exuberance and dynamic realism of his work may be seen in his fresco, *Mexican Revolution*, for the National Anthropological Museum in Mexico City, which he completed in 1965 after an interruption caused by his arrest and imprisonment on political charges. His easel pictures, including portraits, still lifes and landscapes, are painted with the same vivid individualism as the murals.

**Sisley, Alfred** (1839–99) French Impressionist painter. Although of English parentage (his father had a business in Paris) he lived most of his life in France after being sent to England as a boy to train for a career in commerce. He studied at Gleyre's *atelier* in 1862, where Monet, Renoir and Bazille were among his fellow students, then contributed to the Salon des Refusés (1863) and to the first Impressionist exhibition (1874). He confined himself to landscapes painted in the multi-hued palette of Monet but also close in mood to those of Pissarro, with whom he shared a liking for riverside scenery on the fringes of the Paris suburbs. Always struggling to make a living, Sisley did not achieve full recognition in his lifetime.

At his death, Monet organized an exhibition of the paintings he had left behind. It was an instant success, and his reputation was made.

**size** A dilute solution of a resinous substance which is sometimes applied to a canvas or other surface before it receives any paint, in order to make it less absorbent.

**size colour** Paint made by mixing pigment with size and oil, used to cover large areas with uniform colour. It is frequently used for painting stage scenery, and is similar in effect and application to poster colour.

**sketch** A rough, preliminary drawing intended to serve as a basis for a more finished picture, or executed as part of the process of working out what form the final work is to take. It is distinct from a study, which is a detailed working out of one part of a picture such as a hand or folds of drapery. However, the spontaneity and informality of sketches has led to their being increasingly valued during the 19th and 20th centuries. The meaning of the word has broadened to include any drawing or painting of a spontaneous and unpretentious nature. Today the sketches made by Constable or Turner are almost as highly esteemed as their exhibition pieces, and appeal more directly to modern taste.

**skew chisel** A chisel whose blade is at an angle to its shank, as opposed to lying in the same plane.

**Slade** London's most celebrated school of art, endowed by the art collector, Felix Slade (1790–1868) along with professorships at Oxford, Cambridge and University College, London. Its heyday was the early Edwardian era, when its pupils included Augustus John, Stanley Spencer, Mark Gertler (1892–1939), C. R. W. Nevinson (1889–1946), David Bomberg (1890–1957), Edward Wadsworth (1889–1949), William Roberts (1895–1980) and Paul Nash.

**slate hanging** A wall cladding of overlapping rows of slates on a timber substructure. Sometimes shaped tiles are used, producing fish-scale effect.

**Sloan, John** (1871–1951) American painter. He began as a commercial artist on Philadelphia newspapers before taking up painting in 1897, supporting himself as an illustrator for New York magazines. He formed a group known as The Eight, and in 1918 became the first president of the Society of Independent Artists, a position he held until 1944. His long isolation from the academic art world was partly due to his preferred subject matter, the drab realism of urban life, which he captured with a journalist's unflinching eye. At the same time his refusal to use his art as social propaganda did not endear him to the activists. He has been claimed, somewhat loosely, as a founder of the **Ashcan School**.

**Smith, Sir Matthew** (1879–1959) English painter. He studied at Manchester and at the Slade School, then went to France in search of the Gauguin legend at Pont-Aven and to work under Matisse in Paris. He returned a Fauvist in manner, and remained a vivid colourist for the rest of his career. He was particularly successful with still life and with nudes, which he painted with ripe and fluid gusto.

**smoking** In etching, the process by which the etching ground is blackened prior to the artist drawing his design on the plate. It is done by holding the plate, with the ground applied, over burning wax tapers which deposit a coating of soot all over its face. Smoking is carried out to increase the visibility of the design as it is inscribed through the ground, the shiny metal thus exposed contrasting well with the black surface.

**smooch** A deliberately smudged area of a drawing which has been done in a soft medium such as charcoal, pastel or pencil.

**Soane, Sir John** (1753–1837) English architect. He is regarded as the most original of his time, investing the Neoclassical style with an individual touch of Romanticism. He trained in England, spent three years in Italy, and returned in 1780. Eight years later he was appointed Surveyor to the Bank of England.

His personal style, with its daring liberties and touches of the Picturesque, can be seen in Pitzhanger Manor, now the Ealing Public Library; in the Dulwich Art Gallery, purpose built to accommodate the collection left to the College by Sir Francis Bourgeois RA in 1811; and in the house he built for himself in Lincoln's Inn, London, now the Sir John Soane Museum.

**soapstone** A very soft stone, usually greenish or greyish in colour and marbled in appearance, which has a slightly soapy texture; a compact variety of talc. It is too perishable to be used for outdoor sculpture but in many parts of the world it is carved into domestic pieces, particularly by the North American Eskimos. It is easily worked, and takes a good polish.

**Social Realism** A term which has come into use since 1945 to describe painting of the contemporary scene which is realist in approach and contains an implicit social critique. Courbet has been nominated as its originator, but the term is more convincingly applied to modern painters such as those of the American Ashcan and the British Kitchen Sink schools.

The term is distinct from Socialist Realism, which since the 1930s has been the only permissible style in the Soviet Union.

**Sodoma,** otherwise Giovanni Antonio Bazzi (1477–1549) Italian painter, born in Piedmont. He was one of the most gifted followers of Leonardo and Raphael, with an aptitude for graceful, half-melancholy groupings and gestures and winsomely beautiful Madonnas. His frescoes in Siena, where he did most of his work, include the *Life of St Catharine* in S. Domenico. He also did some paintings in the Vatican and frescoes for the Villa Farnesina in Rome.

**soffit** In architecture, the underside of a feature such as an arch, balcony, window, door, cornice or lintel.

**soft-ground etching** A variation on the usual method of etching. It produces prints with a softer line, and can render texture. A metal plate is coated with an etching ground which is mixed with tallow, making it greasy and sticky. Over this is laid a sheet of paper on which the artist draws with a pencil; wherever his lines run, the ground sticks to the back of the paper, so that when it is lifted the ground beneath the lines comes with it. The plate is then bitten in the usual way, often in a bath of Dutch mordant, inked, and printed. The resulting line may be coarse or fine, depending on the type of paper used and the pressure of the pencil.

When the technique was first developed late in the 18th century, it was mostly used for reproductions simulating crayon or pencil drawings. Gainsborough and Cotman, among

**Soft-ground etching** A landscape print by Thomas Gainsborough, who also used the technique in conjunction with aquatint.

others, were quick to see its advantages. Gainsborough used it successfully in combination with aquatint to make landscape prints. In this century many artists have discovered that the impressions of any textured material – fabric, leaves, gauzes and other items – may be bitten into the plate by essentially the same method.

**soldier arch** A flat arch made up of bricks which are laid on edge.

**Solimena, Francesco,** also known as L'Abate Ciccio (1657–1747) Italian painter of the late Baroque. From 1674 he lived and prospered in Naples, where much of his work in the city's churches was lost or damaged in the 1939–45 war. At the height of his fame he headed an academy in Naples where one of the pupils

was the Scottish portrait painter, Allan Ramsay, who was thus responsible for bringing the expansive Solimena manner back to Britain.

**sopraporta** A painting above the door of a room.

**sotto in su** An Italian term which means 'from below upwards'. It applies to the extreme foreshortening of figures and scenes in ceiling decoration, so that they appear to be floating in space rather than contained on the picture plane. The use of this form of perspective was first developed by Mantegna and Romano, and in the 17th century was practised with particular brilliance by Tiepolo.

**Soutine, Chaim** (1894–1943) Lithuanian-born painter. A friend of Modigliani, who encouraged him in his early years in Paris, he was beset with doubts about his own talents, veering from Expressionism to Fauvism and back to Van Gogh, all the time rooting his art in the painterly example of the old masters. His passionate use of paint gives added drama to such subjects as flayed sides of meat, butchered poultry, anguished portraits or landscapes seen as skin and bone. He had enthusiastic supporters in America, but never left France to meet them.

**spall** A chip or sliver broken from a stone carving, whether in progress or finished.

**spandrel** In architecture, the approximately triangular space left between the extrados of an arch and any horizontal boundary line immediately above the crown of the arch. It is frequently used as an area for decoration, especially with relief sculpture.

**spectrum palette** A palette confined to the colours of the spectrum – red, orange, yellow, green, blue, indigo and violet – plus white. This was the palette first used by the Impressionists.

**Spencer, Sir Stanley** (1891–1959) English painter. He was at the Slade School from 1909 to 1912, then served with the army in Macedonia. His wartime experiences provided him with themes which he later introduced into his murals for Burghclere Chapel, Berkshire, and in his *Resurrection: Cookham*, of 1922–7 (Tate Gallery). By relating religious themes to the everyday life of Cookham, his native village, he gave them a contemporaneity which some found objectionable. His powerful use of metaphor and analogy, combined with a stylized realism, invite comparisons with Blake. He fits into no category, but joins the band of English artists whose eccentricities were akin to genius.

**spire** The upright conical or pyramid-shaped structure on a tower or roof common in church construction. It is used largely in Gothic architecture, where it is always octagonal, though square spires are frequently seen in Romanesque architecture, especially in North Germany. The chief quality of a spire is that the main lines are continuous to the apex.

**spolvero** A tracing taken of a cartoon. It is then transferred on to the wall or canvas so that the original cartoon can be left intact.

**sprezzatura** Cultivated carelessness; the appearance of achievement without effort.

**springer** The bottom stone of an arch which supports the beginning of the arc. It is part of the abutment.

**springing line** The starting point of an arch; the top of the abutment where the curve of the arch rises.

**sprue** In casting, the hole in the mould into which the liquid medium is poured. It does not run right through the mould, but subdivides first so that it joins the model through smaller holes called gates. See **bronze**.

**spumato** A term derived from the Italian *fumo*, meaning smoke. It is used to describe the gradation from one colour or tone to another, without abrupt transition.

**spur** A decoration, usually of foliage but sometimes grotesque, on the corner of a square plinth surmounted by a circular column.

**squared drawing** A drawing executed on a surface marked out in squares, either to help the artist with the organization of the picture or to enable him to transfer it to another surface. By marking out a grid or 'gridding', a design can be enlarged simply by duplicating the squares on another surface at the appropriate scale, and copying the contents of each square from the original.

**squeegee** In silk-screen printing, the tool used to force paint through the screen on to the print. It consists of a strip of slightly flexible rubber mounted lengthwise in a wooden handle. An application of paint is made in a single stroke across the screen.

**squinch** or **squinch arch** A series of arch forms built across the angle between two walls which enable the corners of a spire to be supported on a square tower.

**squint** An opening at an oblique angle in the wall of a church enabling members of the congregation in the transepts to catch a view of the altar.

**stabile** The opposite to the mobile. Alexander Calder is credited with inventing it in 1932. Unlike mobiles, stabiles do not move. The term is also applicable to Calder's own static sculpture, in which the forms resemble those of his kinetic work.

**stacco** A method of transferring a fresco painting from its wall. The lower levels of plaster on which frescoes are painted sometimes disintegrate because of damp. In this condition, the pigment and plaster are removed together by sticking sheets of cloth to the surface with animal glue and peeling the surface layer off its rotting key. The painting is given a new support before the paint surface is restored. See also **strappo**.

**Staël, Nicholas de** (1914–55) Russian-French painter. He studied at the Academy of Fine Art in Brussels, then spent five years travelling in Europe and North Africa before returning to Paris. In 1944 he was befriended by Braque and began painting in an Abstract style. His *Compositions*, as he called his work, are remarkable for their refined colour sense and suggestions of figurative elements from traditional painting. They were much admired in New York, where he exhibited in 1950, and have grown in esteem since his death.

**staffage** Figures and animals which are often added to landscapes to enliven and animate their composition, while remaining secondary to the picture's main theme or purpose. Some 17th-century Dutch landscape painters employed specialist artists to perform this function.

**stained glass** Designs made from pieces of coloured glass, either dyed or painted, and held together with strips of lead. The art was a Byzantine invention, but reached its fullest development in the service of western Christendom, having been introduced to France by the 11th century and to England in the 12th, and is at its most sublime in the great churches of northern and western Europe. Coloured glass was produced either by dyeing it with metallic oxides while it was still molten ('pot metal'), or by fusing a layer of coloured glass on to clear glass ('flashing'). In practice these techniques were used in parallel with **grisaille** – hand painting clear glass with enamel pigments – a method which has changed little since medieval times.

The design is first drawn to size as a cartoon on board or paper with the lines of leading picked out in black and the colours of the various pieces of glass noted. These are then cut out of a large sheet of plain glass to the required shape and painted where necessary. The enamel has to be fired on to the glass, and only then can the pieces be inserted into the leads – lead strips with grooves on either side. These were pre-cast until the invention of the lead vice in the 16th century which enabled them to be hand moulded.

Early Gothic stained glass is predominantly blue, with warmer colours in support. In the 14th century primary colours gave way to less vivid tones, and with the advent of the Perpendicular style windows of mostly clear glass were introduced. In England, glass painting has survived a decline elsewhere in Europe, largely through the continued interest of accomplished artists and craftsmen. In recent times, the chapel designed and decorated by Matisse at Vence has helped towards a revival of the art.

**stamnos** A type of ancient Greek urn. Characteristically, it was large with a small, covered mouth.

**Stanfield, Clarkson** (1793–1867) English marine painter. He joined the Merchant Navy as a boy and was later pressed into the Royal Navy, eventually coming ashore in 1818. His next job was as a scene painter in Wapping, which led him to take up painting marine subjects. He went to Paris in 1824 where he became an admirer of Bonington, and soon after his return to London began exhibiting at the Royal Academy. His eye for nautical detail and his seaman's familiarity with the movements of skies and oceans stamped his work with authority. In addition, his handling of paint rivalled even that of Turner, with whose seascapes Stanfield's were compared by the critics. Ruskin praised him as an English realist, adding, 'We should like him to be less clever and more affecting; less wonderful and more terrible.'

**Stapart's ground** An etching ground used in aquatint. The surface of the plate is covered with a white wax ground and dusted with salt, which penetrates and pits the wax when heated. Cold water washes out the salt, leaving a myriad tiny stipples in the ground and exposing the plate beneath to the acid.

**star moulding** An ornamental sculptured moulding with a star motif.

**Stark, James** (1794–1859) English landscape painter. He was a member of the Norwich School and the favourite pupil of John Crome; a member of the Norwich Society of Artists from 1812, and the closest to Crome in bringing the Dutch view of landscape into English painting. He left Norwich for London in 1830, and ten years later moved out to Windsor. By then he had lost much of the Norwich School breadth and lyricism. His watercolours are uncommon and highly prized.

His son, Arthur James Stark (1831–1902), who sometimes painted the animals in his father's pictures, was an accomplished watercolour painter with a free and sunny style.

**state** In print making, each stage in the development of a print is referred to as a 'state'. If when he first takes an impression from a plate or block the artist then decides to do a little more work to it, the next printing, with his alterations made, will constitute the second state. A print may go through many such changes before it reaches its final state. Proofs of early states have a rarity value and appeal to specialist collectors.

**stave church** A Scandinavian church made of timber, dating from the early or mid-11th century.

**Steen, Jan** (*c.*1626–79) Dutch painter. He is best known for bucolic genre and peasant scenes but he also painted landscapes, still lifes and a number of religious subjects, in styles reminiscent of van Goyen (who was his father-in-law), Ostade, Jordaens and De Hooch. He maintained a higher standard than his prolific output might suggest. At his best, he is the equal of any of the artists whose styles he occasionally borrowed.

**Steer, Philip Wilson** (1860–1942) English painter. Trained at the Gloucester School of Art and in Paris, he was a founder of the **New English Art Club** and exhibited at both the Royal Academy and the Salon. His admiration for Degas and Monet, combined with a lifelong attachment to Constable and Turner, resulted in his bright, atmospheric style of anglicized Impressionism. His early beach scene, *Knucklebones* (Ipswich Museum and Art Gallery) was shown at the exhibition of 'London Impressionists' in 1889. His *Children Paddling, Walberswick* (Fitzwilliam Museum, Cambridge) is among his most Monet-like works.

Steer's later work established him among the leading landscape painters of modern times. His watercolours, in the early English tradition, are masterly.

**Steinberg, Saul** (b.1914) American painter and cartoonist, born in Romania and educated in Italy. He is famous for his witty, wayward yet geometric line, which encloses abstract thoughts with wiry precision.

**Steinlen, Théophile Alexandre** (1859–1923) Swiss-French painter, illustrator and graphic artist. He studied in Lausanne, then went to live in Paris (1878), where he recorded the life of the street, the café and the music hall in a series of vivacious illustrations for the magazines, among them *Gil Blas*. His style resembles that of Toulouse-Lautrec. Though he was not in the same class as a draughtsman, his prints and chromo-lithographs cover many of the same subjects with keen observation and good drawing.

**stele** A Greek word for an upright stone, generally a column or obelisk and usually an ancient memorial. In architecture it also applies to the surface of the face of a building which bears an inscription.

**Stella, Frank** (b.1935) American painter. He began in the Abstract Expressionist mode, but has since worked in non-organic materials and metals, as well as with paint, in his quest for what has been defined as **Post-Painterly Abstraction**. To achieve this he has banished all painterly nuances and suggestions of figurative imagery in favour of simple patterns, often in conjunction with the shape of the canvas so as to do away with any conception of the 'parts' of the whole. This formalistic reduction of the medium has given rise to **Minimal art**.

**Stella, Joseph** (1877–1946) American painter. His first work depicted his life as an Italian immigrant on Lower East Side, New York, and the dramas of life in mining communities. On return visits to Europe he made contact with avant-garde artists and was excited by the Futurist movement in Italy. He exhibited with Marcel Duchamp and Man Ray during the 1920s, and was subsequently recognized as the most important American Futurist by virtue of his powerful, architectonic images of New York.

**stellar vaulting** Roof vaulting where the ribs form a star-like pattern.

**stencil** A method of duplicating a design by cutting it out of a sheet of material such as plastic or metal and spraying, brushing or rubbing colour through the holes. Until the invention of silk-screen printing only simple shapes could be printed by this method. It has frequently been used as a means of colouring prints and for printing on fabric. See **pochoir**.

**stereobate** The foundation or basement of a building.

**Stevens, Alfred** (1817–75) English painter and sculptor. He received no formal training, but as a young man spent some nine years in Italy, where he kept himself by drawing portraits and copying old masters. He returned to London, found a teaching job, and in 1856 entered a competition for a memorial to the Duke of Wellington, to be erected in St Paul's. It is his major work.

**Stieglitz, Alfred** (1864–1946) American photographer and art dealer. Over a period of 30 years his Photo-Secession Gallery, the Intimate Gallery and An American Place all showed avant-garde and controversial art, from Picasso and Brancuși to Georgia O'Keefe, who became his wife.

**stiff-leaf** Descriptive term for late 12th-century and early 13th-century sculptured foliage.

**Still, Clyfford** (1904–80) American painter, a leader of the New York School. Like Robert Motherwell, he had an academic background, including six years as an assistant professor at Washington State University. His best-known work belongs to the Abstract Expressionist period, when he joined Jackson Pollock, Barnett Newman and Mark Rothko in New York.

**still life** A picture of an arrangement of inanimate objects, shown with some degree of realism, which may also be intended by the artist to have symbolic, as well as aesthetic, content. The origins of the genre in Western art lie in Roman times, but it was not until the 16th century that it became an independent form. Dutch and Flemish painters, in particular, developed it and still life later became a popular genre in France, culminating in the explorations of Cézanne, Picasso, Braque and Ben Nicholson.

**stipple** In painting or drawing, the technique by which small dots of colour or light and shade are applied with the point of the brush or pencil.

**stipple engraving** A process for engraving in tone, very similar to crayon engraving, and popular in the late 18th century for reproducing master drawings. The plate was covered with an etching ground and the design inscribed with broken lines. After the plate had been bitten in an acid bath the ground was removed and the plate worked with roulettes to build up tone by means of varying densities of dots. The technique was rarely practised outside England, and was rendered obsolete in the early 19th century with the advent of **lithography**.

**stone carving** Stone may be carved either directly or indirectly. In indirect carving, a model is first made in clay or wax, cast in plaster, and transferred to stone by the mechanical method of **pointing**. The predominant method in modern times is direct carving, when the form is hewn directly out of the stone. The way in which the sculptor releases the image from within the stone obviously depends on how he conceives it. If, like the ancient Egyptians, his conception is based on **frontal-**

ity, he will work the stone on four separate faces. Michelangelo, on the other hand, liked to work from the front to the back of the block. Modern sculptors usually conceive their sculptures in the round, and work the block correspondingly.

The stone carver's tools have barely changed since antiquity. The first blocking out is done with a heavy hammer, or *boucharde*, which has a head studded with pyramidal points. It is roughened down with a point or punch – simply a pointed steel bar – and mallet, which chip off large pieces of stone. Next a claw, a curved chisel with four or more teeth on a broad blade, is used to work the stone into better definition, leaving it furrowed and gouged, to be flattened by a variety of flat chisels. The sculptor then works the surface with a series of rasps, files and abrasives until he has achieved the desired texture.

**stopping out** In etching and aquatint, the application of an acid resist, usually a varnish, to selected areas of the plate to protect them from being further bitten by the mordant. The darkness of the printing in these processes is governed by the depth of the bite and accordingly those areas that are to remain light must be covered while the acid eats further into those that are to print dark. Depending on the number of different tones that the artist desires, successive areas of the plate may be stopped out many times.

**Stothard, Thomas** (1755–1834) English illustrator and watercolour artist. His first illustrations were published in 1779, for the *Poems of Ossian*, and he was kept busy for the next 50 years with drawings for editions of the poets and novelists, anthologies, and re-issues of the classics from Ariosto to Bunyan. His style, neat and Neoclassical, was well suited to engraving on a small scale. He shared one commission with J. M. W. Turner: to illustrate the two volumes by the banker-poet Samuel Rogers, *Poems* and *Italy*, published in 1830.

**strappo** Like **stacco**, a method of transferring a fresco from its original wall. Strips of cloth are attached to the paint surface with animal glue. The paint layer is then peeled from the intonaco and given a new backing of cloth.

This method is used when the intonaco is too decayed for the stacco method to be successful.

**strapwork** Interlaced bands and fretwork shapes used in screens and in ceiling decoration.

**Street, George Edmund** (1824–81) English architect, a pupil of George Gilbert Scott. He set up in Oxford in 1852, moved to London three years later, and proceeded to build a number of notable Victorian churches in his High Church manner: St James the Less, off Vauxhall Bridge Road; St Mary Magdalen, Paddington; and in 1879 Holbury St Mary, which he paid for out of his own pocket. In 1866 he won a competition for a design for the Law Courts, which remains his best-known London building.

**stretcher** The wooden framework on which a painter's canvas is stretched.

**string-course** A moulding run horizontally along a wall to mark a division in the vertical spacing of an architectural design. Sometimes it is used as an indication of an interior division of the storeys, or run along beneath or between a series of windows or openings to connect them architecturally. It occurs in Gothic architecture, where towers are often divided in this manner into storeys.

**Stuart** Period of English architecture 1625–1702, encompassing the Carolean period. Essentially, the age of Inigo Jones and Wren.

**Stubbs, George** (1724–1806) English animal painter. He was born in Liverpool, where his father was a currier and leather seller. He worked at the trade as a boy, but was making anatomical studies by the age of eight. He taught himself to paint, and earned money as a portraitist while studying anatomy at York Hospital. From 1756 he undertook dissections for his classic work, *The Anatomy of the Horse*, the plates for which he engraved himself. By this time he was well known, and received numerous commissions to paint racehorses and hunters, farm animals and wildlife. He became a Royal Academician in 1781, but declined to deposit a picture and so did not receive the diploma. At this, the high point of his career, he painted the *Phaeton with Cream Ponies* (Paul Mellon), the *Reapers* and *Haymakers* (Tate Gallery, London) and *Hambletonian with Trainer and Stable-lad* (private collection). Far more than a sporting painter, Stubbs is an acknowledged master of the English School.

**stucco** A form of ornamentation, Oriental in origin, achieved by applying a mixture of plaster to the wall surface and modelling or brushing it to attain the desired effect.

**Stuck, Franz von** (1863–1928) German painter, graphic artist and sculptor. In 1893 he became a founder member of the Munich Sezession. Two years later, as a teacher at the Munich Academy, his pupils included Wassily Kandinsky and Paul Klee. He is remembered for his contribution to the *Jugendstil*.

**studio** An artist's workplace. The term also refers collectively to an artist and his assistants and, by extension, has grown to mean 'School'. 'Studio work' can mean either an outdoor subject executed indoors or a work that is the product of a studio rather than of the master whose name it bears.

**study** A highly wrought drawing or painting, or sometimes only a detail, done for practice or to explore a particular aspect of a projected work.

**stump** A cigar-shaped implement made of cork or rolled leather or paper, used during the 18th and 19th centuries to rub chalk, crayon or pencil drawings so as to soften them in order to achieve tonal changes.

**stun** In stone carving, to bruise or chip the stone.

**style** The distinctive mode of expression of an artist or group of artists. As well as describing an artist's individuality, styles are classified according to period, manner, locality, school, nationality and movement.

**stylization** Art which is representational, yet departs from strictly naturalistic norms in favour of other modes.

**stylus** A pointed metal instrument about the shape of a pencil, used to impress the ground or surface but not to mark it. Originally they were used by the Greeks and Romans in ancient times for writing on wax tablets, but more recently for incising ornaments on gold grounds, tracing the outline of a cartoon on to plaster, or ruling lines on paper for squaring or to work out perspective.

**Sublime** An 18th-century term for a new aesthetic concept which entered the fine arts through the literature of the period, anticipating the Romantic sensibility that was to follow. The Sublime was closely allied to the cult of the Picturesque in nature, but went beyond mere rustic beauty to embrace all that is wild, awe-inspiring and magnificent. The key work on the concept in English was Burke's *Philosophical Enquiry into the Origin of our Ideas of the Sublime and Beautiful* (1757), which stressed the power of the Sublime to evoke terror and 'the grander passions'.

**Suffolk School** An invention of the picture dealers, but convenient for rounding up the assorted 19th-century followers of the two great Suffolk artists, Gainsborough and Constable, many of whom exhibited at the Ipswich Art Society. The 'School' is usually taken to include the Smythes of Ipswich, Edward Robert (1810–99) and Thomas (1825–92); John Moore (1820–1902); Robert Burrows (1810–83); the animal painter, John Duvall (1816–92), and the still-life artist, Henry George Todd (1846–98).

**sugar aquatint** see **aquatint**

**Suiboku** Japanese for ink painting. Suiboku is a style of painting on silk or paper in black ink practised in Japan throughout the 14th to 17th centuries. It derived from China in the Sung and Yüan dynasties, and was characterized by bold composition, tonal nuance, and meditative simplicity. Later practitioners tended to elaborate the form in virtuoso displays.

**Study** Leonardo da Vinci: *Study for Virgin and Child with St Anne and the infant St John* (Accademia, Venice).

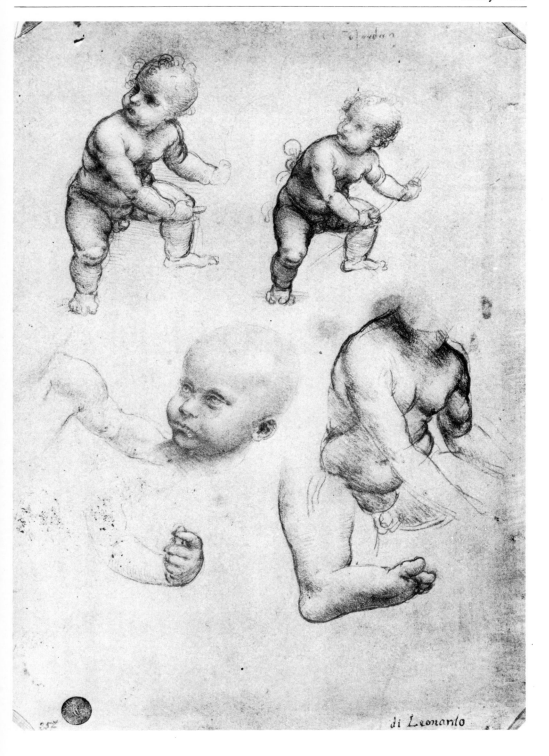

**Sullivan, Louis Henry** (1856–1924) American architect, born in Boston. After studying at the Massachusetts Institute of Technology he moved to Chicago, where in 1879 he set up in partnership with Dankmar Adler. The firm became successful builders of tall, metal-framed buildings, including the Wainwright Building, St Louis (1890), the Guaranty Building, Buffalo (1894) and the Carson, Pirie & Scott Store in Chicago (1899).

**sumi** Japanese ink.

**Super-Realism** Highly representational art, aiming to bring the image so close to the original as to be indistinguishable from it. The style is mainly confined to America and its subjects are taken from mundane, unheroic activities, heightened by immaculate photo-painterly technique. Its purpose is to shock the spectator into reacting to a familiar image as if he had never seen it before. A golf bag hanging from a hook, made of plastic (Marilyn Levine, b. 1933), or a top coat on a hanger, made of carved wood (Christian Renonciat, b. 1947), are typical of the **tromp-l'oeil** ambiguity which Super-Realist painters aim at. The *Colposcopy* by Maina-Miriam Munsky (b. 1943) and the lifesize *Couple with Shopping Bags* by Duane Hanson (b. 1925), in cast vinyl, achieve a chilling realism consistent with the artists' illusionist skills.

**support** The canvas, panel, paper or other substance on which the ground or paint is laid. For example, an oil painting support may be a stretched linen canvas or a panel or board support.

**Suprematism** An Abstract movement which flourished in Russia between 1913 and 1919 based on the ideas of Kasimir Malevich. He believed that art should employ only the basic geometrical shapes of the square, circle, triangle and cross, through which he hoped to express pure feeling. The movement had strong ties with **Constructivism**, and had a considerable influence, particularly on the Bauhaus, until well into the 1920s.

Malevich carried his theory to its most natural conclusion in his famous *White on White* series, which he exhibited in 1919. In his essay *The Non-Objective World* (1927), he described the black square on a white field as being 'the first form in which non-objective feeling came to be expressed. The square equals feeling, the white field equals the void beyond this feeling . . . The Suprematist square and the forms proceeding out of it can be likened to the primitive marks or symbols of aboriginal man, which represented in their combinations not ornament but a feeling of rhythm.'

**surbase moulding** The moulding which forms the cornice of a pedestal.

**surbased** Descriptive term for an arch where the height of the curve above the impost is less than half its span.

**surmounted** A term referring to an arch in which the height of a curve above the level of the impost is more than one half of the span.

**Surrealism** The movement in modern art that succeeded Dada, though with a literary and intellectual basis that gave it more validity and substance. It spanned virtually the entire inter-war period, at a time of intense curiosity about the working of the unconscious mind and the illusory nature of the physical world. To its proponents, realism extended into a psychic domain, beyond reason or precognition. They found precedents in such artists as Bosch, Piranesi and Goya, and in the writings of a 19th-century fantasist, Lautréamont, whose *Poésies* and *Maldoror* were rediscovered and claimed as proto-Surrealist texts.

The theories of Freud on the workings of the unconscious underpinned the Surrealists' conviction that dream and reality are not contradictory conditions but one 'super-reality'. André Breton, its first champion and spokesman, published a manifesto in 1924 defining Surrealism as 'pure psychic automatism through which the real functioning of thought may be expressed either verbally or in writing or in any other manner', and as 'dictation of thought completely uncontrolled by reason and independent of all aesthetic or moral preoccupations'. The artists who remained most true to this dictum over the next two decades included Max Ernst, Joan Miró, Giorgio de Chirico, Hans Arp, Man Ray, René Magritte and Yves Tanguy. Dali, a brilliant recruit in 1929, was later furiously rejected. In England,

**Surrealism** *Celebes* (1921) by Max Ernst, one of the leading figures in the Surrealist movement (Tate Gallery, London).

where Surrealist painting arrived late (1937), brought over by Roland Penrose (b. 1900) and the poet David Gascoyne (b. 1916), the impact was short-lived. However, it left its mark on such painters as Paul Nash, Graham Sutherland and Francis Bacon, and an entire generation of artists in collage have grown up in its wake.

**Sutherland, Graham** (1903–80) English painter. He studied at Goldsmith's School of Art, where he was among the group of students who together 'rediscovered' Samuel Palmer. The English strain of visionary Romanticism runs through his subsequent work, which is an exploration of the organic nature of landscape, rocks, roots and seemingly inanimate forms. His favourite painting country was Pembrokeshire, where he came upon the realization that 'reality is a dispersed and disintegrated form of imagination'.

His *Somerset Maugham*, in the Tate Gallery, London, painted in 1949, was the first in a series of portraits of prominent contemporaries. It included *Sir Winston Churchill*, a presentation portrait which the Churchill

family later destroyed. His tapestry, *Christ in Majesty*, was placed in Coventry Cathedral in 1962. In later life he returned to print making. Two series of aquatints, *The Bees* and Apollinaire's *Bestiary*, were completed in his last years.

**swag** Any decorative design based on festoons of flowers or drapery.

**Symbolism** A term used to describe a new attitude in painting and poetry that emerged in the mid-1880s, marking a watershed in the development of Western art, particularly in France. The Symbolists sought to express subjective, spiritual states through external images: as the poet Jean Moreau put it in 1886, 'to clothe the idea in sensuous form'. The visual elements of a Symbolist painting were therefore symbolic equivalents of an experience or emotion, transformations of reality rather than representations of it. Behind Symbolist art lay an anti-rationalist spirit, reflecting a preoccupation with the realm of dreams that was shortly to exercise Freud and the philosophical beliefs of Hegel, Schopenhauer and Bergson that ultimate reality lies beyond mere appearances.

The dominant Symbolist painter was Gauguin, whose style – often known as Synthetism or Cloisonnisme to distinguish it from the literary side of the movement – consisted of generalizing from specific shapes, so that figures and objects became flat and simplified, defined

**Symbolism** *The Poor Fisherman* (1881) by Puvis de Chavannes, in which a dominant colour tone helps to express the spiritual message (Louvre, Paris).

by a strong outline enclosing fields of non-naturalistic colour. Gauguin left France for Tahiti in 1891, but his followers, the Nabis – who included Maurice Denis, Edouard Vuillard, Pierre Bonnard and Paul Sérusier – continued in their various ways to develop his ideas in Paris.

Among other painters who produced Symbolist work are Gustave Moreau, Puvis de Chavannes, Odilon Redon, and Eugène Carrière (1849–1906). The work of Van Gogh, Edvard Munch, James Ensor and others is customarily described in Symbolist terms. The English Pre-Raphaelites, especially Rossetti and Burne-Jones, shared many Symbolist attitudes.

The movement pre-figured many later developments in 20th-century art, including **Surrealism** and **Expressionism**. Its achievement in finally freeing painting from an obligatory realism did much to pave the way for the development of abstract art.

**Synchronism** A movement founded in Paris in 1912 by the American painters Stanton Macdonald-Wright (1890–1973) and Morgan Russell (1886–1953), based on a theory of pure colour as the basic concomitant of form. Both painters were influenced by Cézanne, Matisse and Robert Delaunay. They were joined by two other American artists working in Paris, Patrick Bruce (1880–1937) and Arthur Frost (1887–1917), and in 1913 the group exhibited at the Armory show in New York. It is chiefly remarkable for being the first American movement with a formulated theory.

**Synthetic Cubism** see **Cubism**

**Synthetism** A Post-Impressionist manner, associated with members of the **Pont-Aven School**, which sought to express forms in a stripped-down, synthesized style, bounded by a strong outline.

**Tachisme** A term derived from the French *tache*, meaning spot or blob. Tachisme is very different from **blot** painting, in which a random mark is used to prompt a formal composition, in that the whole picture is made up of splotches of colour applied in a spontaneous and dynamic manner. The term was first used in the 1880s to describe Impressionist techniques, but acquired its modern meaning in the 1950s when it was used to describe the European counterpart to Action Painting.

Tachisme is opposed to all formality in art, whether abstract or naturalistic. Instead of seeking expression or representation, it seeks to *be* a dramatic record of the creative state of mind.

**tactile values** A term introduced by Bernard Berenson in *Florentine Painters of the Renaissance* (1896) to describe the sense of tangibility and texture first manifested in the works of Giotto, and characteristic of many Renaissance paintings. Berenson's term remains a useful one in art criticism, though his insistence on this property above all others as a prerequisite for high achievement has since been recognized as an anachronism.

**taenia** The small moulding along the top of the architrave in the Doric order.

**taille douce** see **line engraving**

**Talman, William** (1650–1719) English architect. He served under Wren, probably worked on the designs for Hampton Court, and rivalled Vanbrugh as an architect of country houses, in which he introduced elements of French and Italian Baroque. He was responsible for the east front of Chatsworth, Dyrham Park, and the state apartments at Burghley, since destroyed.

**Tamayo, Rufino** (b. 1899) Mexican painter, born at Oaxaca, where a museum contains his collection of pre-Columbian art treasures. Unlike the politically motivated mural painters, he confined himself largely to easel painting, in which European influences from Cubism to Expressionism are apparent. The cultural tensions inherent in modern Mexico are given expression in the angular Abstraction of his later work, which won him a reputation in the United States and Europe.

**Tanagra figurines** A class of small painted terracotta statuettes made in Greece during the late 4th and 3rd centuries BC. They are named after a small town in Boeotia that specialized in their production, and are valued for their depiction of contemporary life.

**Tanguy, Yves** (1900–55) French-American Surrealist painter. He began painting in 1923, after being introduced to Lautréamont's *Maldoror* and other Surrealist literature, and to a picture by Giorgio de' Chirico. Encouraged by André Breton, he exhibited with the Surrealists until 1938, when he emigrated to the United States. His imagery owes much to Salvador Dali and Jean Arp, but he found original themes in rugged landscape, which he gradually turned into interlocking forms amid which unearthly creatures have their spooky abode.

**Tanner, Robin** (b. 1904) English etcher. He studied under Stanley Anderson (1884–1966) at Goldsmith's College with Graham Sutherland, and captured for himself the visionary gleam of Samuel Palmer. After his retirement as an Inspector of Schools he resumed his early career as an etcher in the English pastoral tradition with a succession of plates inspired by his devotion to the Wiltshire countryside. *A Wiltshire Village* (1939), written by Heather Tanner, contains some of his most admired etchings and drawings.

**Tassi, Agostino,** otherwise Agostino Buonamaci (*c.* 1580–1644) Italian painter of the early Baroque period. He was a specialist in **quadratura**, the Illusionist architectural painting of floors and ceilings, which can be seen to striking effect in his setting for Guercino's *Aurora* (Casino Ludovisi, Rome). With Paul Bril and Adam Elsheimer he was instrumental in forming the landscape style of Claude Lorraine, who was his pupil.

**Tatlin, Vladimir** (1885–1953) Russian painter and sculptor, a founder of Constructivism. Born in Kharkov, he was trained in Moscow and influenced by the Analytical Cubism of Picasso, which took him on the first step to the constructions and hanging reliefs which he exhibited from 1913 to 1916. His most ambitious work was his projected *Monument to the Third International* (1919–20), a tower of wood and glass for a structure intended to be 1200 feet high. He reconciled his talents and ideas to Soviet aims, working as a theatrical and industrial designer in Kiev and Moscow.

**Taylor, Sir Robert** (1714–88) English architect. He began as a sculptor and was commissioned to make the Captain Cornewall monument at Westminster Abbey in 1744. As an architect he was content to follow in the Neo-Palladian tradition that was popular in his time. Of his surviving buildings, Asgill House, Richmond, and Stone Building, Lincoln's Inn, are typical.

**Tchelitchev, Pavel** (1898–1957) Russian-American painter and theatrical designer. He worked on theatrical design in Berlin and Paris in the 1920s, and used theatrical subjects in his first paintings. He moved on to portraiture, and in the 1930s to Constructivist works involving triple perspective and simultaneous images. His *Leaf Children* (1939) and *Hide and Seek* (1940) are in the Museum of Modern Art, New York.

**Telford, Thomas** (1757–1834) Scottish architect. He first trained as a mason, and left Edinburgh for London in his twenties. In 1784 he was made supervisor of the works at Portsmouth Dockyard. His subsequent career was in industrial building, which included the Buildwas Bridge, the Chirk Aqueduct, the Caledonian Canal and St Katherine's Docks. His most lasting achievements are the Menai Straits Bridge and the Conway Suspension Bridge, both of iron.

**temper** To improve the hardness of a metal by heating it and then plunging it into water. During the Renaissance the term was also applied to the preparation of paint. Tempered or tempera colours, in which a binder or vehicle is used, were distinguished from fresco, in which none were. Later tempera came to apply only to paint in which egg yoke or another emulsion was used.

**tempera** A technique of painting which employs pigments suspended in an emulsion vehicle. The emulsions can be natural (egg or milk of figs), artificial (casein and glue) or saponified (oil, wax or soap mixed with alkalis). Historically the most important of these is egg tempera, which was established in Europe by the 13th century and was the dominant technique for panel painting until the 15th, when it gradually gave way to oil painting. In modern times it has enjoyed a modest revival, most notably in the work of the American realist painter, Andrew Wyeth.

**template** A thin sheet usually of plastic or metal from which has been cut a variety of standard shapes, symbols or letters, used by draughtsmen as a stencil.

**Tenebrism** A term derived from the Italian word *tenebroso* (murky), which is used of paintings executed in a low key, such as those by Neapolitan and Spanish painters of the early 17th century who imitated the style of Caravaggio.

**Teniers, David** (1610–90) Flemish painter. He is known as Teniers the Younger to distinguish him from his less conspicuous father David Teniers the Elder (1582–1649). His first work consisted of religious pieces, but he found his most typical subjects in rustic genre scenes such as the *Peasants Playing Bowls, Peasants at Archery* and *Backgammon Players*, all in the National Gallery, London. He was made Dean of the Antwerp Guild of Painters, and shortly afterwards Court Painter to the Austrian governor of the Netherlands, Archduke Leopold Wilhelm. His records of the Archduke's collection, both in catalogue form and as copies of particular works, are in the Museum of Art History, Vienna.

**Tenniel, Sir John** (1820–1914) English cartoonist and illustrator. Born in London, he studied at the Clipstone Street Academy with Keene and Edward Dalziel. He illustrated an edition of *Aesop's Fables* in 1848, joined *Punch*, and became the paper's principal cartoonist in 1864. His 2000 cartoons cover the epoch of Imperial power, often with incisive humour. His masterpiece, however, is his contribution to Lewis Carroll's *Alice in Wonderland* in 1865, followed by *Alice Through the Looking Glass* in 1872. He was knighted in 1893.

**Terbrugghen, Hendrick** (1588–1629) Dutch painter. He was a leading member of the Utrecht School, but with a style and palette that separate him from his teacher, Bloemart, and look forward to the lighter graces of the Delft School. Two paintings of this character, *Jacob Reproaching Laban* (1627) and *A Man Playing a Lute* (1624), are in the National Gallery, London.

**terrace** or **terrase** In sculpture, any flaw in a piece of marble that can be remedied by filling with cement.

**terracotta** Clay baked in an oven or kiln until it is hard: literally, baked earth. The term is more loosely used of any clay suitable for firing in this way, with the exception of the finest porcelain clays. Terracotta sculpture and pottery are among the earliest of man-made objects.

**terrazzo** A flooring of marble chips set in cement.

**tertiary colours.** The range of hues that is produced by mixing secondary colours, usually chromatic variations of greys and browns.

**tessella** Small tesserae.

**tessellated** Descriptive of a cement floor in which tesserae are decoratively inserted.

**tesserae** Small cubes of hard, durable material used in the execution of a **mosaic**. The earliest tesserae used in the ancient civilizations were simply differently coloured pebbles. Later, ceramic, marble, glass, mother-of-pearl and even gold were used.

**tetrastyle** A Classical style of building with a four-column portico.

**Thornhill, Sir James** (1675–1734) English decorative painter. Alone among English artists, he was fully at home with the Baroque manner of the great European painters. His work at Greenwich between 1708 and 1727 is his most sustained achievement, including the Painted Hall, the Lower Hall and the Vestibule. Other important work by him includes the Queen's Bedroom at Hampton Court and the grisaille panels inside the Dome of St Paul's Cathedral.

He was appointed History Painter to George I in 1718 and was knighted in 1722. Hogarth, who studied under him at the St Martins Lane Academy, married his daughter in 1728.

**throw** To shape on a potter's wheel.

**tie beam** In a roof truss, the large horizontal beam which rests at each end on the walls and confines the thrust of the principal rafters, the feet of which are partially let into it.

**Tiepolo, Giovanni Battista** or Giambattista (1696–1770) Italian painter, the last and greatest of the Venetian decorative painters. His first major commission was to decorate the Archbishop's Palace at Udine (1725–8), where he showed a novel and spectacular grasp of steep perspective. The airy brilliance of his style was soon in demand all over northern Italy, from Venice to Milan. In 1750 he was invited to decorate the Kaisersaal at the Prince of Würzburg's residence, where his *Olympus with the Quarters of the Earth* reveals his imaginative energy at full stretch. In 1762 he went to Madrid to paint frescoes in the Royal Palace, and stayed there until his death.
His son Giovanni Domenico or Giandomenico (1727–1804) assisted him at Würzburg, and later received important commissions in his own right. His particular fancy was for genre scenes of a knockabout kind, including *commedia dell'arte* figures.

**tilehanging** Tiles overlapped and mounted on a wooden structure to form a covering for a wall.

**tincture** An archaic name for a tinge.

**tinge** A light stain or permeation of colour, faint yet perceptible.

**Tinguely, Jean** (b. 1925) Swiss sculptor, associated with Happenings involving the spectator. His work from 1945 is primarily in metal and constructed in moving parts. His 'meta-mechanical' reliefs developed into automatic painting machines, which he demonstrated in 1960 at the Paris Biennale. His more recent work has been concerned with destruction by, or of, mechanical structures.

**tint** A colour subtly modified by the addition of another – for example, light blue tinted with red turns lavender. Also, in the graphic arts, an area of uniform shade produced by the regular repetition of dots or lines to achieve shading.

**tint tool** A fine-pointed graver, named after its use in creating an even tint by regular, fine hatching, used in line and wood engraving.

**Tintoretto, Jacopo** (1518–94) Italian painter of the Venetian School. He may have worked briefly in the studio of Titian, whose influence persists throughout his long career. His *St Mark Rescuing a Slave*, painted in 1548 (Accademia, Venice) shows his skill in bringing together a wealth of narrative incident in a dramatic composition. His *Christ Washing the Disciples' Feet* (National Gallery, London) combines the powerful colour sense of Titian with a design that evokes Michelangelo. The cycle of paintings in the Scuola di S. Rocco, which occupied him from 1565 until 1587, is a sustained achievement of great nobility and force. The *Crucifixion*, in particular, has the impact of a spectator's-eye view, the entire drama both suspended and alive. The Mannerism of his late works looks forward to El Greco.

**Tissot, James** (1836–1902) French painter and etcher. Born in Nantes, he studied at the École des Beaux-Arts in Paris, exhibited costume pieces at the Salon from 1859, and in the 1860s was associated with the Impressionists, particularly Manet and Monet. He came to England after his involvement in the Commune of 1870–71, and stayed for 20 years. His conversation pieces and group paintings were exhibited regularly at the Royal Academy, many of them including Mrs Kathleen Newton, a beautiful divorcee who became his mistress. She died in 1882, and he went back to Paris where he produced further figure-pieces and a number of religious paintings before retiring into obscurity.

**Titian,** otherwise Tiziano Vecellio (c. 1487–1576) Italian painter, the dominant master of the Venetian School. He is thought to have been a pupil of the Bellini, but the obvious influence is that of Giorgione, some of whose works he was invited to finish after 1510, when Giorgione died.
By 1516 Titian had succeeded Giovanni Bellini as official painter to the Republic of Venice. His *Assumption*, in the S. Maria dei

Frari, begun in the same year, is a huge exercise in the High Renaissance manner. It was followed by altarpieces on a similar scale, resounding in force and colour, by mythological compositions such as the *Worship of Venus* (Prado, Madrid) and the *Bacchus and Ariadne* (National Gallery, London), and by a number of remarkable portraits, among them the scathing *Pope Paul and his Nephews* (Museo Nazionale, Naples). His series of commissions from the Emperor Charles V culminated in a picture, *La Gloria* (Prado), showing him and the dead Empress being received by the Trinity.

The piety of works like these contrasts with the fleshy sensuality of his *poesie*, as he called them, for Philip II: *Danae* and the *Venus and Adonis* (both in the Prado) are typical examples. He ended with a *Pietà*, now in the Accademia (Venice), which he painted for his own tomb but did not live to finish.

**Tobey, Mark** (1890–1976) American painter. He has travelled extensively in the East and has been influenced by oriental art and ideas. His aim has been to 'smash' form by eliminating perspective. His calligraphic compositions in 'white writing' are characteristic.

**tondo** A relief carving or easel picture of circular shape.

**tone** A broad term, used variously to apply to the degree of brightness in colour, to its saturation (deep or pale tone), value (light or dark tone) or chroma (bluish or reddish tone, cool or warm).

**toning** The application of a glaze or **scumble** in oil painting, so as to alter the pervading colour of the surface.

**Toorop, Jan** (1858–1928) Dutch painter, born in Java. He studied in Amsterdam and at the Académie des Beaux-Arts, Brussels, became a friend of Ensor, and exhibited with him in 1883. He painted in the Neo-Impressionist style from about 1887, then turned towards Symbolism under the influence of his friend Maeterlinck and the poet Emile Verhaeren. His most exotic work, *The Young Generation*, painted in 1892 (Boymans-Van Beuningem Museum, Rotterdam), is an allegory in luxuriant Art Nouveau.

**tooth** The coarse granularity in a **ground**, which helps the adhesion of the paint.

**topographical art** A term for the pictorial depiction of buildings and towns. It is distinguished from landscape in placing a higher degree of importance on literal accuracy, being primarily intended as a pictorial means of conveying information. However, the two categories frequently shade into one another: topographical features in a landscape may be depicted by the artist with the same freedom and looseness as the purely natural aspects of the scene. A scene in which both terrain and features are rendered with a high degree of accuracy is sometimes referred to as a topographical landscape.

**toreutics** The technique of working in intaglio or relief. It covers carving, engraving, and embossing.

**torso** The trunk of the human body, a statue without head or limbs. Classical statues have often lost their extremities, but have nevertheless been admired since the Renaissance, even in their mutilated state. Towards the end of the 19th century sculptors, led by Rodin, began to create torsos expressly for their incomplete, yet powerful effect.

**tortillon** A small twist of tightly rolled paper, pointed at one end, used to smear or blend charcoal or pastel. See **stump**.

**torus** A large semicircular convex moulding.

**tracery** In Gothic architecture, the stone framing in the head of a window treated as a decorative design springing from and supported by the mullions. The early forms of tracery were made up of geometrical figures fitted together and butted against each other. Later Gothic tracery bars show a greater freedom and flow of line. One of the architectural advantages of traceried windows is that they carry the texture of the wall surface over the windows, instead of leaving them as blank openings in the wall.

**tracing** A drawing copied from another, using the original as a guide. This may be done by laying a piece of thin paper over the outline and simply copying its shape. Heavier paper may be used if it is placed over the original on a tracing box, a device which shines light through the two layers of paper from underneath. A drawing may also be transferred to another surface by rubbing its back with charcoal, placing it that side down on another surface, and going over its lines with a pencil or stylus, causing the charcoal beneath to adhere to the new surface.

**transept** In church architecture, the arms of the cross projecting north and south, separating the apse from the nave.

**transfer lithography** An adjunct of lithography, which enables the artist to draw his design on paper and have it transferred to the stone by a professional printer. The design must still be executed in litho crayon, but working on paper allows a freedom and spontaneity not attainable by direct application to the stone.

**transom** The horizontal crossbar in late Gothic traceried windows, inserted at right angles to the mullions. It is also the word for the crosspiece separating a door from the fanlight above it or, in the United States, the fanlight itself.

**transparent base** In silk-screen printing, a medium for giving normally opaque colour a degree of transparency, so making it more workable. It usually consists of a mixture of aluminium steatrate, acrylic resin and mineral spirits.

**transverse rib** In roof vaulting, a rib that crosses the roof at right angles to the walls.

**travesty** As used in art criticism, a ludicrous parody or burlesque of a serious work or genre. Duchamp's famous painting of the *Mona Lisa* with a moustache is an example.

**trecento** The 1300s, that is, the 14th century. The word is often used as a comprehensive term for Italian art of that period.

**trefoil** Tracery consisting of three lobes or arcs.

**trial proof** In print making, a proof pulled from any particular state of the block or plate

so that the artist can see how his work is progressing, or in order to perfect the inking.

**triforium** In Gothic architecture, an arcade occupying the space between the top of the nave arcade and the sills of the **clerestory** windows. It is a decorative treatment of the part of the wall against which the roof of the aisle butts, and where there can therefore be no windows.

**triglyphs** In architecture, the rectangular blocks between the metopes in a frieze of the Doric order, each with two vertical grooves in the centre and a half groove at each side.

**triptych** see **altarpiece**

**trompe l'oeil** A painting that deceives the eye by being three-dimensionally realistic. See **Illusionism**.

**trucage** The French word for fakery.

**trullisatio** An Italian term for the first coat of plaster that makes up the support for a fresco. In English, the scratch coat.

**Tudor** The period between 1485 and 1603. It is essentially a domestic style, covering as it does a period when the church's fortunes were at a low ebb. The predominant material was brick, often made from adjacent clay pits, the diggings being turned into a lake or moat. Gentlemen's houses had small windows, steep roofs and tall, ornamented chimneys (coal was by now being burned as a fuel). Yeomen's houses were timber framed with panels of brick or wattle-and-daub plaster.

**Tudor flower** An upright, conventional ivy-leaf motif, used in English late Gothic and Tudor architecture.

**tunnel vault** see **barrel vault**

**Turner, Joseph Mallord William** (1775–1851) English painter and watercolourist. He was the most important English artist of the 19th century and among the greatest in European art. The son of a barber, he was born in London and showed his first drawings in his father's shop. He studied at the Royal Academy Schools, exhibited at the Royal Academy

**Trompe l'oeil** Hans Holbein: *The Ambassadors* (1533). The optical trickery arises from the · perspective rendering of the skull in the foreground which can only be perceived from a certain angle (National Gallery, London).

from 1790, and became a full member at the age of 22. With Girtin he was among the young artists patronized by Dr Monro.

His early oils vary in manner from Dutch-style landscapes and marines in the manner of Cuyp, Ruisdael and Van de Velde to classical compositions in the style of Claude. His visits to Europe produced original themes, notably from the Swiss Alps, which he treated with unprecedented power, and Venice, whose qualities he translated into watercolours of an almost magical delicacy. His obsession with light and colour and with the fusion of elements was expressed in subjects as varied as *The Burning of the Houses of Parliament* (1834), *Norham Castle* (1835) and *Rain, Steam and Speed* (1844).

His 'colour beginnings' and late, visionary oils, mostly unseen in his lifetime, pre-date the birth of the Modern Movement by some 30 years.

**Tuscan** see **order**

**Tudor** Barrington Court, Somerset. The twisted, ornamented chimneys are typical features of Tudor architecture.

**tusche** A greasy ink used in lithography for drawing the design on to the stone or plate, and used to create effects not possible with the lithographic crayon. It is also used in silkscreen printing to paint the design to be printed on to the screen. The screen is covered with a glue which does not adhere to the tusche, though it has the effect of stopping out the remaining areas.

**tympanum** The triangular space left between the horizontal and raking cornices of a pediment in Classical architecture. It was usually occupied by a sculpture in the centre, standing free of the wall behind it.

**type-high** A term describing a block or plate that is made to the exact depth of type used in letterpress printing, so that it can be incorporated as an illustration to the text. Type height is usually 0.9 in.

**typography** The art of printing with type, from design through to composition (typesetting). The technique of printing by movable type was developed in the 15th century, chiefly by Johann Gütenburg, and quickly superseded the more laborious hand copying and block book printing then in use. Type was set by hand in frames until the invention of mechanical processes – Monotype and Linotype machines – at the beginning of this century.

The typographer's art is concerned not only with the selection of a particular face – its font, size, boldness, whether serif or sans-serif – but also with the overall proportions of the page, the width of the margins, breadth of the columns, placement of headlines and illustrations, and use of initial letters. Commercial standardization has restricted the typographer's role, but it is kept alive within the private press movement and by publishers of limited editions.

**Uccello, Paolo,** otherwise Paolo di Dono (1397–1475) Italian painter, mosaicist and craftsman. He was an assistant in the workshop of Ghiberti, went to Venice around 1425, where he was employed as a mosaicist at St Mark's, then returned to Florence and embarked on the four frescoes in the S. Maria Novella depicting scenes from *Genesis*. Of these, *The Deluge* is regarded as a masterpiece of perspective, demonstrating Uccello's imaginative use of what was still a novel and imperfectly understood device. In Padua he painted the three panels of the *Battle of San Romano* (Uffizi Gallery, Florence, Louvre, Paris, and National Gallery, London), under the patronage of the Medici. His last works, painted in Urbino, were an altarpiece for the Confraternity of the Corpus Domini, which he was unable to finish, and the romantically mysterious *Hunt* (Ashmolean Museum, Oxford).

**Ukiyo-e** The term used to describe a form of genre painting and print making in Japan, from the 16th to the 18th century. The subjects were usually of contemporary life, such as theatre scenes, street entertainers, brothels and public baths. From the 1740s they began to be printed in colour, often with the use of as many as 20 separate blocks, and to introduce landscape, bird and animal subjects. The art enjoyed no prestige in Japan, but was eagerly taken up by 19th-century European painters, notably the Impressionists. Its influence subsequently worked through to the Post-Impressionists, the Nabis, and Art Nouveau.

**Ultraism** A pejorative term rather than a designation, used by traditionalists to refer in a general way to all 20th-century art movements of which they do not approve.

**undercroft** In a church or chapel, a room below ground, usually vaulted.

**undercut** The part of a sculpture that protrudes from the main form and leaves an indentation beneath it.

**underpainting** The preliminary layer of colour in which, until the advent of **alla prima** painting, the drawing, composition and tonal relationships of a painting were worked out. Underpaintings were often executed in **grisaille**. Colouristic aspects were left to the glazes, scumbles and impasto with which the underpainting was covered. It was also known as dead colouring or abozzo.

**undertone** The perceived colour of a pigment when seen by transmitted light – light which has already passed through a substance such as a transparent glaze. The undertone of a pigment may be different from its overall tone: for example, alizarin crimson has a bluish undertone.

**Unit One** A group of English painters which included Paul Nash, Ben Nicholson, Edward Wadsworth, Henry Moore, Barbara Hepworth and Edward Burra (b. 1905). They exhibited together once in 1933 in what they called 'a truly contemporary spirit', but after that Unit One was hardly ever heard of again.

**Unwin, Raymond** (1863–1940) English architect and town planner. His lasting achievement is the 'garden city', of which the prototype was the one at Letchworth (1903). The most successful is the Hampstead Garden Suburb, begun in 1907 and still discernible amid the encircling Brutalism.

**Upjohn, Richard** (1802–78) English-born architect. He emigrated to the United States, where he became a leading church architect in the Gothic style. His son Richard Michell Upjohn (1828–1903) became his father's partner. He is known for his design of the State Capitol in Hartford, Connecticut, in the Victorian Gothic mould.

**Utamaro, Kitagawa** (1753–1806) Japanese master of the colour print (**Ukiyo-e**). He was an habitué of brothels, whose inmates he drew with fastidious skill. His series of the *Twelve Hours in the Green Houses* shows the stylized routines and preparations for the night's work. The *Calendar of the Green Houses* is a conducted tour of the Yoshiwara, a red-light district where the artist spent most of his life. His career coincided with the beginning of the end of the Ukiyo-e figure print. The art was overtaken by its own popularity, and slowly died.

**Utrillo, Maurice** (1883–1955) French painter. He was the illegitimate son of Suzanne Valadon (1867–1938), an artist's model turned painter, and took his name from his adoptive father, a Spanish architect and writer. Utrillo's career was a conflict between his addiction to drink and drugs and his startling talents as a painter. His street scenes in Montmartre and in Montmagny show a poetic sense of form which places him among the most gifted artists of his time.

**Valadon, Suzanne** (1867–1938) French painter. The daughter of a bricklayer and laundress, she became an artist's model, mistress of Renoir and protégé of Degas, who rated her talents as a painter highly. Her style contained elements of the painters she knew, including Gauguin. She was the mother, at 18, of Maurice Utrillo.

**valley** The interior angle formed where two adjacent roof surfaces meet.

**valley tile** A concave tile shaped to fit the angles of the roof valleys where two roofs meet.

**Vallotton, Félix** (1865–1925) Swiss painter, born in Lausanne, Switzerland. He went to Paris as a youth, trained at the Académie Julian, and began exhibiting at the Salon in 1885. He switched his style from Nabis to Pointillist, then took to woodcut illustrations of a sharp, sophisticated brilliance. It is mainly on these that his reputation rests.

**values** A term for the gradations of tone on a scale of greys running from black to white. Chromatic colours can be calibrated in the same way: the darker they are, the lower their value or key. In nature the scale is a continuum, as revealed by a monochrome photograph, but painting involves differentiations of tone or colour values.

**Vanbrugh, Sir John** (1664–1726) English architect. He had already established himself as a popular dramatist when he turned to architecture. His first commission was to design Castle Howard for the Earl of Carlisle (1699), who then secured him the office of Comptroller at the Office of Works, where he became a colleague of Wren. His greatest achievement is Blenheim, a fitting palace for the nation's hero, the Duke of Marlborough. With money no object and an opportunity to create a sumptuous monument for living in, he brought English Baroque to a brilliant summation.

**Vanderbank, John** (c. 1694–1739) Portrait painter, the son of Peter Vanderbank (1649–97). He was born and trained in Paris. He was a busy and competent follower of Kneller, with a taste for dressing his lady sitters in Rubens-type costume. He painted Queen Caroline and Sir Isaac Newton and a series of illustrations for *Don Quixote* (1731).

**vanishing point** The distant point to which all receding parallel lines in a picture lead. It is used as a means of achieving depth.

**vanitas** A still-life composition illustrating the inexorable passage of time, and hence the vanity of human wishes. It was popular in the 17th century, especially in Holland.

**Varley, John** (1778–1842) English watercolour artist. Though largely untrained, he achieved an eminence in his art equalled by only a few of his contemporaries. He passed on to numerous pupils the classic principles of laying a watercolour wash and of composition in the quasi-academic Picturesque tradition. His early work is under the influence of Girtin, whom he met at Dr Monro's. His travels in Wales, Northumberland, Ireland and along the Thames yielded typical subjects, often treated with a freedom and looseness not always to be seen in his exhibition pictures. David Cox, John Linnell and Samuel Palmer

were among the artists who profited from his teaching.

His brother Cornelius (1781–1873), who accompanied him on early sketching tours, also occupies a distinguished place among the early English watercolour painters. Both he and John Varley were founder members of the Old Water Colour Society in 1804.

**Vasarély, Victor** (b. 1908) French painter and sculptor. His explorations of the ways in which sets of lines or geometric forms operate on the optic nerve anticipated Op art. In his sculpture he aspires to what he has called a 'universal folklore' in an abstract, architectonic form.

**Vasari, Giorgio** (1511–74) Italian painter and architect. He was the author of the *Lives of the Most Eminent Painters, Sculptors and Architects* (1550, enlarged 1568), a source of much that is known of his contemporaries, in particular Michelangelo. He trained in Florence in the circle of Andrea del Sarto, travelled all over Italy, and maintained a large workshop to help him carry out his commissions. In 1555 he was appointed architect for the Palazzo Vecchio, and in 1563 he founded the Accademia del Disegno, both in Florence. He is remembered as a painter mostly for his Mannerist decorations and frescoes. His own house at Arezzo has been converted into a Vasari museum.

**Vaughan, Keith** (b. 1912) English painter. He belongs with Sutherland, Minton and Colquhoun in the tradition of romantic naturalism that continues in English painting. He remained a figurative painter, though with a variety of Abstraction after the example of Nicholas de Staël.

**vault** Any solidly built arched roof over a building, other than a dome. Types of vaulting are listed under separate entries.

**vaulting surfaces** The filling in between the ribs of a Gothic vault, known as the 'web' of the vault.

**veduta** A picture of a sizeable part or whole of a town, most frequently Venice and other Italian cities. A *viduta ideata* is an imaginary, though realistically depicted, location. Piranesi, Canaletto and Guardi are probably the most accomplished practitioners of the genre. See also **capriccio**.

**vehicle** The liquid in which pigments are dispersed to make paint. The word can be applied to either the medium or the diluent. A vehicle may serve to make the colour malleable, to bind pigment into a cohesive mass, to cement it as it dries to the ground, and sometimes to enhance its optical effect.

**veil** A transparent layer of thin glaze applied over a white ground to give it colour while not detracting from its reflective properties. If a tint is mixed into the ground rather than applied over it, it loses its characteristic reflection.

**Velazquez, Diego Rodríguez de Silva y** (1599–1600) Spanish painter. He was born in Seville of Portugese parentage, and trained in the academy of Francisco Pacheco (1564–1654), his future father-in-law.

In his religious paintings he soon forsook the academic dryness of Pacheco for a naturalistic manner, heightened with warm Venetian colour. He went to Madrid in 1622 and in the following year was invited back as Court Painter to Philip IV. His courtly portraits have the vivacity of Titian, whose work he saw in the Spanish royal collection. Rubens, a visitor to Madrid in 1628, may have suggested his visit to Italy, 1629–31, which introduced him to the work of Renaissance masters. There followed the splendid series of royal and equestrian portraits and the *Surrender of Breda* (1634, Prado, Madrid), a dignified celebration of a Spanish victory in the Netherlands, painted for the Buen Retiro Palace.

A second visit to Rome, 1649–51, produced his portrait of *Pope Innocent X* (Doria, Rome) and the *Rokeby Venus*, the only nude he ever painted (National Gallery, London). His cryptic 'painting about painting', *Las Meninas*, in the Prado, is a statement and a conundrum, containing much of what Velazquez felt about the painter's relationship to his art.

**Velde, Adriaen van de** (1636–72) The younger brother of Willem van de Velde, known as Willem II, he was taught by his father and by Jan Wijnants. His subjects were landscapes, portraits, genre and biblical scenes. He was also an etcher, notably of cattle in landscape settings.

**Velde, Esaias van de** (c. 1591–1630) Dutch painter. A pupil of Gillis van Coninxloo (1544–1607), he was one of the first of the Dutch School of realistic landscape painters, taking his subjects direct from nature. The *Winter Scence* (1623) in the National Gallery, London, is a typical example. Jan van Goyen and Salomon van Ruysdael were pupils of his.

**Velde, Henri van de** (1863–1957) Belgian painter and architect. He studied in Antwerp and in Paris, where he met Monet, Pissarro and Signac. Returning to Belgium in 1885 he combined painting with art criticism. He gradually abandoned art for furniture making, interior design, and ultimately architecture.

As a painter, he was lastingly influenced by Seurat's *La Grande Jatte*, which he saw in 1887. His interest in the decorative arts was quickened by William Morris's Arts and Crafts Movement and by the influence of Japanese art on that of Paris.

**Velde, Willem van de** (1611–93) and his son, also called Willem (1633–1707) They were among the leading marine painters of the Dutch School. They came to London in 1672, and two years later were paid retainers by Charles II to illustrate the Navy's sea fights against the Dutch. The son, often known as Willem II, emerges as the busier and livelier painter. Some of his studies were done from the deck of a small vessel at the scene of the action. They made a profound impression on English painters, laying the foundations of the English School of marine painting. Father and son are well represented at the National Maritime Museum, Greenwich and in the Rijksmuseum, Amsterdam.

**vellum** A fine parchment, traditionally made from the skin of newborn calves, kids or lambs, later superseded by heavy drawing paper.

**Venetian window** An arched opening with a rectangular opening on either side.

**Verism** A pure form of realism, which repudiates all idealization in favour of the belief that the most mundane and vulgar subjects are imbued with aesthetic value, and deserve to be depicted with scrupulous art. An essentially 20th-century concept, it has been retrospectively applied to a number of early artists, including the Roman portrait sculptors.

**Vermeer, Jan** (1632–75) Dutch painter, born and worked in Delft. He has been awarded his position among the great masters only in the last hundred years. Before 1880 his work was unrecognized or attributed to other Delft painters such as Nicolaes Maes and Pieter de Hooch. He is thought to have been a pupil of Carel Fabritius, who was taught by Rembrandt. He became a Master of the Delft Guild in 1653, and Dean ten years later. When he died, he left his wife and eleven children in dire poverty and heavily in debt.

Only 36 paintings by him are known to exist. The earliest of them, from about 1655, are the *Diana* (Mauritshuis, The Hague) and *Christ in the House of Mary and Martha* (National Gallery of Scotland, Edinburgh). He reaches his full mastery of interior light in the *Young Woman with a Water-jug* (Metropolitan Museum of Art, New York), *c.*1660, and *The Lace Maker* (Louvre), *c.*1664.

**vermiculation** Ornamentation of masonry with shallow, scraped marks that look like worm tracks.

**Vernet, Claude-Joseph** (1714–89) French landscape and marine painter. He lived for 20 years in Rome, where he painted works which were hailed by the proto-Romantic art pundit Diderot as superior to Claude. Louis XV later commissioned him to paint a series of the *Ports of France*, which number 16 works, now in the Louvre. He knew Richard Wilson, and had several English patrons for his stormy marine subjects.

His son Antoine-Charles-Horace, otherwise known as Carle Vernet, painted sporting pictures for Louis XVIII and battle scenes, including the *Gallery of Battles* at Versailles. His son Emile-Jean-Horace Vernet (1789–1863), also a specialist in battle pieces, was director of the French Academy at Rome.

**Veronese, Paolo** (*c.*1528–88) Italian painter. The son of a sculptor, he trained as a painter at his birthplace, Verona. In Venice in about 1553 he painted the ceilings of the Doges' Palace and decorated the church of S. Sebastiano. At the Villa Barbaro at Maser he worked with Palladio and the sculptor Alessandro Vittoria (1525–1608), contributing exuberant Illusionist frescoes.

He was much in demand as a painter of large-scale religious pieces, which he carried out with a wealth of natural detail in the **Grand Manner** of the Renaissance masters. The *Adoration of the Kings*, originally painted for the S. Silvestro, Venice, and now in the National Gallery, London, is typical of what Ruskin called the 'manly, simple, everyday natural grandeur of Veronese'. His painterly conception of landscape, and the use he made of architectural features, extended into the work of Poussin and Claude.

**Verrocchio, Andrea del** (*c.*1435–88) Italian painter and sculptor of the Florentine School. He is thought to have been a pupil of Donatello, whom he succeeded as the first sculptor of Florence. His style, however, is of a lighter, more flexible and interpretative kind. His best-known painting, the *Baptism of Christ* (Uffizi Gallery, Florence), includes a kneeling, curly-headed angel which is generally accepted as the earliest work of Leonardo, who as a boy was an assistant in his workshop. The equestrian statue of *Bartolomeo Colleoni* (1479–88) in Venice and his bronze *David* (Bargello, Florence), are his most characteristic sculptures.

**Vertue, Robert and William** (active 1475–1527) English master masons. They were jointly responsible for the rebuilding of Bath Abbey, for the Henry VII chapel in Westminster Abbey, and probably for King's College Chapel, Cambridge. Robert Vertue also designed Corpus Christi College, Oxford.

**Victorian** Style of architecture between about 1850 and the end of the 19th century. The period covers the post-Regency decline of middle-class architecture, the growth of the suburbs, the Gothic revival and the birth of the garden suburb. There is therefore no single Victorian style of architecture any more than of painting or the fine arts generally. It was, however, an age of notable architects, for example William Butterfield, A. W. N. Pugin,

Kark Schinkel, Louis Sullivan, Charles Voysey and the two Webbs, Sir Aston and Philip.

**Vienna Sezession** A radical and relatively self-contained movement in 20th-century art launched in 1897 when a group of young artists, architects and designers seceded from the Austrian artistic establishment to exhibit as an independent group in their own art centre. They formed a new society under the presidency of Gustav Klimt, supported by Egon Schiele, Oskar Kokoschka, the painter and graphic artist Kolo Moser (1868–1918) and the architects Josef Hoffman (1870–1956), Otto Wagner (1841–1918), Adolf Loos (1870–1933) and Josef Olbrich (1867–1908), who was responsible for the new Sezession building. Despite their different talents the members succeeded in creating a coherent and distinctive manner, redolent of Symbolism and of Art Nouveau (Jugenstil). They achieved popular esteem, and left a mark on most aspects of artistic life in Vienna during the last years of the Empire. In architecture and applied design they were markedly influenced by the work of Charles Rennie Mackintosh.

**Vienna Sezession** *Mme Adèle Block-Bauer* by Gustav Klimt, the movement's first President until 1905.

The energies of the Sezessionists were dissipated after 1918, the year in which some of its leading members – Klimt, Schiele, Wagner and Moser – died.

**vignette** In painting and photography, a small picture without distinct edges in which the borders shade off into the background. In traditional book printing, a small ornamental design, usually at the beginning or end of a chapter, whose edges similarly fade off.

**Vignola, Giacomo Barozzi da** (1507–73) Italian architect. Born at Vignola, near Modena, he studied in Bologna and in 1530 settled in Rome, where he became the most important architect following the death of Michelangelo. He completed the Palazzo Farnese, Caprarola, which had been begun by Peruzzi, and designed the Mannerist villa of Pope Julius in collaboration with Ammanati and Vasari (1551–5). His church of Gesu, in Rome, begun in 1568, brought together the basic Renaissance scheme and the longitudinal form of medieval times, with chapels leading off the nave and emphasis on the focal positioning of the high altar: a design that has been widely followed into modern times. At St Peter's, Rome, Vignola took over Michelangelo's role as Chief Architect.

**Vignon, Pierre** (1762–1828) French architect. He was the builder of the Madeleine in Paris (1806–43). The commission came from Napoleon, whose concept of the building, which at that time had been envisaged on a less grandiose scale, was that it should be a temple to French glory. It could equally be called a temple to the glory that was Rome.

**Villon, Jacques** (1875–1963) French painter, brother of Marcel Duchamp and Raymond Duchamp-Villon. He began as an illustrator, becoming involved in Cubism and in the Section d'Or. He turned to Abstract painting in the 1920s, usually in a low-toned palette of greys and browns. In the 1930s he painted with an almost Fauve brightness. His reputation has advanced considerably in recent years.

**Vingts, Les** A group of 20 Belgian artists, the members of which varied from year to year, who exhibited between 1883 and 1893 and invited prominent foreign artists to come to Brussels and exhibit with them. The idea was initiated by a local patron of the arts, Octave Maus, in the belief that established institutions were failing to recognize the artistic talents then emerging in Belgium. By this means, developments in Paris were rapidly communicated to Brussels. Rodin, Whistler, Redon, Renoir, Monet, Signac, Cézanne, Van Gogh, Seurat, Toulouse-Lautrec and Gauguin were among the artists who exhibited with Les Vingts.

**Viollet-le-Duc, Eugène-Emmanuel** (1814–79) French architect and engineer. His researches into the Gothic style led him to publish a theory equating medieval Gothic with 19th-century iron-ribbed structures. His work as a restorer of medieval monuments included Nôtre-Dame de Paris, and the city of Carcassonne.

**virtu** The Italian word for excellence, used into the 18th century to refer to a refined artistic taste. It also meant a curio, a usage that persists in the salerooms today. Similarly, virtuoso was originally used of a collector or connoisseur, and later of a professional artist.

**Vlaminck, Maurice de** (1876–1958) French painter. With Derain he founded the 'Dalou' school, a precursor of Fauvism. Resolutely non-academic, he refused to take Cubism seriously or to contribute to the intellectual 'isms' of the time. After the wild colours of his Fauve period he adopted a relatively restrained naturalism, the style of his *Still Life with Lemons* (National Gallery of Art, Washington) and *Bougival* (Musée d'Art Moderne, Paris), derived from Cézanne.

**volutes** The distinctive spiral ornaments on each side of an Ionic capital.

**Vorticism** An English art movement founded by Wyndham Lewis in 1913. Its members included William Roberts, Edward Wadsworth and Henri Gaudier-Brzeska, with the poet Ezra Pound acting as general instigator and impressario. Lewis claimed later that 'Vorticism, in fact, was what I, personally, did and said at a certain period.' It was born out

**Vorticism** Wyndham Lewis: *Composition*, 1913 (Tate Gallery, London).

of Cubism and Futurism and the belief, taken from Boccioni, that artistic creation must take place in a state of emotional vortex. The aim was 'to establish what we consider to be characteristic in the consciousness and form content of our time; then to dig to the durable simplicity by which that can be most grandly and distinctly expressed.'

The Vorticist style was based on angular and machine-like forms, anticipating many of Fernand Léger's themes. But the essence of the movement lay as much in the social and cultural energy that it sought to inject into a complacent and conservative epoch in British history, as in its purely aesthetic aims. In 1914 Lewis and his friends announced the end of the Christian era on the cover of the first issue of their magazine *Blast*. The following year they published a second issue and held a Vorticist exhibition. But wartime conditions were too much for the movement, and by 1918 its moment had passed.

**voussoirs** The stones which are used for building an arch. Because of their wedge shape, they are self-supporting.

**Voysey, Charles Annesley** (1857–1941) English architect and designer. He was one of the first to lead domestic architecture away from the frills and embellishments of the late Victorian age towards a quasi-rural simplicity, designing from the centre outwards rather than from a preconceived idea of external form. Interior furnishings and fittings, from lamp brackets to door handles, were designed in the same spirit of dignity and respect for natural materials. His ideas, in the tradition of William Morris and the Arts and Crafts movement, were anti-revivalist. However, translated into the mass market they account for much of the mock-Tudor development between the wars.

**Vuillard, Edouard** (1869–1940) French painter. He was a student at the École des Beaux-Arts, Paris, in the last days of Impressionism, a friend of Maurice Denis, Sérusier, Félix Vallotton and Pierre Bonnard. He belonged to the Nabis circle and exhibited at the Salon, worked in the theatre and music-hall as designer and decorator, and mastered the art of colour lithography, through which much of his most typical work is best known. He worked outside the art coteries, sticking to his own beliefs, and carrying the flavour of Impressionism into the 1930s.

**Wadsworth, Edward** (1889–1949) English artist. He studied at Bradford and the Slade School, and was a member of the Vorticist group headed by Wyndham Lewis. He exhibited with the New English Art Club from 1921, and in the 1930s turned to painting in tempera in a style that had affinities with Léger and Surrealism. His murals include the De La Warr Pavilion, Bexhill, and decorations for the liner Queen Mary. His graphic style, in sharply defined abstract shapes, epitomizes the Vorticist ideal of an aesthetic mechanical age.

**Walker, Frederick** (1840–75) English painter and illustrator. He studied art at the British Museum and at the Royal Academy Schools and learned the craft of wood engraving from Josiah Wood Whymper. He worked for the *Cornhill Magazine*, where he took over the illustration of Thackeray's novel *Philip* from the author, and was soon in demand for his intelligent, animated figures. His watercolours, exhibited from 1870, established a second reputation for him.

**wall shaft** In Gothic architecture, a half or three-quarter shaft projecting from the wall but forming part of the masonry. It is generally used to lead up to the springing of the vault.

**walling wax** Beeswax which, when warmed, can be used to form a raised edge around an etching plate so that the mordant can be poured directly on to it instead of immersing the whole plate in acid.

**Wanderers, The** A movement organized in Russia by Nicholas Kramskoy in 1872. The paintings were realistic treatments of social themes, often thinly disguised propaganda against the Czarist government. The group used to send touring exhibitions throughout the provinces in the belief that art exists to educate the people.

**Ward, James** (1769–1859) English painter. He was the brother-in-law of George Morland (1763–1804), a pot-boiling painter of animal and rustic subjects whom Ward at first emulated. He soon took Stubbs as his model, and developed a reputation as an animal painter with such works as *Bulls Fighting* (Victoria and Albert Museum, London) and *Fighting Horses*, a subject inspired by Gericault. His landscapes have breadth and grandeur and are infused with the Romantic spirit. His massive *Gordale Scar* (Tate Gallery, London) is his most ambitious composition in the Rubens tradition. Watercolours and drawings by him also have a prominent place in the English School.

**Warhol, Andy** (b. 1930) American painter. After a successful career as a commercial artist he began turning the techniques, imagery and products of the media, from soup cans to film actresses, into manufactured art: 'I am painting this way because I want to be a machine'. He became the most influential of the American Pop artists, then turned to film making as an extension of his feeling for mechanized expressionism. He was given a retrospective exhibition at the Tate Gallery in 1971.

**warm colours** Colours in which red and yellows are dominant are called warm, as opposed to the cool colours at the blue end of the spectrum.

**wash** A transparent coat of diluted ink or watercolour spread over a broad area, such as the sky in a landscape. It is usually applied with a thick, soft brush. Originally, washes were used as an adjunct to pen drawing. The early English watercolourists built up their paintings in a series of superimposed washes over a pen or pencil outline, in imitation of the oil painter's glazes. See **watercolour**.

**wash drawing** Brush drawings in one or two diluted washes of ink or watercolour, often over a pencil or pen-and-ink outline.

**waste mould** A plaster mould used for casting sculpture which can be used only once, since it must be broken in order to remove the cast within it.

**water leaf** Descriptive architectural term for the leaf-shaped decorations used in late 12th-century capitals. It is usually broad, tapering and curving in shape.

**watercolour** The technique of laying on colour with pigments bound with a water-soluble medium, usually gum. It is therefore a transparent medium as opposed to the opaque characteristics of oils, pastels, tempera or gouache. In a 'pure' watercolour, light is reflected both from the surface and from the white paper underneath the pigment. The surface of the paper can also contribute to this translucent quality by allowing the brush to be drawn across it in such a way as to achieve the sparkle of scattered lights.

As a medium in its own right, watercolour developed in Europe from the tints, washes and stains with which painters have embellished their working drawings since the Renaissance. Dürer used it with a mastery unknown in Western art up to that time, and Van Dyck was instrumental in demonstrating its usefulness as a means of sketching landscape out of doors. From its 18th-century beginnings among topographical artists it grew into a widely popular medium. A group of watercolour artists were encouraged to form the 'Old'

Watercolour Society in 1804, in conscious emulation of professional oil painters. The medium produced some of the most popular English artists of the 19th century, many of whom were also in demand as drawing masters, among them David Cox, Peter de Wint, John Varley, Samuel Prout and Copley Fielding (1787–1855).

Some French painters have also used watercolour professionally, notably Cézanne, Signac and Dufy. In America, Winslow Homer and Edward Hopper, among others, helped to establish an indigenous tradition. English watercolour landscape lives on in the work of Edward Seago, Rowland Hilder (b. 1905), and of the members of the Royal Watercolour Society.

**waterglass painting** A technique of mural painting in which pigment is applied with water and then coated with a solution of sodium silicate. When it dries it seals the painting behind a thin transparent film; but because it is alkaline it can only be used with certain pigments.

**Watteau, Jean-Antoine** (1684–1721) French painter. He worked first with Claude Gillot (1673–1732), from whom he acquired his liking for costume subjects, and in 1708 joined Claude Audran, Keeper of the Luxembourg Palace with its cycle of Rubens paintings on the life of Marie de Medici. After Rubens, the main influence on him was the Venetian School, especially Veronese.

Watteau's paintings evoke the cultivated amusements of the French leisured class of his time, though not without theatrical exaggeration and stylized fantasy. The vague melancholy that pervades these scenes was both poetic and involuntary: he knew his days were numbered. A visit to London in the winter of 1719, for medical treatment, may well have hastened his end.

**Watts, George Frederick** (1817–1904) English painter. Of all Victorian artists he was perhaps the most high-minded, believing in the 'moral purpose' of his profession more than in any of the current schools or movements. He went for high art on the grand scale, attempted fresco painting, and produced moral allegories such as *Mammon*, 1884 and *Hope*,

1886, both in the Tate Gallery, London. *Hope*, in particular, was enormously popular in its day: prints of it hung in front parlours throughout the land.

Watts was also a sculptor of impressive talent, harking back to Michelangelo and the Elgin Marbles. He was honoured with the Order of Merit in 1902.

**wave moulding** In architecture, the moulding formed by a convex curve between two concave curves.

**wax** see **bronze, modelling** and **encaustic painting**

**Webb, John** (1611–72) English architect. He was trained by Inigo Jones and became his right-hand man, standing in for him in the Civil War and subsequently carrying on his work as a stage designer. The King Charles building at Greenwich Hospital is one of the few important works by him that have survived.

**Webb, Philip Speakman** (1831–1915) English architect. His best-known work was Red House, Bexley Heath (1859), which his friend William Morris had built to move into on his marriage to Jane Burden. He designed furniture for Morris's firm, and also attempted stained glass. With Norman Shaw (1831–1912), who followed him as chief draughtsman to George Edmund Street, he represents the brave, brief, English domestic revival.

**Webb, Sir Aston** (1849–1930) English architect, the son of Edward Webb (1804–54), engraver and watercolour artist. His works in London at the turn of the century include the Victoria and Albert Museum; Imperial College, Kensington; Admiralty Arch; and the façade of Buckingham Palace. He also designed the new Christ's Hospital, Horsham; the Royal Naval College, Dartmouth; and Birmingham University.

**welding** The process of joining two pieces of metal together by fusion, used in making direct metal sculpture. Heat is applied to the edges to be joined until they are sufficiently plastic to be fused. In the process known as brazing, a rod of metal is melted along the joint to increase adhesion.

**West, Sir Benjamin** (1738–1820) American painter. He came to England via Rome (1759), having acquired sufficient prowess en route to set up as a portrait painter in London (1763). His advance was rapid, due largely to the fashionable Neoclassicism which he brought with him from Italy. George III took a liking to him and appointed him his historical painter in 1772. The *Departure of Regulus from Rome*, in the Royal Collection, was his first commission from the King.

West scored his biggest success with the *Death of Wolfe* (National Gallery of Canada, Ottawa), which was a sensation at the Royal Academy of 1771. It broke away from the traditional form of history painting by showing the figures in contemporary dress. West's later paintings carried this innovation into medieval history subjects. He was appointed President of the Royal Academy in succession to Reynolds in 1792.

**Westall, Richard** (1765–1836) English painter and illustrator. Having studied at the Royal Academy Schools, he was apprenticed to a silver engraver and spent much of his career illustrating, including biblical subjects and editions of the poets. His paintings and watercolours are mostly sentimentalized country subjects, now out of fashion. He seems to have been permanently hard up, perhaps because he dabbled in buying and selling old masters. His drawings have a Neoclassical base, though with an idiosyncratic touch that is reminscent of Blake.

**Westmacott, Sir Richard** (1775–1856) English sculptor. He trained under his father (who had the same name) and in Rome under the Neoclassical sculptor Antonio Canova (1757–1822). From 1797, when he returned to London, he built up a prosperous practice. His works include the bronze *Achilles* in Hyde Park, reliefs on the Marble Arch and the pediment over the portico of the British Museum. He is also responsible for the tomb of Charles James Fox in Westminster Abbey.

His son, Richard Westmacott RA (1799–1872), is best known for his portrait busts. He was Professor of Sculpture of the Royal Academy from 1857 to 1867.

**Weyden, Rogier van der** (1400–64) Flemish painter. His early career is vague, but he is thought to have been a pupil of Robert Campin, who was active in Tournai from about 1406. His work is distinguished by the depth of emotion expressed in his figures, whose poignant humanism is absent from the work of his great contemporary, Jan van Eyck. His *Descent from the Cross* (Prado, Madrid) and *Calvary* triptych (Vienna), and his versions of the Crucifixion, combine tragedy with ineffable tenderness.

By 1436 he was the leading painter of Brussels, esteemed and wealthy. In the 1450s he was patronized by the Burgundian court and by the Bishop of Tournai, for whom he painted the *Seven Sacraments* (Antwerp). His pupil Memling adopted his style, which became the dominant form in northern Europe for the rest of the century.

**Whistler, James McNeill** (1834–1903) American painter and etcher. After training for a military career at West Point Academy he came to Europe and studied in Paris at Gleyre's Academy. Through Fantin-Latour he met Courbet, whose Realism influenced his early work. In 1859 he settled in London, where his work shifted towards the Japanese-like semi-abstraction of his *Nocturnes*. In 1877 one of these, *Nocturne in Black and Gold: the Falling Rocket*, (Tate Gallery, London) prompted the attack on him by Ruskin, followed by the libel action in which he was awarded one farthing damages.

During the 1880s his provocative aesthetic creed gained him more supporters. He was elected President of the Society of British Artists in 1886 and helped to secure the Society's royal charter. His etchings, particularly the *Thames* set, are among the most brilliant of modern times.

**Whymper, Josiah Wood** (1813–1903) English landscape painter and wood engraver. Born in Ipswich, he was largely self-taught and at first made his living in London as an illustrator. He exhibited watercolour landscapes from 1844, but his business as a wood engraver kept him busy working for publishers and magazines. He had several successful pupils, including Charles Keene and Frederick Walker.

**Wijnants, Jan** (*c*. 1630–84) Dutch painter, born in Haarlem. His landscapes of paths through sand-dunes and peasants driving sheep usually have figures in them which have been contributed by Philips Wouwerman or Adriaen van de Velde. There are six typical examples in the National Gallery, London.

**Wilkie, Sir David** (1785–1841) Scottish painter. Born near Edinburgh, he made his way to London at the age of 20 with a letter of introduction to the Earl of Mansfield, for whom he painted a rustic group that is still in the family collection. He had a gift for genre in the tradition of Hogarth, often raising the quality of the subject above its content, as in *Chelsea Pensioners Reading the Gazette of the Battle of Waterloo* (Apsley House, London) 1822.

Travels in Spain and Italy broadened his subject matter. The *Defence of Saragossa* (1828), in the Royal Collection, shows his debt to Delacroix, whose manner he also adopted for portrait sketches brought back from the Middle East. He was held in high regard by his fellow painters, especially Turner, whose *Peace–Burial at Sea* (Tate Gallery, London) commemorates Wilkie's end.

**Wilson, Richard** (1713–82) British landscape painter. He was born in Wales and came to London in 1729, where he worked under Thomas Wright, an obscure and unrecorded painter of portraits. In 1752 he set out for Italy, and in five years of travelling absorbed the manner and material of Claude. In Rome he met Claude-Joseph Vernet, who urged him to give up portraiture for landscape painting.

Back in London, Wilson secured occasional commissions to paint English country seats, such as *Croome Court, near Worcester* (Birmingham City Art Gallery), which he treated in the manner of Claude and Poussin. In these, and in his studies of wild English and Welsh landscape, he based his designs on the classical balance between foreground trees, one dense, the other slender, and a picturesque distance, often marked with an architectural feature or ruin. However, he had sufficient genius not to let methods stand in the way of imaginative insight. In the greatest of his landscapes he comes closer to Romanticism than any painter of the 18th century.

**wiping** The process of removing ink from the surface of an etched plate in print making. Artists who prefer to leave a small amount of ink on the uncut surface so as to soften the lines and reduce contrast use the method known as **retroussage**, blotting the plate with gauze or muslin until an evenly spread residue of ink is left. It is also common for a little ink to be drawn from the incised lines on a wiped plate so as to blur its edges slightly, an effect similar to that produced by the burr in drypoint.

**Wolgemut, Michael** (1434–1519) German painter and woodcut illustrator. He was born in Nuremberg, and seems to have known the work of the Netherlandish master, Rogier van der Weyden. Only two paintings by him can be attributed with certainty: altarpieces in Zwickau and Schwabach. He is known less for these than for his woodcuts, which include illustrations for Hartman Schedel's *Weltchronik*, 1493. The young Dürer learned the craft in Wolgemut's workshop, with historic results.

**wood carving** Wood is one of the oldest and most universal media for sculpture, though being organic it has a shorter life than stone. It has been used widely for both free-standing sculpture and works in relief. It can be carved with nothing more than a knife or adze, though the modern wood sculptor is also equipped with a range of saws, drills, gouges, chisels, files and other abrasives.

**wood engraving** A form of relief printing from wood. It differs from the woodcut in that the block is sawn across the grain. The block, hard and highly polished, is cut to make lines that will print white against a black background. It is more suited to fine work than the woodcut, capable of delicate modelling and fine tonal variation, allowing the artist to cut curved lines without meeting resistance caused by the direction of the grain.

Wood engraving was revived in England during the latter years of the 18th century by Thomas Bewick, who brought the art to a point where, for delicacy and detail, it could rival

Wood engraving *The Stag or Red Deer,* from *A General History of Quadrupeds* by Thomas Bewick, published in 1790.

metal engraving. By the middle of the 19th century wood engraving was established as the dominant illustrative method. The wooden blocks could be made type high, and picture and text printed in one operation.

The advent of photo-mechanical methods of reproduction in the 1880s brought an end to wood engraving's pre-eminence in illustration. However, the technique has since flourished in book illustration and in the work of private presses.

**Wood, Grant** (1891–1942) American painter, born in Iowa. He was one of the native-born artists who tried to lead American painting away from European conventions, and to look for material within the American experience. He studied in Paris at the Académie Julian, and on his return replaced the Impressionism in his work with the indigenous realism of the Regionalist movement.

His paintings include *American Gothic* (Art Institute, Chicago), 1930. The *Midnight Ride of Paul Revere,* 1931, and the *Daughters of the American Revolution,* 1932, are both in private American collections. His murals at the Iowa State College Library have the characteristic title *When Tillage Begins, Other Arts Follow.*

**woodcut** The oldest relief printing technique. The artist draws his design on the smooth surface of a block cut longitudinally from a hardwood tree so that the grain flows across it. Using a selection of chisels, gouges and knives, he cuts away all the areas which are to print white, leaving the design upstanding in relief. A roller is used to ink the surface, and the design is then transferred to paper, either by hand or in a press.

Woodcuts are characterized by boldness and simplicity of design, qualities imposed by the medium. Many modern artists have exploited the texture of the wood grain, often deliberately coarsening the surface still further. Since they are produced by a relief printing method, woodcuts are most suitable for book illustrations. They can be made type high, and locked in a frame of movable type, so that the text and picture are printed together. Colour woodcuts are made by cutting several blocks and printing them in register (see **colour prints**).

The origins of the woodcut are obscure. It began to be used in Europe towards the end of the 14th century for making religious prints, and in the 15th century established the direct connection between word and image that has always been an aspect of the medium. In the 16th century the art was greatly advanced by

Woodcut *The Kiss* by the Norwegian artist Edvard Munch shows how the grain of the wood can be dramatically exploited.

Cranach, Dürer and Holbein. During the 17th and 18th centuries the supremacy of **intaglio** techniques relegated the woodcut to popular printing work. At the end of the 19th century, artists such as Gauguin and Munch revived the process, finding in the directness and muscularity of the woodcut a means of powerful and original expression.

**workshop** Paintings are described as being from the workshop of a master if, though not in his own hand, they were done under his supervision. During the Renaissance and later it was common for a master painter to employ apprentices to execute parts of a picture, or on occasion the whole of it, from the original cartoon.

**Wouwerman, Philips** (1619–68) Dutch painter, probably a pupil of Frans Hals, though most of his early life is undocumented. His landscapes, delicately painted and busy with horsemen and figures, have always been among the most popular of the Dutch School, and made him a fortune in his lifetime. Typical subjects are *Cavalrymen Halted at a Sutler's Booth*, *Stag Hunt*, and *Sortie from a Fort on a Hill*, all in the National Gallery, London. His military subjects suggest a first-hand acquaintance with service in the Thirty Years War.

**WPA/FAP** The Works Progress Administration/Federal Arts Project was a programme established by the US government in 1935, an extension of the New Deal projects that had been set up to help America through the Depression. The idea was to provide employment, broaden interest in American art, and set up centres for art education by commissioning artists to embellish public and government buildings, usually with themes dealing with American life. Virtually every notable American artist of the time was in some way involved.

**Wren, Sir Christopher** (1632–1723) English architect. His genius was first revealed in mathematics and the sciences. He held academic posts at Gresham College, London, and at Oxford University before he was 30, and in 1660 was a foundation member of the Royal Society. His earliest buildings are the chapel at Pembroke College, Cambridge and the Sheldonian Theatre, Oxford, both started in 1663. Two years later he visited France to study French architecture, and met Bernini in Paris.

Before leaving England he had been appointed to a Commission looking into the state of disrepair at Old St Paul's and after the Great Fire of London, 1666, he produced a master plan for rebuilding the city. It was rejected, but he at once became actively involved in replacing 51 churches destroyed or damaged in the fire, along with St Paul's. With no tradition or precedent to help him, Wren devoted to each design the inventiveness, variety and grace that distinguish such masterpieces as St Stephen, Walbrook, St James's, Piccadilly, and St Bride's, Fleet Street. St Paul's, with its courageous and noble dome, immortalized him.

His later works include Greenwich Hospital, with its Painted Hall; Trinity College Library, Cambridge; Tom Tower, Oxford; Marlborough House, London (since altered); Chelsea Hospital; and Hampton Court Palace.

**Wright, Frank Lloyd** (1869–1959) American architect. He began by working with Louis Henry Sullivan (1856–1924) designing domestic buildings before branching out on his own in 1893. Over the next decade he devised the 'prairie-house' concept that was to sweep America: low, horizontal, L-shaped and T-shaped houses with free space between the living areas. In the 1920s, after travels in Europe, he introduced concrete-block houses in California, well suited to the light and climate, with patterned wall surfaces and flat, invisible roofs. In a career that embraced many public building projects as well as domestic ones he rarely, if ever, repeated himself, holding to his ideal of a universal, organic architecture to the end.

**Wyatt, James** (1747–1813) English architect. In his day he was rivalled only by the brothers Adam. He studied for six years in Venice, and on returning to London built the *Pantheon* in Regent Street, sensationally adapting the Byzantine S. Sophia, Istanbul, for the purpose. He was capable of turning out smoothly fashionable country seats, such as Heaton Hall, Lincolnshire (1772), for the Earl of Wilton, and Doddington House, Gloucestershire (1798–1808), with its columns wide enough apart for a carriage to drive through. But his heavy hand as a restorer or 'improver' of Gothic buildings earned him a reputation as 'Wyatt the Destroyer.'

**Wyeth, Andrew** (b. 1917) American painter. He was taught by his father, Newell Convers Wyeth, an illustrator and mural painter, and was from the outset of his career a Realist, working in a clear, linear style with a subdued palette. His painting grounds have been Chadds Ford, Pennsylvania, and Cushing, Maine, where he has spent his summers. The atmosphere suggested by these solitary locations is one in which Wyeth's paintings, in tempera or watercolour, are most at home. The lonely spaces of his homelands lay a peculiar spell on the American imagination.

**xylography** A little-used term for wood engraving and woodcut.

**Yeats, Jack** (1871–1957) Irish painter born in London, the brother of William Butler Yeats, the poet. He exhibited in Paris and at the Armory Show, New York. He developed a deep-felt sense of involvement in the troubles of Ireland, revealed in brushwork of an Expressionist intensity.

**yellowing** The term for the discoloration of a painting as it ages. It may be caused by using pigments inherently prone to yellowing; by excessive use of linseed oil; by over-exposure to sunlight (especially in the case of works executed on paper); or simply by the build-up of grime on the picture surface.

**Zoffany, Johann** (1734–1810) German-born painter. He was a leading portraitist in England, popular also for his conversation pieces, which included some of the leading theatrical figures of the day. George III thought well enough of him to finance a stay in Florence (1772). He had not been back long before he went to India on a portrait-painting mission. He seems to have enjoyed painting the Rococo trappings among which many of his sitters posed for him. He was a founding member of the Royal Academy.

**zones of recession** In **Costruzione Legittima**, receding depth is expressed in a series of disconnected planes, according to strict rules of linear perspective. Although not always so sharply delineated, these zones of recession exist in any composition that attempts to represent spatial depth, even if they are nothing more than the categories of foreground, middle distance, and background. The use of aerial perspective to introduce a gradation of hazing as the picture recedes into depth is one way of blurring the edges of the zones.

**zoophorus** Animal reliefs used in the decoration of a frieze.

**Zorn, Anders** (1860–1920) Swedish painter and etcher, who worked mainly in Paris. He had a talent for watercolour, which he used with an Impressionist sparkle and freedom. His society portraits and his oils of Paris street scenes show a similar lightness of touch. His real achievement is as an etcher, notably of portraits (*Rodin, Verlaine*) and bathers.

**Zuccarelli, Francesco** (1702–88) Italian painter. He worked in the pastoral landscape manner derived from Marco Ricci. In Venice in 1751 he met Richard Wilson, who painted his portrait, and in the following year he came to London. His work was readily saleable in England, and he eventually stayed for 16 years. He became a founder member of the Royal Academy, and on his return to Venice in 1771 was made President of the Venetian Academy.

**Zurbarán, Francisco de** (1598–1664) Spanish painter. In 1628 he was established as official artist to the town of Seville, where he was based for much of his subsequent career. His *Vision of the Blessed Alonso Rodriguez* (Academia de S. Fernando, Madrid) and the *Apotheosis of St Thomas Aquinas* (Museo de Bellas Arts, Seville) are among the finest work of this fruitful period, in which he built up a busy export business to Spain's American colonies, as well as supplying monasteries and churches nearer home. Zurbarán's single figures of praying monks and saints are typical of his work in the 1630s. They show the weighty, sincere realism of his manner, which in later years gave way to the more ingratiating style of Murillo, who overtook him in popularity. But he has lasted the better, to make his mark on such formative painters as Courbet, Manet and Picasso.

# ACKNOWLEDGEMENTS

Arabesque 9 — Hamlyn Group Picture Library
Art Nouveau 11 — Photographie Giraudon, Paris
Baroque 15 — Hamlyn Group Picture Library
Byzantine Art 29 — Photographie Giraudon, Paris
Camera obscura 31 — Kodak Museum, Harrow
Caricature 33 — Guildhall Art Gallery, London
Caryatid 35 — Bildarchiv Foto Marburg
Cave art 36 — Roger-Viollet, Paris
Collage 41 — Philadelphia Museum of Art © SPADEM 1981
Cubism 49 — Berner Kunstmuseum © ADAGP 1981
Decorated 52 — British Tourist Authority, London
Deposition 53 — Alinari, Florence
Divisionism 55 — Photographie Giraudon, Paris © SPADEM 1981
Early English 60 — British Tourist Authority, London
Engraving 63 — British Museum, London
Etching 64 — Hamlyn Group Picture Library
Flying buttress 68 — Archives Photographiques, Paris
Foreshortening 69 — National Gallery, London
Found Object 70 — John Webb, London © SPADEM 1981
Glasgow style 77 — University of Glasgow
Gothic Revival 79 — Country Life, London
History painting 86 — Royal Ontario Museum
Icon 89 — Azad, Beyruth
Illumination 90 — Hamlyn Group Picture Library
Illumination 91 — Photographie Giraudon, Paris
Jacobean 93 — Hamlyn Group Picture Library
Japonaiserie 93 — Bildarchiv Foto Marburg
Jones, Inigo 94 — Trustees of the Chatsworth Settlement
Kouros 97 — Alinari, Florence
Linocut 102 — Victoria & Albert Museum, London
Lithograph 103 — Art Institute of Chicago
Marine painting 108 — National Maritime Museum, Greenwich

Mezzotint 111 — Hamlyn Group Picture Library
Mobile 113 — Adolph Studly, New York © ADAGP 1981
Mosaic 116 — Alinari, Florence
Naive art 118 — Photographie Giraudon, Paris
Neoclassicism 120 — Hamlyn Group Picture Library
Neue Sachlichkeit 121 — Kunstsammlung Nordhein-Westfalen, Düsseldorf
Norman 123 — Hamlyn Group Picture Library
Odalisque 124 — Photographie Giraudon, Paris
Op art 126 — Peter Stuyvesant Foundation, London
Palladian 129 — Alinari, Florence
Pargeting 131 — British Tourist Authority, London
Perpendicular 134 — British Tourist Authority, London
Pietà 136 — Leonard von Matt, Buochs
Pop art 140 — Tate Gallery, London
Pre-Columbian art 142 — Staatliche Museen für Völkerkunde, Berlin-Dahlem
Pre-Raphaelite 143 — Tate Gallery, London
Regency 148 — Hamlyn Group Picture Library
Relief 148 — Gabinetto Fotografico, Florence
Rococo 153 — Hamlyn Group Picture Library
Romanesque 154 — Roger-Viollet, Paris
Soft-ground etching 168 — Denis Thomas
Study 175 — Cameraphoto, Venice
Surrealism 177 — Hamlyn Group Picture Library © SPADEM 1981
Symbolism 177 — Archives Photographiques, Paris
Trompe l'oeil 184 — National Gallery, London
Tudor 185 — Country Life, London
Vienna Sezession 190 — Hamlyn Group Picture Library
Vorticism 192 — Tate Gallery, London
Wood engraving 197 — Hamlyn Group Picture Library
Woodcut 197 — Victoria & Albert Museum, London